Enlightenment in the Colony

Enlightenment in the Colony

The Jewish Question and the Crisis of Postcolonial Culture

Aamir R. Mufti

PRINCETON UNIVERSITY PRESS
PRINCETON AND OXFORD

Published by Princeton University Press, 41 William Street, Princeton, New Jersey 08540
In the United Kingdom: Princeton University Press, 3 Market Place, Woodstock, Oxfordshire OX20 1SY

Library of Congress Cataloging-in-Publication Data
Mufti, Aamir.
Enlightenment in the colony : the Jewish question and the crisis of postcolonial culture / Aamir R. Mufti.
p. cm.
Includes bibliographical references and index.
ISBN-13: 978-0-691-05731-6 (alk. paper)
ISBN-10: 0-691-05731-1 (alk. paper)
ISBN-13: 978-0-691-05732-3 (pbk. : alk. paper)
ISBN-10: 0-691-05732-X (pbk. : alk. paper)
1. Secularism—India—History. 2. Nationalism—India—History. 3. India—Colonial influence. 4. Muslims in literature. 5. Jews in literature. 6. Jews—Europe—Identity—History. 7. Liberalism—Europe—History. I. Title.

DS428.2.M82 2007
211'.60954—dc22 2006050393

British Library Cataloging-in-Publication Data is available

This book has been composed in Times Ten LT Std

Printed on acid-free paper. ∞

pup.princeton.edu

Printed in the United States of America

10 9 8 7 6 5 4 3 2 1

یہ سخن جو ہم نے رقم کیے، یہ ہیں سب ورق تری یاد کے
کوئی لمحہ صبحِ وصال کا، کئی شامِ ہجر کی مدّتیں

ये सुख़न जो हम ने रक़म किए ये हैं सब वरक़ तेरी याद के

कोई लमहा सुबह-ए विसाल का कई शाम-ए हिज्र की मुद्दतें

In memory of my parents,
Fakhrunnisa Mufti and Mufti Rashiduddin Ahmad,
in belated recognition of the journey they made

Contents

A Note on Translation and Transliteration

For all texts originally in a language other than English, I provide standard English translations where these are available but alter these translations as I see fit. Citations for the original are also provided wherever necessary, but extracts of the text are reproduced in the original only where I engage closely with a text and feel it necessary for the purpose of the analysis. Translations from the Urdu-Hindi, and the occasional one from the French, unless otherwise indicated, are my own. For translations from the German, I am deeply grateful for the help of Willi Goetschel, who has been my ready reference source over long distances and for many years.

In matters of transliteration from the Urdu-Hindi, I follow the revised scheme proposed by the *Annual of Urdu Studies* (2005), with a few small changes of my own: *ch* instead of *č*, *ḳh* instead of *kh*, and *ġh* instead of *ġ*, with the last two changes meant to facilitate reading by exclusively Devanagari readers. For all personal, place and organizational names I use the standard English versions, without diacritics. The only exception to this is made in the names of publishers in the notes and bibliography. In the case of some of these, either not well known in English or based on an Arabic or Persian morphological form or both (especially the *ʾiḍāfa/iẓāfat*), I give the transliteration with full diacritics in parentheses only at the first appearance of the name. Words of English origin used in Urdu-Hindi—for instance, in organization names—are reproduced with their English spellings: hence *Bureau*, rather than Biyūrō. Also, words and phrases transliterated here from the Urdu-Hindi that have a strong and continued basis in Arabic—as Islamic terms, for instance—are rendered as if from the written Arabic: hence *waḥdat al-wujūd*, instead of *vaḥdat ul-vujūd*. Otherwise, Arabic-origin words are rendered as they are inscribed in Urdu script but with attention to how they are meant to be pronounced in Urdu-Hindi: hence *vaṭ̤an*, not *waṭ̤an*. All Indic words are transcribed as written in the Urdu script, not Devanagari. In giving the Urdu names of organizations, English rules of capitalization are followed, but not in the case of titles of works in Urdu.

Acknowledgments

THE LARGEST INTELLECTUAL DEBT accrued during this project's period of gestation is to the late Edward Said, my teacher, mentor, and friend. It is a cause of abiding sadness for me that his life was cut short before the appearance of this book, in whose composition his intellectual influence and support had played such an enormous role. I first met Edward in 1984 but did not formally become his student until late in 1989. All of us who started working with him in the 1980s were attracted to him in large measure by the role he played in making the question of the imperialization of the world indispensible to the study of modern culture. I realized only gradually that my own reasons had been somewhat different and had to do with the relationship in his work between the colonial question and the particular themes he spoke of as "secular criticism" and "exile." It is this nexus of issues that constitutes the core of this work.

I also want to acknowledge here the intellectual influence of a long list of other teachers, many of whom will be unaware of this influence: John Briggs, Henry Rutz, Hy Van Luong, Maurice Bloch, Alfred Gell, Jonathan Parry, Robert Murphy, Allan Silver, Gauri Viswanathan, Jean Franco, Gayatri Spivak, David Lelyveld, and, in particular, Andreas Huyssen and Jean Howard. Professor C. M. Naim did me the honor of treating me as if I were his student when, without knowing it, I needed it most. It was an incalculable gift for which I am deeply grateful. His influence is everywhere visible in my engagements with the history of modern Urdu literature in part 2 of this book, even where I diverge significantly from his views, and final responsibility for all errors of fact or judgment must, of course, remain my own. Willi Goetschel was my first guide through Jewish cultural studies, and I shall always be grateful for his generosity.

Over the long period that I have worked on this book, I have been blessed with some unique friendships. Without Rob Nixon's encouragement many years ago, I might never have entered a Ph.D. program in literary studies—a dubious favor, clearly. Bruce Robbins and Andrew Ross introduced me to the argumentative pleasures of journal life, which have become an addiction that has been fed in recent years by Paul Bové, Ronald Judy, and Jonathan Arac. Jyotsna Uppal and Qadri Ismail have kept the stakes real for too many years, and Mazen Arafat has been an unflinching interlocutor across oceans and continents. Gyan Prakash,

P. A. Skantze, Stathis Gourgouris, Pankaj Butalia, and Nilofer Kaul Butalia have been generous and indulgent friends at various times over these years. Michael Howley and Hugh Crean have sustained and restored me on more occasions than it is possible to remember, and Hugh's unique home in Harlem has been my home away from home for a decade now, a gift for which there can be no return. Finally, Nick Dirks and Janaki Bakhle opened the doors of their home to me during a crucial year of my life, in Ann Arbor, Michigan. For this inexplicable act of generosity, and for their continuing and unconditional friendship from across a continent, I shall always be grateful.

The work in this book has been presented in fragments, in early versions and in précis, at a number of institutions around the world, including, in no particular order, the National University of Ireland, Galway; Princeton University; Harvard University; University of Chicago; University of Pennsylvania; University of Michigan, Ann Arbor; Columbia University; University of California, Santa Cruz; University of California, Los Angeles; University of British Columbia; University of Illinois, Chicago; Hong Kong University; University of Pittsburgh; University of Rochester; Notre Dame University; New York University; Wayne State University, Detroit; University of Texas, Austin; Center for the Study of Developing Societies and Sarai, Delhi; and Delhi University.

Among all those who have read or heard earlier drafts of various parts of the book and offered valuable suggestions, encouragement, and critique, I am especially grateful to Dipesh Chakrabarty, Partha Chatterjee, Nick Dirks, Charles Hirschkind, Janaki Bakhle, Qadri Ismail, Joe Cleary, Homi Bhabha, Simon Gikandi, Anton Shammas, Andreas Huyssen, Martha Vicinus, Yopie Prins, Ronald Judy, Akeel Bilgrami, Paul Bové, Jonathan Arac, Lauren Kruger, Bill Brown, W.J.T. Mitchell, Jim Chandler, Gyan Prakash, Gail Minault, Kamran Asdar Ali, Milind Wakankar, Sanjay Krishnan, Kowshik Ghosh, Carla Petievich, Kathy Hansen, Adela Pinch, Patsy Yaeger, John Gonzalez, Stathis Gourgouris, Eduardo Cadava, Jonathan Boyarin, Kathryn Babayan, Michael Szalay, Tejaswini Niranjana, Susie Tharu, C. M. Naim, Ravikant, Shail Mayaram, Tarun Saint, Alok Rai, Harish Trivedi, Emily Apter, Gil Hochberg, Mahmood Farooqi, Donald Pease, Nauman Naqvi, Deniz Kandiyoti, Afsaneh Najmabadi, Sandra Berman, Joe Buttigieg, Willi Goetschel, Dorothea von Mücke, and the three reviewers for Princeton University Press.

I am deeply grateful for the research support provided over the years by the Graduate School of Arts and Sciences, Columbia University; the Office of the Vice-Provost for Research, University of Michigan; and the International Institute and the Senate, University of California at Los Angeles. The Humanities Institute at Michigan provided me with a luxurious and stimulating environment for research and writing as a Steelcase Research Professor during 1999–2000; and residence at the Huntington Library during 2004–2005 with a Burckhardt Fellowship for Recently Tenured Scholars from the American Council of Learned Societies allowed me to bring the book to a conclusion. I want to thank the directors and staff of these institutions for providing me with these opportunities, especially Tom Trautman, Roy Ritchie, Susie Krasnoo, and Pauline Yu. My thanks also to the staff of the libraries of Columbia University; University of Michigan; UCLA; the Leo Baeck Institute, New York; the British Library and the India Office Reading Room, Nehru Memorial Museum and Library, Delhi; and the Quaid-e Azam Academy, Karachi. This book has benefited from the help of a number of research assistants over the years, and I wish to acknowledge in particular the able and uncomplaining assistance of Indra Mukhopadhyay, my research assistant over the last three years of this project.

Earlier versions of sections of the prologue and of chapters 1, 4, and 5 have appeared as part of the following articles: "Secularism and Minority: Elements of a Critique," *Social Text* (1995); "The Aura of Authenticity," *Social Text* (2000); "A Greater Story Writer than God: Genre, Gender and Minority in Late Colonial India," in *Subaltern Studies XI*, ed. Partha Chatterjee and Pradeep Jeganathan (2000); and "Towards a Lyric History of India," *boundary 2* (2004).

I offer thanks to my friend and former editor Mary Murrell at Princeton University Press for her enthusiasm for this book from very early on, and to Hanne Winarsky and Debbie Tegarden for their support and guidance during the last year of its life as an ongoing project.

For the unconditional love and support of my dispersed extended family—the Muftis, the Ahmeds, the Sultans, and the Mathurs—there is no repayment. I hope I have been occasionally able to do for each of them a fraction of what they daily do for me.

For Saloni and Jalal, words do not suffice. Without Saloni's seemingly endless line of emotional credit, I would soon be bankrupt. She has been a companion equally in dark moments and light, and my best and most indispensable intellectual partner. To Jalal, in the hope that some day in the distant future he might read these words—is that really too much to ask of one's child?—I would like to say, find out where this is from and what it means: "opaṛ dī guṛguṛ dī anēksi dī bē-dhyānā dī mung dī dāl āf dī lālṭain" (it is part of our story).

Abbreviations

A Jawaharlal Nehru, *Autobiography*
AGN Johann Gottlieb Fichte, *Address to the German Nation*
AV Leslie Fleming, *Another Lonely Voice*
BB Anita Desai, *Baumgartner's Bombay*
CW Rudyard Kipling, "On the City Wall"
DD George Eliot, *Daniel Deronda*
DE Max Horkheimer and Theodor Adorno, *Dialectic of Enlightenment*
DI Jawaharlal Nehru, *The Discovery of India*
G Maulana Abul Kalam Azad, *Ġhubār-e k̲hāt̤ir*
I Walter Scott, *Ivanhoe*
J Moses Mendelssohn, *Jerusalem*
JS Heinrich Heine, *Jewish Stories and Hebrew Melodies*
K Maulana Abul Kalam Azad, *K̲hut̤bāt-e Āzād*
KE Saadat Hasan Manto, *Kingdom's End*
M Salman Rushdie, *The Moor's Last Sigh*
MD Saadat Hasan Manto, *Mottled Dawn*
MK Saadat Hasan Manto, *Manṭō kahāniyāñ*
MLS Salman Rushdie, *The Moor's Last Sigh*
MN Saadat Hasan Manto, *Manṭōnāma*
MR Saadat Hasan Manto, *Manṭōrāmā*
N Gotthold Efraim Lessing, *Nathan the Wise*
NV Faiz Ahmed Faiz, *Nusk̲hahā-e vafā*
PI E. M. Forster, *A Passage to India*
PF Faiz Ahmed Faiz, *Poems from Faiz*

Enlightenment in the Colony

Prologue

TOWARDS A GENEALOGY OF POSTCOLONIAL SECULARISM

THE IDEA FOR THIS PROJECT BEGAN to emerge in the weeks and months following the destruction of the Babri Mosque at Ayodhya in northern India on December 6, 1992. Communities across what was once North India—that is, the region now including Pakistan and Bangladesh—were in flames. Each day brought news of more and more towns and cities erupting in "communal" violence. The city of Bombay, long a symbol of a cosmopolitan Indian modernity, ground to a halt, as the reality took hold that, for the first time in its post-Partition history, middle-class and even elite Muslim families were not safe from their neighbors. From Lahore, which had been cleansed of its substantial Hindu and Sikh populations half a century earlier, we were treated to the extraordinary sight of a Hindu temple, abandoned and unused for almost fifty years, being razed with the help of municipal bulldozers, a startling reminder that the citizens of that city were still not free of their former neighbors. And if the destruction of the Babri mosque itself was a primitive and chaotic affair, all sledgehammers and pickaxes, its aftermath was brought up to date in Surat, in the form of videotapes of gang rapes of Muslim women which reportedly became popular entertainment in middle-class living rooms across the country. An outrage in one place brought out a worse response in another. It was as if the nation-state boundaries implemented in 1947 had ceased to exist. Once again communities all across the subcontinent seemed to be communicating with one another in the only language permitted by the postcolonial states, that of collective violence—violence now becoming the only act of communication that could not be interdicted at the borders of the nation-state. Whoever you spoke to, wherever you turned for comprehension, one perception repeated itself like a refrain: nothing like this had been seen since India's Partition.[1]

In the event, it proved to be a particularly clarifying moment, bringing into sharp relief the larger movements of India's modernity. It made evident the fact that the crisis over Muslim identity, which first emerged in the decades following the great rebellion of 1857, continues to be one of the central dramas of political and cultural life in the three successor societies to British India. It became clear that the form of political and intellectual secularism that had been tied to the postcolonial state in India, and whose founding figure was Jawaharlal Nehru, was in a state of irreversible collapse, regardless of the fortunes of those political organizations most closely associated with it. This collapse was apparent in the crisis surrounding the language of secularism itself, whose characteristic pose—its "neutrality" regarding two supposedly symmetrical "communalisms"—first required that the mosque be converted into "the disputed structure." Then, in the aftermath of its destruction, when officials and liberal media alike spoke of undoing the work of the mobs in Ayodhya, the word "mosque" could not even be uttered, and they spoke, with a straight face, of *rebuilding* "the disputed structure." Thus the last vestiges of a connection between state secularism and the principles of Enlightenment rationality and critique, on which it had drawn at least since its first elaborations in the "heroic" thought of Nehru and his contemporaries, appeared to be broken. It became increasingly clear that what came crashing down that day in Ayodhya was the very structure of Indian citizenship, that what was being eliminated in the pogrom-like atmosphere of the weeks and months following "December 6," as the event has come to be called, was the figure of the secular citizen subject itself.[2]

This book is about the crisis of modern secularism, and of postcolonial secularism in particular, at whose center I identify the terrorized and terrifying figures of minority. It is in part an attempt to formulate some ways of thinking about the meaning of the crisis of Muslim identity in modern India. It is a study in particular of the literary dimensions of this crisis, an exploration, at the level of form, content, and literary institution, of the dialectic of selfhood in a colonial and postcolonial society. But my basic premise is that the crisis of Muslim identity must be understood in terms of the problematic of secularization and minority in post-Enlightenment liberal culture as a whole and therefore cannot be understood in isolation from the history of the so-called Jewish Question in modern Europe. I argue that in the "question" of the Jews' status in modern culture and society, as it first came to be formulated in the late eighteenth century, what emerges is a set of paradigmatic narratives, conceptual frameworks, motifs, and formal relationships concerned with the very question of minority existence, which are then disseminated globally in the emergence, under colonial and semicolonial conditions, of the forms of modern social, political, and cultural life. My goal is to delineate central categories and narratives of liberal culture and thought concerning the question of minority existence—assimilation, emancipation, separatism, conversion, the language of state protection and minority rights, uprooting, exile, and homelessness—and the dialectic within which they are produced. It is important therefore at the outset to establish at least an initial sense of the way I use such terms as "imperialism," "capitalism," "Enlightenment," "citizenship," and "nation-state." Number and "equivalence," Max Horkheimer and Theodor Adorno once argued, famously, are the rule and "canon" of bourgeois society.[3] For the purposes of this project, I regard post–Industrial Revolution (and thus post-Enlightenment) imperialism to be a multifarious movement of expansionism whose ultimate goal—in the final instance, as it were—is the global establishment of the market, and thus of the rule of equivalence (but not equality). The reshaping, to this end, of the diverse and heterogeneous social formations that come under its grasp thus results in the creation of polities consisting of equivalent "values," that is, citizens. That "the nation" (of supposedly equal citizens) in the colonized world emerges out of the very socioeconomic processes that it comes to oppose is now a well-known and well-understood story.[4] It is the contradictory nature of this transition, and the resultant crisis of its structures in the form of minoritized social groups and cultural practices, that I am concerned with in this book.

I begin, therefore, by exploring the crises that have encircled the attributes of Jewishness in the process of elaboration of the structures, narratives, and forms of bourgeois culture and society in the West. Among these crises, of concern to us here, are the purported indifference of the liberal state and the troubling difference of the Jews; anxious and impossible claims about the autochthony of the people; the irrationality of bureaucratic rationalism; the uncanny (*unheimlisch*) inflections of the mother tongue in "alien" hands; "mature" subjectivity and the force of tradition; patriotism and the terror of divided or ambiguous loyalties; and the recurrent specter of Hebraism in modern literature and culture. It is in the eruption of such crises around the meaning of Jewishness that we get the earliest elaborations of minority cultural practice as a critique of dominant culture and its majoritarian affiliations. In recent years a growing number of literary scholars, including, inter alia, Sander Gilman, James Shapiro, Bryan Cheyette, Michael Ragussis, Ira Nadel, Irene Tucker, and Jonathan Freedman, have been charting this centrality of the question and crisis of Jewish difference to the literature of the liberal West.[5] In this book I attempt to reinterpret this central role of the Jews to modern Western culture from perspectives made possible by the contemporary crisis of secularism in postcolonial societies and, in particular, the nation-states of the South Asian subcontinent. My aim is to resituate certain aspects of the larger problematic of Jewishness within an extra-European, global frame, and to clarify its location within the process of emergence, dispersion, and universalization of these liberal narratives and forms by examining their reappearance in the crisis of minority in colonial and postcolonial India.

What this book offers, therefore, is, first, a distinctly Third World and postcolonial understanding of those forms of constitutive failure of the idea of Europe that come to us coded as the "Jewish Question," bringing to the trajectories of Europe's modernity modes of analysis that have emerged in recent years out of the critique of colonial culture and a globalized postcolonial modernity. One premise of this book is that the present moment in the history of postcolonial societies allows a unique vantage point on the particular trajectory of the modern that we call secularization. At the same time, the book is an attempt to make the cultural and critical legacies of the Jewish Question speak to debates and dilemmas that are distinctly postcolonial. This effort to revisit our understandings of the conditions and resources of that "minor," exilic, or diasporic Jewish intellectual culture, as part of a larger endeavor to fashion a truly more planetary critique of contemporary forms of "settled" thinking and the social asymmetries they justify and often even help to produce, is all the more imperative today with the intensification of the political and economic oppression of the Palestinian people precisely in the name of that history of dispossession of the Jews. What is sought here, in other words, is, on the one hand, a specifically internationalist and postcolonial understanding of the scenarios of Jewish minoritization and exile, and an acknowledgment of affiliation with the modes of critique produced out of them; and, on the other, the conceptual and historical basis for a critique of the Zionist "solution" and its consequences for the Palestinians, for Arabs more generally, and for the global culture of decolonization as a whole. These are inseparable elements in a Third Worldist and postcolonial understanding of the Jewish Question, and, without the first, as Edward Said so tirelessly pointed out in his work as in his politics, the second risks collapsing into a reflex of ressentiment and revenge.

Finally, a word about the concept of "Enlightenment" as it is elaborated here. As standard narratives of the bourgeois Enlightenment would have it, to make public and political life secular was one of the most cherished goals of the Enlightenment, a claim I examine critically at some length in the following chapter. And whether or not the non-Western societies of the colonized world could move in that secular direction became the litmus test for their entry into modern civilization. Throughout the nineteenth and early twentieth centuries, writers, thinkers, and public figures of all stripes in the West and elsewhere speculated about the chances of Enlightenment in the colonies. This book addresses this central preoccupation of the bourgeois Enlightenment and its fate in a colonial and postcolonial setting. It examines the shifting relationship between colonial culture, Indian nationalism, and the Enlightenment ideal of a public sphere cleansed of the signs of religious difference. Its particular stance on this question emerges out of a study of, and conversation with, two distinct discourses on the significance and legacy of the bourgeois Enlightenment for modern culture, namely, Frankfurt School critical theory and the critical historiographic project of Subaltern Studies. If this book aims, on the one hand, to reconsider the former's critique of Enlightenment from the perspective of subject positions that cannot be subsumed within the narrative of a seamless universalization of modern Western culture, it is, on the other, to nudge the latter away from an undialectical rejection of Enlightenment as colonial domination. In one sense, therefore, the book is an attempt to think about how and where to proceed beyond the powerful critical perception near the end of Partha Chatterjee's monumental work, *Nationalist Thought and the Colonial World*: "That is the story of Enlightenment in the Colonies. It comes in the hands of the policeman, and the marriage is consummated in the station-house."[6] It may be read as an extended argument for the view that this perception not be allowed to degenerate into the banality of the anti-secularist gesture but lead instead to a more difficult, and also more truthful, negotiation with the history of colonial domination and the political and cultural situations and legacies we call Enlightenment.

Jews and Others: Minority and the Forms of Modernity

Observers of modern anti-Semitism, including Hannah Arendt, Horkheimer, and Adorno, have long recognized that the forms of organized violence, scapegoating and collective punishment, coerced and unfree labor, race theory and race thinking, and overall instrumentalization and destruction of human life that came to characterize the treatment of the Jews in Europe following the rise of the Nazis bear a striking resemblance to practices of governance and forms of culture that had been developed in the colonies. Arendt's *The Origins of Totalitarianism* is, of course, an extended argument about the interconnections between the development of colonial racism and anti-Semitism since the nineteenth century. And scattered in the works of Adorno and Horkheimer are numerous insights, often expressed aphoristically rather than developed at length, about the commonality of powerlessness and "minority" status among "colonial natives," Jews, and even women. Such claims about the continuities or overlaps between colonial and Jewish experience have also long and repeatedly been made by those, like Nehru, whose internationalist and disinterested commitment to the struggle against fascism was continually tested by their own oppression as colonial subjects by the European nation-states that claimed leadership of that struggle. Thus, for instance, writing in prison during the war, Nehru argued, in *The Discovery of India*, that "we in India have known racialism in all its forms ever since the commencement of British rule. The whole ideology of this rule was that of the herrenvolk [*sic*] and the master race, and the structure of government was based upon it." Writing a decade later, Aimé Césaire infused his *Discourse on Colonialism* with the insight that the events of the previous two decades in Europe could only be understood as the continuation of Europe's treatment of various non-European peoples over the previous several centuries: "[Hitler] applied to Europe colonialist procedures which until then had been reserved exclusively for the Arabs of Algeria, the coolies of India, and the blacks of Africa." In the same spirit, Amilcar Cabral once referred to the Nazis as "the most tragic expression of imperialism and thirst for domination."[7]

More recently work within the emerging field of Jewish cultural studies has sometimes sought to compare and affiliate Jewish marginalization within dominant forms of European culture to colonial and postcolonial forms of alienation; perhaps exemplary in this regard is the work of Bryan Cheyette, Jonathan Boyarin, and Daniel Boyarin. To a certain extent, then, this recent scholarship has been attempting to dismantle the anti-comparatist impulse of much of Jewish studies since its founding in Germany in the *Wissenschaft des Judentums* in the early nineteenth century.[8] It is becoming increasingly clear, moreover, that many of the often contradictory facets of social and cultural life familiar to us from prewar Jewish experience in Europe—cultural mobility, adaptability, resolute attention to social life in the face of hostility from the "host" culture, intense separatism and religious revival, political radicalism, cosmopolitan elites, a cultural taste for transgression, irony, and the irreverent gesture—have reappeared in Europe in the experience of the "postcolonial" migrants, displaced people, and refugees who have largely replaced Europe's annihilated Jews as the continent's "Other within."[9] Comparative research in this direction is bound to shed new and defamiliarizing light on Europe's internal life in the modern era, and this book allies itself with this effort. My overall purpose in this context is to contribute to the ongoing effort to explore the possibilities for the convergence of perspectives made possible by the problematic of "Jewish difference" with those emerging out of the forms of difference that mark the trajectories of colonial and postcolonial cultures and societies. In the final chapter of the book I turn to the metaphorical possibilities of Jewishness for contemporary postcolonial culture, through a reading of their elaboration in a number of recent Indian narrative works in

English. But my more proximate goal, in the first part of the book, is to locate the troubled and recurring question of Jewish emancipation-assimilation as an early, and *exemplary*, instance of the crisis of minority that has accompanied the development of liberal-secular state and society in numerous contexts around the world. As in the case of Europe and the Jews, the question of what it means to be Indian, I argue later in the book, has remained a cultural formation brought to crisis by the question of Muslim identity, in which at stake is the minoritization of language, culture, and memory. I am especially interested in the inflections that the question of minority existence undergoes between its early emergence in Europe and its reemergence in colonial India with the development of a nascent nation-state formation, the experience of citizenship and national belonging, and the cultural crisis and conflict that have centered ever since around the marks of "Muslim" particularity and difference.

In turning to the history of the Jewish Question in this manner, I am acutely aware of the pitfalls of appropriating Jewish existence for allegories of non-Jewish lives, a form of appropriation that has itself produced a sort of canonical tradition of conceptualizing Jewishness in the theoretical literature of the modern West. I fully share Arendt's critique of Sartre's *Anti-Semite and Jew*, for instance, or Daniel Boyarin and Jonathan Boyarin's concern with that same work and with Lyotard's *Heidegger and "the jews"*, namely, that these works reduce the Jews to a figment of the non-Jewish, and, in the case of Sartre at least, anti-Semitic, imagination.[10] Whether and to what extent I succeed in not lapsing into such appropriative moves myself in what follows is for others to decide. But this form of critique of the dominant, and ultimately majoritarian, accounts of the meaning and place of Jewish experience is itself of central importance to the argument developed in this book. I am interested precisely in the effort to rethink European selfhood itself from positions marked by the dilemmas, vulnerabilities, and ethical and critical possibilities of Jewishness-minority. Explored specifically are aspects of the relationship between Jewish experience in Western Europe and secularism and *critique* as they have developed since the eighteenth century, and therefore the metaphorical (or rather, metonymic) possibilities of Jewishness for oppositional culture as a whole, including the ongoing project of decolonization and its critique of colonial and postcolonial culture and society. Therefore of interest to me here is what the Boyarins call the diasporic and exilic "ground of Jewish identity"—Jewishness as the very disruption and disaggregation of the categories of identity—and its relationship to secularism and critique.[11] From their earliest Enlightenment elaboration, the projects of secularism—secular citizenship, separation of church and state, national language, literature, and culture, to name just a few—have circled around the question of the Jews. Thus a key concern here is the Jewish intellectual attachment to—and, as I shall argue, immanent critique of—the Enlightenment and its legacies, above all its secularist concepts, narratives, and values. Hence the emphasis in the book on the figure of the Jewish intellectual and the problematics surrounding it, such as the question of assimilation, whose dominant conception as the dissolution of a (minority) particularity by immersion in a constant and unchanging majority culture is repeatedly and consistently challenged and undermined by at least some of those individuals at whom it is directed. Arendt's formulation of what she called the "hidden" Jewish tradition of the "conscious pariah," derived from the fin de siècle polemics of Bernard Lazarre but which may also be read as a reinscription of Max Weber's ultimately dismissive characterization of the Jews as a "pariah" people, was key in formulating my own conception of minority experience as a site for the critique of dominant conceptions and narratives of collective life.[12] I am interested, in other words, in the figure of the Jew as *subject*, not just object, of the processes we know as emancipation and assimilation. A larger purpose of the book as a whole, therefore, is to outline cultural possibilities for groups deemed minorities that take neither the form of assimilation in the official sense nor of separatism of the political sort, which, I shall try to show, is often the most complete form assimilation can take, despite being presented as its opposite. This approach to the question of modern culture—that is, its examination through the prism of minority experience—might appear quaint in the present moment, given the larger context of the utter domestication of (at least some) minority struggles within the official multicultural refashioning of contemporary U.S. culture, including and above all in the academy. However, what I am attempting here, by turning to the fraught histories of European Jews and Indian Muslims, is in part precisely to make the history of such struggles available once again as resources for critical practice.

Finally, if the theoretical presence of such figures as Adorno, Horkheimer, Arendt, Georg Lukács, and Edward Said looms large in this project, it is far from accidental. The modes of critique generated from the history of the Jewish Question and in response to it, with their deep exploration of the implications of marginality, homelessness, exile, and uprooting, resonate in a powerful and complex way for an examination of the dialectic of minoritization, displacement, and partitioning of language, culture, and memory in modern India. This book is concerned, to some extent, with exploring whether and how these European theoretical elaborations can be said to belong to the same *archive* as the textualities produced out of the trajectory of the Indian modern, and how our reading of the one may influence and alter our reading of the other.

It is this mutual alteration, this *translation*, that I attempt to facilitate here. It will, I hope, become evident as the argument develops that these mid-century Indian formulations have a great deal to contribute to contemporary global debates about culture, critique, and community.

Therefore, with respect as well to the history of Jewish assimilation-emancipation, my goal is to reexamine that history from the perspective of twentieth-century events and formulations. In the first part of the book I turn, in particular, to a number of eighteenth- and nineteenth-century texts and preoccupations in terms of the significance they acquire in their reflections on the Jewish Question for such twentieth-century (émigré) figures as Adorno, Horkheimer, Arendt, Lukács, Gershom Scholem, Erich Auerbach, and Isaiah Berlin. A number of these reflections were, of course, sometimes produced in dialogue with, and at other times at least with knowledge of, one another in the 1930s, 1940s, and 1950s, that is, in the decades of the radical reorganization of European life and the final catastrophe of the dispersal and decimation of the Jews. Although these writers represent a wide range of political attitudes, theoretical and philosophical positions, aesthetic views, and personal identities, many of their reflections on the fate of culture in the modern world share an understanding of the late eighteenth century as a key moment and point of departure in the drama of (Jewish) difference and modernity, an understanding I take as my own starting point. The late eighteenth century is thus the exemplary moment for a number of developments: the elaboration of the philosophical problematic we call Enlightenment (Horkheimer and Adorno); the transformation of the absolutist state and the emergence of the question of political emancipation (Arendt); the reformulation of the dialectic of reason and redemption, of Haskala and Hasidism (Scholem); the historicist critique of the extreme abstraction of Enlightenment thought (Auerbach and Berlin); and the emergence of the forms of historicism that bring about notions such as world literature and culture as ideals and points of arrival in the drama of human cultural development (Auerbach). This large and highly diffuse body of critical, philosophical, and scholarly writings contains some of the most profound reflections on culture produced in the modern era, and our understanding of them have become indispensable to how we think about culture and critique. But I wish to expand our understanding of this mid-century situation by relating it to the fin de siècle perspectives embodied in the work of Edward Said, which—and not just his history of the exploration of the Palestine question but also the entire critical project as it developed at least since *Beginnings*—may be read at one level as a complex engagement with this critical, cultural, and political legacy.[13] The recurring turn in his work to such figures as Auerbach, Adorno, Lukács, and, to a lesser extent, Arendt represents a detailed engagement with this tradition from perspectives made possible by the devastation of Palestinian life in the realization of the Zionist "solution" to the Jewish Question. It also marks his own perception of the continued imbrications of the figure of the modern intellectual, and of the vocation of critique, with the history of the Jewish Question. *All profoundly affected themselves by the history of the Jews in the modern era*, these intellectuals and their reflections on the historical past provide the context out of which I myself turn to those earlier moments and trajectories. In sum, my aim here is to understand the manner in which the Jews of Europe became a *question*, both for themselves and for others, and the implications this being put in question has for elaborating responses—literary, philosophical, popular-cultural, and political—to the crises and conflicts of the projects of modernity in European and non-European, specifically colonial and postcolonial, settings.

Because it turns in this manner to the history of the Jews in modern Europe, this study of the crisis of secularism in contemporary South Asia is best viewed as a search for *beginnings* rather than *origins*, to use a distinction familiar to readers of Said.[14] The book is an attempt to answer the question, What would the genealogy of a non-Western secularism look like? But since it is a genealogy that attempts to cross the treacherous and heavily policed oceans that separate the narratives and figures of modernity in Europe from their reappearance in the colonies—an unavoidable passage for students of colonized societies—it lends to the terms of genealogy itself a contingent or heuristic quality.[15] The necessity for such a move lies in the paradoxical fact that the nation-state and its subsumption of culture can be understood not within the confines of a single and discrete national culture, or even by means of a comparison of such discrete entities, but only cross-nationally, by standing, at least partially and momentarily, outside national identification. This paradox seems not to have been fully understood even by such radical critics of the nationalization of culture and society as Benedict Anderson and Chatterjee. Radical historicism of the Foucauldian sort, which informs in various visible and invisible ways contemporary critiques of the national forms taken by politics and culture, continues to replicate these national configurations of literature and culture as well as the "contexts" appropriate to their production and relevant to their reading. As Wlad Godzich has pointed out, it remains very much the case that, "in spite of its global pretensions, discourse analysis accepts the dominant framework of the nation-state as its geographical boundary and generally follows the periodizations set in literary history."[16]

The answers I offer in this book are based, first of all, on the assertion, which I elaborate and defend at different points in the book, that the crisis of secularism be examined from the point of view, and at the site, of minority existence. Furthermore, I argue, that an account of the "beginnings" of the crisis of Indian secularism around the identity of the Muslims must lead to the history of the involvement of European liberalism with the question of the Jews. This argument is counterintuitive in some ways, but the discomfort produced by such a move, from which I myself am not entirely immune, is a sign of the presence of a notion of culture ultimately tied to an organic model of regeneration and descent. The charting of *this* particular genealogical route for the crisis of culture and community in India is a means of insisting that it be understood as arising out of the conflicts of modernity. The past, or rather the question of the past, plays a crucial role in this crisis, and part of my purpose here is precisely to document this role. But my aim here is also to advise caution against the tendency to view this crisis in terms of the interactions simply of "Islam" and "Hinduism" on Indian soil, as merely the latest phase in a "primordial," that is, millennium-long religious, metaphysical, or cultural conflict.[17] Hence the book's emphasis on the *minoritization* of culture, language, community, and identity as irreducible processes inherent in the transition to modern forms of culture and society, both in the metropolitan and colonial settings. Minoritization is thus viewed here as a continuing process and recurring application of pressure at numerous points across the social field. My goal here, however, is not to suggest the existence of a straightforward historical route by which a European problematic may be said to have "arrived" in colonial India. On the contrary, this book stresses precisely the disjuncture, discontinuity, and lack of fit that are the basis of the Indian reinscription of the narratives and figures of secularism and minority experience.

Readers will not find in this book an inventory of "anti-Semitic" or, in the Indian context, "anti-Muslim" or "communalist" themes or representations in European and Indian literature, respectively. Nor am I concerned here with Zionism or Muslim separatism per se. Instead, this book targets those moments at which liberal culture attempts, *sincerely*, as it were, to resolve the question of the Jews—or, in India, of the Muslims. I am interested, in other words, in how liberalism historically has talked about the modes of apartness of the Jews and the history of their persecution in Western society, and the kinds of solution it has offered: "uniform" citizenship, religious "tolerance," secular "national" literature and culture. Thus this book charts a number of ideological interactions between, on the one hand, modern political and social experience—citizenship, national belonging, minoritization, "partition," uprooting, and exile—and, on the other, modern literature at the level of theme, form, and literary institution. Above all, it attempts to describe the dialectic out of which a certain kind of *minor critique* of modernity is produced. I am concerned, in particular, with the formal qualities and affinities of minority as a cultural and literary location, and my intention is to explore the forms in which minority is inscribed within the larger problematic of the relationship of self to the world. But if, on the one hand, minority is to be understood in this book as a set of formal relationships within literature as a whole, the specifically literary, on the other hand, constitutes for it an exemplary site for the writing of the problematic of national culture, minority existence, and representative selfhood. The relationship of the individual consciousness to totality, which Lukács identified as the central problematic of narrative form, and which, at least in Adorno's handling, is also of significance with respect to modern lyric poetry, constitutes the ground on which the drama of minority is staged. The current renewal of interest in "minor" and "minority" literary practices owes a great deal conceptually to the exploration of this space in Gilles Deleuze and Félix Guattari's *Kafka: Toward a Minor Literature* (1975). In that milestone work, the authors suggest something like a definition of "minor literature": "it is . . . that which a minority constructs within a major language."[18] They thus link the deterritorializing impulse of minor literature to displacements in the mutual relationships of language, literature, culture, place, and people. In a number of reworkings of Deleuze and Guattari's formulation, David Lloyd has introduced the concept of "state" as a mediating term between minority and literature.[19] Lloyd conceives of the state as the locus of practices and narratives of representative ethical development against which, and in relationship to which, the disruptions of minority are produced. Similarly my aim throughout this book is to show the manner in which the *effects* of minority experience are produced. My real focus is therefore on the *process* of minoritization, the *pressures* exerted on language, literature, culture, and identity in the process of becoming minoritized. The significance of India in this examination of comparative minoritizations is that it allows a certain clarity of perception of the relationship between these pressures and the *partition* of a culture, a society, and a state out of which the minoritization of "the Muslims" was actualized. Thus the broader literary concern here is to raise some fundamental questions about how we read literature in terms of certain dominant models of social cohesion, namely, those that have been tied historically in varying ways in the modern era to the cultural forms of the nation-state. But instead of arguing for a *superceding* of these forms in the current global conjuncture of "transnational" flows, identifications, loyalties, affiliations, and forms of performance and consumption of culture and difference, I hope to point out some of the ways in which those "national" (and hence canonical) forms have *always* been open-ended, incomplete, and impossible to achieve.

Currently influential theoretical critiques of nationalism, such as Anderson's *Imagined Communities* and Chatterjee's *Nationalist Thought and the Colonial World*, although divergent in many important respects, share the underlying assumption that the great historical achievement of the nation-form is its unifying project, its desire (even if not ability) to produce the one out of the many. This is to read nation and nationalism on their own terms, however, the terms in which they demand we read them. What these critics fail to account for fully is that nationalism has historically been a great *disrupter* of social and cultural relations, that its reconstitution of societies and populations in terms of distinct narratives of collective life always implies setting forth an entire dynamic of inclusion and exclusion within the very social formation that it claims as uniquely its own and with which it declares itself identical. Thus the great "accomplishment," we might say, of nationalism as a distinctly modern form of political and cultural identity is not that it is a great settling of peoples—"*this* place for *this* people." Rather, its distinguishing mark historically has been precisely that it makes large numbers of people eminently unsettled. More simply put, whenever a population is *minoritized*—a process inherent in the nationalization of peoples and cultural practices—it is also rendered potentially *movable*. Minority, in the sense in which I use this term, is always potentially exile, and exile is an actualization of the threat inherent to the condition of minority. This premise about the conditions and modalities of uprooting, which follows the spirit if not the letter of Arendt's understanding of citizenship and the nation-state in *The Origins of Totalitarianism*, is the basis of my argument in this book, which I extend here into the literary and cultural domain: thus a possible uprooting of populations, and an "entire social texture,"[20] as Arendt puts it, but also, more precisely, of linguistic and cultural practices, and of narratives and memories of collective life. I should clarify, however, that the book does not see its task as one of identifying what Pièrre Nora calls *les lieux de mémoire*, "places" or "sites" that become loci for the generation of shared memories of collective life, a conception which I consider a sort of updating of the Durkheimian *conscience collective*, and which therefore shares the latter's shortcomings.[21] Where Nora attempts to make a stable distinction between memory and history, this book aims to recover minority as a place of disruption of that distinction and to affiliate critical practice itself to these disruptive forms of remembering.

In the remainder of this introductory chapter, I shall attempt to reopen the question of decolonization, postcolonial selfhood, and the legacies, broadly conceived, of the Enlightenment. The goal in this sense is to elaborate the terms of a secularist critique of modern secularism, a *critical secularism* whose affiliations are with the dilemmas of minority existence.[22] Such a critical practice does not claim for itself an external and uncontaminated position. Its critique of the categories of nation and state is a self-consciously immanent one, and seeks to dislodge their stability from within. It therefore confronts the *risk* of reproducing those categories as the only possible way to elude their reproduction. Criticism of the state of contemporary society and culture in South Asia can only begin with a keen sense of the enormity of what has taken place. The (secularist) critique of Partition, the religio-political event that is the material condition of nation-statehood in South Asia, and of the forms of "communal" consciousness and conflict in the twentieth century must avoid the temptation of explaining them away by simply pointing to the accidental twists and turns of political and diplomatic history—the Nehru Report, the Simla Conference, the Cabinet Mission; to the bad faith of various historical agents—the colonial state, the Congress, the Muslim League; or to the false consciousness of social collectivities—the Muslim *ashrāf* elites or the Hindu-*savarna* elites. The historical process explored here is part of us, part of the very critical thought that seeks to comprehend it. On the other hand, the critique of state secularism is reduced to conceptual and practical incoherence, as I shortly argue at some length, if it fails to take stock of its own reliance on the secular culture of critique. In sum, this book is concerned with the fractures of modern experience, with the differing experience of modernity at majority and minority locations, and sees itself as contributing to an immanent critique of the forms of belonging in modern culture, whose great price has always been a great uprooting—of "other" peoples and other problematics.

The Aura of Authenticity

Colonialism is a form of human suffering, one of the historically determinate forms of suffering specific to the modern age. Frantz Fanon is one of the best-known cartographers of this experience and has left us a vocabulary, as much a revised psychoanalysis as a "stretched" Marxism, for tracing out its contours in the culture and politics of the colonial world.[23] Referring as much to the sufferings of the individual under colonial rule as of the sufferings of society as a whole, Fanon wrote that, "because it is a systematic negation of the other person and a furious determination to deny the other person all attributes of humanity, colonialism forces the people it dominates to ask themselves the question constantly: 'In reality, who am I?' "[24] In a remarkable essay on the phenomenology of colonial conquest, Ranajit Guha has reopened this question for the postcolonial moment, exploring its links to the narrative traditions in which the ascendancy of Europe and its encounters with non-European cultures and peoples continue to be told and retold: "Whenever I read or hear the words *colonial India*, it hurts me. It hurts like an injury that has healed and yet has retained somehow a trace of the original pain linked to many different things—memories, values, sentiments."[25] Guha produces a gestalt shift in our understanding of anticolonial nationalism by pointing out that its principal affect is a desire to tell and retell this same painful story, although from the perspective not of the colonizers' victory as such but rather of the defeat and subjugation of the colonized.

Modes of transition to modern forms of culture that have been mediated through the experience of colonial subjugation share the inability to produce narratives of cultural continuity that can absorb the dislocations of modernity. The breaker of tradition—the canonical figure of modernity—is in such contexts fully a *colonial* subject and becomes so precisely in that act of iconoclasm. This stain of treachery against one's own people and of loyalty to the foreign rulers spreads throughout the cultural terrain, coloring even the most radical critiques of indigenous society. The question of tradition in such contexts thus takes a distinct form, with the past appearing not exactly to be dead and buried, even if present in ghostly form, but *murdered* (by or at the behest of an other) and still remaining inappropriately and insufficiently mourned.[26] Thus tradition, which is the realm in which a cultural object is restored its lost aura, here becomes imbued with a melancholy that attaches not to any single object but to the sense of the past as a whole. It appears as that which has become alien to the self, a marginal and threatened fragment of life, but a fragment out of whose lineaments one might attempt to recall what was once *all* of life. The task of a postcolonial literary criticism, therefore, as G. N. Devy has noted, is to attempt to think across the "epistemological stumbling block" represented by colonial culture. And no critical practice that underestimates the difficulty of this task can hope to evade reproducing the hierarchies of thought made possible by colonial rule. In India, as Devy suggests, modern critical consciousness is confronted by the mid-nineteenth century as a sort of cut-off point, "incapable of tracing [its] tradition backwards" beyond that moment. It is a profoundly significant perception, one that helps illuminate the aporia of a range of disciplines in the humanities, as of literary production itself.[27]

To further explore and clarify the issues at stake here, I turn now to their elaboration in the school of Urdu criticism known as *jadīdīyat* and, in particular, to the work of Muhammad Hasan Askari, its leading light and founder, and a widely influential and hugely controversial figure.[28] A magisterial intellect, a polyglot and polymath of staggering erudition, but also deeply conservative in his cultural inclinations, Askari began writing criticism in the 1940s as an enthusiastic interpreter for the Urdu literary world of European modernism, of the entire series of formal developments from Baudelaire and the impressionists to Joyce, Eliot, and Lawrence. In a series of brief essays contributed to the literary magazine *Sāqī* during the late 1940s and 1950s, and in a large number of longer works, Askari explored the relationship of Urdu writing to the literature of the modern West and argued that the former could no longer find its way except insofar as it came to terms with the latter. Thus, in an essay on modernism titled "The Last Stage of Western Literature," he argues that,

> While living in *this* world, we cannot produce an Eastern literature of the traditional sort. Such a literature can only be produced in a society that has its foundation in a metaphysical tradition. For this reason it has become inescapable for our writers to accept Western influences. But we must be alert to which influences we accept and to their significance. My own opinion is this: that until the writers of the East absorb within themselves the literary process that began with Flaubert and Baudelaire, as well as Joyce, Pound, and Lawrence, they will not be able to produce a meaningful literature.[29]

A great deal of Askari's work of this period is an attempt to explore what this *absorption* would mean. The cultural fissure represented by British ascendancy in South Asia—usually located in Urdu literary culture in the Rebellion of 1857—and by the introduction and dominance of "modern" or "English" education is, for Askari, irreversible at this point. In Urdu literary culture in the last century and a half, 1857 has been the object of repeated and obsessive attention, with the revolt and its aftermath coming to mark the moment of catastrophe, and this obsessive reopening of the question of rupture has itself become the condition of possibility of creativity for successive literary generations. In Askari's work, and in that of his leading disciple, Saleem Ahmed, it marks the moment at which the social order that was the world of classical Urdu literature is destroyed and human experience becomes a fragmented and alienated one. The horizon of Urdu writing in the twentieth century is provided by this fragmentation, and the writer's task is to produce an adequate response to it. The literature of a period, movement, or school, or the oeuvre of an individual author, may thus be evaluated in terms of the kind of response it embodies and the social, cultural, and psychological implications of that response.

During the 1950s and 1960s Askari's positions underwent a series of subtle shifts whose cumulative effect is dramatic. In a series of long essays he began to rethink the meaning of "tradition" (*rivāyat*), arguing that it could not be reduced to convention, habit, or "culture." Traditional ways of living are now seen not only in opposition to the modern West but as essentially the same everywhere. Thus at one point he speaks of the essential unity of all "Eastern civilizations," which resides in their adherence to the principle that certain forms of Islamic thought have termed *waḥdat al-wujūd* (the oneness of being, immanence) and that Hinduism has elaborated as the unitarian philosophy of *advaita* (nonduality, monism).[30] Even Europe before the Renaissance is absorbed in this notion of tradition, and Askari is able to make the following far-reaching claim: "The basic tradition is everywhere the same; the difference is one of outward appearance only."[31] But by the end of his life, his work was focused on the reconstruction of the tradition of Urdu literature—which he deemed "Islamic"—a hermeneutic effort across the break represented by British ascendancy in North India. And in his last work, *Jadīdīyat*, published posthumously in 1979, Askari turned, in a new shift of emphasis, to an enumeration of the "errors" and misconceptions of "the West" concerning Islam and religion in general, errors that had been disseminated through "English education" among Muslims themselves.[32] The very word that had designated the kind of critical practice he inaugurated was now seen as the sign of the destructiveness of the culture of the modern West towards the cultures of "the East" in general and Islam in particular. I do not contend, however, that these transformations are steps in the development—or, depending on one's point of view, degeneration—of an individual career and critical project. I suggest instead that they are the results of a common underlying problematic and that Askari himself surely would not have seen his later views as an abandonment of his earlier ones. The incongruous presence in Askari's work of Lawrence and Joyce, on the one hand, and Islamic exegesis, on the other, points to his perception of the paradoxical nature of the problem of Urdu literature. For modernism, in Askari's reading, is the appropriate aesthetic response to inappropriate existence in modernity. Modernism makes available a kaleidoscopic perception of the fragmented reality of modern subjective experience, of modernity as a fallen condition. This perception allows the critic to begin the work of recovery both of tradition and of self through tradition. While the effort to recall and reproduce an auratic consciousness of the (precolonial) past and to reanimate it in the present must be alert to the plurality of the present, to the continued survival of "our" tradition, it can *begin* only by fully inhabiting and working through this (colonized) condition. Furthermore, the interpretation of tradition belongs to its traditional upholders, the *ʿulamā*, but their education prevents the *ʿulamā* from understanding "Europe" as it has arisen even in our midst, and so they are unable to comprehend fully our present. Therefore it is the critic's role to function as mediator, to interpret their exegeses to the larger national public sphere, on the one hand, and, on the other, to enable the *ʿulamā* to comprehend better the culture of the modern West so they can more effectively refute their Westernized and rationalist critics. Thus Askari's larger project here is nothing less than a transformation of the modern public sphere into the domain of traditional disputation. However, we must not confuse this project with those of what has come to be called Islamic fundamentalism, as his less careful critics are wont to do, for the shattered totality his work struggles to reconstruct is not *sharīʿa* or Islamic law per se but the Sufi worldview (*taṣavvuf*) of the medieval Islamic world as interpreted in the work of such twentieth-century exegetes as Ashraf Ali Thanavi—a far cry, for instance, from the hyper-rationalist and hyper-literalist techno-Islamism of an increasingly global sort that now makes headlines worldwide.

It is in the explication of the first-person plural, which stands at the center of his project, that Askari's elaborate hermeneutic effort encounters its limit and makes visible its own reliance on the structures of modern state and society. For the attempt to contain the premodern past of Urdu in a coherent and self-contained structure of meaning—"tradition"—inexorably replicates the conflation of language, literature, and religious "community" that is an ongoing process in the development precisely of the modern nation-state formation in colonial and postcolonial South Asia. Thus, in a strong sense, the subject of Urdu writing is, for Askari, "Muslim," which he spent the better part of his intellectual life elaborating. And the search for the traditional font of Urdu writing leads him exclusively to such Arabic and Persian sources as Ibn al-Arabi, Rumi, and Hafiz. It is a familiar gesture associated with the official historiography of Urdu literature but repudiated in the work of a number of writers who are Askari's rough contemporaries, such as Intizar Husain, whose attachment to the Shia Muslim culture of Lucknow and its environs is simultaneously qualified and enriched by a sense of its deep rootedness in linguistic and cultural practices that quietly and unself-consciously create havoc for the categories of nationalized religious identity. In Askari's work, the complex interplay of indigenous-popular and élite-Persian elements in the emergence and continued performance of Urdu as a spoken and literary register, as well as its fundamental homelessness throughout the modern era, in other words, its minoritization implicit in the nationalization of Indian culture and society, which is the context proper to his own effort at resettling and recovery, are erased from literary historical memory. So while Askari's project is quite different from the conceptual framework that, for instance, is associated with Ashis Nandy, it manages to arrive at the same cul-de-sac as the latter, although from, as it were, the opposite direction: if Nandy's effort for the recovery of an authentic Indian self often leads him to forget the contested and conflicted history of Indianness, Askari's search for the "tradition" of Urdu requires a forgetting of the (ambivalent and problematic) Indianness of Urdu itself.[33] The auratic attempt to resolve the crisis of postcolonial culture can thus be taken in either a "Hindu" or "Muslim" direction. But at no point can either account of Indian reality open itself up adequately to the other. In such a context the central question of how these "traditions" are located within the national-cultural space we call India cannot even be formulated.

My critique of such "auratic" gestures in criticism is not animated by a desire to disavow or *defuse* the crisis of authenticity. It does not attempt to settle, once and for all, this question, which under no circumstances do I take to be a spurious or illusory one. The enormity of what has been ruined is not in doubt, and evidence of its destruction is everywhere to be seen. In this, as in so much else, the forms of postcolonial remembering evoke those "mass-graves for the forgotten" in which Arendt once placed the products of European Jewish creativity, contrasting them with the "enduring monuments" to those who are "remembered and cherished."[34] When we consider some of the South Asian and Islamic contexts at stake in the discussion of Askari, for example, an individual text from the medieval or premodern corpus—whether theological or poetic or both, as is often the case—cannot be approached except through the Orientalist archive. It comes to us already constituted as an object of (Orientalist) knowledge. The ("post-Orientalist") critical task is to undermine the inevitability of this circle, but this project cannot be conceived of as simply *reanimating* the text and claiming a living and unbroken connection to it. The authority of the Orientalist archive is not ultimately displaced by this posture of return to a reanimated past, whether this gesture is made in the context of literary criticism or of militantly politicized "Hinduism" or "Islam." A claim Abdallah Laroui once made for postcolonial Arab culture may be repeated for contemporary South Asian society: "In contemporary Arab ideology, no form of consciousness is authentic: no more so in the religious scholar than in the technophile; he reflects a different image of contact with the West, but the center of his thought is no more his own than that of the technophile belongs properly to him."[35] The premodern corpus can only be approached from a position of *exile* from it, that is, through a careful elaboration of the forms of displacement, distance, alienation—and, yes, remembrance, familiarity, and recognition—that characterize our contemporary relationship to it. (I shall return to these questions at some length in later chapters.)

I am concerned here, in other words, with the possibilities of living *with* the crisis of authenticity and coming to understand the social and ethical stakes in that struggle to live. The wound cannot be healed by the attempt to resurrect an undifferentiated tradition. The equation of the modern with the Western, and of the non-modern with (contemporary) religiosity, seeks to settle the question once and for all in favor of the rejection of everything marked as modern (and Western) and the recuperation and strengthening of surviving, "lived" traditions, wherever they are to be found. In part this book is motivated by the desire to examine critically the casualness of these equations and to give substance to such concepts as "liberal," "secular," "modern," "post-Enlightenment," and "citizenship" as they appear in the critique of postcolonial culture—terms sometimes used in contemporary criticism with the utmost vagueness and abandonment of rigor. The tendency to look for an Archimedean point outside "modernity"—as embodied, for instance, in Nandy's famous interpretation of the life of Gandhi or in Askari's attempted recuperation of medieval *taṣavvuf*—marks a failure to recognize that there is now no *unmediated* recourse to an outside. To the gesture in criticism that would pretend to reanimate an auratic recollection of the past, we may counterpose what I call *vernacular modernities*, a formulation I shall return to shortly.[36] When a writer like Salman Rushdie, who is now almost iconically identified with the thematics of postcolonial secularism, is invoked in that context in either avowal or disavowal, it is not often understood, least of all by Rushdie himself, that a number of these secularist formulations are not unique to the postcolonial migrant, or Anglophone (or Francophone), contexts. Despite huge differences of impulse and emphasis from the latter, one may point in the Indian and Urdu context, for instance, to numerous precedents: to the unapologetic urbanism and irreverence of the fiction of Saadat Hasan Manto, to Faiz Ahmed Faiz's immersion in, and secularization of, the language of Sufism in classical Urdu lyric, and to the *Islamic* polemic of Abul Kalam Azad (Abū al-Kalām Āzād) against the cultural claims of Muslim separatism, embodying a religious but *non-auratic* view of the space of national politics, to cite a handful of writers who reappear in subsequent chapters. Each of these writers opens up the question of relationship to the past in a manner consistent with his material: respectively, modern narrative and epic ambition, the modern lyric and its recollection of the polyvalence of love in *taṣavvuf*, and life-writing and its production of cultural memory for the staking of political claims. But each writer is alert in his own way to the ethical consequences of this reopening of the question of the past and views social space as inherently secular, as that which is always in excess of narrative claims about the past and must be shared with others. Later in the book I turn to each of these figures in order to situate them and their writings of the 1940s and 1950s, and Urdu literary production more generally, within the literary landscape of late colonial and early postcolonial South Asia. It is with such vernacular projects for modern selfhood and collective life that criticism must affiliate itself in its struggle to point toward and perhaps even momentarily achieve authentic forms of culture and memory. Above all, my readings of these writers are meant to highlight that the anti-secularist position in debates about the crisis of postcolonial culture—by which I do *not* signify only the contemporary migrant intellectual context—is *majoritarian* in nature, to the extent that it places outside the bounds of critique and leaves intact normative notions of tradition and culture that have the nation-state as the historical horizon of their emergence and codification.

Dialectic of Enlightenment in the Colony

For a critique of the sort I attempt to elaborate here, it is not sufficient to make the historicist argument that all traditions are invented. What is needed, instead, is an immanent critique of the aura of authenticity itself, a critique that seeks to *displace* terms such as "tradition," "culture," and "homeland" in which the problematic of authenticity is produced. In outlining such a critique, I turn first to a seemingly unlikely figure, namely, Adorno, and to an unlikely Adornian text, namely, one of the fragments (no. 32) of *Minima Moralia*, which carries the aphoristic and famously provocative title, "Savages are not better humans."[37] In the pious populism that is increasingly our common sense in the humanities, the title and text of the fragment can be easily dismissed as signs of the elitist Adorno, of a mandarinism unable to see history as anything but the history of European man. That would be an incorrect reading, however, for these seemingly Eurocentric emphases must be read within Adorno's larger concern here with a critique of historical agency as it has traditionally been conceived of in Western Marxism. This segment appears in part 1 of the book, marked by the author as compositions of 1944. It is part of a set of paragraphs that begin the transition from elaborations of the private experience of exile to larger cultural and political concerns, a transition which, according to the dedication, structures each of the parts of the book as a whole.[38] They chart a twin process: on the one hand, the decline of bourgeois liberal culture and society into administration but also, on the other, the containment of genuinely emancipatory politics in the cult of the commissar. Thus, in no. 30, "progress" and "barbarism," as these terms apply to contemporary mass culture, are shown to be in a dialectical relation, "so matted together . . . that only barbaric asceticism towards the latter, and towards progress in technical means, could restore an unbarbaric condition."[39] Progress in the productive means available to society, although real in itself, is no guarantee of social and cultural progress as such, which now requires a critical relationship to the language and paraphernalia of progress itself. And in no. 31 Adorno marks the decline of solidarity, which had been the intersubjective dimension of progressive politics, into the ruthlessness and "cold shoulder" of "the organization men."[40] Solidarity has turned into the "confidence that the Party has a thousand eyes," and the psychic energies of individuals are now wasted in surviving the capriciousness of the bosses rather than in testing the weaknesses of the class enemy. It is this twin process—the descent of liberalism into administered mass society, and of organized political opposition into the psychology of totalitarianism—that opens up for Adorno the question of a newcomer on the world-historical stage constructed by "the conflicts of industrial society": the non-Western, the underdeveloped, the primitive, the native.

The dominant and characteristic posture of Adorno's text is a studied avoidance of and caution against political sentimentality. Adorno anticipates, in a remarkably prescient manner, the rise of the postwar figure of the anticolonial insurgent and warns against its romanticization within an ultimately unaltered and Eurocentric history of the realization of Man. A classic, even canonical, formulation of this romance is to be found in Sartre's preface to *The Wretched of the Earth*, where, in stark contrast with Fanon's own studied hesitation in the face of precisely such a move, Sartre situates the native as the agent of a more comprehensive and universal humanism than that which had so far been achieved, in a world divided between "men" and "natives," between colonizer and colonized. Sartre describes his own text as an attempt to take the argument further, beyond the point where "Fanon stops," and, in the process, reinscribes the native as more European than the European (at present). In Sartre's text, anticolonial insurgency cancels out a humanism tainted by colonial racism, a contradictory mode of "laying claim to and denying the human condition at the same time." By inflicting violence on the settler, by murdering him, the native becomes "a different man; of higher quality." The conclusion of this process is the final disappearance of racism, a "full-grown" humanity, and hence the "end of the dialectic."[41]

Adorno, like Fanon, resists this resolution. For Fanon, the mere substitution of Third World for Europe, of native for European, is a ruse of the colonial status quo itself: "If we want to turn Africa into a new Europe, and America into a new Europe, then let us leave the destiny of our countries to Europeans. They will know how to do it better than the most gifted among us."[42] Adorno points to the hard reality that the non-Western and anticolonial renewal of humanism and Enlightenment is in itself no guarantee against the mode of domestication of critical rationality whose most visible theoretical expression for him is modern positivism. The allusive reference in the fragment to "Carnap-worshipers in India"[43] is itself a remarkable anticipation, and an imaging in condensed form, of the complex of relations between "positivism" and the rationalities of the postcolonial, developmentalist nation-state. But in concluding the fragment, Adorno opens up a constellation even more complex and paradoxical than Fanon's: "There is some reason to fear that the involvement of non-Western peoples in the conflicts of industrial society, long overdue in itself, will be less to the benefit of the liberated peoples than to that of rationally improved production and communications, and a modestly raised standard of living."[44] This remarkable passage, each of its phrases opening up a prospect onto the problematic of decolonization and modernity, will recall for readers Adorno's better-known critique of jazz.[45] In both cases the real emphasis is not on the thing itself—jazz or decolonization—but on the ability of an increasingly integrated world to *administer* it. Faced with the prospect of the "involvement of non-Western peoples in the conflicts of industrial society," Adorno opens up the question: involvement on what basis, in what terms, in whose interest? Unlike Sartre, for whom the native simply takes us to a higher, more complete humanism, Adorno's skepticism leads us to ask the question of the fate of humanism itself: How will "the non-Western peoples" narrate their humanity out of their struggle against colonialism? Adorno's answer to these questions is, of course, cautionary. It calls, above all, for the recognition that the system can absorb and work over that which claims to be unequivocally *outside* it. *Effective* critique of capitalist modernity, and of Enlightenment as such, therefore cannot take the form of a gesture merely of self-distancing and disavowal: "It presupposes experience, a historical memory, a fastidious intellect and above all an ample measure of satiety."[46] As is well known, the social equivalent of this critical posture for Adorno is the experience of exile, the indeterminate, threatened, and threatening location at the cusp of outside and inside. That Adorno could not anticipate the "weariness" or "satiety" (and therefore "experience") of the *colonized* with Western culture, that he could not recognize the emergence of an antagonistic and exilic "historical memory" not reducible to that of the principled *Western* critic of the West, marks the limit of his own comprehension of the dialectic of Enlightenment in a decolonizing world. We might even say that today a comprehensive critique of "Western" modernity is not possible without an intimate experience of the imperialization of the world, from one side or the other of the imperial divide. But Adorno's skepticism is also salutary, a refusal to speak in the name of the colonized, a refusal to append their struggles to a narrative of the self-realization of a Euro-centered humanity.

Adorno and Horkheimer's most far-reaching contribution to a rethinking of the dominant narrative of secularization is, of course, *Dialectic of Enlightenment*, in which the opening paragraph signals this concern with the narrative of the emergence and fate of secular consciousness. The first (and unmarked) textual reference in "The Concept of Enlightenment" is to Max Weber, the most significant early-twentieth-century theorist of secularization, and precedes the explicit reference to Bacon: "Enlightenment's program was the disenchantment of the world."[47] Notoriously the term "enlightenment" undergoes a recurring, almost cyclical, expansion and contraction of designation in Adorno and Horkheimer's text, from being a category in modern intellectual history to its most expansive use as the concept of a philosophical anthropology, as in the essay's very first sentence: "Enlightenment, understood in the widest sense as the advance of thought, has always aimed at liberating human beings from fear and installing them as masters" (*DE*, 1). Knowledge and power are one; hence the cataclysmic dangers (and utopian possibilities) that accompany any movements in knowledge and culture. One conceptual consequence of this philosophical anthropology, this understanding of "enlightenment" as a *human* phenomenon—and, beyond the Greek and Jewish materials, *Dialectic of Enlightenment* makes repeated references to Egyptian and Indian ones, in addition to numerous "primitive" cultures as documented and codified in modern Western ethnography—is that the bourgeois Enlightenment also be considered, momentarily at least, as simply an event and process in human history rather than in Western history alone.[48]

Whether or to what extent Horkheimer and Adorno's argument is able to coexist with, if not actually encourage, a concern with Enlightenment in the colonies is a discussion for another day, although below I attempt to show its relevance for such analysis by performing one. It is no longer possible, however, to give a critical account of the modern Enlightenment's global career except through a careful examination of its deep involvement in the history of colonialism, from ideologies of the civilizing mission to the very structure of state and society to emerge in the colonies. Far from being suspended or dissolved, therefore, the question of the Enlightenment's Western provenance currently stands at the heart of this critical enterprise. A *comprehensive* understanding of modernity today requires that it be treated as an articulation of metropolitan and colonial constellations and forms, and no attempt to rearticulate the mutual relations of "tradition" and "modernity" in postcolonial societies themselves can simply bypass this question. But it is a false perception to view the colonial reenactment of the modern, bourgeois Enlightenment as entirely the imposition of an external form, whose removal is synonymous with the end of the sovereignty of colonial rationality. In fact, this reappearance does not lack its own dialectic. Those among the colonized who propagated it misperceived this themselves when they trumpeted their "enlightened" and secularizing projects under the sign of the discovery of universal and immutable principles. That these were, properly speaking, élite projects, hardly settles the question in favor of the critics of their purported alienness, such as Askari, Nandy, and Devy. As Adorno and Horkheimer so painstakingly demonstrate, most pointedly in their allegorical reading of Odysseus's encounter with the Sirens, Enlightenment in its "widest sense" is always inextricably linked with power and proceeds with asymmetrical consequences for rulers and ruled. The trajectory of the modern in colonial and postcolonial India is marked by the fact, which imbues this trajectory with both an innocence and an unrelenting melancholy, that the "nature"—"external" and "internal"—which is sought to be mastered, as it were, anew within the conceptual antinomies (and techniques) of industrial civilization is a long manipulated and devastated one, reflecting a far longer civilizational history than the one Horkheimer and Adorno draw upon for their speculative history of knowledge in the West. The perceived gulf that separates the élite's modernizing slogans and projects from the culture of the Indian masses is thus itself a feature of indigenous society at the moment of its encounter with the forces of colonial modernity.

The larger paradox of Enlightenment in the colony is that it brings to an auratically hierarchized social space, to an "enchanted" world, a dialectic whose context proper in the metropolis is precisely the dissolution of heterogeneous subjectivities and the social spaces they inhabit. The objective substratum here is not an unfinished or incomplete progress, however, but rather the distinct articulation of power and knowledge under conditions of colonial capitalism, whose logic Ranajit Guha has identified, in a succinct formulation, as "dominance without hegemony."[49] As a form of knowledge, this domination—of human beings as of nature—arises at the "coalescence" and "divergence," Guha argues, of two conceptual systems, the one post-Enlightenment and European, the other traditional and indigenous. Guha's account of colonial power stresses the preeminence within it of *coercion* over *persuasion*, and therefore the absence of hegemony, properly speaking, in the relation of rulers to ruled. In the exercise of this coercive domination, the articulation of these "alien" and "indigenous" logics makes possible forms of knowledge of dominated groups and society whose claims correspond to the interests of the élite groups in society. Guha, perhaps the most rigorous and unsentimental contemporary theorist of "élitism" as it pertains to the production of knowledge, makes clear what the critique of the élitism of (colonial) knowledge entails: a *displacement* of the categories of such knowledge from the perspective of those heterogeneous subjectivities, which he designates "subaltern," that the knowledge claims attempt to domesticate or even annihilate.[50] There is undoubtedly a partial convergence here with Adorno's conception (which he attributes to Benjamin) of the necessity for knowledge to attend to the "waste products" of history that have fallen "by the wayside," materials which have not been fully taken over by the production of history as a succession of "victory and defeat."[51] The procedure of such critique for Adorno is not the *substitution* of a purportedly true idea for a false one but, rather, "to read from [the latter's] features the admission of falseness which cancels its power and hands it over to truth" (*DE*, 18).

For a representative, perhaps even canonical, elaboration of the themes of Enlightenment, disenchantment, and domination in colonial India, we turn to a passage in Nehru's *Discovery of India* (1946), the famous section in chapter 3 titled "Bharat Mata" (Mother India). Nehru describes his travels across the length and breadth of India during the electoral campaign of 1936–37:

> Often, as I wandered from meeting to meeting, I spoke to my audience of this India of ours, of Hindustan and of *Bharata*, the old Sanskrit name derived from the mythical founder of the race. I seldom do so in the cities, for there the audiences were more sophisticated and wanted stronger fare. But to the peasant, with his limited outlook, I spoke of this great country for whose freedom we were struggling... Sometimes as I reached a gathering, a great roar of welcome would greet me: *Bharat Mata ki jai*—"Victory to Mother India." I would ask them unexpectedly what they meant by that cry, who was this *Bharat Mata*, Mother India, whose victory they wanted? My question would amuse them and surprise them, and then, not knowing exactly what to answer, they would look at each other and at me. I persisted in my questioning. At last a vigorous Jat, wedded to the soil from immemorial generations, would say that it was the dharti, the good earth of India, that they meant. What earth? Their particular village patch, or all the patches in the district or province, or in all of India? And so question and answer went on, till they would ask me impatiently to tell them all about it. I would endeavour to do so and explain that India was all this that they had thought, but it was much more. The mountains and the rivers of India, and the forests and the broad fields, which gave us food, were all dear to us, but what counted ultimately were the people of India, people like them and me, who were spread out all over this vast land. *Bharat Mata*, Mother India, was essentially these millions of people, and victory to her meant victory to these people. You are parts of this *Bharat Mata*, I told them, you are in a manner yourselves

> *Bharat Mata*, and as this idea slowly soaked into their brains, their eyes would light up as if they had made a great discovery.[52]

All the elements of the dialectic I attempt to describe here are present in this passage. In it we encounter a nationalist pedagogy whose aim is the disenchantment of the (peasants') world, and the moment of their recognition of *themselves* as "Mother India" is that moment of Enlightenment, which, in other words, consists of, and is identical with, entering a sense of national belonging. I have a great deal more to say about the gendered nature of this resolution in chapter 4. Here suffice it to note that what is defeated in this moment is myth, namely, the inchoate association of the nation with the mythical ancestor. But further revealing is the role assigned in Nehru's text to the élite male subject. The urban, "sophisticated" consciousness that is the nationalist has transcended its reliance on the modes of thought implicit in veneration of the nation as cosmic Mother, which comes to appear to him as a species of superstition. His use of it is entirely self-conscious and instrumental: it is the language he must speak when he addresses the masses, even as his goal is to shake its hold over their minds, to lead them to a secular and rational sense of themselves as the nation. Moreover, the negation enacted here is a determinate one (in the Adornian-Hegelian sense)—a negation not of "myth" in general but of a concrete historical form it takes in the history of nationalism and of modern Indian culture, which in its own turn had marked a progressive or enlightening moment, namely, the "rebirth" or "renaissance" of the Indian nation. Negated here, in other words, is the elaboration of this master trope in the culture of anticolonial nationalism since the late nineteenth century; also negated, in terms of *Discovery*'s own textual prehistory, is the history of figurations of Bharat Mata from Bankimchandra Chatterjee's novel *Anandamaṭh* (1888) to Bipin Chandra Pal's *Soul of India* (1923), a trajectory Partha Chatterjee has characterized as nationalism's "moment of departure," just as he has situated Nehru and *The Discovery of India* as exemplary of its "moment of arrival."[53] In Nehru's text, "Bharat Mata" is the means not to the interpellation of the nationalist subject, as it is in Bankim's novel, but of its manipulation of the collectivized object that is the peasant masses. At work here is an instrumental rationality, a consciousness to whose relation to the masses Guha has attributed the implicit slogan "discipline and mobilize."

The political logic at work in this relationship of the nationalist to the masses is therefore not one of representation per se but of *exemplarity*. The urban and "sophisticated" consciousness that is the "secular" nationalist claims to represent the nation, to act in its interest, not because it is representative of the people, that is, because it belongs to the world of the people, but because it exemplifies the *highest form of consciousness* one can attain in this colonial society. Hence its sense of isolation in Indian society, and its peculiar reliance, so brilliantly analyzed by Chatterjee, upon the thought and practice of Gandhian politics and on the figure of Gandhi himself, whom it considers a true representative of the masses, with their irrationalism and non-modern worldview—he "almost *is* peasant India."[54] Chatterjee has conceived of the trajectory of nationalist thought in terms of three "moments," a schema which has led to the misreading that he is proposing a stagist narrative of development. As Chatterjee explicitly states at numerous points in his study, his aim is precisely to attempt to dislodge the self-representation of Nehruvian nationalism as the end point of a natural national development.[55] At its "moment of departure," nationalist thought takes the form of a project of "national-cultural regeneration" for the new middle class that seeks to synthesize the "material" superiority of the modern West with the "spiritual" greatness of "Indian" culture, a synthesis to be achieved through (Hindu) religious reform—an engagement, in other words, with modern culture as Enlightenment. The colonial obstacles in the development of the nationalist middle class, then, produce the necessity of taking nationalism to the subaltern classes, and this moment of "maneuver" requires the incorporation of the culture of the rural masses into the culture of middle-class nationalism itself, a historical task whose most visible facilitator is Gandhi. At its "moment of arrival," Chatterjee argues, nationalism takes the form of secular statecraft, an ideology whose most consistent elaborator and proponent is Nehru. Nehruvian *étatisme* and governance by expertise do not represent a canceling or transcending of the Gandhian critique of modernity. Their mutual contradiction at the level of content conceals their articulation or "imbrication" at the level of function.[56] "Maneuver" and "arrival" therefore represent not *successive* "moments" here but an articulation of non-synchronous ones: the populism and indigenism of Gandhian politics allows the hyper-élitism and Anglocentrism of Nehruvian thought to clothe itself in the garb of the popular and the indigenous, while the securing of the "leadership" role of the "expert" élites at the helm of the state-to-come allows for the (Gandhian) gesture of inclusion towards the culture and ethos of the peasant masses. Thus the paradox of Nehruvian Enlightenment is its reliance on social forces and modes of thought that it considers premodern and even reactionary, which lends to the Nehruvian persona its characteristic and melancholic sense of its own (élite) isolation and hence vulnerability. Nowhere perhaps is this paradox more poignantly visible than in Nehru's personal identity itself, and may be read in the seemingly trivial fact that this untiring proponent of egalitarianism and rationalism, who writes of the institution of caste that "in the social organization of today it has no place," was universally referred to and addressed in the public realm, often even by colonial officials, as Pandit Nehru (*DI*, 620).

A critical secularism in South Asia today must confront the contradictions of its own genealogy, even as it challenges the accusation of its purported alienness to Indian (and South Asian) society. A critique of culture and society in contemporary South Asia must produce the conceptual resources necessary to put "Hindu" and "Muslim" (and "Indian" and "Pakistani") in question, to make visible the dialectic of majority and minority within which they are produced, which in itself constitutes the larger part of the movement of Indian modernity. The main lines of development of Subaltern Studies, despite the best and repeatedly expressed intentions of its leading practitioners, have failed to take up this constellation of issues with the seriousness it deserves.[57] I am not suggesting, however, that "Hindu" and "Muslim" have no meaning in precolonial South Asia; on the contrary, the aim here is, in part, precisely to excavate those buried meanings. As Muzaffar Alam has recently shown in his work, *The Languages of Political Islam: India, 1200–1800*, there was no single overarching principle of the governance of its subjects in the political culture of either the Sultanate or the Mughal Empire but rather a shifting ground of negotiation between local forms and traditions and those with Central Asian or other foreign lineage, elaborated and formalized to various extents in the *tahzīb*, *akhlāq*, and Sufi literatures, with the latter, in what became a characteristic of Sufism in India, attempting the convergence of Indian-Hindu and Islamic theosophical concerns.[58] Unique to modern society is our contemporary political experience of religion as political identity, in which identification within a "world" community, the will to cultural uniformity, and political interest are fused together as if in a seamless whole, and the emergence of this experience converges with the rise of a modern middle class, of its chief mode of political and cultural expression (nationalism), and the political structure it characteristically seeks to build for the protection of its interests as a class (the nation-state). A considerable body of scholarship in recent years indicates that this process still remains incomplete, and this more than two centuries after colonial rule emerged for the first time on a mass scale, with the ongoing pervasiveness of forms of social and cultural differentiation (and non-differentiation) that make a daily mockery of the homogenizing machinery of the state and the arenas of politics defined by the state.[59] The present study therefore takes its lead from *Castes of Mind: Colonialism and the Making of Modern India*, Nicholas Dirks's monumental investigation of the colonial invention of the uniform language of "caste" for the comprehension of a vast tapestry of social differentiation.[60] Dirks provides a detailed history of the emerging discourse of caste in the course of the nineteenth century, its relationship to what he calls the "ethnographic state," the numerous paths by which it entered a "nationalist sociology" and, more important, came to reshape large sectors of Indian society and stamp it with the (now) uniform institution of caste. A critical history of colonial conceptions of religious community that would parallel Dirks's account of caste remains to be written. Partly for reasons of disciplinary location, the present book moves in a decidedly different manner, although in basic agreement with Dirks's critical account of the emergence of social and cultural technologies for the fixing of identities in colonial India. Through a close engagement with a range of texts, mostly but not exclusively literary, the aim is to provide a critique—which I see as inevitably an immanent one—of a wide terrain of secularist culture in modern and contemporary South Asia, a critique which, as already discussed at some length above, is not to be confused with the anti-secularist gesture. Such a critique confronts Nehruvian secularism with the demand that it radicalize and, in fact, *secularize* itself. As I previously noted, the "postcolonial" critique of Nehruvian nationalism that has emerged in recent years—and I am thinking here primarily of Chatterjee's work, which remains the most compelling and influential move in this direction—has been directed primarily at what is taken to be the élitism of its thought and practice, the distance from the masses inherent in its secularizing and rationalizing worldview, while leaving untouched Nehru's reputation as the figure of "tolerance" and the champion of Muslim-minority "rights." The basic veracity of this reputation notwithstanding—and the liberal champion of minority rights from a majority position will be a recurring figure in this book—this championing itself must be opened up to a reading as an essential element in the middle-class culture associated with the figure of Nehru. Nationalism's cult of statecraft, technocracy, and expertise, on the one hand, which implies relegating the life-worlds of the masses to the realm of the unverifiable and hence of ritual and mythology, as well as its claim, on the other, to encompass all of society irrespective of denominational or linguistic heterogeneity, are equally signs of the *positivism* of the modes of thought associated with it. It is the social and cultural residue of this positivist concept of the nation that concerns me in this book.

That such polarities as universal and particular or cosmopolitan and vernacular figure decisively today in debates about the crisis of postcolonial culture in numerous sites across the globe is as sure a sign as any that, to paraphrase Adorno, non-Western societies have now entered fully into "the conflicts of industrial society."[61] To say this, however, is in no way to prejudge the exact nature of this entry and its consequences for societies on either side of the imperial divide or for our understanding of those conflicts themselves. I fully share the skepticism, voiced by, among others, Fredric Jameson recently, that the "formula" of "alternate" or "alternative" modernities seems hardly adequate to giving a critical account of the emergence of global society over the last several centuries; furthermore, as Slavoj Žižek has noted, given the cultural logic of the global market system today, "multiplication functions as the disavowal of the antagonism that inheres to the notion of modernity as such."[62] The answer, however, does not seem to me to be the postulation of an undifferentiated and "singular" modernity whose concept is derived largely from the canonical sites and formulations of the modern—France, Britain, Germany—a portable template into which we may fit any social and cultural contents from anywhere across the globe. As Dipesh Chakrabarty has noted, the "problem of capitalist modernity cannot any longer be seen simply as a sociological problem of historical transition . . . but as a problem of translation as well."[63] Thus, if the critical thrust of this book is directed, in the first instance, against the fetishization of the local and the particular, it is at the same time pointed at too uncritical an acceptance of the system's claims concerning its own efficacies. It is with this purpose that I deploy the seemingly oxymoronic term "vernacular modernity" here in order to signify those responses to the pressures of the expanding liberal order—the pressures of Jewish assimilation into the emerging national societies in Europe, in the first instance, and of Muslim minoritization within colonial-national modernity, in the second—that do not simply reproduce its governing antinomies.

In the first part of this book I begin with the emergence and dissemination of the question of minority existence, whose early and exemplary form I chart in the dialectic of Jewishness as minority in post-Enlightenment European culture. The larger aim in chapters 1 and 2, which comprise part 1, is to describe the dialectic of abstract citizenship and national belonging, and to delineate the meanings of Jewishness within each moment of this dialectic. In the first chapter I trace the tension between the universalism of late Enlightenment formulations of emancipation and citizen subjectivity and the particularism and historicism of emergent "nation-thinking," as I call it, in a trajectory that leads from the late works of Gotthold Lessing and Moses Mendelssohn (1780s) to Walter Scott and Heinrich Heine (1810s to 1840s). My aim here is to construct a *European* stage for the literary elaboration of Jewishness as crisis for modern, liberal subjectivity. Chapter 2 brings this exploration of liberalism's Jewish "question" to the end of the so-called era of emancipation, in a reading of the moment, and the text, of George Eliot's last novel, *Daniel Deronda*, the canonical and, as I shall argue, pan-European text of the Jewish Question for the late nineteenth century, in which this persistent question of post-Enlightenment culture and society is offered up for a resolution made possible by the imaginative geographies of modern imperialism. I then turn to an account of how the figures and forms of minority are reinscribed, in Britain's late imperial culture, into an exploration of the nature and meaning of its Indian colony. This chapter traces, to be more precise, a possible trajectory of the problematic of minority from the figure of the Jew in *Deronda* to that of the Muslim in Kipling's Indian stories and Forster's *A Passage to India*.

Part 2 of this book takes as its starting point *The Discovery of India* as a canonical nationalist elaboration of the question of identity in late colonial India, in which Nehru seeks, in the classic liberal manner, to comprehend the crisis surrounding "Muslim" difference within the rubric of "the problem of minorities." What follows in chapters 3, 4, and 5, which comprise part 2, is a discussion of Urdu as a literary-linguistic formation at odds with the cultural geometry of the nation-state, examined here in the work of three mid-century writers who, we might say, are "on the verge of India": that is, individuals whose writings are an elaboration of forms of individual and collective selfhood that cannot be entirely contained within the categories of the emerging nation-state system. Azad, Manto, and Faiz reject the narrowness and political and cultural poverty of Muslim separatism, and yet their oeuvres, together so utterly defining of Urdu writing in the mid-twentieth century, cannot be said simply to affirm in an unmediated form the antinomial terms—majority and minority, indigenous and alien, tradition and modernity—of the nationalist resolution of the question of culture and identity. It is these mediations that the chapters in part 2 attempt to elaborate, with a view to highlighting the always unfinished nature of the nation-state project and the persistence of forms of consciousness that point to hitherto unrealized and utopian possibilities for individual and collective existence. The epilogue brings the argument of the book full circle—to the question of Jewishness—but, as it were, by ending up in a different place. It attempts to read the significance of the thematics of Jewishness that have emerged—and apparently so seamlessly—in a number of recent works of Indo-English fiction, particularly in major novels by Anita Desai and Salman Rushdie.

A final word on the use of the term "postcolonial" in this book. A small industry has appeared in recent years that allows individuals to make a tidy living within the increasingly institutionalized terrain of postcolonial studies by denouncing this terrain and its problematics, and by claiming piously to refrain from the use of the concept itself. I myself deplore this institutionalization and the inevitable academic ghettoization, however privileged, it clearly indicates as well as the stultification of critical thinking it obviously has produced. And, as I have argued elsewhere, modes of analysis associated with categories like postcolonial literature have failed so far to facilitate an adequate response from the literary discipline in the United States at least to the challenge of undoing the Eurocentric structure of its knowledge forms and incorporating non-Western literary traditions on something like an equal footing.[64] One impetus of this book is precisely to suggest ways to resist this ghettoization of concern with the nature of culture in colonial and postcolonial societies and to suggest one possible means of bringing a modern non-Western literature into comparative literary studies in a way that poses productive challenges to its core practices. This effort is thus meant to contribute to the emergence of what Gayatri Spivak has called "planetary" forms of critical practice.[65] But I also reject the dishonest piety of the anti-postcolonialist gesture, made from any number of political positions, including sometimes Marxism, but always in the name of being, as it were, more radical than thou, although entirely limited at the same time to the academic terrain. The concept and its constellation are with us for now, for better and for worse, and the critical task is to disturb their certainties, to prevent their reification, and to reclaim and reanimate their radical energies, rather than this anxious and dishonest claim to having been free from them from the beginning or to have transcended them once and for all.

Permit me to end on a personal note: the skeptical yet engaged critical practice I attempt to outline here has been formed in significant ways by the history of my own family. My parents, in their twenties and thirties, went from being colonial subjects of one of the last great classical empires of the modern era to being citizens of an at least nominally sovereign postcolonial state—a historical shift that defined intergenerational relations within hundreds of millions of families worldwide. That political decolonization as a global process has resulted in the emergence of a new system for the production and management of global inequality—whether it is called neo-colonialism, dependency, globalization, or simply Empire—does not vitiate the fact that it nevertheless represented a real and dramatic change in lived experience on a global scale. Critique of contemporaray, postcolonial globality does not require that we not recognize and pay tribute to what was historically achieved by those who struggled in and against the colonial world; in fact, it requires it. We have all been shaped by that achievement, and to fail to recognize this in the name of an anti-systemic politics is to betray that politics itself. Finally, the distinctness of the process of decolonization experienced by millions of my parents' generation in South Asia—Hindus, Muslims, Sikhs, Parsis, and Christians—is that, within this process, they became not just physically displaced from, but also radically alien to, the places and practices of their origins. It is the larger story of colonial rule and decolonization, national sovereignty and displacement, and the settling and unsettling of peoples and cultures in the modern era, reflected in my parents' individual journey, that I attempt to tell in this book, as a means of paying belated and insufficient homage to it.

PART ONE

Emergence: Europe and Its Others

CHAPTER ONE

Jewishness as Minority

EMERGENCE OF A EUROPEAN PROBLEMATIC

In the fall of 1843, in the process of becoming a political refugee himself, Karl Marx turned his attention to the genesis of liberal state and society in the eighteenth century in order to ponder the failure of what he called "political emancipation": "The decomposition of man into Jew and citizen, protestant and citizen, religious man and citizen, this decomposition is no trick played upon political citizenship, no avoidance of political emancipation. It is political emancipation itself, the political manner of emancipating oneself from religion."[1] The failure of emancipation, he concluded, did not derive from its having been thwarted; it lay instead in its success. The appearance of a crisis around the particularism of the Jews was intrinsic to the successful realization of liberal state and society, for the figure of the Jew, as it emerged from the collapse of the social space of the ancien régime (and hence of the ghetto), continually and paradoxically undermined the universalist claims of the emerging liberal order. With characteristic clarity, Marx noted the centrality of the Jews to the emergence of the forms of modernity—capitalist relations of economic production, the secular and universalist state, the money form, Enlightenment legacies of tolerance and critique, uniform and abstract citizenship—not simply in sociological terms but rather as a site for the elaboration of the constitutive narratives of modern life.[2] The subsequent century of European politics was to confirm Marx's prognosis, as at key moments in the political history of Europe and its relations with the rest of the world—the Damascus Affair, the Revolutions of 1830 and 1848, the unification of Germany, the Dreyfus Affair, the defeat and dissolution of the Ottoman Empire, the rise of National Socialism, and the beginnings of the era of decolonization—the Jews were repeatedly thrust into the foreground of an increasingly global drama about the meaning and fate of the projects of European modernity, the meaning and fate in the world of the idea of Europe itself. The drama that had begun a half-century before Marx's declaration, in the revolutionary declaration of the Rights of Man and of the Citizen, and renewed during the Napoleonic reorganization of the continent and then the retrenchment at Vienna, was thus established as the source of some of the most often recurring motifs of the nineteenth century. And the history that had begun as a series of questions, explorations, aspirations, and crises in such places as Königsberg, Paris, the Rhineland, and Berlin, played itself out a century and a half later in upheavals and displacements in such faraway places as Jaffa, Jerusalem, New York, Shanghai, Buenos Aires, Istanbul, Bombay, and Los Angeles. But if it is widely understood that the crisis over the Jews represents an irreducible feature of modern Western life, it is not generally perceived that its consequences are global in nature, that is, that it now represents an irreducible feature of a globalized modernity as such.[3] It is in and through the external displacement of the purportedly internal Jewish Question, as much as through the imperial management of other peoples and continents, that the problematic of European modernity itself achieves a global significance. In the present, post-genocide phase of the Jewish Question, that is, in the conflict over the meaning and inhabiting of historical Palestine, the question of Europe's "other without" is brought together and into articulation with that of its "other within."[4] The inherent failure of the modern nation-state system, the recurring crises it engenders about "national" peoples and "minorities," is condensed in concentrated form, and revealed with unrelenting clarity, in the conflict over Palestine and the nature of the Jews and the Palestinians as distinct peoples. In this book I take seriously, and with an eye to its many implications, the assertion that the fate of the Jews of Europe carries implications not simply for Europe and its peoples but for the projects of modernity as a whole. I begin, therefore, by attempting to reinscribe certain elements of the literary and cultural history of the Jewish Question within a global frame in order to reopen the question of liberalism, secularization, and the crisis of minority, and to explore the mutual relations of these formations as a problematic of global dimensions and significance.

The figure of the Jew has faced a paradoxical predicament in the culture of the modern West, and has typically been met with a contradictory set of representational demands: on the one hand, as a figure of particularity, it has generated anxieties about the undermining of the universalizing claims and ambitions embedded in the constitutive narratives of modern culture, with the Jews coming to be seen as slavishly bound to external Law and tradition, ritualistic and irrational, and incapable of the maturity and autonomy called for in the development of enlightened, modern subjectivity; on the other, as a figure of transnational range and abilities, it raises questions about deracination, homelessness, abstraction, supra-national identifications, and divided loyalties. Marx pointed precisely to this paradox of Jewish particularity as the basis of Jewish cosmopolitanism in outlining the contradictory relationship of the Jews to the emerging liberal order (and each of the two parts of his essay on the Jewish Question corresponds to one side of this contradiction):

"the Jew" of modern Western imagination is both the threat of particularism confronting the secularizing and universalizing state and the figure of universal exchange that serves as a marker for the uprootedness and abstraction of bourgeois culture. "Jewish emancipation" is thus for Marx an impossible idea so long as emancipation is conceived of in liberal terms and the crisis around the Jews marks the inherent limit of this form of emancipation.[5]

This chapter itself is structured into two main parts, each one broadly corresponding to one side of this contradictory configuration. In the first section I examine the figure of the Jew from the perspective offered by the question of enlightened subjectivity, the universal and abstract citizen subject on whose emergence the projects of Enlightenment are predicated.[6] In the second part I approach the figure from the direction of the problem of national culture and belonging. It has become a commonplace method in the comparative study of minority-majority relations to counterpose what is seen as the universalism of liberal citizenship to the exclusivism and narrowness of national belonging, a procedure inherent to the practice and self-perception of liberal politics itself. This sometimes takes the form of a historical narrative—Enlightenment followed by Romantic-nationalist reaction—and sometimes the form of ideal-type analysis in which different nation-state formations are compared for their more or less inclusive political traditions, with Germany and France often representing the two oppositional poles.[7] Very often the two strategies work in tandem, as in the various arguments that see Germany–Nationalism itself as a rejection of and response to France–Enlightenment–Revolution. This chapter, and the book as a whole, opens up, on the one hand, the legal or political question of citizenship towards an exploration of wider notions of personhood, community, and subjectivity, which the legal or political discourses themselves repeatedly rely upon, point towards, and blend into; on the other, this chapter dismantles the self-abstraction of liberal culture from the more patently troubled history of romantic nationalism. Abstract citizen subjectivity and national belonging constitute moments in the dialectic of modern selfhood, with the figure of the Jew coming to mark the inherent limit of *each* moment of identification, to mark the disruption of the categories of identity, becoming in the process the site of crisis and its attempted containment. This tension between, as it were, emancipation and assimilation is a central problematic in the history of the Jewish Question, often misperceived as a tension between practices (as well as theories) of social cohesion that differ in their treatment of the Jews. It is, instead, a constitutive tension in the emergence of the forms of liberal culture and society as a whole and marks the centrality of the Jews to this emergence. As Arendt pointed out long ago, this tension is embodied in the (hyphenated) idea of the nation-state itself, even as it has taken different forms in concrete historical situations.[8] Thus the relationship between the subject of national belonging and the eighteenth-century figure of citizen, whose dignity and rights were supposed to be derived entirely from a uniform human nature, and not from received culture or tradition, is one of tension and not mere contradiction, as certain forms of intellectual history have conventionally suggested. Rejecting such a historical narrative, Isaiah Berlin viewed this relationship as one of *reliance* as much as negation, drawing our attention to the "paradoxical" possibility that the figure of the autonomous and autochthonous people *assumes* the self-determining individual subject posited in Enlightenment thought and is a displacement of it from one plane of existence to another.[9] To be more precise, one can only conceive of the collective and sovereign subject of national belonging once the "freedom" of the subject as such—its "self-legislation," in Kantian terms—has been achieved. This constitutive freedom of the abstract subject, as much as the myth of autochthony of an individual people, is brought to crisis in the *minor* practices, narratives, and locations of Jewish existence. The ultimate collapse of this tenuous balance concerning the status and meaning of Jewish existence, which opened the door to the final catastrophe, represents, as Arendt noted, the complete overpowering of the claims of citizenship and state by those of *Volk* and national belonging: "the transformation of the state from an instrument of the law into an instrument of the nation had been completed; the nation had conquered the state, national interest had priority over law long before Hitler could pronounce 'right is what is good for the German people.' "[10]

In the following chapter I turn to the rhetorical complexities of the attempt to normalize and *settle* the unsettling figure of the Jew through the form of territorialization that we know historically as Zionism, in which the Jewish Question, this recurring and seemingly intractable crisis of post–Enlightenment European culture, is offered up to a solution in terms of a social, political, and cultural geography made possible by Europe's colonial domination of non-European societies. I am particularly interested here in the involvement of liberalism with this manner of conceiving of a resolution to the question of the Jews. Finally, in keeping with the larger thesis of this book, I turn in the second half of the next chapter to an exploration of the manner in which the question of minority and modernity is transformed in the literary culture of late imperial Britain, as the figures and narratives of Jewishness in the metropolis are displaced and reinscribed in a consideration of the colonial relationship and the crisis of the identity of England's empire and its Indian colony—the passage, to be precise, from the formal and thematic preoccupations of *Daniel Deronda* to those of *A Passage to India.*

At various points in these two chapters I take individual texts or fragments of texts as starting points for an exploration of a larger cultural moment and constellation. Beginning with readings of a number of literary, philosophical, and polemical texts from the late eighteenth to the latter half of the nineteenth century, I chart the emergence of the problematic of Jewishness in these early decades, from the first formulations of the question of emancipation to the moment when the "question" of the Jews becomes available for a Zionist and hence colonial solution. The social, political, and cultural history of Jewish emancipation has, of course, taken rather different forms in the various European countries, as well as in different regions within individual countries themselves, depending upon a host of factors ranging from long-standing cultural traditions to varying processes of economic, social, and political modernization, and I draw here upon material from the British, German, and French contexts. It is certainly possible, however, to speak of the emergence of a *European* problematic in the mutual interaction of these individual histories, and my purpose throughout is to place individual texts, persons, events, and discourses within this larger perspective, even concerning the question of national belonging, for it is precisely the normalization of European selfhood in terms of *national* identities in the nineteenth century to which Jewish identity poses a number of insurmountable difficulties. In other words, I attempt to read the works that concern this book as European texts, a task that will also involve, wherever possible, an endeavor to make visible the *translation* of these local or national themes and questions into that pan-European context.

Jewishness, Philo-Semitism, and the Antinomies of Emancipation

It is customary in the historiography of Jewish emancipation to see the beginnings of the era of emancipation in the developments of the late 1770s and the 1780s, for example, in such events as the publication and performance of Gotthold Ephraim Lessing's reputedly philo-Semitic play, *Nathan the Wise* (1779); the wide-ranging public debate following the appearance of Christian Wilhelm Dohm's plea for Jewish emancipation, *On the Civic Improvement of the Jews* (1781); the Austrian Edict of Toleration (1782); the publication of Moses Mendelssohn's *Jerusalem* (1783); the appearance of Königsberg *Ha-Me'asef* (1783); the discussion surrounding the writings of Mirabeau and Grégoire of the late 1780s on the subject and the National Assembly debates of 1789–91, which concluded with the emancipation proclamations of 1791; and the publication, in 1792–93, of Solomon Maimon's *Autobiography*.[11] I follow this convention to the extent that it identifies a new configuration of the problem centering around the status of the Jews, with the polemics now taking the form of a call for uniformity of rights based on the notion of uniformity of human nature. The difference from even the so-called Jew Bill controversy of 1753 in England is a marked one. Although the bill was repealed after an eruption of both popular and organized Tory anti-Semitism, it had in fact been concerned with the smallest of changes in the civil status of the Jews, easing to a degree some of the conditions for naturalization of foreign-born Jews alone. The controversy introduced for the first time into the emerging liberal public sphere such ancient features of European anti-Semitism as the charge of ritual murder. Not even the proponents of the bill, who hastily withdrew in light of the public outcry, imagined anything like the notion that uniformity of citizenship would be a basis for their views, which routinely would be the case from the 1780s onwards not just in France and Germany but in England as well.[12]

Such is the case, for instance, with Lessing's play, whose influence on the subsequent history of assimilation-emancipation can hardly be over-estimated, and also with Mendelssohn's influential philosophical discourse on the vexed question of Enlightenment and religious particularity and difference. The two works cap a remarkable relationship, legendary in its own time for intellectual collaboration, held up then and throughout the nineteenth-century as exemplary of the Enlightenment cult of friend-ship across the divisions of religious difference.[13] If Lessing came to symbolize the inclusive humaneness of a distinctly German Enlighten-ment, Mendelssohn became something like the archetype, or *Vorbild*, of the enlightened German Jew, with a celebrated reputation throughout Europe in his own time as the *philosophe Juif de Berlin* (as the French locution had it), in whom *Haskala* and German Enlightenment spilled over into each other.[14] Each text itself has had an extraordinary history of reception as exemplar of the Enlightenment attitude toward religious co-existence and tolerance. *Nathan the Wise*, in particular, came to acquire in the nineteenth century something like the status of a banner for the project of assimilating Jews into the *Bildungsbürgertum*, and became a sort of ur-text of the liberal concern with the equality of the Jews, leading the historian George L. Mosse, himself one of the late inheritors of this tradition of Jewish assimilation, to refer to Lessing's play as the "Magna Charta of German Jewry."[15] The play influenced later champions of Jewish rights on a pan-European scale, including Maria Edgeworth, who, already in *Harrington* (1817), ironically cites knowledge of the play as essential to displays of concern for Jewish affairs, and George Eliot, who attended a performance of the play in Berlin during her visit in 1854 with G. H. Lewes.[16] We also know that Eliot read *Jerusalem* in 1872 as part of the wide reading and research she did for *Daniel Deronda*.[17] The eponymous Jewish protagonist of Lessing's play, a defining example of the literary type of the "noble Jew" and widely interpreted as modeled on Mendelssohn himself, was seen as the embodiment of the ideal of *Bildung* on the basis of which Jewish equality was to be achieved.[18] His restraint and lack of bitterness at the fate of his own wife and sons, murdered by Crusaders years before the time frame of the action of the play, already pointed towards the "enlightened self-control" and forgetting of "the painful scars of domination by others" which Horkheimer and Adorno ascribed to the psychology of assimilation as a whole.[19] The nineteenth-century figure of the cultivated (*gebildet*) German Jew was, as it were, prefigured and announced in Lessing's play.[20]

But while both *Nathan* and *Jerusalem* give expression to a classic Enlightenment concept of religious coexistence and tolerance, based on notions of the shared rational and moral nature of all human beings, they also reveal, below the calm surface of claims about a universal and uniform human nature, signs of the threatened and threatening forms of difference embodied in Jewish life. Mendelssohn's *Jerusalem*, written after Lessing's death, represents a critique of the notion of citizenship implicit in *Nathan*. Both works explore the relationship between citizenship in the narrow, legalistic sense and the wider experience of enlightened subjectivity or personhood, but *Jerusalem* is an attempt to rethink, from within the Enlightenment project, the structure of relations to state and society which define the Enlightenment citizen subject. It is produced, in other words, from the position I described in the introduction as *minority*: it resists, from within, the resolutions and narratives of ethical development produced within the "major" work that is *Nathan*. Far from being content with "tolerance" of Jewish existence in enlightened modernity, *Jerusalem* calls for a rethinking of the very terms within which the toleration of minority by majority is conceptualized. My point here is not to challenge Lessing's philo-Semitism, his status as a champion of Jewish emancipation, but rather to understand what this championing actually means, to explore its inherent limits and contradictions and what it ever *can* mean. Lessing's play is of singular importance to an effort at a critical understanding of that recurring figure of modern European culture, the champion of the Jews.[21]

In the famous, central episode of Lessing's play, the Jewish protagonist is asked by the sultan Saladin, then ruler of Jerusalem and much of Palestine, to declare which of the three great monotheistic faiths of Abrahamic origin is the true one. The background to the action of the play, and to the sovereign's question about the conflicting faiths, is therefore provided by the Crusades, or, to be historically more precise, by the period of sporadic confrontation and tenuous truce between Christian and Muslim forces in Palestine known as the Third Crusade. *Nathan the Wise* is illustrative of the uses to which the religious conflicts of the medieval era have repeatedly been put in modern writing. The Crusades and the *Reconquista*, those twin fevers of the medieval world, which preoccupied (and affected in profoundly different ways) communities of Muslims, Christians, and Jews over the course of centuries throughout the Old World, have provided powerful motifs and topoi in modern literature for navigations of the terrain of culture and violence, secular life and religious difference, Enlightenment and community. But if Lessing's play is exemplary in this regard, we may also note here the reworking of these motifs and strategies in such works as Heine's *Rabbi of Bacherach*, "Jehuda Ben Halevy," and "Almansor"; Scott's *Ivanhoe* and *Talisman*; and, with a view to the South Asian and Urdu contexts discussed later in this book, Abdul Halim Sharar's *Flora Florinda*, Salman Rushdie's *The Moor's Last Sigh*, Amitav Ghosh's *In an Antique Land*, Tariq Ali's *The Pomegranate Tree* and *The Book of Saladin*, and, in one comparatively small but crucial respect at least, even Abul Kalam Azad's *Ġhubār-e ḳhāṭir*. It is in fact as a partial engagement with the larger literary history of preoccupation with these medieval cultural conflicts that, for instance, the famous, and, for non-Muslim Indian nationalists, often perplexing, attachment of Indian Muslims to Arab Spain becomes meaningful. Urdu literary imagination at least from Sharar onwards, in the life and work of Muhammad Iqbal, above all, but also with a number of non-Urdu writers like Rushdie, whose origins lie within the larger milieu of the Urdu-speaking world, has repeatedly been sparked by engagements with the motifs of this medieval Spain of modern literature. I return to this tendency at greater length at some points later in this book; here suffice it to say that collectively these engagements represent a rewriting both of colonialist as well as nationalist narratives of colonial and postcolonial identity from within the linguistic and literary problematic that is marked by its "Urdu" and "Muslim" affiliations in the culture of modern India.[22]

Finally, Eliot's last novel may also be read fruitfully, as I argue in the next chapter, as a reinscription, and a return to the nineteenth-century present, of these resonant historical themes and motifs: the meaning of the Holy Land, the power of the West and its history of confrontation with Islam, the long story of Christian persecution of the Jews, the intertwined (Christian) ideologies of conversion and restoration, and the nature and destiny of the Jews. We might say of *Daniel Deronda*, in fact, that it *secularizes* the literary constellation which is the Crusades by returning it to the historical present and identifying the Jewish Question as at the center of the formation of English national and modern European identity more broadly, of which this medievalist constellation was an inscription and displacement in the first place. "Moorish" Spain and "Turkish" Palestine are thus the source of recurring motifs of great significance in modern literature, providing the site for complex explorations of ideological intersections—between colonialism, national identity, the concerns of secular liberal culture, and religious difference and identity—that are germane to the argument of this book as a whole and will provide the means of mooring its analyses from time to time.

At the heart of the reception of Lessing's play is the well-known parable-like story which Nathan eventually tells in response to Saladin's question about the one true faith, the story that is the basis for the play being read as revolving around religious tolerance and coexistence.[23] More notable for my purposes here, however, is the speech immediately preceding the telling of the parable. Nathan, left alone by Saladin to think through his answer, launches into a soliloquy. Recall that this is their first meeting, and that Nathan has been summoned because Saladin is short of money—"Accursed, wretched money!" he calls it[24]—and hopes to borrow some from the merchant. Given his discomfort at his ever precarious financial situation, and also given the Jewish reputation for shrewd tight-fistedness which he assumes, Saladin has deliberately kept Nathan in the dark about the true nature of his summons. Instead of asking the merchant straight out for a loan, Saladin decides, as he puts it, to dissemble—hence the question about the one true faith, and hence Nathan's soliloquy.

Nathan immediately recognizes that he is being dissembled with. What a question, he wonders to himself, asking for the "bare and blank" truth—bare and blank, as he puts it, like "coin from modern mints [*neue Münze*]," which "but the stamp creates" (3.6.6–7). He must be cautious and not allow himself to be trapped:

> To be a Jew outright [*Stockjude*] won't do at all.—
> But not to be a Jew will do still less.
> For if no Jew, he might well ask, then why
> Not Musulman?—That's it! And that can save me!
> Not only children can be quieted
> With fables [*Märchen*].
>
> (3.6.19–24)

I argue that *Nathan* may be read as a staging of the political dilemmas of the Enlightenment. The play enacts a utopian scenario in which the absolutist state is confronted with the need for the legitimation of authority and is transformed in that moment of self-recognition in accordance with the universal laws of reason. Further, philosophical criticism comes to see itself as the state's collaborator and heir. Saladin functions within this structure as the sign of state authority, of the authority of the absolutist state in the process of *enlightening* itself or, more precisely, being *brought* to Enlightenment through interaction with the Jew. The conclusion of the ring parable is such a moment, in which Saladin, this Frederick the Great figure, as it were, is confronted by the Jew with an unsettling truth: that the magical ring, which is meant to bring its wearer the blessings of God and the love and loyalty of man, that is, political authority, works only when its wearer acts according to principles; in itself the ring is nothing. Ecclesiastical authority appears in the play in the form of the Patriarch of Jerusalem, disloyal to Saladin to the point of conspiring against him, yet insistent on seeking his, that is, the state's protection. The state is therefore shown as guaranteeing the civil authority of the Church, and held hostage morally by the latter, which keeps in its possession the original of the compact between them, complete with the state's "hand and seal" (4.2.106).

The principles of Enlightenment philosophical criticism and rationality, figured here as the manly refusal to allow external authority to guide one's thoughts and actions, are embodied in the form of the taciturn and aloof Swabian Knight Templar, the captured crusader whose life has been spared by Saladin because, it is rumored, of a resemblance between him and Saladin's late brother. Initially, of course, an opponent of Saladin's reign over Jerusalem, this "Frank" is seen through most of the play as troubled and reflective about the sovereign's pardon. We are told at first that he shuns all Jews (1.4.23), avoiding a requested encounter with Nathan on the grounds that "Jew is Jew" whereas he is a "Swabian blunt" (1.6.55–56). He holds Judaism responsible, moreover, for giving birth to the "pride" of religious exclusivism and transmitting it to the other monotheistic faiths (2.5.94), an attitude toward Jews and Judaism not unlike that attributed to the *philosophes*, especially Voltaire.[25] Of the many varieties of philosophical-critical attitudes towards Judaism in Lessing's own time, perhaps the most common tendency was to distinguish between Mosaic and post-Mosaic Talmudic Judaism, with the latter seen as riddled with superstition, sophistry, and irrationality in general. This attitude is present, for instance, in the works of enlightened religious criticism that provide the immediate context for the writing of Mendelssohn's *Jerusalem*, to which I return below. Lessing himself suggests such a view in *The Education of the Human Race* (1780). Also, the image of a massively intricate and Byzantine Talmud, as against the humble and simple little Bible, came to be a defining motif of the Evangelical Revival's "fever," as Michael Ragussis has characterized it, for the conversion of the Jews in nineteenth-century Britain.[26] Thus it is not surprising that, at the beginning of his encounter with Nathan, the Templar would display an attitude of contempt towards what he considers the exclusivism of all organized faith, and feel a sense of revulsion at, and desire to escape from, what he expects will be the Jew's sophistry and volubility; but, significantly, that attitude is changed to one of affection and protectiveness following this extended encounter and exchange of typically enlightened ideas with Nathan (2.5). And it is he, of course, who rescues Nathan's daughter, Recha, from a blazing fire. When later in the play, the Templar (incorrectly) believes Recha to be an adopted Christian orphan, and the Patriarch insists that any Jew who has raised a Christian child as a Jew must be burned at the stake, he rejects this proposal, especially since he has heard, he claims, that the Jew has "taught this child no more or less of God" than required by reason (4.2.89). This statement by the Templar is of one with Lessing's own defense, throughout the play and elsewhere, of the claims of natural over positive religion: "The best revealed or positive religion is that which contains the fewest conventional additions to natural religion, and least hinders the good effects of natural religion."[27]

As for the merchant himself, he is the only Jew left standing, so to speak, at the end of the play; his daughter, it is revealed, is adopted and is not Jewish. Reminiscent at the same time of the "court Jew" financiers on whose capital the absolutist state historically depended and of the Jewish sage—the reputed model for whom, namely, Mendelssohn, was himself a merchant-scholar—the merchant appears as a sign of the anomalous position of the Jew within enlightened society: the Jew as crisis for modernity.[28] Nathan reads Saladin's question as a characteristically modern one about identity. The modern state, in other words, is asking the Jew to explain himself in terms of the simple question: Who are you? The state's demand for "truth" is experienced as a trap: Nathan can be neither "Jew outright" (*Stockjude*), for then he is, by definition and forever, different from the subject of the enlightening (Christian) state; nor can he be "no Jew at all," for that means he is now a "Muslim" (that is, Christian). In enlightened society, that is, the Jew cannot simply be a sign of himself in his difference, as he is so long as he remains contained within the late medieval and early modern structure of the ghetto. Implicit within Nathan's soliloquy is therefore a narrative about the breakdown of the ghetto as social space and paradigm, a narrative that turns around the possibility and threat of Jewish diffusion in enlightened civil society. The Jew is necessarily faced with the now fraught question of identity: Who *are* you? It is a tenuous and paradoxical path that Nathan must tread—neither "bare and blank" citizen nor the latter's negation, that is, a subjectivity with intrinsic value and content, like ancient coin (*uralte Münze*) minted from precious metal (3.6.5)—becoming in the process a sign of the indeterminacy, the non-closure, the always incomplete universalism of Enlightenment. The displacement, moreover, of this eighteenth-century Berlin problematic to twelfth-century

Jerusalem, this formal conceit at the center of Lessing's play, itself generates a complex set of meanings about the thought and practice of Enlightenment: the displacement of the absolutism of Christian state authority onto medieval Islam is at one level an attempt to escape the censor while simultaneously pulling off an unflattering comparison of absolutism with the despotic "Musulman." It is a familiar strategy of the literature of the Enlightenment, recalling in some ways Montesquieu's famous displacement of his critique of the old order onto a Persian traveler. More significantly, however, it opens up Enlightenment itself to a reading as a universal project, conceived of here as the interrelations of the three major monotheistic faiths of Abrahamic origin.

When Nathan reads Saladin's apparently philosophical question as an unavoidably political one, in seeking to formulate an adequate response he immediately resorts to a metaphor, as already noted, that relies on the representational possibilities of money. Nathan suspects Saladin of leading him into a trap, implicitly recognizing that inherent within the latter's question is an attempt by the state to impress upon the Jew a value as it does upon an ingot destined to circulate as coin of the realm; to interpellate him, in other words, as subject (3.6.11–15). This *value* is, of course, political identity or, put more precisely, citizenship. Lessing thus invokes money here in its role as "the functionary of the improper," to borrow from a formulation of Gayatri Spivak's in a different context. For money, as Marx noted, lives a double existence, its "material existence" as substance "absorbed," but not erased, by its function as representation of value.[29] The money-commodity functions as a medium of exchange merely by virtue of the inscription of the issuing authority, the state, which *compels* this "objective social validity" of the commodity as "symbol."[30] In money, in other words, "the real content and the nominal content begin to move apart," but in its pre-capitalist forms the value of the money-commodity—gold, say, or silver—as commodity continues to assert itself over its value as money: "The history of these difficulties," writes Marx, "constitutes the history of the coinage throughout the Middle Ages and in modern times down to the eighteenth century."[31] In the terms of Lessing's play, therefore, "ancient" coin signifies a pre-capitalist, premodern past as a whole, conceived of as social relations characterized by the production and consumption, by the domination, of use-values. In terms of political identity—the issue at hand in Saladin's question to Nathan—ancient coin represents an attempt at imagining the possibility of the self-presence of the political subject: the Jew simply as himself in his difference from the Christian subject of the prince.[32]

Implicit in this use of the metaphor of money-as-sign, and in Saladin's question and Nathan's soliloquy as a whole, is therefore a representational theory and narrative of progress. The elements of this eighteenth-century semiotic paradigm are often traced to the influence of Condillac's *Essay on the Origin of Human Knowledge* (1746), especially its second part, to which I return later.[33] Lessing's fullest development of these questions is in *Laokoön* (1766). The key terms in Lessing's theory of representation are "arbitrariness" and "naturalness" (or what one might identify in contemporary terms as "motivation"). A sign is arbitrary when it has no intrinsic resemblance to that which it signifies, for which it functions as a substitute; it is natural when it bears a likeness to the object, simulating its inherent qualities. Enlightenment consists of the demystification of the sign and of systems of signs, that is, it means a foregrounding of their nature as signs. Unlike with Condillac, however, the question for Lessing is not simply that of a historical progression from an originary "natural" system of signs—Condillac's gestural *langage d'action*—to increasingly arbitrary ones, culminating in a purely rational-critical *langage de calcul*. Naturalness and arbitrariness coexist in a complex fashion within the (enlightened) present. But while Lessing gives us a typology of the sign, it is one that continues to be over-written by a narrative of rationalization, formalization, demystification, and progress.[34] The history of language and human knowledge is a movement away from the simplicity of immediate, intuitive perception, away from sensation to the reflection and distance that the sign makes possible. Nathan's soliloquy stages a parallel representational narrative, one concerned with the opposition and transition between two forms of political experience and the relation of political subject to state. In fact, one might say that, in the use of money-as-sign as metaphor for the citizen, the two narratives of progress—the representational-semiotic and the political—are fused and made one. Implicit within this narrative superimposition is an attempt to see the structures of modern political experience in semiotic terms, not simply an account of democracy as "representative," as working through surrogates—to recall Rousseau's famous critique—but also the deeper perception that citizen subjectivity itself is constituted as a representational structure, as a sign-relationship.

The condition of citizen subjectivity therefore seems to require in *Nathan* something like what Suzanne Gearhart has called the "generalized mimesis" inherent in contemporary notions for the reform of theatrical practice, in whose elaboration Lessing's own work of course figured prominently.[35] In Diderot's theatrical writings, for instance, which Lessing helped to propagate in Germany, we find a conception of the consummate performer not as a person of great sensibility, one who actually experiences the psychical states he renders onstage, but rather as a great imitator, reproducing the "external signs" of those states with such precision and deliberation that the audience is "taken in."[36] Actors are great, Diderot writes in a striking phrase, in those moments of performance "*suspended*" between nature and its theatrical imitation (309), producing the anxiety that this possibility of generalized mimesis inherent in acting implies the unsettling truth about actors that "they're only good at playing all [characters] because they haven't got one of their own" (350). Citizenship as a form of individual identity is thus like acting in that the latter is, as Diderot writes, that "vanishing moment," in which the question of identity is indefinitely postponed. The pedagogical orientation of the actor towards the citizen-spectator is thus not limited to the transmission of positive virtues; it extends to the teaching of "imitation" itself. The crisis of modern subjectivity is therefore the threat of artificiality and arbitrariness that hangs over it, its implicit imitativeness and protean nature. But if this possibility is real, so, too, is the fact that the "imitative" subject is better capable of rendering nature than the one with "sensibility": the former, "fully master of himself and playing entirely from observation and judgment, would be what daily experience shows, that is, *more uniform* than [plus un que] the one who plays half from nature, half from observation, half from a model and half from himself" (375; emphasis added). And this is, as Gearhart points out, the real "paradox" of the actor: it is precisely when he is without any sensibility and capable of rendering any passion that he *is* the character. If there were elements of passion he could not render, if, in other words, actor could be distinguished from character, it would indicate that a natural sensibility or passion had intruded into his art.[37] That the citizen subjectivity of "daily experience" is a *uniform* performance, a constant and regularized relationship of individual to state and society, is therefore simply another way of saying that it is protean, "imitative," the very opposite of "being oneself." The paradox of the citizen (as actor) is therefore that his is an "artificial sensibility," a mediated nature (342).

Like the great actor, therefore, the private individual is not himself when he appears in public in the role of citizen. Like the successful theatrical performance in Diderot's text, citizenship consists in giving such faithful rendering of the external signs of the "sentiment" that others are "taken in." This is the basis of the indifference or neutrality that characterizes the relationship of the citizen to the state (and to his fellow citizens). Within the discursive elaboration of bourgeois civil society, a body politic apparently composed of "free" and "equal" citizens, a corporate relationship to other citizens and to the state, such as embodied in the ghetto as social experience, appears to make individuals *sensible* in a communal manner, and is therefore experienced as the opposite of Enlightenment, as the sign of the past; it becomes an anachronism. The trap Saladin lays for his Jewish subject is meant to render the latter a citizen like any other, equivalent to all others, a subjectivity without intrinsic content, or at least a subjectivity whose content is a matter of indifference to state and civil society. This is the Jewish emancipation that liberalism promises from its very inception. Enlightenment for Lessing thus requires the privatization of religious affiliation, that is, its confinement to the (patriarchal) realm of the (bourgeois) family under the rubric of practice and belief. The signs of religious affiliation and community must cease to have a public existence. But most interesting here is Lessing's staging of Nathan's response to that demand: the latter hesitates in making the choice offered him, neither opting for a corporate relation to the state, which would place him outside the universalism of bourgeois civil society while at the same time negating that universalism, nor agreeing to a dissolution in this civil society composed of exchangeable, equal "values." ("Money is in the first instance that which expresses the relation of equality between all exchange values: in money, they all have the same *name*.")[38] That which constitutes the Jew as crisis for enlightened community is therefore not that he is other to the citizen of the state but rather precisely that he becomes indeterminate, neither outsider nor one of us. (It is this role, "this unity of nearness and remoteness," that Georg Simmel, thinking above all of the experience of the Jews, would come to give the name of "the stranger.")[39] On the one hand, with his prominent function in the emerging bourgeois economy, the Jew is the sign par excellence of the impersonal contractual relationship, "cosmopolitanism," and the exchangeability of values. On the other hand, his very (communal and thus corporate) existence threatens continuously to expose the bourgeois claim to universality. In the figure of the Jew, a whole series of oppositions—tradition and modernity, past and present, corporation and citizen, privilege and right, motivation and arbitrariness, use(-value) and exchange(-value)—become dislocated, unstable, untenable. Hence the contradictory charge that bourgeois society directs at the Jew: the latter is both accused of being not rooted and hence cosmopolitan, *and* resented for having that which society as a whole is being denied, that is, meaningful community.

In Lessing's play the forms of Enlightenment universalism, like citizenship, are seen to be resisted "in reality" by the very existence of the Jews. In other words, the continuing crisis that the Jews represent for the discursive production of the citizen is posed, in social terms, as the intransigence of (a segment of) social reality in the face of a universal principle, its failure *so far* to realize that ideal. In his staging of the transition to liberal society, Lessing struggles with the meaning of Jewishness, seeing it simultaneously (and paradoxically) as situated near the outer limits of society, as that which, by definition, would leave its center unchanged, and as the core problem facing the emergence of enlightened society. As Etienne Balibar has noted, "the citizen's becoming-a-subject takes the form of a dialectic . . . precisely because *both* the necessity of 'founding' institutional definitions of the citizen and the impossibility of ignoring their contestation—the infinite contradiction within which they are caught—are crystallized within it."[40] In Lessing's text Jewishness constitutes such a site of crisis, "infinite contradiction," and "contestation" for the universalism of bourgeois citizen subjectivity, a crisis that was to resurface repeatedly in nineteenth-century culture despite attempts at its defusion. Marx was the first theorist to point out this paradoxical nature of the relationship between the secular liberal state and the Jewish minority: the former continuously produces and sustains, through such constructs as tolerance and rights, precisely that structure of difference which undermines its claims to a universalist project. He therefore identified the Jewish Question as itself a fundamental feature of the development of the forms of liberal state and society, a fact ignored in those contemporary Marxist critiques of liberal citizenship that view its crisis only in class terms, counterposing the fact of wage-slavery to equality-in-citizenship as a means of exposing the latter as merely formal and therefore untrue.[41]

In its suggestion that the dynamism of bourgeois civil society is merely *like* the mobility of values in the bourgeois economy, in this monetary metaphor and its consequences, Lessing's liberal discourse encounters its own limit. Marx noted this limitation of liberalism in his characteristic fashion: the Jewish Question, (only) as old as liberalism itself, cannot be resolved until the fundamental condition of possibility of liberal society, "the division of man into the *public person* and the *private person*, the *displacement* of religion from the state to civil society," is itself canceled and overcome.[42] But the significance of Lessing's play for the larger argument being developed here resides in the fact that the familiar Enlightenment theme of tolerance and freedom from established religious authority is elaborated in the detailed and careful staging of Jewishness as a distinct site of crisis and containment in modernity. The question so elaborately staged in *Nathan* concerns the (impossible) conditions under which the Jew may acquire the attributes of citizen. In order to be the citizen of an enlightened state the majority of whose subjects are Christian, a Jew must be both a Jew and not a Jew—this dilemma is, as Nathan puts it, a fairy tale or tall yarn ("Märchen"), but one, ironically, that is not for "children." It is, in other words, a fairy tale for *adults*, for those with the "mature" ability, as Kant would respond five years later in his famous contribution in the *Berlinische Monatsschrift* to the question "What is Enlightenment?" "to use [their] understanding without the guidance of another," namely, the *Aufklärer*.[43] In this staging of Enlightenment, then, the Jew emerges as a central figure. It is through him that the non-identity of "citizen" is staged, and he becomes in the process the vehicle for a defining irony: the "mature" subject of Enlightenment Reason reverts, in the very process of its genesis, to a childlike reliance on fable—the Jew is not a Jew, the citizen is not a citizen. Nathan's dilemma thus prefigures the concrete, historical dilemma of Jewish existence in the era of emancipation. It reveals that emancipation is precisely this dilemma: declared in country after country to be citizens, technically speaking, at a par with non-Jews, no longer subject to the elaborate structures and stipulations that had regulated ghetto life, the Jews remained nevertheless excluded from large areas of social life, not just in the context of voluntary associations in civil society but within state structures as well, ranging from the bureaucracy and military to the academy, becoming in the process, as Jacob Katz writes, "a kind of social hybrid," simultaneously "recognized by law as citizens, but still excluded from the essential benefits entailed in this status."[44]

In the final scene of the play the relationships between all the major characters, which we had initially taken for granted but about which we had become increasingly confused as the play progressed, are radically transformed. The initially removed and contemplative Templar, signifier for the Enlightenment temperament, is revealed to be Saladin's long-lost nephew. Enlightenment Reason, in other words, is made to recognize that it has a world to inherit—"And now, you contrarian [*Trotzkopf*]," Saladin tells the Templar, "now you'll have to love me!" (5.7.146)—and state authority is confronted with the fact that it has an organic connection with the principle of reasonable governance. Recha, the girl whom Nathan has raised as his own daughter, and who has become amorously infatuated with the Templar as a result of being rescued by him, is also revealed to be the latter's sister (and hence, like him, half "Musulman," half "Christian"). This remarkable play closes, then, with the consolidation of a family group—Saladin, his sister Sittah, and their newly found niece and nephew—a utopian community coming into existence in a moment of Enlightenment, when what was previously obscured is clarified and the true nature of the relationships between the various figures becomes visible. But this tableau of family happiness, in which time itself appears to stand still, is undermined by a sense of crisis threatened and barely averted, a knowledge of incestuous union prevented in the nick of time. For the Templar, the moment of his recognition of his connection to Saladin, and the moment of Recha entering the space of the sexually taboo, are one and the same. It is in that act of enlightened self-control that the new community comes into being.[45] The threat of arbitrariness, artificiality, and dissolution of community and meaning that Enlightenment continually poses is therefore contained within an affective economy based on a kinship structure formed in the implementation of the incest taboo.

Even more significant in this regard, however, is Nathan's final situation. The Jew, as I have tried to show, creates an ongoing crisis for the notion of society as community of citizens, both highlighting and undermining the arbitrariness that underlies the concept of citizen itself. For the same reason, however, he can also be figured as a source of moral persuasion, as in Nathan's recounting of the parable to Saladin, an act with clearly pedagogical consequences. The figure of the Jew is therefore both a threatening sign of the instability of central categories of the Enlightenment and at the same time indispensable as the means to avert the threat of abstraction and loss of persuasiveness hanging over modernity. In the era of emancipation, the liberal imagination turns repeatedly to the possibility of secular redemption of the Jews as a means to the redemption of society, as in *Daniel Deronda*, a key work for an understanding of these thematics in the literature of the modern West, to which I turn in the next chapter. But this paradoxical relationship of Jew to Enlightenment is made visible in the final fate of Nathan himself. For, as the other characters onstage are integrated into a utopian community, Nathan is left standing alone: loved, revered, respected for his "wisdom," welcomed into the family group, but ultimately unrelated; at the end of the play he is a haunting image and a striking reminder of what it means, in the transition to modern culture, for a group to become a minority. The ending of the play is thus a highly charged moment, in which the central dynamic tensions of the play as a whole are made apparent, and the ending itself has a resonant history in the cultural politics of the Jewish Question. When, in 1933, after the forced Nazi exclusion of Jews from cultural life, the newly formed Kulturbund Deutscher Juden inaugurated its first season in Berlin with a performance of *Nathan the Wise*, the ending was slightly but significantly changed: instead of Nathan and the family making separate but happy exits, in this production "Nathan stayed behind, proud and lonely at the front of the stage, as the curtain fell."[46]

Arendt's critique of Jewish emancipation, so controversial in her own lifetime, is productively viewed alongside the situation of the Jew in Lessing's play, as she herself seems to suggest in her Lessing Prize lecture, in a rather different reading of the parable scene than I have presented here: "I cannot gloss over the fact that for many years I considered the only adequate reply to the question, Who are you? to be: A Jew. That answer alone took into account the reality of persecution. As for the statement with which Nathan the Wise (in effect, though not in actual wording) countered the command: 'Step closer, Jew'—the statement: I am a man—I would have considered as nothing but a grotesque and dangerous evasion of reality."[47] The tradition of Jewish emancipation into the *Bildungsbürgertum* remained predicated on the assimilation of the Jews to the "universal" culture and subject position of the majority, coded as the standpoint of humanity. But this promise itself—the "treacherous promise of equality"—is for Arendt in its own terms an untruth.[48] For emancipation has never meant the dissolution of the forms of difference in modern European culture that have come to us coded as the Jewish Question; if anything, it has reinscribed the crisis around this difference in ever more menacing forms. What it does accomplish is to strip the Jews of the possibility of having a distinct political identity that might become the basis for a struggle for rights, a distinctly Jewish political struggle, as Arendt puts it, alongside other oppressed peoples.[49] It is certainly the case, as Richard Bernstein has pointed out, that Arendt never attempts comprehensively to solve the riddle of what she means by being Jewish, although it is clear, at least in her case, that it cannot simply have a religious content.[50] Thus in "The Jew as Pariah," for instance, Jewishness takes a series of unexpected forms: the everyday culture of ordinary Jews and the figure of *schlemiel* so loved by Heine; Bernard Lazarre's moral and political contempt for the "parvenu" Jewish elites and his championing of the rights of the powerless; Kafka's keen perception of the hypostasization of the forms of modern culture; and the innocence, bravado, and instinct for survival of "the little Yid" so compellingly performed and celebrated by Charlie Chaplin.[51] For Arendt, the question of Jewishness is never meant to be answered comprehensively and in advance, even as she insists on the mere facticity of being Jewish in the world, as in the famous letter to Gershom Scholem in response to his critique of *Eichmann in Jerusalem*: "I have always regarded my Jewishness as one of the indisputable factual data of my life, and I have never had the wish to change or disclaim facts of this kind."[52] Above all, she finds the basis of her Jewishness in what she considers the "hidden Jewish tradition" of the "conscious pariah," the artist or intellectual who, aware of the marginal status of the Jews in European society, adopts this location consciously as the place from which to produce a critique of the dominant forms of culture and society rather than "ape the gentiles" or "play the *parvenu*."[53] It is this alternative tradition of assimilation, of assimilation with a difference, which becomes for Arendt the social basis for a distinctly Jewish culture of critique and a concrete, historically inflected humanism.

My attempt thus far in this chapter has been to outline what it means to be "philo-Semitic" in the Enlightenment, to bring to the fore the crisis of representation that characterizes the liberal ideal of tolerance. What begins to become apparent here is an early expression of the liberal involvement with the question of Jewish existence; my effort in this book is to chart the history of elements of this involvement. The abstract and universal figure of the secular citizen subject, in which all religious and cultural particularity is to be suspended, remains densely inscribed with the signs of Jewish difference. This is a constitutive ambivalence of liberal citizenship, and it is reinscribed and reemerges in one form or another in all later attempts to claim modern subjectivity through a proclamation of citizenship. If it has been the goal of modern, post-Enlightenment imperialism—that is, of expansionist industrial capitalism—to establish globally the rule of equivalence, which Adorno and Horkeimer called the "canon" of bourgeois society, then it is the figure of the citizen that embodies the logic of this rule at the level of subjectivity and society.[54] But as I have tried to show, the citizen is not so much a figure as a problematic, a tense imbalance and interplay between "major" and "minor" terms, and liberal citizenship, in all its historically varied forms and locales, is unthinkable without it. The anticolonial claim to citizenship, for instance, whose entire impetus derives from a rejection of the indignity of colonial subjecthood, reproduces the ambivalence and maldistribution of "dignity" whose exemplary elaboration and situation with respect to the Jews we have just seen in Lessing. The nineteenth-century Indian version of this claim is perhaps best known in Western literature through its cruel but brilliant parody in Kipling, to which I turn in the next chapter. Here I examine at some length the possibilities of the emergence of distinctly minor-Jewish claims for emancipation and equality out of these unstable, tenuous spaces of liberal culture, and of calls for the withdrawal of the demand that the Jews adjust to the forms of an external modernity. It is in this context that the paradox of the Jewish intellectual attachment to, and critique of, the Enlightenment and its legacies becomes meaningful. This paradox takes different forms at different moments and in different figures in the era of emancipation and beyond—for instance, as we see a bit later in this chapter, in Heinrich Heine's uncanny and ironic reinscriptions of the Romantic image of the homeland from the viewpoint of Enlightenment and emancipation—and reaches a kind of climax when it is reinscribed by Adorno and Horkheimer, in the midst of the rationalized annihilation of the Jews, as the dialectical perception that if Enlightenment means the demystification of everything, it must ultimately lead to the demystification of the idea of Enlightenment itself.

Signs of Citizenship: Jewish Existence and the Critique of Enlightenment

Lessing and Mendelssohn became involved in a controversy concerning the status of the Jews—Mendelssohn only anonymously—as early as 1754. The occasion was a review of Lessing's play, *The Jews* (1749), an early instance of the entanglement of Jewish emancipation with assimilation in the literature of the Enlightenment.[55] The reviewer, the Göttingen Orientalist Johann David Michaelis, had complained of Lessing's implausible portrayal of a Jewish character endowed with the noble virtues of a Christian citizen, a Jew literally able to pass himself off in the world as a Christian. In his published response, Lessing had included an anguished letter from an anonymous Jew, "one from this nation itself... a man who is as intelligent as he is honest," but had felt the need to assure the public that it was not a fake, but had genuinely been written by a Jew.[56] Then, in 1769–70, Mendelssohn was challenged publicly by the Zurich theologian Johann Caspar Lavater to either disprove the truth of Christianity or abandon his ancestral faith, an invitation to religious controversy that carried the thinly veiled threat, for this "protected Jew" in Berlin, of confrontation with Christian state authority and public outrage.[57] In 1782 Mendelssohn was once again challenged in this manner by the author of an anonymous pamphlet, who declared that Mendelssohn's ideas concerning liberty of conscience meant in effect that he had abandoned Judaism and entered Christianity and should openly declare so.[58] The "enlightenend"—that is, philosophical, as opposed either to the merely Pietistic-theological or the customary and popular—gentile demand for Jewish conversion, repeatedly directed at Mendelssohn throughout his lifetime often even by friends and admirers, was to become a recurring, defining motif of the era of emancipation, and was experienced as a pressure, often internalized, in the lives of intellectuals of German Jewish origin even into the twentieth century, as amply demonstrated by the example of such diverse figures as Franz Rosenzweig and Emil Ludwig.[59] Moritz Oppenheim's famous painting of an imaginary meeting between Mendelssohn, Lavater, and Lessing presents a sort of primal scene of this asymmetrical historical encounter from the perspective of the mid-nineteenth century.[60] And, in nineteenth-century Britain, the call for conversion acquired the dimensions of a national obsession at the intersection of a range of discourses concerning nationalism, colonialism, and citizenship—the "English madness," as one commentator called it, whose complexities and contradictions came to be most clearly visible in the person of the (baptized) "Hebrew prime minister."[61]

In *Jerusalem*, written two years after Lessing's death, Mendelssohn was seeking to respond to recent commentators who had framed the question of Jewish emancipation and integration in terms of the obstacles posed by the nature of Judaism itself; among the commentators was his friend, the Prussian state official Christian Wilhelm Dohm, writing in his widely disseminated pro-emancipation tract, *On the Civic Improvement of the Jews* (1781). Dohm, although himself a proponent of the demand for the Jews' civil emancipation, held on to the thesis of the Jews' moral degeneration and their present incapacity for rational political thought and action, a notion shared by many *Aufklärer* who opposed Dohm's call for emancipation, including Michaelis and his circle.[62] The wide-ranging debate set off by the publication of Dohm's treatise, whose arguments for Jewish emancipation had themselves been inspired by Mendelssohn, was the first systematic and detailed public discussion of the question in Europe and took place on the philosophical terrain of human nature and rights.[63] Upon its translation into French in 1782, it achieved wide dissemination in France as well and deeply influenced Mirabeau and Grégoire, and therefore the National Assembly debates of 1789–91 concerning the granting of citizenship to the Jews.[64]

Mendelssohn's simultaneous identification with some of the most advanced ideas of the German Enlightenment and what he considered traditional Judaism had long confounded at least some of his interlocutors and sometimes even produced derision.[65] But he emerged from this debate with a set of positions concerning religion more radical than his Christian interlocutors, demolishing the claims of all forms of established religious authority, including rabbinical authority over such matters as excommunication.[66] The overall effect of Mendelssohn's intervention in *Jerusalem* was to invert the terms of this interaction, with Jewish experience now providing the location for an interrogation of the philosophical arguments of its interrogators. Mendelssohn's text is, in particular, a critical engagement with certain concerns and motifs that are important in Lessing's later work, above all the account of secular and abstract citizen subjectivity that appears in *Nathan*. This critical and political register is present throughout the book, a set of concerns that linger below the surface of the text even when the explicit concern seems to be theological or epistemological. The form of Mendelssohn's text, in other words, is the indirect, covert or discreet, even *parabolic* one so brilliantly anticipated by Lessing for the enlightened *Jewish* claim for emancipation and given the form of Nathan's parable. Mendelssohn manages to formulate a detailed philosophical case for Jewish emancipation without, as Alexander Altmann has noted, recourse to a single word of "direct appeal."[67] But whereas Lessing's indirectness—the overall displacement of an eighteenth-century Berlin problematic to twelfth-century Jerusalem, just as much as Nathan's indirectness with the Sultan—is oriented toward the absolutist state, Mendelssohn's is concerned also with the enlightened intelligentsia itself.

Jerusalem begins by giving a classic and consistent philosophical account of the imperative for a separation of church and state. Elements of this Enlightenment position are scattered throughout Lessing's play and also appear sporadically within Dohm's pragmatic and political discourse on the case for the granting of citizenship rights to the Jews; in the first part of *Jerusalem*, however, they are developed as elements of a consistent philosophical position. In seeking to influence the convictions of men, the state can rely on persuasion alone and does not have the right to coerce an avowal because that right could not have been ceded to it in the first place. The social contract can apply only to "my dispensable goods" and not to those that are inalienable, as convictions are, and which, being an internal matter, do not enter a case of collision of interests (*J*, 64, 70). However, like Kant in "What Is Enlightenment?" the following year, Mendelssohn concludes that while the individual may pass judgment on laws with which he does not agree, he may not disobey them. Civil society is based precisely on the renunciation of the right not to obey a law one does not believe in. The inalienability of convictions, furthermore, applies not only to the state but also to the church. The church, unlike the state, is not even based in a social contract, for it is founded on a relationship between man and God. Who, then, is to be the arbiter if disputes or conflicts arise over religious matters? Mendelssohn's answer is unequivocal: neither the state nor the church but, rather, the one with the ability to convince others. That contract is unimaginable by which the members of society could have granted either state or church the right to arbitrate a conflict of religious convictions among them. A major consequence of this separation of church and state, and of their defanging in matters of conviction, is that it is impermissible for the state to exact religious oaths from its citizens as a condition of public office. This rather concrete issue, a recurring concern in the history of emancipation throughout Europe, is, of course, what Mendelssohn's philosophical derivation is leading up to and is all about. But the arguments against oaths are sought in the nature of the act itself, not simply in a political claim on behalf of the Jews. The administration of oaths is an interrogation regarding the *internal sense* and is thus an invitation to lying; it *necessarily* means a disjuncture between avowal and belief:

> Count all the men who occupy your academic chairs and pulpits, and have their doubts about many a proposition to which they swore when they assumed office; take all the bishops who sit in the House of Lords, all the truly great men who hold high office in England and can no longer accept the Thirty-Nine Articles, to which they have sworn, as unconditionally as they did when they were first set before them. Count them, and then still say that civil liberty cannot be granted to my oppressed nation because so many of its members think little of an oath! (*J*, 68)

Mendelssohn is deeply aware, however, of the links between the call for disestablishment and state indifference in matters of religious faith and practice, on the one hand, and the call for the dissolution of the particularity of the Jews, on the other. It is this slippage that, in the end, *Jerusalem* is meant to argue against and prevent.

In looking more closely at the precise nature of this threat of dissolution inherent in the liberal promise of emancipation, we might consider the following remarks, made in the National Assembly on December 23, 1789, by Clermont-Tonnerre, during the inconclusive debate regarding the granting of citizenship rights to Jews:

> The law cannot affect the religion of a man. It can take no hold over his soul; it can affect only his actions, and it must protect those actions when they do no harm to society. God wanted us to reach agreement among ourselves on issues of morality, and he has permitted us to make moral laws, but he has given to no one but himself the right to legislate dogmas and to rule over [religious] conscience. So leave man's conscience free, that sentiments or thoughts guided in one manner or another toward the heavens will not be crimes that society punishes by the loss of social rights. Or else create a national religion, arm yourself with a sword, and tear up your Declaration of Rights.[68]

While made from within a far more radical political and social situation, the argument here so far is essentially identical in conceptual terms to the one we just saw in Mendelssohn. For Clermont-Tonnerre, the dismantling of the hierarchies and privileges that constituted the ancien régime has made of the unnaturalized Jews a striking anomaly, the revolutionary Declaration of the Rights of Man and of the Citizen, that crowning practical achievement of Enlightenment political thought, requiring the indifference of the state towards the religious convictions of individuals. However, as Clermont-Tonnerre, one of the most outspoken protagonists of emancipation, immediately points out, this indifference is made impossible if the Jews insist on entering the state as a distinct "political formation or class" and not as isolated individuals. It is in isolation as individuals that they can claim the rights and perform the duties, that is, acquire the attributes, of citizen. Any other course on the part of the Jews can only imply that "we shall then be compelled to expel them."[69] The "political emancipation" of the Jews is thus caught in a contradiction it cannot overcome: it can only conceive of granting rights to *individuals* as a solution to the *corporate* denial of rights to the Jews as Jews, and keeps reverting in its treatment of the Jews to precisely the methods and forms it seeks to eliminate. With each new phase of the process of emancipation throughout the continent, as the final resolution of the Jewish Question seems in sight, the contradiction is reinscribed and the crisis renewed. In the second part of *Jerusalem*, Mendelssohn anticipates this recurring and periodically renewed burden of Jewish existence in the era of emancipation and makes visible its reliance on the structures of Enlightenment itself.

Mendelssohn's most controversial move in *Jerusalem* is the well-known claim that Judaism knows no revealed religious truth, only social legislation, for religious truth cannot be other than what is accessible to, and demonstrable in, human reason. Knowing no revealed elements of faith, Judaism is therefore the closest of the positive religions to the natural religion of reason. The purpose of Mosaic Law is to regulate not belief but actions, not perceptions of eternal truth but man's behavior as a member of human society. It is this concern with the regulation of men's actions by Jewish ceremonial law that leads Mendelssohn to offer, in a few pages, a history of the written sign in the development of human knowledge, a narrative that seeks to alter in significant ways the conception of semiosis dominant in the Enlightenment, the "tradition of Condillac," to cite Aarsleff once again.

Mendelssohn's narrative follows Condillac's in positing an original state of immediacy, presence, and plenitude, in which every human action is its own sign, spontaneously produced and understood, a fully transparent *langage d'action*. The overall thrust of Condillac's narrative is from self-explanatory, "natural" signs to arbitrary ones, and the final telos of this process is a fully abstract and rationalized *langage de calcul.*[70] The first visible signs of things used by man, Mendelssohn argues, must have been the things themselves. In time, it would have proved more convenient to make two- or three-dimensional images of things. These would have evolved over time into mere outlines and their segments, and finally a mode of creating out of heterogeneous parts a meaningful whole—hieroglyphs. Hieroglyphs acquire a central position in Mendelssohn's account, as they also do in Condillac's.[71] With their ambiguous status as both naturalized depiction and conventionalized sign, they represent a double reality: while their invention meant that the "observations, experiments, and reflections in astronomical, economic, moral, and religious matters were multiplied, propagated, facilitated, and preserved for posterity," hieroglyphs nevertheless also hold the possibility of becoming confused for the things themselves, the possibility of corruption, error, seduction, and fetishization: in a word, "idolatry" (*J*, 108, 110, 117). So although the written sign was both necessary and inevitable for the development of human knowledge, it could also become "the road of corruption," leading to the worst forms of mystification, hypostatization, and priestly esotericism (*J*, 120):

> They saw the signs not as mere signs, but believed them to be the things themselves. As long as one still used the things themselves or their images and outlines, instead of signs, this error was easily made. For besides their signification, the things also had a reality of their own. The coin was, at the same time, a piece of merchandise which had its own use and utility; therefore, the ignorant person could easily misjudge and wrongly speculate its value as a coin. Hieroglyphic script could, to be sure, partly correct this error . . . [but the] enigmatic and strange character of [its] composition itself afforded superstition the material for all sorts of inventions and fables. (*J*, 111)

As in Nathan's soliloquy, here money provides a means of conceptualizing the inherent dangers of signification.[72] Our interest in this account of the significance of hieroglyphs is this: the latter represent both a *stage* in the history of writing and the *ever present danger* of regress, of losing sight of the referent, which, of course, is the actual eighteenth-century Western experience of hieroglyphs as "enigmatic and strange," namely, their undecipherability.[73] The biblical references are clearly striking. Egypt-hieroglyph represents in Mendelssohn's account the possibility of "idolatry" or exile from truth, while Enlightenment and the restoration of law and reason are figured as an escape from this Egypt of undecipherable signs.

Thus far the argument accords fairly closely with Condillac's and, of course, with the aesthetic-representational narrative implied in Lessing's metaphorical use of money-as-sign. But where Condillac's resolution of the epistemological difficulties of writing relies on the unrelenting thrust of a linear narrative, in Mendelssohn's text this progressive movement is arrested and made subject to the signs of Jewish difference. The operative poles in Mendelssohn's schema are images and hieroglyphs, on the one hand, and alphabetic writing, on the other. The former, we have seen, can lead to fetishization, either in the form of popular superstition or priestly esotericism. And a culture based in the latter is also subject to a crisis—namely, abstraction, arbitrariness, distance from real life, lack of persuasive or pedagogical power, bookishness, and "speculation." But it is the third term in Mendelssohn's account that makes it possible to view the present as other than a choice between a past and a future. This third term, which continually interrupts the movement from concreteness to abstraction, which checks the opposed tendencies to myth and to atomism, is none other than Judaism's ceremonial law in its function as a means to the regulation of the human body. Jewish ceremonial laws, rules governing such factors as physical appearance, preparation of food, and observation of the Sabbath—precisely those signs of Jewish difference which are, for many an "enlightened" Christian, the signs of Jewish *intransigence* in the face of modernity and hence cause for the Jews' disqualification from emancipation—become in Mendelssohn's account the means through which the promise of Enlightenment can be realized. A "script" that uses actions is superior to scripts based on images or the written word. The former surrounds the individual with concrete and ubiquitous "tokens" of religious faith. It does not claim to reveal truth but merely brings it within the grasp of the individual's intuition. Obedience to the ritual commandments, therefore, not only does not contradict the requirements of natural religion, but it is entirely in accordance with reason, though indirectly, through its function as a way to avoid both its regression into dogmatic belief—"idolatry"—and excessive speculativeness and abstraction. In *Jerusalem* the concrete language of actions appears not simply as not primitive but in fact as essential for Enlightenment itself. It is that crucial third term which prevents Enlightenment from degenerating into an endless oscillation between the other two poles.

As we have seen, Jewish ceremonial law, for Mendelssohn, compels actions, not beliefs, actions, furthermore, that are directed at other human beings. It therefore impels the individual towards "social intercourse" (*J*, 119). The advanced culture of writing and print, of the "dead letter," is a culture of impersonal relations: "man has almost lost his value for his fellow man" (*J*, 103). The Jewish body, subject to a communally recognized body of revealed law, thus stands as a living, concrete critique of the structure of *indifference* within which the citizen subject is located and produced. If in Lessing's play Condillac's model of movement from concreteness to abstraction in human affairs becomes a means of describing the emergence of the modern citizen subject, Mendelssohn's destructuring of that linearity suggests another model of citizenship, non-uniform and discontinuous, in which the Jew appears not as crisis but as an indispensable term within the utopian community that is Enlightenment. Jewish specificity for Mendelssohn, therefore, cannot represent a mere stage in human development, neither in the sense implicit in the crude demand for conversion nor, for that matter, in the significance Lessing attached to it, as a superseded stage in a cosmopolitan "education of the human race":[74]

> I, for my part, cannot conceive of the education of the human race as my late friend Lessing imagined it under the influence of I-don't-know-which historian of mankind. One pictures the collective entity of the human race as an individual person and believes that Providence sent it to school here on earth, in order to raise it from childhood to manhood. In reality, the human race is—if the metaphor is appropriate—in almost every century, child, adult, and old man at the same time, though in different places and regions of the world. (*J*, 96)

Mendelssohn's use of the metaphor of age is indeed inappropriate, for it displaces, or is not appropriate to, the image of the Aufklärer as "adult" subject of human reason.

This does not mean simply that a space is being created here for a Jewish existence in at least an angular relationship with the Enlightenment discourse of citizenship and civil society but rather that the very terms in which we conceive of Enlightenment are being rewritten from the vantage point of that existence. The infamous "materialism" of the Jews is thus made the basis and guarantor of Enlightenment itself. The consequences of this rewriting, in other words, are not merely to fall upon the Jewish minority but upon society as a whole. The burden of movement and adjustment in the creation of the enlightened community rests not with the minority but with the majority: "if civil union cannot be obtained under any other condition than our departing from the laws which we still consider binding on us, then we are sincerely sorry to find it necessary to declare that we must rather do without civil union. It does not rest with us to yield on this matter" (*J*, 135). The call for a "union of faiths," that is, dissolution of minority into majority, which is supposedly made from within the viewpoint of Enlightenment, is in reality a trap which "fanaticism," weakened by the triumphs of reason, wants to put in the way of the principle of liberty of conscience, for in order to achieve felicity "under the care of this omnipresent shepherd the entire flock need neither graze in one pasture nor enter and leave the master's house through a single door" (*J*, 135).

Mendelssohn began the second section of *Jerusalem* by answering the recent charge of an "enlightened" commentator that, in his espousal of a rational religion, Mendelssohn had in fact abandoned the faith of his fathers, had practically entered Christianity, and should therefore openly acknowledge it. Mendelssohn's response is novel, for it does not consist simply of providing an argument for why he is very far from taking such a step. He turns the tables on his interlocutor, questioning not so much the latter's right to make that call for conversion as the reasonableness of that demand: "If it be true that the cornerstones of my house are dislodged, and the structure threatens to collapse, do I act wisely if I remove my belongings from the lower to the upper floor for safety? Am I more secure there? Now Christianity, as you know, is built upon Judaism, and if the latter falls, it must necessarily collapse with it into *one* heap of ruins" (*J*, 87). In this image of the two-storied house Mendelssohn manages to displace the very structure within which the call for conversion is voiced—a Christian representative of the Enlightenment asking the Jew to recognize that laying claim to personal enlightenment means abandoning Judaism. The assumption that it is the Jew who must change fundamentally is rejected, and the onus of providing proof of his enlightened principles is transferred onto the Christian himself. Mendelssohn's two-storied house is therefore a political and not a strictly theological structure. It contains not the relationship of one religious tradition to another, the emergence of the Christian Bible out of the Hebrew one, but rather embodies the secular structure of citizenship within which Jew and Christian are mutually inserted. If the Jewish or minor stratum is made to "fall," Mendelssohn suggests, so will the entire edifice. A century and a half after *Jerusalem* was written, Arendt concluded her reflections on her own status as a stateless refugee in a statement remarkably resonant with Mendelssohn's caution: "The comity of European peoples went to pieces when, and because, it allowed its weakest member to be excluded and persecuted."[75]

The city of Jerusalem became in early Christian tradition the spot on earth where history began and where it would reach its apocalyptic consummation. In the stories and traditions of the Haggadah it also represented the messianic promise of restoration, after the in-gathering of the exiles, when "all nations and all kingdoms" would come to "gather together in the midst of it." "Jerusalem," and the promised restoration to that city, thus became a metaphor for the coming of the Messiah, for "an end of the wandering that characterizes human existence."[76] Beginning in the seventeenth century there emerged from these traditions a new set of secular meanings—the "New Jerusalem" as a symbol of the struggle and yearning for a better and nobler form of society. In the last major works of their respective careers, Lessing and Mendelssohn both turned to the image of the Holy City in leaving us with sketches of enlightened community. In these key textual elaborations of the question of Jewishness and modernity, therefore, "Jerusalem" is an image of an enlightened, or self-enlightening, world; the overcoming of sectarian difference and conflict, which alone can make "the human" possible, is to be staged in this imagined Jerusalem. In other words, "Jerusalem" here already marks a space for the resolution of the crisis of European modernity marked by the difference of the Jews. The very manner of Mendelssohn's invocation of Jerusalem implies a *secularization* of the ritual and eschatological meaning of the Holy City and the Holy Land, which are now to play the role of the *worldly* ground for the narrative resolutions of European modernity—a secularization that would later become the ground for the Zionist appropriation and reworking of the *ritual* idea of the Promised Land as the secular (because national) home of the Jewish people.

Conversely, however, secular, "political" emancipation itself retained within it a redemptive, even messianic dimension, so that when, for instance, Napoleon called for a centralized Jewish authority in 1806 to underwrite the incorporation of Jewish life into the structures of the postrevolutionary secular state, he conceived of this action as the reconvening of the Sanhedrin, an event with clearly messianic overtones linked to the city of Jerusalem.[77] The grandiosity of the plan may be judged by the following remarks by the emperor to his minister of the interior, regarding the decisions that were to be ratified by this gathering of the so-called Sanhedrin: "[these] will be turned into compelling ecclesiastical or religious law and will become a second legislation of the Jews, which, while keeping the essential character of that of Moses, will adapt itself to the present situation of the Jews, to our ways and our usages."[78] Already in 1798, as he pushed from Egypt toward Syria and Palestine, Napoleon had "dreamed of great things" and reportedly called upon the Jews of the Near East to organize under his banner for a rebuilding and restoration of Jerusalem and Palestine.[79] Edward Said has spoken of the Napoleonic excursion into the Near East, and its particular mechanisms and attendant production and use of knowledge, as one of the first great "projects" through which modern Orientalism comes into being: "with Napoleon's occupation of Egypt processes were set in motion between East and West that still dominate our contemporary cultural and political perspectives."[80] The aim was nothing short of a reorganization not only of Egyptian life but, more generally, of Near Eastern and Muslim life, through a grand enterprise in which military, political, scholarly, and artistic activities were to work in elaborate unison. In other words, the result of the Napoleonic expedition was to put in place the *machinery for the management of otherness* that has regulated relations between Western and non-Western societies in the modern era. To Said's conception of these Napoleonic Orientalist "projects" we must add the project for the reorganization of Jewish life and for redefining its relation to state and society—an undertaking with which Napoleon was almost obsessively concerned throughout his military and administrative career, from the early encounter with the ghetto in the Italian campaigns to the various emancipation decrees in the German principalities that came under French occupation or influence toward the end of the first decade of the century. As Said demonstrated at length in his work, the modern, secular Orientalism that emerged in the late eighteenth century "retained, as an undisclosed current in its discourse, a reconstructed religious impulse, a naturalized supernaturalism."[81] This "reconstructed religious impulse" reveals itself at various points in the history of the Napoleonic attempts to settle the question of the Jews, producing repeatedly the messianic idea of their restoration to Palestine—an idea with a long Christian history, shared in Napoleon's own time, for instance, by the Evangelical Revival in England.

Napoleon's reputation as the great emancipator of the Jews survived his personal and often publicly expressed dislike of the Jews and even withstood the great reversal of the decree of 17 March 1808, not only among the Jewish masses of central and Eastern Europe, within whose scattered communities he acquired a mythic, even messianic stature, but also among the intelligentsia for generations to come. The lifelong and effusive enthusiasm of Heine, for instance, who had as a child seen the emperor during his visit to Düsseldorf in 1811 and viewed him as the quintessential modern man, is a case in point. And Marx and Engels in their early writings viewed his conquests across the Rhine as Germany's great good fortune, crediting the conqueror with "cleaning out Germany's Augean stables."[82] It is certainly partly the case that in 1806 Napoleon had conceived of calling for an Assembly of Notables, and then the so-called Great Sanhedrin, as a result of the debt crisis in the Alsace countryside, which had been blamed both in popular and official discourse on the usurious practices of the Jewish petty moneylenders. Made patently visible by this crisis was that the Jews, emancipated citizens of France since 1791, could still not expect to be treated by the state as individual citizens but rather as a corporate group, in contradiction not only specifically of the constitution but of wider revolutionary principles. Thus one of Napoleon's measures in response to the Alsace situation in 1806 was to freeze the repayment of bonds for a certain period only if the bond were held by a Jew.[83] But as significant as these local and national concerns were in the convening of these Jewish bodies, they were seen by contemporaries as having historical importance far beyond the moment and even the reaches of the empire. The twelve questions put by Molé, the emperor's chief representative, to the Assembly of Notables were all "leading" ones, and were meant to deal with the problem of the persistence of the corporate identity of the Jews.[84] Their overall aim was to compel a choice between Jewish law and community and fealty to the secular state, but the outcome of the process was the infamous decree of 1808, which revived a panoply of the methods of the ancien régime, including the proclamation of various laws of exception and the discriminatory distinction between northern and southern Jews, the so-called *nation allemand* and *nation portugais*, respectively, with the Sephardic Jews of Bordeaux excluded from the laws of exception and granted full citizenship rights. And, undoubtedly, the mode of response adopted by the Jewish deputies in the Assembly in the case of the most troubling questions was evasive, as Molé and his fellow commissioners noted in their reports.[85] The most disturbing of the questions, the fourth—"In the eyes of the Jews, are the French their brothers, or are they strangers?"—crystallized the peril represented by this interaction between the representatives of the modern state and those deemed "notable" among its population of Jews. In internal correspondence, Napoleon made no secret of what was at stake in the answers being solicited and spoke of "the danger of a refusal, whose result will be the expulsion of the Jewish people."[86] Clearly the interrogative encounter represented in the episode of the Assembly and the Sanhedrin in 1806–1808 recalls, in important ways, the classic relationship of the "enlightened" but Christian absolutist state to its Jewish subject, which we have seen elaborated at length in *Nathan the Wise*. The fundamental paradox and lacuna of this encounter between the state and the Jew is now familiar: the Jews are asked *collectively* to prove their *individual* state citizenship, and the state envisions collective measures directed at the Jews as a socius in order to put a final end to this form of sociality—"the national character of Jewish existence in France"[87]—and render them individual citizens of the state like any other. In the same instance that the state attempts to "hail" them, in the Althusserian sense, as (individual) citizen subjects within the state, it fixes their collective identity as a sovereign group outside the life of the state.

The significance of *Jerusalem* from my present perspective is thus not in its contribution to religious thought per se but rather in its anticipation, and opening up, of this lacuna inherent in the categories of citizenship and political emancipation. Mendelssohn responds to the pressures of Enlightenment reason on Jewish faith and experience by arguing that a chasm separates superstition—whose danger is potentialized for him in the form of writing he calls hieroglyphs—and rational abstraction—represented by alphabetic writing. If the former involves myth and a kind of reification of the sign, the latter leads to social isolation. It is this chasm that Judaism fills with *action* as prescribed by Mosaic legislation. The very basis of Judaism, and hence Jewish identity, is therefore tied to the possibilities of the dialectic of Enlightenment; its rationality lies in that it offers action—that is, our orientation toward our fellow human beings—instead of symbols as signs of religious truths. He makes of the regulations of Mosaic Law the particularity of Jewish social life and insists not so much on the right of this particular to exist but rather the necessity from the perspective of Enlightenment itself that it do so: the concrete, even physical signs of Jewish particularity, these *markers of distinctly Jewish community*, are mediating terms, the means of preventing Enlightenment from either hypostasizing into an abstract universalism or degenerating into myth and reification of the concrete. In this sense the very body of the Jew, visibly governed by Mosaic legislation, becomes a means of averting the collapse of true Enlightenment, not just in the lives of the Jews themselves but of society as a whole. The problem that Mendelssohn's philosophical discourse attempts to tackle is the classic dilemma of minority existence: how to remain distinct and at the same time enter into the fullness of political experience as citizens. The theological formulation in Mendelssohn's work is therefore, at the same time, a secular and political one, concerned with the question of the structure of citizenship. (This splitting of Judaism into a private, natural religion and a public, embodied legislation would have significant and unanticipated political consequences, which I return to later.) But here it is important to note that the radically democratic aspect of this formulation is its insistence that Enlightenment itself requires that it is the majority, and not the minority—which faces, in every demand that is made of it, the possibility of extinction—that must yield on the question of those cultural accommodations that make enlightened community possible.

The Napoleonic wars, of course, mark a turning point for the intellectual history of the modern West. But the rise of Romantic literary and philosophical culture, with its attendant notions of the uniqueness and coherence of national genius—in short, "nation-thinking"—which overshadowed the abstract universalism of Enlightenment thought during these upheavals on a continental scale, did so in a manner that preserved and reinscribed one of the latter's crowning achievements: the logic of equivalence and equality.[88] This is nowhere clearer than in the French instance, where the revolutionary ideals themselves became signs of the uniqueness of a national culture. Thus Sieyès was able, already in 1789, to draw the famous conclusion that an aristocrat, or anyone else whose social identity was marked by privilege instead of rights, could not, by definition be a Frenchman.[89] The question around the Jews is reinscribed and renewed in the new nation-thinking, with its emphasis, on the one hand, on equality, and, on the other, on organic community and the bonds of common descent.

Into a Europe of Nations: Jewishness and National Culture

Arguably no two texts of the postrevolutionary era in Europe have been as closely scrutinized for signs of this emergent nation-thinking as Johann Gottlieb Fichte's *Addresses to the German Nation* and Walter Scott's *Ivanhoe*. But only occasionally have they been examined for the significance they attach to the question of the Jews. In each of these works the question of modern identity is linked in complex ways to the nature of linguistic practices and the boundaries of language. Fichte and Scott are interested in the ways in which languages interfere with one another, the hierarchies that define the mutual relations of linguistic communities, and the consequences of these inequalities for the languages themselves. What these texts offer is nothing short of accounts of the linguistic dimension of the formation of nations, and the Jews come to occupy in them a special position within the narrative of the emergence of the nation. I return shortly to the emergence of the historical novel and Scott's imbrication of the Jews into the question of (English) national history. But first, let us look at the linguistic nationalism that emerges in Fichte's *Addresses*, which were delivered as a series of public lectures in Berlin during the winter of 1807–1808 and were hailed by contemporaries as the "Bible of nationalism," "one of the 'spiritual sponsors' of the new Germanness," and "one of the most precious products of the German spirit."[90] In our own time as well, the work has been seen as an originary work of nation-thinking in the modern era. Balibar, for instance, speaks of it as "the most typical and, up to our day, the most influential of all elaborations of the theory of the elect nation."[91] The political backdrop of the lectures was, of course, the Napoleonic defeat of Prussia and occupation of Berlin in 1806, events largely credited with delivering a final blow to the already weakened spirit of Enlightenment in Germany. Fichte gave expression to a virulent German nationalism, seeing in the authenticity of German culture the last remaining hope for European humanity faced with the disruptiveness, alienation, and abstraction of "Western" modernity as represented by revolutionary France: "If we have hitherto proceeded correctly in the course of our investigation, it must here be obvious at once that only the German—the original man, who has not become dead in an arbitrary organization—really has a people and is entitled to count on one, and that he alone is capable of real and rational love for his nation."[92] Fichte's is an overblown and metaphysical conception of national cultural life, seeking to place, to paraphrase Foucault's description of the metaphysical impulse, present needs at the origin.[93] The life of the modern nation, the most modern of political communities, is placed in a line of continuity with the life of the ancient Germanic tribe, which comes to serve as an origin already pregnant with the former as possibility. In sum, the tone of Fichte's work reflects that "high-flown expression" that Marx and Engels attributed to the typical products of the German intelligentsia under Napoleonic occupation.[94]

It is therefore not surprising that the Jews occupy a central, if unmarked, place throughout Fichte's text. They make an unannounced appearance, for instance, in the fourth address, which is, for my purposes, the central section of the work, in which the conceptual resources of German idealism are brought to bear on the elaboration of a theory of national culture and language, a theoretical account, as David Martyn has suggested, with deeply allegorical resonances. The organizing move in this account is the attempt to draw a boundary around the truly native or domestic elements in any existing language and to distinguish those unambiguously from the foreign or extraneous, an attempt that, as Martyn has shown, characterizes the language of Fichte's text itself, which is shaped by an "unrelenting repression of the foreign provenance of its [own] metaphors."[95] In Fichte's reckoning the chief distinction of the Germans as a people is not so much racial purity as that among them the native language has been retained with little or no influence from foreign sources. The linguistic distinctness of the Germans therefore rests primarily in this history of "uninterrupted communication" (*AGN*, 47–49). Fichte's text seems here to give the lie to Liah Greenfield's characterization of German nationalism as "essentially an identity of race, and only superficially that of language or anything else" and to support Balibar's claim that at stake in this national community is not "race" but the "ethics of communication." A closer reading of the text, however, reveals a more complex set of relationships between race and language. "Language" is already defined in "racial" or genetic terms, and anxieties that are racial are displaced onto the terrain of language for their attempted resolution.

The account of the relationship between the German language and the German people that emerges in the *Addresses* is thus a highly tautological one, as the living language is defined by reference to the people who have continually spoken it, and the people themselves are defined as the collectivity that form their language in continuous communication (*AGN*, 61–62). The higher or supersensuous concepts of any language can only take the form of images provided by the sensuous domain, so that the body of supersensuous conceptions of a given culture depends in very crucial ways on its accumulated sensuous perceptions deposited in the common language. Furthermore, both the sensuous and supersensuous domains are differently developed and inflected in each language, with German displaying a distinct talent for the latter. Contrary to the Condillac tradition, therefore—and here we may include the Lessing of *Laokoön*—progress in human knowledge does not mean the progressively greater formalization and arbitrariness of language. On the contrary, the production of higher conceptions in any language always depends on the accumulated knowledge already contained within it. So long as "the people of this language have continued in unbroken communication," their higher ideas will develop "continuously out of the actual common life of this people," and therefore there will be no element of arbitrariness to them (*AGN*, 53). So while German has a special aptitude for philosophical speculation, this figural or abstract richness of the language emerges out of, and is dependent upon, the everyday life of the people and its representation in language. Words such as *Humanität*, *Popularität*, and *Liberalität* are thus dead and incomprehensible to Germans, foreign words forced into German but never becoming truly a part of the collective wisdom of the speakers of this language (*AGN*, 53–58).

Fichte's choice of examples here is interesting, for the etymologies of these "foreign" words point not just to the distant Latin and Roman social experience but also to the more proximate French—the French of the eighteenth century, the Enlightenment, and the Revolution—through which they have entered into the German-speaking lands. This distrust of the abstractions of the Revolution thus marks a distinct departure from Fichte's vehement advocacy of the Revolution in the 1790s, although this disavowal is more consistent with the anxieties the text is unable to suppress regarding the possibility of Jewish emancipation. Moreover, as Martyn has noted, Fichte's call to replace these words with words of native provenance, such as *Menschenfreundlichket* for *Humanität*, fails inevitably to achieve the linguistic purism that is Fichte's stated goal: the translation of a "foreign" word into a morphological structure that *sounds* "native" or "domestic"—a so-called loan translation—already reveals the superficiality of the claim to indigenousness.

However, it is when Fichte's text confronts a hypothetical linguistic situation rather similar to the contemporary condition of the German Jews that it is disturbed by a powerful anxiety, which rises to the surface with all the force of a return of the repressed: what, Fichte asks, of a situation in which the continuity of people and language has been disrupted, and "many individuals of other race and other language are incorporated with the people speaking this language" (*AGN*, 53)? In this instituting text of German national identity, first addressed to a public in 1807 in occupied Berlin, this anxiety about the possible influx of outsiders into the German linguistic community and their influence on the mother tongue cannot but take as one of its objects the beginnings of the process of assimilation of the Jews—these individuals of "other race and other language" who are assimilating into German culture and society precisely, in part, through linguistic self-transformation. I am not speaking here of political emancipation. The first formal emancipation decree was to come in Prussia only in 1812, although the granting of civic rights to Jews in the western provinces, and especially the Rhineland under French occupation in the 1790s, had made Jewish emancipation a visible enough reality. By assimilation, I mean, in particular, that process of cultural accommodation and interchange whose most dramatic sign in Fichte's Berlin was the Jewish salon. The last two decades of the eighteenth century had seen a gradual but significant change in the place of Jews in Berlin society. Not constitutional change, certainly, and not a material change in the lives of the great majority of Jewish Berliners, but a remarkable change in the role Jews came to play in Berlin high society. Upper-class Jewish homes became indispensable meeting places for the enlightened segments of the aristocracy and the cream of the German intelligentsia: Alexander and Wilhelm von Humboldt, the brothers

Schlegel, Goethe, Schleiermacher, and von Chamisso, to name only a few, were all regular guests at the salons of fashionable young Jewish women, such as Henrietta Herz (wife of Markus Herz, the physician), Dorothea Mendelssohn Veit (née Brendel, daughter of Moses Mendelssohn, and later mistress and then wife of Friedrich Schlegel), and the famous Rahel Levin (later Varnhagen), Heine's friend and correspondent and arguably the inventor of the Goethe cult. Fichte himself, as Deborah Hertz has noted in her fascinating social history of the Berlin Jewish salon, was to be seen regularly at Rahel's salon, and it became, she writes, his "intellectual home" on escaping to Berlin in 1799 from the public battle in Jena over his professed atheism.[96] This culture of salons and literary societies received a severe blow with the Revolutionary wars and the ultimate humiliation of the French occupation, and, within the resultant mood of anti-Western and German national sentiment, the now indefinable Jews came to represent an internal presence of the outside threat.[97] The question of Jewish emancipation was already linked in complex ways to the exportable politics of the Revolution, the experience of the Rhineland under French occupation since 1795 having made clear to everyone the link between the fate of the Revolution and the fate of the Jews. It was in the confusions and ambiguities of this period that even such an early enthusiast of the Revolution as Fichte could pen his famous remarks in 1793 about the Jews constituting a threatening "state within a state" in every European country.[98] Now the fate of the Jews became historically inseparable from the upheavals of the French occupation. Patriotic anti-French feeling and disdain for the slogans of the Revolution were on a continuum with the growing hostility toward the Jews. As Arendt noted of this period in her interpretation of Rahel's life, "patriotic anti-Semitism, to which Fichte too was not averse, poisoned all relationships between Jews and non-Jews."[99]

It is at least the perceived threat of Jewish access to civil society in these conditions that Fichte's allegory of language attempts to deflect. The incorporation of a "foreign" group into the national linguistic community can take one of two forms. When a group gives up its own language and "adopts a foreign one which is already highly developed as regards the designation of supersensuous things," it receives only "the flat and dead history of a foreign culture but not in any way a culture of their own" (*AGN*, 54). The symbols of this foreign tongue appear arbitrary to the group, since they are not derived from a collective life that is the group's own. On the other hand, this incursion of a foreign culture into an original one need not be a threat to the latter so long as the foreign individuals "are not permitted to bring the sphere of their observations up to the position from which the language is thereafter to develop [and] remain dumb in the community and without influence on the language, until the time comes when they themselves have entered into the sphere of influence of the original people," so that "they do not form the language [and] it is the language that forms them" (*AGN*, 53). Persons of "other race and other language" who have assimilated into the "original" language can have, Fichte's audience would be relieved to know, only an external command of their new tongue; they can master the realm of sensuous designations but never the higher or supersensuous. And the "original" people itself may be protected from this incursion, this displacement of linguistic and national communities, so long as the intruders are kept "dumb" and "without influence" on the language.

Fichte's theory of language and identity thus constitutes an allegory of the predicament of European culture at the beginning of the era of the nation-state. It clarifies the importance that historical continuity has for nation-thinking as the narrative and conceptual structure within which the displacements of minority are to be contained. The space of the national is thus susceptible, in its very constitution, to the intrusion of minority cultural and political practice, and the Jews, the exemplary figure for the disruptions of minority, are to be kept marginal to the core of the national culture if the integrity of that culture is to be achieved. Fichte thus inaugurates in the *Addresses* the recurring theme in German intellectual life of the artificiality of the Jewish acquisition and performance of the German language, especially in the "higher" linguistic domain of philosophical speculation. That this claim had a certain life even in the postwar era becomes evident when we recall that Jürgen Habermas felt the need, on the threshold of the 1960s, to defend at length "Jewish philosophers" such as Cohen, Rosenzweig, Buber, and Benjamin against the judgment that they "at best attain stardom of the second rank."[100]

Given the subsequent influence, in nineteenth- and twentieth-century German culture as in European culture as a whole, of Fichte's early elaboration of (German) nationality in its relation to (the German) language, it is hardly surprising that Adorno's most significant remarks on the fabrication of "national collectivities" have come in connection with language as an ideological domain.[101] In a number of late essays, originally delivered as radio talks, Adorno formulates a far-reaching critique not only of German nationalism and its troubled history but of the terrain of nation-thinking as such.[102] For Adorno, as for Fichte, the question "What is German?" can best be answered by turning to the domain of language. And for both these practitioners of the German language, the specificity of the language lies in its ability to speculate about the things of the world beyond their mere "given-ness." But here the parallel movement between this early expression of German idealism and its late materialist critique comes to an end. For, in Adorno's formulation, the "German tradition" is precisely that which makes possible a certain "vigilance" against the belief that "the metaphysical excess of the German language in itself already guarantees the truth of the metaphysics it suggests, or of metaphysics in general." It is an uncanny image of the mother tongue, the language that at the same time is and is not one's own. In Adorno's reckoning, therefore, no one is more German, as it were, more true to the "German tradition," than "the returning émigré," who, having "lost the naive relation to what is his own, must unite the most intimate relationship to his own language with unflagging vigilance against any fraud it promotes." It is thus the exile's special relationship to the German tradition that prevents its reification and commodification, becoming simply "a German brand-name product."[103]

I turn in the final chapter to the postcolonial affinities for such a view of language, but we should note that there is a certain replication here, in historical materialist form, of the vulnerable and deeply touching claim so often made by German Jewish survivors that they, and not the bustling German nationalists, to say nothing of those who participated or acquiesced in mass murder, are the true heirs of the tradition of Lessing, Kant, Goethe, and Schiller—that is, the true bearers of German *Bildung*. More important, however, these remarks represent a rewriting of the entire gamut of notions of belonging and locatedness, such as nation, tradition, and culture. This critical effort requires a clear recognition of the impossibility of standing entirely outside the language of national belonging, of nation-thinking, even as it seeks to shatter the myth of origin the latter simultaneously produces and relies upon. Thus Adorno makes possible the perception, as our reading of Fichte's *Addresses* has already made clear, that the myth of the autochthony of the nation arises precisely out of a displacement of the mutual relationships of language, nationality, and citizenship, out of a crisis of community. To paraphrase a formulation from Said, itself produced in part through an engagement with Adorno, home is already a form of exile, or, as Horkheimer and Adorno put it in the Odysseus essay: "Homeland is a state of having escaped" (*DE*, 61).[104] It is in this context that we must read Adorno's theory of what he calls "foreign words," a theory directed precisely against the will to closure of indigenous discourse that we have seen in Fichte's text. A foreign word whose sense of foreignness has not been fully assimilated in the host language, and its foreign origin not forgotten, can be used strategically for the "explosive" and "negative" power it carries within it. The prosthetic quality of the foreign word becomes a means to unnerving linguistic nationalism by subjecting the organicism of the native tongue to interrogation. It is with this function of foreign words in mind that Adorno spoke of them aphoristically, while in Californian exile, as "the Jews of language."[105]

If in Fichte's *Addresses* we find the elaboration of a linguistic nationalism on the premise of the purity of the language, in Walter Scott's *Ivanhoe* we encounter a seemingly rather different constellation, with the hybridized nature of the English language and culture emerging precisely as its unique and distinctive quality. Such discordances in *Ivanhoe* are, in fact, highly revealing of the ideological tensions of what is Scott's first "purely English" tale,[108] and his most popular and influential fictional work not only in Britain and on the continent but also in many parts of the colonial world, which quickly became, in Katie Trumpener's apt phrase, "the paradigmatic novel of empire, appealing to nationalist, imperialist, and colonial readers alike."[106] For in *Ivanhoe*, Walter Scott, the Scots inventor of a disappeared Scottish world, turns his attention to the dominant culture in Britain and invents a narrative of the emergence of the English nation out of the admixture of conflicting races, languages, and cultures. The predominant preoccupation of the novel—the conquest of one people, culture, and language by another—helps to elaborate the myth, in Christopher Hill's evocative phrase, of "the Norman yoke,"[107] and the Norman Conquest and resulting conflict between Norman and Saxon elements in language and culture becomes the originary moment of English history. The novel begins with an account of the linguistic hierarchies put in place by the Norman victory over the native sons of the soil, as Wamba the fool instructs Gurth the swineherd in the relationship of language to conquest and power:

> There is old Alderman Ox continues to hold his Saxon epithet while he is under the charge of serfs and bondsmen such as thou, but becomes Beef, a fiery French gallant, when he arrives before the worshipful jaws that are destined to consume him. Mynherr Calf, too, becomes Monsieur de Veau in the like manner: he is Saxon when he requires tendance, and takes a Norman name when he becomes a matter of enjoyment. (*I*, 15)

But the novel is at pains from the start to chart the movement beyond this conflict and provides in the end an account of the emergence of modern English identity out of the intermingling of these elements:

> Cedric lived to see this union [that is, of Norman and Saxon] approximate towards its completion; for, as the two nations mixed in society and formed intermarriages with each other, the Normans abated their scorn, and the Saxons were refined from the rusticity. But it was not until the reign of Edward the Third that the mixed language, now termed English, was spoken at the court of London, and that the hostile distinction of Normans and Saxons seems entirely to have disappeared. (515)

However, while Norman and Saxon are ultimately fused into a composite English identity, and indeed are shown to be members of the same family, namely, the European, whose unity is itself based on its common struggle to wrench the Holy Land away from the Saracens (Richard, Ivanhoe, the Templars) and by the effort to convert the Jews (Rowena, the Templars), the Jewish element—secretive, magical, particularistic, and "Asiatic," on the one hand, but also mobile, artificial and adaptable, on the other—remains ultimately inassimilable to the linguistic and cultural synthesis that comes to represent the people. In his own important and revisionist reading of Scott's novel, Michael Ragussis has argued that it belongs, along with *Harrington* and *Daniel Deronda*, to a revisionist English tradition of the novel of Jewish identity, which portrays the history of Jewish persecution within English society as a way of insisting upon the centrality of the Jewish Question to the formulation of the identity of the English nation itself. *Ivanhoe* brings to the surface, Ragussis argues, the secret national guilt of the persecution and uprooting of the Jews, Rebecca's and Isaac's final departure for Spain prefiguring retrospectively, as it were, the expulsion of the Jews from England that was to come in A.D. 1290. However, such an account of Scott's, and for that matter Eliot's, installation of the Jewish Question within (English) national history is ultimately too sanguine and one-sided. Scott's fictional recollection of the predication of English identity on the exclusion of the Jews is a deeply ambivalent one. For the novel also suggests that, for better or for worse, that is what Englishness simply *is* and ought to be. It is only with the departure of the Jews from England that English history proper may be said to begin.

When, in the concluding chapter of *Ivanhoe*, Rebecca comes to meet Rowena for the last time (and openly for the first time), she informs this descendant of the royal Saxon ancestor Alfred, and who, for the purposes of the plot, is Rebecca's (unknowing) rival for the love of Ivanhoe, of her family's plans to leave England forever and seek refuge in the far less hostile and more tolerant environment of Moorish Spain, or in the kingdom of Granada, to be exact, "secure of peace and protection, for the payment of such ransom as the Moslem exact from our people" (516). And earlier in the novel, while imprisoned by the Templars and awaiting near certain execution for allegedly practicing witchcraft, she had advised her father in a letter to leave England for Spain after her death, because "less cruel are the cruelties of the Moors unto the race of Jacob than the cruelties of the Nazarenes of England" (433). Rowena, however, moved by what she correctly perceives as Rebecca's mental anguish, and beginning to feel empathy, friendship, and a sense of gratitude toward her, who saved Ivanhoe's life by healing the battle wounds he suffered in jousting with the Norman overlords, and thus also helped to secure the domain of Richard Coeur-de-Lion from usurpation by John, tries to convince the young Jewish woman to stay in England and accept conversion to Christianity: "the counsel of holy men will wean you from your erring law, and I will be a sister to you" (518). Tolerance toward and affection for the Jew and the will to convert therefore go hand in hand in this encounter, as Ragussis noted in his singular account of the conversionist impulse in nineteenth-century English writing.[109] This conversionist scene in *Ivanhoe* draws upon contemporary Evangelical and millenarian discourse, and anticipates numerous later nineteenth-century formulations of tolerance and conversion from Evangelical but also secular liberal positions.

But if, on the one hand, *Ivanhoe* links the possibility of toleration to the ideology of conversion, on the other, it raises complex questions about the interconnections between the conversion of the Jews and the end of their wandering existence, including the possibility of their restoration to Palestine. Here again the novel draws upon prevalent discourses and concerns about the meaning of Jewish existence in a Europe of nations. In the thought of the Evangelical Revival, for instance, conversion of the Jews and their restoration to Palestine, or removal from Christian Europe, are inextricably linked and intertwined. Concern with their conversion inevitably leads to the idea of their restoration, and those painstaking and baffling textual exercises in the identification of biblical prophecies of restoration take place in the context of the "mania" for conversion, derided by an early critic of the seemingly endless but unfruitful efforts of the London Society for Promoting Christianity among the Jews, as "this English madness."[110] The enormous body of restorationist literature in this period can only be understood alongside the efforts of the various conversionist societies, above all, the London Society since its founding in 1808–1809, and these rather concrete and practical endeavors—painstakingly recorded in semiannual reports, official correspondence, lists of subscribers, and the like, often published for examination by the larger interested public—never wander too far from the end-of-the-world tremulousness of Christian restorationist thought. Equally significant is the redemptive role Evangelical thinking assigns to the event of restoration, not just for the Jews but for humanity as a whole. Conceived within the biblical plot for the coming of the Messiah, restoration becomes a means of imagining the final resolution of the political crisis of the modern world and becomes sublated into secular politics in the second half of the century in the rise of Zionism, both the Jewish and non-Jewish varieties. (I return at some length to the precise nature of this sublation in the next chapter.) As for the recurrence of the figures of conversion in English culture, that was to reach its climax in Victorian times in the person and works of Benjamin Disraeli, a seemingly sincere convert to Christianity who nonetheless never stopped referring to himself as a Jew. In *Ivanhoe*, the conversion-restoration constellation is rearranged and the plot given a further twist in the Templar Bois-Guilbert's offer to Rebecca, with whom he has become romantically obsessed, to "return" with him to Palestine and be at his side in his treacherous abandonment of the Crusaders' cause in favor of a personal, worldly, and hence *secular*, conquest of Palestine: "Thou shalt be a queen, Rebecca: on Mount Carmel shall we pitch the throne which my valor will gain for you, and I shall exchange my long-desired batoon for a scepter!" (442). Represented here is the atheistic Frenchman's ambition for Palestine and the Jews, an ambition historically available to the British imagination in the form of the Napoleonic "projects" directed at the Jews and at the Near East. The restoration of a Jewish queen on the throne of Palestine, in other words, could come about through (the paradox of) a secularization of the Western claim on the Holy Land, ascribed in this novel to the atheistic Frenchman. The episode points to the absence of a properly English alternative to the French, the former either obsessed with converting the Jews or indifferent to their fate. So it is significant that this possible alliance of Jew and secular Gentile is figured by Scott as an illegitimate union. As for the offer of conversion Rowena makes to Rebecca—the (Christian) assimilationist option, in other words—for the novel's readers, who by now have waded through seemingly endless evidence of the corruption, debauchery, and overall unholiness of the Christian clergy, to say nothing of that of the Templars, such an appeal cannot but appear in a decidedly ironic light. In the end the Jews are shown to prefer exile in Islamic lands to this Euro-Christian assimilation.

Thus we must read this set of historical-narrative moves in *Ivanhoe* as part of, and a contribution to, a larger context in the early nineteenth century for making use of the treatment of Jews as a way to derive a comparative definition of national identities among the emerging European nation-states. Thus the conditions of the Jews during the Crusades, in Moorish Spain, during the *Reconquista* and the Inquisition; the "enlightened despotic" reforms in Frederick II's Prussia and other German lands in the late eighteenth century; the French emancipation of 1791; and the concerted Napoleonic efforts directed at the Jews of Europe and the Islamic Near East—all these conditions regarding Jews are utilized in multifarious literary and cultural projects for the elaboration of English, Spanish, French, and German national identities in the early nineteenth century and beyond. In Edgeworth's story, "The Prussian Vase," for instance, Prussian experiments with ideas about citizenship and military service are gently satirized in the form of Frederick's effort to stage at Potsdam a military review consisting entirely of his Jewish subjects, a spectacle so comical that it sends the king into hiding at Sans Souci Palace to nurse his resulting depression; in Heine's "Almansor" (the short poem and the play in verse) the secret homecoming of an expelled Moor to Grenada is used to explore the psychological predicament of being Jewish in modern Europe, while in his narrative fragment, *The Rabbi of Bacherach*, written under the immediate effects on the author of a reading of *Ivanhoe*, and to which I return below, Moorish Spain appears as the lovingly recalled location for the flowering of Jewish civilization, in contrast to the precariousness of Jewish existence on the banks of the Rhine, the author's own native homeland; and in Eliot's *The Spanish Gypsy* (1868) and *Romola* (1863), the secretive and potentially treacherous figure of the crypto-Jew is revived in order to contemplate the pressures of conversion on Jews in modern Britain in comparison with the fate of the Jews in Spain under the Inquisition, while in her final novel, the protagonist's discovery of his descent from "a line of Spanish Jews that has borne many students and men of practical power" recalls the invention of a similar genealogy by the then prime minister.[111]

In *Ivanhoe* itself, the opposition of Saxon to Norman, while at one level resolved in the "marriage" of two cultures, which is symbolized and prefigured in the marriage of the Normanized Ivanhoe to the Saxon heiress Rowena, at another level remains resonant with the opposition of Protestant to Catholic, and at another still with a sense of the fundamental differences between the national characteristics of the French and the English. This latter distinction is also infused with the historically more recent experience of the various Napoleonic "projects" directed at the Jews—political emancipation, communal and theological centralization, the projected restoration to Palestine—as well as the myriad concrete consequences that the victories of the Revolutionary and Napoleonic armies had recently had for Jewish populations throughout the continent. The departure of the Jewish characters from Christian Europe at the end of the novel therefore recalls the ongoing consequences of the defeat of Napoleon for Jewish hopes for political emancipation and survival in Europe. In *Ivanhoe*, in other words, the new political order emerging in Europe is explored from the perspective offered by the question of the existence of the Jews, and Scott gives his readers an account, by means of a displacement onto the medieval world of Plantagenet England, of the dilemmas of Jewish life on its entry into a Europe of nations. Given its enormous popularity in the nineteenth century in many parts of the world, including the colonial world, the novel may thus be considered a global object lesson in the significance of the Jews for European modernity, a lesson in the contours and locations of Jewishness as minority. Through this book, more than any other work of Western literature, readers in faraway places made their first acquaintance with the narratives, themes, and motifs of Europe's "question" concerning the Jews.

The twentieth-century reader of Scott who attends most fully to the pre-1815 conjuncture in Europe is, of course, Lukács, for whom the historical context appropriate to an understanding of Scott's historical novels is this entire trajectory of developments, from the outbreak of the French Revolution to the rise and fall of Napoleon. For Lukács, it is through the agency of the Revolutionary and Napoleonic wars that the masses in Europe experience their history for the first time as a mass phenomenon and on a continental scale. What "previously was experienced by isolated and mostly adventurous-minded individuals, namely an acquaintance with Europe or at least certain parts of it, becomes in this period the experience of hundreds of thousands, of millions." The raising of mass armies instead of mercenary ones—by the revolutionary French, in the first instance, but subsequently also by their various Legitimist enemies—transformed the relationship between the army and the masses, requiring educating the latter, through numerous means of propaganda, concerning their relationship to the former. It is in this context of the emerging need for a national pedagogy that the new historical fiction acquires its immense popularity. In other words, the historical novel, as exemplified in Scott's work, is, for Lukács, the major aesthetic form corresponding to the social and cultural transformations that made the "national idea" into the "property of the broadest masses," a logical and necessary entailment of the development of bourgeois society, "national" being the form that political and historical consciousness take as a result of a bourgeois revolution. For Lukács, Scott contributes to this literary and cultural development by giving "human embodiment to historical social types." As James Chandler noted in his magisterial study of English literary culture in the year of *Ivanhoe*'s publication, Lukács thus explains Scott in terms of the explanatory method he ascribes to Scott's historical novels.[112]

As for *Ivanhoe* itself, for Lukács it is the work of a progressive national consciousness, which makes available to "his people"—that is, the English people—the history of their emergence out of the antagonistic interaction of the Normans and Saxons, and therefore historical consciousness itself.[113] Scott's "regional" place within the space of British culture, to borrow Trumpener's characterization, is entirely elided in Lukàcs's assessment of his role in the history of the novel and of historicism itself.[114] More significant for the present discussion, Lukàcs portrays the novel's treatment of the question of national history and culture exclusively with reference to the theme of Saxon-Norman conflict and its overcoming in history. It is remarkable, in other words that this major twentieth-century literary critic, historian, and theorist, himself a refugee from the Nazi genocide and thus acutely aware of every aspect of the history leading from the late-eighteenth-century talk of emancipation to the gas chambers, has not a word to say, in *The Historical Novel*, about the theme of Jewish persecution, displacement, and expulsion so central to Scott's novel. Although a remarkable omission, however, it is not unexpected, as it marks a fidelity to the dominant Marxist response to the crisis of minority, namely, a kind of radical assimilationism. The appeal of the Marxist worldview for individual lives caught in the ever deferred liberal promise of emancipation and equal rights cannot be underestimated, proceeding as it does by claiming to *immediately* make available to the purportedly intransigent particularity of the minority the standpoint of totality and the universal—what I term a "strong liberal" approach to emancipation through assimilation.[115] In this context the full significance becomes clear of Lukács's well-known and intriguing declaration that his Party membership card was his ticket into history—an apparent recollection of Heine's often-quoted characterization of baptism, which in his own case was bitterly regretted later in life, as the ticket of admission into European culture. For Lukács to turn to Heine's statement about the latter's conversion to Christianity to explain his own momentous decision to stay loyal to the Party during the Stalinist purges, and to disavow his own neo-Marxist writings, invites us to view this decision in the light not only of the Party intellectual's struggle for survival in the face of the whims of the apparatchik, as Fredric Jameson rightly suggested, but also of the more particular but longer struggle for Jewish survival in modern Europe.[116] These two responses to the Jewish dilemma, although separated by more than a century, are both among the forms taken by assimilation—assimilation through baptism in the first case, and through allegiance to the Communist worldview in the second. They share the attempt to resolve the crisis of minority through the dissolution of (Jewish) particularity into the universal, identified as Europe–Christianity, in the one instance, and Humanity or History, in the second. Thus it is further significant that Lukács historicizes the historical consciousness expressed in Heine's life and work as a partial or momentary one, in the dialectical sense, one that can affirm the full-blown post-1848 revolutionary spirit only with "a tragic cleavage of spirit."[117] According to the account of Heine given here by Lukács, in other words, the political affiliations of the twentieth-century critic are meant to *complete* what the early-nineteenth-century poet's experiments with cultural affiliation could only attempt partially and leave unfinished, namely, a successful assimilation and an end to the crisis of Jewish identity. Lukács's elision of the Jewish theme from his reading of *Ivanhoe* exemplifies the type of response from within the crisis of Jewish identity that proceeds through a disavowal of the forms of difference around which this crisis is centered.

Finally, it should be noted in passing that Gershom Scholem's well-documented discomfort with the attraction that Marxism held for Walter Benjamin—which he ungenerously and dismissively blamed on the undue influence of Brecht and his circle in Berlin in the late 1910s and 1920s[118]—also resonates with this range of theoretical possibilities for Jewish existence. This is because, from a Zionist point of view, Marxism and progressive thought always represent at least a potential rejection of separatist political desires; hence the contradictions and conceptual vulnerabilities of such projects as "socialist Zionism." At the same time this discomfort is also driven in part by a realization that the purported Marxist solution to the crisis of minority identity does not stray far from the (failed) liberal solution. On the other hand, it is important to remember that while assimilationism has been the main response of Marxist thought and practice in the twentieth century to the crisis of minority, this is only part of the picture. In a fuller historical perspective, the response of Marxism may be characterized as a monumental indecision, resulting, at one moment, in a condemnation of minority identity and struggles as epiphenomenal and a reactionary distraction from the class struggle for the body and soul of the larger nation, and at other times, although far less frequently, in championing the separate cultural and political existence of the minority as a distinct "nation" in itself. Each of these positions has been taken at different times, for instance, by Indian Communism, regarding the question of Muslim separatism and the Partition of India. But here my reading of *Ivanhoe* and Fichte's *Addresses* has been an attempt to reveal, to quote Homi Bhabha from another context, those "textual strategies, metaphoric displacements, sub-texts and figurative stratagems" through which these early and influential exercises in nation-thinking "construct the field of meanings and symbols associated with national life."[119] And although Fichte's emphasis on linguistic purism and Scott's on linguistic hybridity might at first suggest polar opposite ways of configuring modern identities, in the end they produce parallel results if we approach them in terms of the fate they envision for those groups and practices that are now deemed minor. Both Fichte and Scott respond to the crisis of modern subjectivity by positing a *national* subject in language, which arises out of the articulation of such figures as "the common life of the people" (Fichte) and the organic "union" of distinct cultural elements (Scott) that attempt to render the Jews an extraneous element.

The critique of this emerging nation-thinking is perhaps nowhere better represented in the early nineteenth century than in the wit and irreverence of Heinrich Heine, one of the linchpins of Western European cultural life in the first half of the century, whose life intersected at various times with the likes of Hegel, Marx, David Friedländer, Leopold Zunz, Franz Bopp, Rahel Varnhagen, Ludwig Börne, Goethe, Balzac, Dumas, Hugo, Liszt, Chopin, Felix Mendelssohn, and Wagner, to name just a few and in no particular order. Heine began his famous narrative fragment, *The Rabbi of Bacherach*, in 1824 under the influence of his association with the founders of *Wissenschaft des Judentums*, and continued writing it again perhaps in 1840 under the impact of the anti-Jewish riots in the Damascus Affair. The narrative begins with the escape of Rabbi Abraham and his wife, Sara, from near certain death at the hands of Christians in the "gloomy and ancient" town of Bacherach to the "free, imperial, and commercial city of Frankfurt-on-Main," a passage, in other words, from the feudal paradigm—represented by the blood-libel—toward the modern one—symbolized by the "protected" but perilous existence of the Jews in their "new" quarter in Frankfurt, an ambiguous and ironic figurative use of that city, given its prominence in the "Hep, Hep" riots that had shaken German Jewry a few years earlier, in 1819, also the year that *Ivanhoe* was published and the Verein für Kultur und Wissenschaft der Juden was founded. Heine is also commenting here on the historical irony that the "modern" is a reversion to the absolutist, in the aftermath of Napoleon's defeat and the repeal of emancipatory laws in the German principalities. He had spent his childhood in that atmosphere of emancipation, and his young adulthood under the conditions of the Restoration.[120]

The Rabbi of Bacherach opens with a description of the Rhine around the town and the wild and stern beauty it acquires in that vicinity. This opening passage leads immediately into a historical narrative, and the present decrepitude of the town is contrasted with its ancient majesty and its relatively free and open communal life in those early centuries. But the lyrical tone of this opening passage is interrupted by the narrator's anguish at the suffering of the Rhineland's—and, by extension, Germany's—Jews, a community that dates back to Roman times. The great persecution of the Jews began, we are told, with the Crusades, and raged furiously in the mid-fourteenth century. Outrage was piled upon outrage, oppression upon oppression, until Jews even came to be accused of the ritual murder of Christians at Passover. Persecution of the Jews became, the narrator tells us, an inherent part of the life of Christianity, purported child victims of the Jews' blood lust coming to be venerated and even canonized by the Church. One such supposed child victim is Saint Werner, in whose honor the magnificent nearby abbey of Oberwesel, now one of the most beautiful ruins on the Rhine, was founded. The lyricism of the image of the Rhine is therefore disturbed by the historical perception of a long and bloody history, one condensed here in the figure of the ruined abbey devoted to the child saint, which, "with the Gothic grandeur of its long, lancet windows, proudly aspiring pillars, and marvelous stone-carving, so strangely enchants us when we wander by it on some merry green summer's day, and do not know what was its origin."[121] With the Rhine thus both established as a Romantic image and undermined in that very function, the narrative turns to the Jewish community of the fifteenth-century town, of whom we are told that "the more hate oppressed them from without, the more earnestly and tenderly did [they] cherish their domestic life within" (*JS*, 23).

The most famous passage in the narrative and the one most often cited is, of course, the description in chapter 1 of the seder in Abraham's home. Along with such poems as "Princess Sabbath," it has been seen as textual evidence of the deeply tender feelings Heine retained for the daily rituals of Jewish life throughout his lifetime.[122] I return shortly to this passage but with a view to understanding the specific manner of its secularization of religious ritual. But continuing here with Heine's intricate rewriting of the signs of national history and culture, as the Jewish couple make their escape by boat on the Rhine, and Sara falls into a kind of trance, the complexity of the river's significations are increasingly brought into play:

> For in truth old, kind-hearted Father Rhine cannot bear that his children shall weep, so, calming their crying, he rocks them on his trusty arm, and tells them his most beautiful stories, and promises them his most golden treasures, perhaps even the ancient long-sunken Nibelungen hoard. Little by little the tears of Beautiful Sara ceased to flow; her worst sorrow seemed to be washed away by the eddying, whispering waves, the night lost its sinister horror, while her native hills bade her the tenderest farewell. (*JS*, 36)

Most striking about this passage is that, first of all, the Jewish couple escaping certain death at the hands of gentile Germans are figured as the *children* of "Father Rhine," guardian of the community's "most beautiful stories." Second, the Rhine, as the repository of German national culture, seeks to comfort its *Jewish* children initially with tales from *Germanic* mythology. The treasures of the Nibelungs, in other words, are as enchanting and comforting for the Jews as they would be for the river's non-Jewish children, and, in fact, Sara is comforted by the rhythmic motion of the river's waters, as "her native hills" bid her a tender farewell.

As Sara's reverie continues, however, these visions are transformed into scenes of her Jewish childhood, and these childhood scenes blend into mythological images of another sort:

> Then the Rhine seemed to murmur the melodies of the *Haggadah*, and from its waters the pictures, large as life and in strange exaggerated guise, came forth one by one. There was the forefather Abraham painfully and hurriedly breaking the idols, who were hastily putting themselves back together; the Mitzri defending himself fiercely against the angry Moses; Mount Sinai flaming and flashing.... Then all at once... the sombre curtain was torn from heaven, and there appeared, far above, the holy city of Jerusalem, with its towers and gates; the Temple gleamed in golden splendour... [and] in the Holy of Holies knelt King David, in his purple mantle and golden crown; sweetly rang his song and the tone from his harp, and smiling happily Beautiful Sara fell asleep. (*JS*, 39, 41, 43)

The Rhine is thus portrayed here as the source not only of Germanic fables but also of the stories of the Hebrew Bible, a narrative move that parallels Heine's inclusion of Spinoza in the history of philosophy and religion in Germany in his famous long essay from the early 1830s.[123] National culture, in other words, is seen by Heine not as a singular trajectory at whose beginning is the image of the Germanic tribe but rather as a historically contingent articulation of different cultural claims. The culture of the modern nation, therefore, has both "Jewish" and "Germanic" roots; it is at the strange intermixing and blending of these images and memories that culture is located and produced. The resources of culture are therefore always *unheimlich*, and thus Heine makes possible a critique of the nation as a form of social existence based on the notion of being at home while at the same time revealing the hoax of this *heimlich* sensibility. A precise image for this narrative strategy is the biblical Abraham in the cited passage itself, engaged in an unending process of breaking the idols—and here it is the secular apotheosis of the modern nation that is in question—which repeatedly re-create themselves.

Finally, as she partially awakens from her dreams, Sara thinks of the loved ones they have left behind facing almost certain death, and suddenly "she seemed to see there her friends and relations, as they, with corpse-like faces and flowing shrouds, passed in awful procession along the Rhine" (*JS*, 39–41). This ghostly procession along the Rhine is a figure for the history of violent persecution of the Jews in German history. These, too, are stories that "Father Rhine" can and does tell his children. In other words, Jewishness-minority becomes here the site and means for arriving at the perception that the canonization of national history requires a forgetting of this ghostly procession, which nevertheless can never be entirely erased from memory. The lyricism of the Rhine is not so much rejected here as opened up to interrogation, as the *heimlich* pleasures of national belonging are disturbed by the *unheimlich* recollection of violent exclusions and discordant histories. The first chapter of *The Rabbi of Bacherach* is therefore an engagement with the language of German national belonging. Heine enters this field by exposing *Rheinromantik* to the dissonances of modern culture. It is a complex strategy. A geographic region—the Rhineland—and its culture are made to stand in for German *national* culture, and this regional-national imagery is then itself placed under a question mark. But, furthermore, with its special historical connection to the Revolution and to emancipation, the Rhineland becomes the embodiment of universal principles and the *center* (rather than a regional locale) in an alternative configuration of the space of the nation. As the emancipatory measures instituted under the Napoleonic Code are being everywhere rescinded in the German lands in the aftermath of Napoleon's defeat, Heine holds on to the *Rhenisch* experience of his childhood as the basis for his projected view of an emancipated German (and Jewish) existence.

The Passover observance in *Rabbi* is often described as the first sympathetic portrayal of an aspect of the traditional Jewish life-world in modern German and perhaps Western literature. The language is tender and nostalgic, and represents an attempt to bring within the purview of Romanticism materials that are distinctly Jewish—the special foods carefully laid out, the particular attire of the men and women, the intoning of passages from the *Haggadah* by the male head of the family:

> Mournfully merry, seriously playful, and mysteriously secret is the character of this nocturnal festival, and the usual traditional singing intonation with which the *Haggadah* is read by the father, and now and then re-echoed in chorus by the hearers, at one time thrills the inmost soul as with a shudder, anon calms it as if it were a mother's lullaby, and anon startles it so suddenly into waking that even those Jews who have fallen away from the faith of their fathers and run after foreign joys and honours [fremden Freuden und Ehren] are moved to their very hearts when by chance the old well-known tones of the Passover songs ring in their ears. (*JS*, 26)

Most notable about this passage is the effort to identify the problematic within which this narrative of Jewish life becomes meaningful, namely, the secularization of that life and the assimilation of Jews to German culture, identified in the passage as "foreign" or "alien." In this sense, this narrative of the affective appeal of Jewish ritual can come only after the principle of the rationalization of religious faith and observance has been established. And it is significant in this episode that it is precisely the moment at which the Jews open their door to non-Jews, or when Judaism opens itself up to politics and community, as it were, that the threat of blood-libel, and hence annihilation, enters the Jewish home. In his exploration of the meaning of Judaism in enlightened society, Mendelssohn distinguished between Jewish faith and ritual observance, assimilating the former entirely to an unrevealed religion of reason in order to preserve the latter as outward tokens of that faith, required by revelation. It is an unintended sign of the success of this rationalization project that these tokens, to which Mendelssohn attributes a religious but merely mnemonic function, are now transformed into the secular signs of (Jewish) *culture*, and hence into the potential means of a political instrumentality. In the third decade of the nineteenth century, in other words, when the question of Jewish emancipation or "civic union" has been established as being central to the question of citizenship and emancipation as such, Heine's citation of the ritual Passover invocation within the secular discourse of modern narrative literature—the Romantic novella, in this instance—transforms the meaning of the invocation, "This year we celebrate it here, but next year, in the land of Israel," which now comes to acquire a secular, cultural, and therefore (at least potentially) political signification. Thus those routine dismissals of the *Wissenschaft des Judentums* by self-described Zionists like Scholem, which characterize it as a variety of apologetics for assimilation, miss the larger point entirely, namely, that the *Wissenschaft* represents in the intellectual history of the Jewish Question the establishment and canonization of the idea of Jewish culture, without which the Zionist idea itself cannot be conceived.[124] Heine himself is, quite literally, a transitional figure in this process, as Lukács recognized with respect to his fluctuating enthusiasm for the growing possibility of proletarian revolution and democracy. But I have in mind here the back-and-forth movements he makes throughout his life regarding the process of intellectual secularization, embodying not an unambiguously secular or atheistic consciousness but one that is still negotiating between emancipation and Enlightenment, on the one hand, and, on the other, various forms of religious belief, identity, and spirituality.

Jeffrey Sammons argued some years ago that to look for explanations for the unfinished nature of *Rabbi* in the individual proclivities of Heine as author is "a version of the intentional fallacy."[125] I follow his lead here in suggesting that the faltering and, in the end, unfinished nature of Heine's attempt is most productively read in a register other than the merely biographical. This formal specificity of this work, its fragmentary nature or "incompleteness," is the inscription, at the level of form, of a wider historical problematic. For at stake here, the question the work confronts, is the location of Jewishness as minority within the emerging discourse of (European) national cultures. If, for Lukács, the rise of the classical historical novel is linked to the emergence of national identities in Europe in the aftermath of the Revolution and the resulting wars, in the fragmentary state of *The Rabbi of Bacherach* we may read an interrogation of the terms for the narrating of German national culture, and one of the authoritative versions of this narrative is Fichte's *Addresses*. One might say that Heine *secularizes* the nationalism of Fichte by returning to the present the cultural dissonance that the latter attempts to resolve through a narrative of continuity with a distant past whose signifier is the life of the Germanic tribe. The nation is an articulation (and conflict or play) of cultural affiliations in the present rather than a common and singular life that emerges out of the dim light of the distant past. We must read this unfinished work not as a Jewish historical novel *manqué* but instead for its success in making Jewishness-minority the site for displacing the authoritative narrative of Europe as a concert of national histories and identities. In other words, *The Rabbi of Bacherach* represents an attempt to reinscribe the problem of national culture from a location within the nation-space that makes visible the produced and tentative nature of that space. By thwarting the epic resolutions of national narrative, by highlighting the impossibility of an epic heroism that takes a minoritized collective as its subject, Heine's text makes the narrative of national identity visible *as* narrative and also makes possible the perception that the right and the ability to attempt those resolutions are not uniformly distributed within culture and society. Heine, the author of "The Lorelei," the anthem of the Rhine, which even the Nazis could not erase from popular memory and were forced to include in their anthologies under the undisguised lie, "author unknown," highlights in his unfinished story the contingent and fabricated nature of national collectivities and refuses to embrace the totalizing narrative of a Europe of nations. The Jews for Heine mark the essential untruth of this narrative, the suppressed element whose very suppression—never fully successful—becomes everywhere the ground for elaborating the fiction of the organic national community. It is with this in mind, perhaps, that Adorno spoke of Heine as a "wound" in the German language and in modern European literature that will be healed only "in a world in which no one would be cast out any more," in a society, in other words, "that has achieved reconciliation."[126]

The "question" that is repeatedly addressed to the figure of the Jew in these early decades of the era of emancipation—"Who are you?"—is, in a rigorous sense, an impossible one to answer, for the impossibility of an adequate response is inherent in its rhetorical form as a question. To respond, for instance, that, "yes, we are French"—or German or English, as the case may be—is to make an utterance whose truth will always be in question. For while the demand may purport to be addressed to the "Jews of France" (or England or Germany), it assumes the existence of

Jews in general, and of Jews as a question in general. The attempt in the nineteenth century to assimilate the Jews into any of the European nation-states, no matter how *sincere*, is thus one almost *intended* to fail and to remain an open question. The cultural position that eventually produces the idea of the Jewish nation and of a Jewish homeland is located within this constitutive failure and represents, paradoxically, the fullest possible assimilation of the Jews to Western modernity, as a (Western) nation among the nations. If the "moment" of *Nathan the Wise*, *Jerusalem*, Maimon's *Autobiography*, and the Proclamation of 1791 inaugurates the era of emancipation, then the "moment" of *Rome and Jerusalem*, *Daniel Deronda*, and the Alliance Israélite Universelle brings it to a close. It is to this latter conjuncture, in Britain and its empire in particular, which were to prove so crucial to the establishment of the Zionist enterprise in Palestine, that I now turn.

CHAPTER TWO

Inscriptions of Minority in British Late Imperial Culture

FROM *DANIEL DERONDA* TO *A PASSAGE TO INDIA*

When, on finding himself responsible for the welfare of Mirah, who is unattached to family and community and thus unprotected, Daniel Deronda begins to make the rounds of Holborn in the hope of discovering some information about her long lost family, on the display table outside a secondhand bookstore he comes upon and purchases a copy of "that wonderful bit of autobiography, the life of the Polish Jew, Salomon Maimon."[1] It is a revelatory moment of George Eliot's preoccupation with the Jews. For Maimon's autobiography is the Jewish *Bildungsgeschichte* par excellence, narrating an individual passage from ignorance to knowledge, from darkness to light, from "East" to "West," from the "medieval" world of the eastern shtetl to Western modernity, and from the Talmud to the Enlightenment and European philosophy. Significantly the autobiographical subject of Maimon's work is a precocious Talmudic scholar as a child and, in adulthood, one of Kant's important interpreters. But it is, of course, a necessarily incomplete passage, embodied in the ambiguous and schlemiel-like figure of Maimon himself, with his reputation for physical and mental eccentricity, never fully assimilated into the Berlin intelligentsia in which he circulated for a few years, at once an uprooted wanderer and deeply rooted in Jewish tradition. When, in 1898, Israel Zangwill fictionalized Maimon's encounter with Mendelssohn in *Dreamers of the Ghetto*, he titled the chapter "Maimon the Fool and Nathan the Wise."[2] Maimon marks in Eliot's text the moment of Enlightenment, *Haskala*, and emancipation, and the ambiguous and ambivalent results of this opening up for the Jews. Notably, Deronda's first encounter with Mordecai takes place over this book, as the former purchases it from the latter in Mr. Ram's bookshop. Mordecai is sufficiently intrigued by this choice of reading matter to examine Deronda closely and ask if he is a Jew, and the latter, having responded no, is left with the curious feeling, "oddly embarrassing and humiliating," of having been judged and found wanting, "as if some high dignitary had found him deficient and given him his *congé*" (*DD*, 327). Thus the process that ends in Deronda's assuming the mantle of

Mordecai's disciple, and the agent of his vision for the regeneration of the Jews, begins with this little interaction over the textual beginnings of the Jewish Question. In pointing in this manner to Maimon's *Autobiography* at the beginning of Deronda's encounter with modern Judaism, Eliot signals her novel's consideration of its own textual prehistory. A great summation of the century of emancipation that preceded it, *Daniel Deronda* in effect brings that century to a close. Where, in its pan-European reception and reputation, Lessing's final play had come to represent the opening gambit, as it were, in the textual elaboration of the question of Jewish emancipation, Eliot's final novel came to perform that pan-European role a century later by bringing that question to a conclusion of sorts. Where *Nathan* established the offer of equality in citizenship, and thus the end of Jewish particularity and "privilege," as the highest form that philo-Semitism could take in European society, *Deronda* endorsed Jewish nationalism as the most advanced form of Jewish consciousness in the final decades of the nineteenth century. It is this role, this preeminence, that Amy Levy gently satirizes in *Reuben Sachs* (1888) just twelve years later, when Leo Leuniger speculates with his extended family that Bertie Lee-Harrison, the aristocratic recent convert to Judaism, had been "shocked at finding us so little like the people in *Daniel Deronda*."[3]

The third quarter of the nineteenth century marks a consolidation of the emerging problematic of minority in a number of events and social and cultural sites worldwide, and therefore also, from our present vantage point, its expansion and diffusion as a global phenomenon intrinsic to the evolution of the nation-state as a global form. These events and cultural sites include the coming into public prominence of Benjamin Disraeli and the admittance of Jews to the House of Commons without the necessity of taking an oath upon "the true faith of a Christian" (Lionel de Rothschild, 1858);[4] the eruption and suppression of the Indian Revolt (1857), the dissolution of Company Raj and emergence of the technologies of a bureaucratic colonial state, and the consequent emergence of a public sphere increasingly preoccupied with and split over the question of the indigenousness (or not) of dominant linguistic, cultural, and social practices; the founding of the Alliance Israélite Universelle (1860) as a project of social and cultural amelioration directed self-consciously at the Jews as a transnationl and transcontinental group; the appearance of small groups of "nationalist" Jewish intellectuals, above all in France, including refugees from German lands such as Moses Hess, whose *Rome and Jerusalem* (1864) marked a turning point in the history of the elaboration of the "question" about the nature and identity of the Jews; the formal end of North American slavery and the attempted "reconstruction" of Southern society (1866–77) through the expansion of practices of citizenship across racial lines; the founding of the Mohammedan Anglo-Oriental College at Aligarh in North India (1877) as a self-consciously Muslim institution and the beginning of the (eventually) massive cultural and political project associated with it; and, finally, the publication and wide dissemination of *Daniel Deronda*, which brought the nationalist aspirations of a small segment of the (assimilated) middle-class Jewish intelligentsia firmly into the mainstream of European liberal culture.

Nineteenth-century British culture is, of course, an imperial culture in a strong sense of the word—a relatively uncontroversial judgment at this time, not only for its critics but also for its defenders.[5] By *late* imperial cultural relations I mean, in part, the systematization of imperial governance brought in play in the wake of the revolt of 1857—the end of Company Raj in the subcontinent and the emergence of a bureaucratic colonial state—and the consequences of this transformation for both the colonizing and colonized peoples. *Late imperial culture*, as I use it here, therefore refers to a period in the history of the British Empire that stretches from the mid-nineteenth-century uprising in India to the explosion on the scene (and on metropolitan consciousness) of nationalism as a mass movement in the late teens and twenties of the twentieth century, when even so "domestic" a novel as *Mrs. Dolloway* is forced to acknowledge the existence, in the metropolis itself, of "a Colonial" who "insulted the House of Windsor which led to words, broken beer glasses, and a general shindy," and a guest at Clarissa's party bemoans the "tragedy" of "the state of India."[6]

In the second half of this chapter I turn at some length to England's relationship to its Indian colony as it is elaborated in a number of representative works of late imperial English literature, particularly in the works of Kipling and Forster; more specifically I address the late imperial preoccupation with the nature of Indian society and its supposed impermeability to such forms of modern political and cultural experience as citizenship and nationality. The figure of the Muslim emerges, I argue, as the site for the elaboration of this impermeability, and in it we may glimpse the contradictions and paradoxes of this colonial discourse. Even as these works proceed with a denial of the possibility that India may be considered a nation in the modern sense, they turn the figures of "Muslim" particularity and difference into the ambivalent signs of minority, thus at the same time *nationalizing* the practices of a modern "Hindu" identity. In the decades following the 1857 Rebellion, "the Muslims" come to appear as a group with a paradoxical social existence—on the one hand, as local and particularistic, caught in a time warp outside the temporalities of the modern world, and, on the other, as formed by loyalties and affiliations that violate and exceed the territorial structure of the (colonial) state. Already in 1858 Syed Ahmed Khan, the great reformer and publicist who was to become the founder of the Aligarh movement for the education and reform of elite *sharīf* Muslim culture, felt the need to produce a treatise titled *The Causes of the Indian Revolt* as a corrective to the universal perception of the treachery of the Muslims, and in 1872 felt compelled once again to enter the public fray on the subject of Muslim political loyalties with a response to W. W. Hunter's *The Indian Musalmans: Are They Bound in Conscience to Rebel against the Queen?* itself a fascinating instance of the late-nineteenth-century imperialist imagination's fantasy encounters with the threat of "Wahhabism" that bears rereading in the early twenty-first century. Sir Syed (as he is universally known in South Asia) refuted vociferously the charge that Muslims in India owed their ultimate political allegiance to the Ottoman Caliphate and therefore represented a fifth column for the colonial state, working in the interest of a foreign and rival power. Nationalism as a political culture inherited this contradictory representational structure concerning the Muslims—as simultaneously a particularist and cosmopolitan group—and nothing makes clearer than this the "derivative" nature of nationalism with respect to colonial culture, as Partha Chatterjee has characterized it, up to and including a figure like Jawaharlal Nehru, universally and rightfully regarded as a defender of Muslim rights in post-Partition India. In the course of the half-century following the rebellion, however, this representational structure undergoes an inversion, treachery against the colonial state having been transformed into betrayal of the *national* struggle and a subservient, client-like posture of the Muslim elites vis-à-vis the British rulers. (As I show later in this chapter, an early story of Kipling's, "On the City Wall," is a brilliant and instrumental utilization of this historical process from the ideological location of mid-Victorian, Anglo-Indian imperialism.) In sum, therefore, this chapter is concerned with the dissemination, in the second half of the nineteenth century, of the modes of representation of social and cultural experiences with a distinctly "minor" relationship to state and society. It charts a particular dissemination of the figures of minority—to colonial India—and is thus an examination of how a problematic that emerged around a concern with the particularity of the Jews in a Europe of nations was transformed into a consideration of what the forms of particularity of the Muslims meant for the question of whether India was a nation.

"A New Evangel": Jewish Redemption in a Europe of Nations

Long ignored or at least held at arm's length by the mainstream critical establishment, Eliot's final novel has in the last two decades become subject to a wide-ranging debate about the intersection of a number of discourses in her work—nationalism, imperialism, liberalism, and, of course, the recurring nineteenth-century crisis concerning the Jews and their place in modern culture and society. Whether it acknowledges this place of beginning, much of this discussion has emerged in response to Edward's Said's reading of the novel—which is a summary one but has been both influential and controversial—in "Zionism from the Standpoint of its Victims," republished as chapter 2 of *The Question of Palestine*.[7] It has thus resonated in complex ways for questions about the historical meaning of Zionism and the contemporary struggle over the meaning and inhabiting of Palestine. For Said, of course, Eliot's elaboration of the theme of the redemption of the land in Palestine, and of European culture and society, by the regeneration of the Jews in their "return" to Palestine erases from view the native inhabitants of the land and the existence of a collective life on it. It is precisely such an "imaginative geography," as he calls it elsewhere, which is for him the most unmistakable trace of modern empire on the elaboration of the forms of culture of the modern West.[8] For Said, this is the ground proper for the emergence of the Zionist "idea," at the intersection of liberalism, imperialism, and the category and domain of culture.

I return at length to some of the questions raised by Said's critique of the novel. But it should be noted here that these questions continue to be at stake in more recent readings of the novel, even where the debt to Said, positive or negative, is left unacknowledged. Amanda Anderson, for instance, in an essay that represents a significant reinterpretation of Eliot's relationship to the Jewish Question, makes no explicit mention of Said's argument but nevertheless seeks precisely to redeem Eliot's Zionism as an expression of a liberal and cosmopolitan view of mankind attempting to overcome the narrowness and partialness of Englishness. She sees the novel as recasting the terms of the Jewish Question in such a manner that "Judaism's ongoing resistance to universalism's assimilationism itself might serve as a basis for a reconstructed universalism committed to dialogical openness in the face of cultural and ethnic multiplicity." She thus defends the novel's Zionism, and the terms of the Zionist "solution" to the Jewish Question more broadly, as compatible with "openness to otherness." Against the critique of historical Zionism and of the Israeli state implicit in Daniel and Jonathan Boyarin's important essay on the "diasporic" ethical ground of Jewish identity, Anderson argues that it "may be that the rhetoric of autochthony surrounding Zionism works against civic nationalism, but this does not mean that we must jettison completely the model of national self-determination."[9] In that casual "may be" is contained the peculiar posture of Anderson's entire argument. Not only is Eliot assured her place as a champion of the

Jews, representing liberalism at its inclusive best, she is such a champion precisely because she puts in place the elements of the cultural and political constellation that by the end of the century would acquire the name of Zionism. In other words, Anderson ties Eliot's championing of the Jews inextricably to her vision, given form in the novel, of a final resolution of Europe's Jewish Question outside the space of Europe itself. Famously the novel leaves entirely up to the reader's imagination what this future life of the Jews—represented in the novel by Daniel and Mirah—will look like. However, it does put in place the basic narrative structure that Zionist thought would come to take for granted and depend on: it seeks to bring a non-European space within the purview of the narratives of European modernity, by reinscribing it as a space appropriate for the resolution of those European narratives. This entire dimension is made to disappear in Anderson's reading, in a move that parallels what Said takes to be the novel's own disappearing act with respect to Palestine and its Arab inhabitants.

In an influential essay whose first publication predates that of Anderson's by a few years, Susan Meyer has taken a dramatically different position on this issue. She highlights the difficulties inherent in trying to redeem Eliot's last novel from the perspective, and in the interest of, Jewish equality and rights by correctly pointing out that in the 1860s and 1870s it was "the English gentiles," and not so much the Jews, "who were fascinated with the idea of the Jewish return."[10] Levy touches on precisely this in *Reuben Sachs*: "Did he expect," Esther asks rhetorically with reference to Lee-Harrison, "to see our boxes in the hall, ready packed and labeled *Palestine*?" To which Leo replies: "I have always been touched . . . at the immense good faith with which George Eliot carried out that elaborate misconception of hers."[11] But Meyer's reading of *Deronda* rests on the somewhat startling claim that *Deronda* is, in fact, "rife with anti-semitism," a conclusion that negates the possibility of asking many more questions than those it answers.[12] My own concern here, as in the previous chapter, is not with whether some individual may or may not be said truly to belong to the liberal tradition of championing the rights of the Jews or, to cite once again the historically more circumscribed category coined by Ragussis, to the "revisionist" tradition of the (English) novel of Jewish identity. Far from being a point of arrival, questions such as these have to be a point of departure for an examination not of the authenticity of the philo-Semitic claim or reputation but rather of the conditions under which such claims and reputations are made, of their rhetorical resources and inherent limitations, and, finally, of their consequences for the human collectivities and ways of life at which they are directed, in whose interest they seem to be made, or which they reorganize or make to disappear in part or even entirely. Said, in focusing on the imaginative imperial geographies inherent in *Daniel Deronda*, that is, on the instrumentalization of non-European places in the interests of the metropolis, and on the price paid by non-European peoples and cultures for the latter's narrative resolutions, shelves the question of Jewish emancipation itself and its fate in the novel's imagined world. It is this question I wish to reopen here and to read alongside and within the questions concerning liberalism and the imperial imagination made possible with respect to the novel for the first time by Said's reading.

Eliot's final novel represents her most far-reaching negotiation of the relationship (and tension) between what she calls the "sweet habit of the blood" (*DD*, 16)—forms of thinking and feeling that are, as it were, "in common," consecrated by such notions as birth, race, tradition, homeland, and culture—and the "civic" ideals of a liberal social and political dispensation.[13] For Eliot this is not a simple or stable opposition between affect and reason but instead a navigation of the spaces around and between them. Affect and reason continually collapse into each other, Eliot repeatedly points out, and any attempt to institute a rational social order without the binds of fellow-feeling itself turns into a kind of superstition, an irrationality, as the narrative persona puts it in *The Impressions of Theophrastus Such*. In *Deronda*, the growing cosmopolitanism of the metropolis is countered not with the moral economy of Old England, as in a number of the earlier novels, but rather is confronted head on in the form of the Jews. In his reading of the Jewish theme in *Deronda*, Said has suggested a link between Daniel's newfound vocation and the sense of diminution at the close of Eliot's previous novel. If *Middlemarch* (1872) ends with its female protagonist chastened to accept, as Barbara Hardy points out, a "reduced consciousness," then Eliot's last work tries, Said argues, to revise "upwards" this "diminished view of things."[14] As David Carroll has shown, early readers of *Middlemarch* saw the novel as "a *cul de sac* of realism and despair." Characteristically a contemporary reader wondered if Eliot could any more be expected to provide a vision of "a humanity which, we hope, is to be," or if she could find a "New Gospel to communicate," or propagate "a new evangel." In Carroll's view, therefore, as in Said's, "*Daniel Deronda* was Eliot's answer" to the readers' expectations generated by her previous novel.[15] If the frustration of ideals suffered by "later-born Theresas" is not the result of what some believe to be "the inconvenient indefiniteness with which the Supreme Power has fashioned the natures of women," then this absence of "epos" must be sought in the conditions of modern society itself, in its singular lack of any "coherent social faith and order which could perform the function of knowledge for the ardently willing soul."[16] The condition for a successful individual life of intense "feeling" is therefore a *collective* life of feeling. And the Jews, with their seemingly obdurate clinging to the distant memories of a collective life, become, for this liberalism in crisis, a source of moral persuasion, and, as Said puts it, of "reproach to the Gentiles."[17]

Unlike so many of Eliot's other protagonists and secondary characters, Daniel does not have to *learn* true "sympathy," that cardinal virtue of Eliot's moral universe, but seems to have acquired it almost naturally.[18] The text repeatedly links this mental orientation—the central concern in so much of Eliot's work—to the protagonist's acutely felt uncertainty of place in his immediate environment and in English society: "Other men, he inwardly said, had a more definite place and duties" (*DD*, 153). Daniel's fears about his own possible birth out of wedlock, triggered by his tutor's explication of the true nature of the relationship between popes or cardinals and their "nephews" (*DD*, 139) and reinforced by numerous experiences—such as a perception of the lack of resemblance between his own physiognomy and those of the Mallingers, both living and dead, who are on display in the portrait gallery, or the casual suggestion from his own "uncle" that he train for a life on the stage—only intensify and make explicit a sense of his own illegitimacy that is, as it were, there from the beginning. This nagging sense of "entailed disadvantage," likened by Eliot to "Byron's susceptibility about his deformed foot" (*DD*, 147, 148), was at the basis, the narrator repeatedly tells us, of the boy's special character: his precocious capacity for self-reflection, his "meditative yearning after wide knowledge," and, above all, his "hatred of all injury" (*DD*, 151). And Daniel's own words later to his mother reveal his understanding of this link in his life: "What I have been most trying to do for fifteen years is to have some understanding of those who differ from myself" (*DD*, 540). Thus, when Daniel's Jewish origin is revealed to him, we realize that he has been prepared for an acceptance, even embracing, of that fact by precisely the life that was meant to remove him from it forever. This capacity for sympathy is precisely what Jewishness is, or at least is capable of. Furthermore, neither the cosmopolitan life of the stage—as in the mother's case—nor the fact of having been raised in utter ignorance of, and disconnected from, one's Jewish origins—as is the case with the son—is enough to achieve what these assimilationist life-possibilities are meant to achieve: to finally erase the particularist sense of being a Jew. It is this paradox that the mother herself senses in her own way when she tells her son, "you are glad to have been born a Jew [...] because you have not been brought up as a Jew. The separateness seems sweet to you because I saved you from it" (*DD*, 540). This linking of Jewishness with the social and psychic effects of illegitimate birth makes crystal clear the relationship of the Jews to the language of national belonging, to nation-thinking, as I have called it here, with its ideological reliance on the family, inheritance, and organic reproduction: the Jews constitute a scandal in national life, surrounded by rumors, suspicions, and crises of (communal) regeneration and of legitimate authority but at the same time, in the very persistence of their communal identification, they represent a kind of hope for a fractured and atomized humanity.

As Eliot has Mordecai tell "The Philosophers" at The Hand and Banner, "Israel is the heart of mankind, if we mean by heart the core of affection which binds a race and its families in dutiful love, and the reverence for the human body which lifts the needs of animal life into religion, and the tenderness which is merciful to the poor and weak and to the dumb creature that wears the yoke for us" (*DD*, 453). Eliot's real concern, in other words, is not the cultural and moral separatism or "alienism" of the Jews but rather the artificiality, atomism, and moral indifference of society itself. Here is Mordecai once again: "They scorn our people's ignorant observance; but the most accursed ignorance is that which has no observance—sunk to the cunning greed of the fox, to which all law is no more than a trap or the cry of the worrying hound" (*DD*, 454). This observation has a certain relationship to the more radical perception in the nineteenth century that the very success of modern capitalist civilization over earlier forms of community and belief, and, of course, over its self-produced specters in 1848, constitutes the greatest threat to its integrity and even to its existence. Therefore Marx's suggestion that all of society under capitalism has become "Jewish," so often misunderstood as an instance of anti-Semitism or German-Jewish *Selbsthaas*—a term that, whatever analytical and descriptive effectivity it once had, has lost any such value in being subsumed into the banality of American pop psychology as "self-hatred"—becomes comprehensible when read against this liberal structure of feeling.[19] It attempts to dialectically invert that structure, thereby displacing the otherness of Jew to modern society: the very social functions that medieval society forced upon the Jews and restricted to them, Marx argues, now provide the very principle of society.

In the conversation of "The Philosophers," Eliot elaborates at great length a constellation of viewpoints and experiences that arise out of the history, and within the problematic, of emancipation. In particular she stages here the tensions, but also the overlaps and slippages, between the emerging Jewish national idea, as expounded in the episode by Mordecai, and the other liberal concept and possibility, namely, assimilation. This opposing possibility is defended most forcefully by Gideon, the optical instrument maker, "a Jew of the red-haired, generous-featured type easily passing for Englishmen of unusually cordial manners" (*DD*, 446). Gideon, a self-professed "rational Jew," who is "for keeping up our worship in a rational way," proposes a secular assimilation, rejecting both religio-communal separatism and the common practice of integration by baptism: "And now we have political equality, there's no excuse for a pretence of that sort [that is, baptism]. But I am for getting rid of all our superstitions and exclusiveness. There's no reason now why we shouldn't melt gradually into the populations we live among. That's the order of the day in point of progress" (*DD*, 449). Furthermore, he links this question to the question of rationality itself. Conceding that Mordecai's is not a millenarian view in the strictest sense, that he does not "hold with the restoration to Judea by miracle," Gideon argues that what constitutes a rational belief is itself determined by "facts," namely, that both Judaism and Christianity, as they are practiced, have mixed "a heap of nonsense" into the question of the Jewish return. The rational option within these circumstances can therefore only be to clear "our liturgy of all such notions as a literal fulfillment of the prophecies about restoration." Cleansed of "a few useless rites and literal interpretations of that sort," Judaism is "the simplest of all religions, and makes no barrier, but a union, between us and the rest of the world" (*DD*, 455). It is clear that in his voicing of the desire to reconcile Jewish belief and practice with a universal, natural religion, Gideon is being presented here as a lineal descendant of eighteenth-century *Haskala* and Enlightenment, which are being interrogated—by Mordecai, above all, but also, we might say, by the narrator—in light of the century-long and paradoxical success/failure of emancipation.

It is well known that Eliot's knowledge of Judaica was acquired above all through a reading of German textual materials—literature, biblical scholarship, historiography, and philosophy—augmented by personal experience of Jewish life in such German-speaking environments as Frankfurt, Berlin, Vienna, and Prague.[20] While the conversation at the Hand and Banner is a genuine exchange, a give and take of ideas, and none of the participants can be identified simply with one major trend in nineteenth-century Jewish culture, or with earlier intellectual antecedents, the overall leanings of Gideon's view of Jewish history, modern Judaism, and the possibility of assimilation into European society are clearly identifiable, as are the contemporary sources for these views, such as the writers associated with the *Wissenschaft des Judentums*, above all Zunz and Geiger, whose works were well known to Eliot and carefully annotated by her, with Zunz, we should note, having been carefully thumbed through even by Deronda himself.[21] The epigraph to chapter 42, which contains the conversation of "The Philosophers," is taken from Zunz's *Die Synagogale Poesie des Mittelalters*, and in her own translation of the passage that "Deronda had lately been reading" (*DD*, 441), Eliot adds the qualifier "National" to the word "Tragedy." The move is of one with Eliot's larger effort to bring the rhetorical frames of nation-thinking to the historical experience of the Jews.

Beyond the historiography of the members of the Verein, Gideon's discourse recalls, in late-nineteenth-century form, the philosophical legacy of the late eighteenth century, above all of *Jerusalem*, which Eliot had read as part of her research for the writing of the novel, and of *Nathan the Wise*, with which she had long been familiar, having seen it performed in Berlin during her visit of 1854–55 with G. H. Lewes, an important journey in personal terms, constituting in effect a public announcement of her association with Lewes.[22] The day following the performance of the play, she wrote home to a friend:

> Last night we went to see "Nathan der Weise." You know, or perhaps you do not know that this play is a sort of dramatic apologue the moral of which is religious tolerance. It thrilled me to think that Lessing dared nearly a hundred years ago to write the grand sentiments and profound thoughts which this play contains . . . In England the words which call down applause here would make the pit rise in horror.[23]

To be more precise, then, Gideon's remarks reflect the late-nineteenth-century fate of Mendelssohn's attempt, "nearly a hundred years ago," to reinvent the Jew as a modern and rational figure, as universal man, while at the same time holding on to visible adherence to the Law as the irreducible sign of Jewish particularity, a balancing act which I discuss at length in the previous chapter. The two projects have now come apart, and adherence to the first has come to mean abandonment of the other, a fate already anticipated by Heine in *The Rabbi of Bacherach* in the figure of Don Isaac, for whom Judaism has become a desirable ethnic cuisine that deserves a trip to the *Judengasse*—that is, has become mere *culture*. The overall approach to the Reform movement in the novel—or, rather, to the assimilationist cultural possibilities associated with it, from "rationalized" liturgy to the abandonment of the literalism of return—is crystallized in the figure of Gideon, who is seen as well-meaning and "generous," but the rationalism he clings to seems now to have reached an impasse, incapable of responding to the profound human needs—for sympathy, community, rootedness, and a sense of continuity—to which Mordecai so passionately gives expression. Daniel's own position in this debate is far from clear—and, of course, this particular exchange predates his own discovery of his Jewish origins. But perhaps this issue ought to be recast as a question about what kind of a Jew precisely we expect Daniel might turn out to be, to which I return shortly.

Also of significance during Elliot's early trip to Germany, which had been undertaken primarily to facilitate Lewes's research for his Goethe biography, had been the couple's acquaintance with Karl August Varnhagen von Ense, Rahel's widowered husband and the official guardian—and, for Arendt, a manipulator—of the Rahel legend. (There is, of course, more than a trace of Rahel's anguish in Leonora's final painful recognition of her inability to escape her Jewish origin.) To this new but close acquaintance—the two apparently saw Varnhagen repeatedly during their three-month stay in the capital[24]—Eliot also owed a rekindling of her interest in Heine, who had of course been a close friend and correspondent of Rahel's. Four review essays dealing with Heine's life and works followed in 1855 and 1856.[25] In the next fifteen years or so Eliot and Lewes made repeated trips of varying lengths to the German-speaking lands, and in 1872 and 1873 made the journey with the explicit intention of acquiring knowledge of German Judaica.[26] In Mordecai's arguments for a national revival of the Jews, Eliot draws on a number of contemporary sources, including Graetz's *History of the Jews*, whose volumes had begun to appear in 1863. Generally thought by contemporaries to be based in part on her friend, the German-Jewish exile and Orientalist Emmanuel Deutsch, author of an article on the Talmud which Eliot read enthusiastically and recommended widely to her friends, Mordecai is the figure of *a different kind of Jewish knowledge*, coincident entirely neither with the traditional learning of the rabbis—the Orthodox Talmudic as well as the mystical or messianic—nor with the new "science" of Judaism with its assimilationist undertones. In sum, then, Jewishness appears conspicuously in *Deronda* as a body of writing. Hence the multiple resonances of the phrase, "the old book-shop" (*DD*, 309)—highlighted here is not only the traditional, religious, and philosophical literature of Judaism but also the already enormous and growing body of modern scholarship on Jewish history, religion, and culture, much of it in German. These judgments of the 1870s about Jewish culture are a far cry from Eliot's notorious response to Disraeli's *Coningsby* some three decades earlier: "Everything *specifically* Jewish is of a low grade."[27]

Mordecai's response to Gideon, full of "fervour" and "feeling," cuts to the heart of the matter: "Can a fresh-made garment of citizenship weave itself straightway into the flesh and change the slow deposit of eighteen centuries? What is the citizenship of him who walks among a people he has no hearty kindred and fellowship with, and has lost the sense of brotherhood with his own race?" (*DD*, 450). Citizenship is a mere garment, an outer covering which, though meant to make us all look alike and interchangeable, is unable to hide the distinctness of our flesh, our substance. It remains external to our being. It is only relationships of "flesh," "love," and "kinship" that can consecrate this raiment (*DD*, 451). Without these bonds of "feeling," equality-in-citizenship is a mere "charter of selfish ambition and rivalry in low greed" (*DD*, 450). And the only authentic "feeling" within which a Jew can participate is that of

Jewish fellow-feeling. This language, in which citizenship is figured as an outer layer of the self, to be changed and exchanged in history like clothing, is repeated later in the most spirited defense in the novel of the will to assimilation, namely, in the discourse of the mother during her encounter with her son, where the former speaks of her baptism as ridding herself of "the Jewish tatters and gibberish that make people nudge each other at sight of us, as if we were tattooed under our clothes, though our faces are as whole as theirs" (*DD*, 544). The most far-reaching claim of a distinctly and exclusively Jewish nationality and the most far-reaching defense of a dissolution into a Europe of nations thus share a conception of citizenship as mere raiment, the one rejecting this outer covering in the name of the irreducibly *Jewish* body-substance, the other putting it on in order to insist on the uniformity of *human* substance. But the novel represents both, not just the first, as distinctly Jewish claims, that is, first of all, as claims emerging in history, in the history of Jewish emancipation, and made from positions within the culture marked by the dilemmas and crises of Jewish difference. The universalism of the liberal ideals is tempered by pointing to their emergence in history, and history itself is viewed as the slow accretion of the collective life in common of a people.

The tensions surrounding the transmission of tradition, self-sacrifice, and self-realization come to the surface most dramatically in Daniel's encounter with his mother, Princess Leonora Halm-Eberstein, once "the greatest lyric actress of Europe," the famous "Alcharisi you have heard of" (*DD*, 548, 543). Thus the encounter also highlights the role of women in the demarcation of community and culture. Leonora's story is overdetermined by a sense of treachery and betrayal—of the Jewish community of her birth, from which she escapes into the life of another race; of her father, whose authority as Jewish patriarch she defies; of her son, whom she denies not only a mother's love but his very identity and heritage; and, finally, of escape from domesticated Jewish femininity to the stage. It is also a story, however, of steadfastness and of remaining true—to her own desires, her "man's force of genius" (*DD*, 541) and sense of artistic self. If, on the one hand, critics have correctly read Leonora's impassioned defense of her course of action in life as the expression of an uncompromising assimilationism, and therefore seen her viewpoint as marginal in the novel and undermined by its overall interest in the assertion of Jewish difference, on the other, we must not forget that Leonora's is a compelling feminist critique of women's sphere of existence in traditional (Jewish) society from a vaguely liberal-reformist viewpoint, which the novel cannot quite reject out of hand, for all its framing of her self-assertion against her designated fate within the theme of her abandonment of her son and her inability to love him. So it is significant that the world that is "repugnant" to Mirah and from which she has sought to escape, even into death—that is, "the artist's life" (*DD*, 570)—is the one *into* which Leonora had once escaped. Thus the life of performance and the stage is both linked to the Jews—Klesmer, Lapidoth, Leonora, and the young Daniel—and at the same time is the site of the potential dissolution of their traditional communality. Being Jewish in the modern world entails something rather like acting, or rather, "what may be called sincere acting," in which "all feeling... immediately became matter of conscious representation [and] experience immediately passed into drama" (*DD*, 539). Hence the "double consciousness" (*DD*, 539) which the narrator attributes to the words Leonora addresses to Daniel is a clear signal that represented here is a distinctly minority consciousness, for the consciousness split in two has, of course, been one of the most persistent signs, and recurring modalities, of elaborations of minority discourse and experience, from Rahel Varnhagen to W.E.B. Dubois and beyond.

It is the self-divisions of this consciousness, the doubts and self-doubts it implies, that, we are led to believe, will be overcome in Daniel's "return" to, and identification with, "his" people. Thus Daniel's confession to Mirah, when asking her to marry him—"I have been in doubt so long" (*DD*, 679)—must be read simultaneously in at least two registers or, more precisely, must be read in the mutual imbrication of these different registers. If, on the one hand, "doubt" here pertains to the narrative of love and marriage, referring to the uncertainties Daniel has had about Mirah returning his love, on the other it pertains to the narrative of discovery of origins and speaks of a more existential condition in Daniel's life, the uncertainty of his place in the world; moreover, the personal and political embracing of a Jewish origin seems to lead, inexorably in the narrative, to marriage to the Jewish woman, and the marriage itself provides the family unit that is to be a microcosm of the new Jewish life. In this sense, then, Jewish nationalism in the novel, like assimilationism, also consists of this paradox and peculiarity: they are both forms of Jewishness that are meant to put an end to Jewishness. Eliot's account of Mordecai's "distinct conception," formed through years of close observation of faces and physiques, of the type of person who could undertake the burden of disciple to his ideas, into whom "he could pour his mind as a testament, some soul kindred enough to accept the spiritual product of his own brief, painful life, as a mission to be executed" (*DD*, 404), clarifies what is at stake—"he wanted to find a man who differed from himself" (*DD*, 405):

> Tracing reasons in the self for the rebuffs he had met with and the hindrances that beset him, he imagined a man who would have all the

> elements necessary for sympathy with him, but in an embodiment unlike his own: he must be a Jew, intellectually cultured, morally fervid—in all this a nature ready to be plenished from Mordecai's; but his face and frame must be beautiful and strong, he must have been used to all the refinements of social life, his voice must flow with a full and easy current, his circumstances be free from sordid need: he must glorify the possibilities of the Jew, not sit and wander as Mordecai did, bearing the stamp of his people amid the signs of poverty and waning breath. (*DD*, 405)

As readers of the novel have long noted, this non-Jewish element in the makeup of the future leader of the Jews is provided by the upbringing of an English gentleman. Clearly the language here draws on later-nineteenth-century discourses on degeneration and the Jews and, in articulating that discourse with the Jewish national idea, anticipates in important ways the thread in the development of Zionism most famously associated with such fin de siècle figures as Max Nordau.[28] The novel considers Daniel's new identity to be the *reclaiming* of a self that has *always been there* but has been forgotten. It is this possibility of identity, with the vast cultural horizons and the swirling movements of historical forces it calls forth, which is so unexpected and baffling to Gwendolyn's consciousness as to shatter the boundaries of her world.

Significantly, however, the novel also attempts both to conflate, and undo the conflation, of language and (racial) identity. Thus in the famous scene that takes place in the Frankfurt synagogue—in the Orthodox *"Rabbinische Schule,"* we might add, and not in "the fine new building of the Reformed" (*DD*, 309)—where Daniel (unknowingly) encounters Joseph Kalonymos, his late grandfather's friend, there is a moment of identity affirmation that also turns out to be a moment of linguistic indeterminacy. When approached by Kalonymos and asked—"in German," the text tells us—for his mother's maiden name and thus whether he is a Jew, Daniel recoils from this cloying presumption, is "inclined to shake off hastily the touch on his arm," and answers coldly, "I am an Englishman" (*DD*, 311). The language of this final utterance, however, is not identified in the text, and this indeterminacy, on the one hand a banal consequence of reported speech in realist narrative, on the other enacts what V. N. Vološinov calls the "decomposition of the authorial context" in the interaction between reported and reporting speech.[29] The manner and mode of determining Englishness, or any expression of sharing in common or belonging together, is rendered contingent in this strange encounter in a strange place and in an unidentified language. As Irene Tucker has noted, the generational model of commonness advanced repeatedly in the novel—as in the passage about the portrait gallery of the Mallinger family or in the queries triggered repeatedly by Daniel's physiognomy about his possible Jewish ancestry—is moved to the margins here in favor of another model, one based on achieving commonality through action and behavior.[30] And, with the revelations about the existence of his mother, as he is about to be projected out of the realm of Englishness initially into a kind of indeterminacy of self, this movement is marked, first of all, in linguistic terms: he could not, we are told, "even conjecture in what language she would speak to him" (*DD*, 535). The mother tongue itself, in other words, is under a question mark and indeterminate. In fact, the entire process of Daniel's slowly gathering discovery of his Jewishness culminates in the midst of something like an explosion of languages, scripts, and dialects—Italian, Spanish, German, Hebrew, the "Jew-dialect" (*DD*, 309) "and, I think, Arabic"(641). At a very fundamental level, then, being Jewish in Europe puts into question any settled identification of *this* place with *this* people and *this* language.

The conclusion of *Daniel Deronda*, turning as it does on the departure of the central Jewish characters from English soil, represents an engagement with the ending of *Ivanhoe*, references to which abound in Eliot's novel, as do references to Scott in general, whom Eliot read voraciously early in life.[31] It is to him she attributes, in the famous review of Harriet Beecher Stowe's *Dred*, sustained attention to what she calls the "conflict of races."[32] Deronda himself is identified, by Miller of "The Philosophers," with Scott—"Is the gentleman anonymous? Is he a Great Unknown?" (*DD*, 445)—surely a hint at the possibility of Deronda as a chronicler of his people, "one of these historical men," as Mr. Vandernoodt puts it to him (*DD*, 372). The most significant of these intertextual references, however, concern Mirah, who is repeatedly compared by a number of characters, and by the narrator, to Rebecca. With that textual model in hand, for instance, the Meyricks attempt to comprehend Mirah's nature (*DD*, 165, 305). In fact, we may arrive at a better understanding of the "Jewish" ending of *Deronda* if we see Mirah's relationship with her father as part of a longer literary trajectory of the pairing of Jewish father and (virtuous) Jewish daughter, which links *Deronda* not only to *Ivanhoe* but also *Nathan the Wise*. In Lessing's play, as we have seen in the previous chapter, the "wise" Jewish father is revered and respected at the end of the play but is left by himself and alone, his presumed daughter having been reclaimed by the (now enlightened) state; in *Ivanhoe* the Jewish father reappears as the conniving and cowardly usurer, the prototype for the nineteenth-century figure of the Jewish financier—as in any number of Trollope's anti-Semitic portrayals—whose daughter's unquestionable love for him does not imply her unquestioning approval of his behavior, especially in his financial dealings with gentiles; and in Eliot's novel, finally, he is reinscribed yet again, now appearing as a threat to the very life and liberty of his daughter. In *Nathan*, as in *Deronda*, father and daughter are separated at the end of the story. But where in the former this separation is necessary for the reformulation of an enlightened universal community, with the Jew accorded an ambivalent relationship to that community, in the latter the separation is required for the realignment of cultural affiliations necessary for the birth of a new and normalized Jewish subjectivity, which the novel itself views as the historical passage from the cowering Isaac to the upright ("English") Daniel.

It has long been argued, from various critical positions, that *Middlemarch* and *Daniel Deronda* bring the development of the realist novel as a genre near to completion to such an extent that it begins to reach out beyond itself toward formal possibilities that become fully apparent only some decades later. While Eliot continues to affirm the values of Victorian humanism, such as the consistency of the self as moral agent, at the same time she undercuts this affirmation with an image of the individual as node of semiotic energy, itself a cluster of signs, described in the famous passage about the pier-glass in chapter 27 of *Middlemarch*.[33] Something similar, of course, could also be said of *Daniel Deronda's* treatment of the Jewish Question, anticipating as it does the settling of Palestine by European Jews and the birth of a cultural movement tied to that goal. But it is in the narrative *structure* of *Deronda* that the relationship of liberal culture to the Jewish minority is most conspicuously inscribed. Reception of the novel has historically voiced discomfort with the manner in which the Jewish theme—these "Disraelian dreams" and "this Semitic mystery," as an early-twentieth-century edition of the *Cambridge History of English Literature* called it—"fits" with the narrative that centers on Gwendolen.[34] F. R. Leavis's famous prognosis that if the Jewish sections were surgically removed, it would leave behind a healthy and significant Eliot novel, makes starkly visible the relationship of late imperial liberal culture, as embodied in the novel form, to the Jews.[35] Drawn irresistably to the Jewish minority, and to its predicament, as a source of moral instruction—and we should note that Daniel is drawn to Mordecai and his ideas well before he has any definite knowledge that he himself is a Jew—liberalism can nevertheless not conceive of this experience as having anything but a tangential relationship to modernity itself. It is in this formal context that the Jewish *theme* of the novel finds its full significance. The imperial structure of global geography that the nineteenth-century novel, according to Said, takes for granted is here brought to bear upon what is usually taken to be a domestic problem in order precisely to make it a global one. The Jewish Question can be evicted from the European home, to be solved elsewhere—a strategy made possible by European global power itself. The narrative of European wholeness and integrity can thus reclaim its continuity. Eliot's narrative simultaneously affirms her commitment to the collective existence of the Jews and affirms the imaginative geography of imperialism, and thus the right of the West to bring the world under its purview, by making it the means to the concrete realization of that existence, whose full flowering it can only conceive of as the normalization of the Jews as a national and colonizing people the *center* of whose collective life lies outside the bounds of Europe. Thus it is only under the most ahistorical strategies of reading that one could read the ending simply as "utopian," as Tucker seems to have done.

In the final chapter of *The Impressions of Theophrastus Such*, and therefore at the conclusion of the very last book she wrote, Eliot again expresses the view voiced by Daniel's mentor. Speaking of the liberal reproach that Jews inexplicably refuse to abandon the feeling of belonging to a dispersed "national family," Theophrastus, the narrative persona of the book, asks: "Will any one teach the nullification of this feeling, and call his doctrine a philosophy? He will teach a blinding superstition, the superstition that a theory of human well-being can be constructed in disregard of the influences which have made us human." There is a value to "the modern insistence on the idea of nationalities." A "fusion of the races" may be the dominant and inevitable tendency of modern life, readily visible in the growing presence of European and other immigrants within the imperial metropolis, but it must be made subject to a conscious moderation of pace and intensity. An uncompromising cosmopolitan belief in a universal humanity and the subjugation of all other attachments to that highest ideal would thus constitute a "blinding superstition." The heroic, collective, and *national* project of a segment of (European) humanity, which is presently dispersed among the European nations, to reclaim their historical home will thus be an exemplum to society as a whole. What is needed, therefore, is "a new Ezra," an individual who can lead his people by heroic example.[36] In *Deronda* the prototype for this modern prophet is, of course, not Mordecai himself, who burns too feverishly with zeal—literally, for he will die of consumption before reaching Palestine—to undertake this deliberate and balanced task, but Deronda, in whom the sense of primordial belonging is tempered by the liberal upbringing of an English gentleman.

Finally, it is not necessary, as Mordecai explains to his friends, in a passage clearly written under the influence of Moses Hess's *Rome and Jerusalem*, that *all* Jews return to the ancient homeland in order for the Jewish condition to be normalized: "Let the reason of Israel disclose itself in a great outward deed, and let there be another great migration, another choosing of Israel to be a nationality whose members may still stretch to the ends of the earth, even as the sons of England and Germany, whom enterprise carries afar, but who still have a national hearth and a tribunal of national opinion" (*DD*, 457). Nothing can better elucidate that what Eliot seeks is the normalization of the Jews by being rendered like a nation among the other (European) nations, but a normalization that cannot, paradoxically, take place within the European home itself. In this, her last novel, we are witness to liberalism not so much abandoning the ideal of liberal citizenship and assimilation into individual European societies as expanding this constellation in order to restage it on a pan-national—"European"—and then global stage. If, within the national space, the assimilation of the Jews can only be conceived of as their disappearance into the larger society, on this larger stage it means assimilating into a Europe of nations *as* a nation. And if, as Said argued, the problem of Jewish citizenship becomes solvable by this extension of the mental horizon, by its projection onto a geography made possible by imperialism, the precise nature of the proposed solution is also interesting: it is not so much (all) the people as the *problem* itself that needs to be transported, in a move we may think of as the secularizing of the restorationist impulse in nineteenth-century English culture, an elaboration of which we have seen in *Ivanhoe* in the previous chapter, and for whose sources in Eliot's life we need turn no further than her Evangelical formation. It is thus not so much the *presence* of the Jews in Western societies that is itself the problem but rather their *non-national relationship* to any of these societies.

Visible within the interstices of this project of advocacy for the rights of the Jews is therefore a deep ambivalence. Responding to the widespread unease within late imperial culture with the exclusivism, ambitiousness, and "success" of the Jews, whose most visible living emblem in the mid-1870s was the Jewish prime minister, Eliot is forced to concede that there is "some truth in these views of Jewish social and political relations."[37] The question simply is, what is the solution? The answer, Theophrastus argues, cannot be "that we should repeal our emancipatory laws."[38] The possibilities of a liberal solution to the Jewish Question are therefore contained within that limit, the imperative to political progress, beyond which, as we have known since the early twentieth century, other kinds of solution become possible. In *Deronda* Eliot had turned to the figure of the Jew in public life, available to the public imagination in the career of Disraeli, who had become prime minister for the second time in 1874 after three decades of prominence among the Tories and in national politics, and rewritten this figure in significant ways. If Disraeli was repeatedly accused of being a crypto-Jew, Eliot made Deronda affirm his Jewishness openly and proudly; if

Disraeli was accused of working secretly in the interest of the Jews, Deronda was to do so honestly, transparently, and publicly. The anxieties of Theophrastus, however, put these transformations in a clearer light. The persistence of the Jewish Question poses a threat to the very accomplishments of liberal politics and culture in Europe, making it imperative to solve the problem by displacing it onto non-European spaces.

If, as I have suggested in the previous chapter, *Nathan the Wise* may be treated as the "first" text of the era of emancipation, then *Deronda* might be considered its "last," bringing to a conclusion of sorts a century of concern with the manner of existence of the Jews within the newly national European societies, releasing into view the paradox that the fullest flowering of assimilation would mean not the disappearance of the Jews as a separate people but rather their reorientation and resettlement as a separate (and "equal") nation. This manner of settling the Jewish Question is thus *the first instance historically* of those modes of thinking that seek resolution of the minority crisis of the (majoritarian) nation-state through a *partition of society*, modes of thinking that have become the political norm globally in the course of the twentieth century. The massive transfers of populations that these modes of thought routinely envision, legitimize, and often precipitate therefore carry within them something like the imperial impetus of this originary attempt in nineteenth-century European society to solve its crisis of minority, in the will to restructure and reinvent (often more than one) society that is inherent in them. Because of its, as it were, universal nature, that is, because by its very nature it takes *every* society (with a Jewish population) under its purview, Jewish nationalism provides a sort of privileged instance for a critical understanding of the trajectory of romantic and political nationalism in the modern era. This was grasped by those early—that is, pre-1948—critics of Zionism, like Arendt, who had a complex, insider-outsider relationship to it. In her essay, "Zionism Reconsidered" (1944), for instance, Arendt pointed out that the complete nationalization of the Jewish Question—represented for her in the wholesale takeover by mainstream Zionism of the ideas that had until then been seen as belonging properly to Revisionist extremism—had left "practically no choice for the Arabs but minority status in Palestine or voluntary emigration."[39] The so-called partition of the Indian subcontinent, an event contemporaneous with the partitioning of historical Palestine, offered this same choice to "the Muslims" as a group. At the same time, however, it was organized Muslim separatism that abrogated to itself the "imperial" right to massive social reconstitution of the regions—Punjab, Sind, and Bengal—that it claimed for itself as parts of its Muslim homeland.

"Great Men" and "Fellow Citizens": Hindu, Muslim, and Indian in Late Imperial Culture

In post-1857 British India, owing in part to their perceived role in the uprising, "the Mohammedans" came to be constituted as the object of a vast and multifarious effort at systematic comprehension, produced in historical and scholarly works, travelogues, missionaries' reports, fiction and poetry, biographies, memoirs, official reports and memos, pamphlets, and newspapers and other periodicals. The *jihādī* reformist movements of the early nineteenth century—the Farā'iẓīs in Bengal, Syed Ahmed Barelvi's followers in northern and northwestern India—had already helped to foster the belief among the British, as P. Hardy has noted, "that the Muslims were by nature fanatical and irreconcilable," always on the verge of revolt against British supremacy in India. In the aftermath of the 1857 rebellion, this belief was extended to the rebels as a whole (who had, of course, been drawn from all segments of society in the affected regions) to such an extent that for "most British observers in 1857 a Muslim meant a rebel." Even such a relatively traditional historian of British India as Hardy seems to have understood that the seemingly uniform collective produced in this body of colonial knowledge did not exist in Indian society, and that the conception itself had a certain *predictive* quality, given the interconnections between the knowledge forms and concrete colonial policy across a wide range of domains, including the recurrent "settling" of property ownership and land tenure, judicial practice, education, census taking, political representation (however nominal the latter may have remained until the end of the nineteenth century), and, above all, with the law as it intersects with, penetrates, and transforms most of these areas of social life.

The rebellion and its massively violent suppression destroyed the social basis of traditional *ashrāf* culture in northern India, to a large extent a *composite* elite culture that had included within itself Hindus (especially Kayasthas and Kashmiri Pandits) as well as Muslims, but in which "the Muslims" had not been subject to the logic of representation and number to which they would become subject in the latter half of the nineteenth century. When Bahadur Shah II, emperor in name but in fact the pensioned and powerless "King of Delhi," was exiled to imprisonment in Burma in 1858, the fiction of British rule in the name of the Mughal emperor was finally put to rest, and the final disappearance of the nominal Mughal Empire wiped away "the last illusions that an education in Persian and Urdu and in the Muslim religious sciences would serve both a Muslim's eternal and his worldly welfare."[40] The *education* of *ashrāf* Muslims, in particular, would henceforth become an engrossing preoccupation of both colonial officials and "loyalist" survivors of the cataclysm among the *ashrāf.* The official call for developing "a rising generation of Muhammadans, no longer learned in their own narrow learning, nor imbued solely with the bitter doctrines of their medieval Law, but tinctured with the sober and genial knowledge of the West" was answered by "reformers" like Syed Ahmed Khan and Syed Ameer Ali with institutions and projects whose most visible emblem was the college at Aligarh.[41] The *ashrāf* Muslim elites of northern India thus underwent a process of social transformation that is traditionally described in nationalist historiography as underdevelopment or partial development (compared to their Hindu counterparts) but that is more adequately characterized as a *reluctant* transition to bourgeois society, a *reluctant embourgeoisement,* as it were, that imbued an entire social and cultural milieu with a distinct structure of feeling—a dogged and melancholic response to the emergence of the new world and an almost panicky sense of forever needing to catch up with other groups in Indian society. This class, which Muhammad Mujeeb once described succinctly as a class "which consisted of big and small landlords, and the lawyers, doctors, government servants who belonged to the families of these landlords," found perhaps its most characteristic political voice in Syed Ahmed Khan's infamous anti-Congress rhetoric of the late 1880s, where even the modest demands—requests, really—of the Congress for greater access of Indians to the lower levels of the colonial bureaucracy through open, competitive examinations were treated as extreme perversions that would overturn the natural hierarchy and order of Indian society. Thus its encounter with the conditions of a modern (and colonial) society—representation, politics, citizenship, nationalization of culture, and (at least as a potential) democracy—produced a class "sentiment," as Mujeeb put it, at odds with nationalist consciousness and ultimately developed into the demand for Muslim "sovereignty" and statehood.[42] Classical Urdu literature—and, above all, its powerful poetic tradition—which had its heyday in the period of Mughal imperial decline in the course of the eighteenth and early nineteenth centuries, may be said, in this final convulsion of *ashrāf* society, to have entered into modernity. The great upheaval that engulfed northern India in 1857–58 thus marks a watershed in the history of culture and identity in the subcontinent, and, more specifically, in the history of Urdu literature and culture, which now came increasingly to be put in question in the new debates about *national* cultural practice, with their reliance on such emerging concepts as the indigenous and the popular.[43] (I return to this set of questions at greater length in subsequent chapters.)

In his stories of the 1880s, as in *Kim* (1901), Kipling returned repeatedly to that mid-century moment of insurrection in order to explore what appeared to him to be the settled nature of British colonial rule in India in the late nineteenth century. In the story "On the City Wall" (ca. 1888) Kipling presents a scathing critique of the very idea of an Indian modernity in which the coalescing of a modern Indian nationhood appears as a sham, necessarily doomed to failure.[44] As critics have noted, it is a rare Kipling attempt to deal directly with Indian political matters.[45] It is also, in some ways, a work well ahead of its time, written probably in 1888, twenty-seven years before Gandhi's return to India from South Africa and a year before Nehru's birth, that imagines and explores, as Benita Parry has put it in her pioneering study of the ideology of Anglo-India, "an incipient nationalism," that is, political realities that would only have been present in its own time in embryonic form.[46] A classic expression of the structure of ambivalence within which citizen, nation, and empire are placed in late imperial culture, the story also portrays the failed Indian modernity as split along the lines of Hindu and Muslim, a majority population with a settled and ancient claim on the land, on the one hand, and, on the other, a mobile and yet recalcitrant group with a non-national relationship to state, place, and society. In the story Lalun, a courtesan of unmatched beauty and accomplishments, lives in a small house perched on the city wall. Her home is the scene of nightly get-togethers to which "all the City"—itself unnamed, but presumably Lahore—seems to find its way:

> Shiahs of the grimmest and most uncompromising persuasion; Sufis who had lost all belief in the Prophet and retained but little in God; wandering Hindu priests passing southward on their way to the Central India fairs and other affairs; Pundits in black gowns, with spectacles on their noses and undigested wisdom in their insides; bearded headmen of the wards; Sikhs with all the details of the latest ecclesiastical scandal in the Golden Temple; red-eyed priests from beyond the Border, looking like trapped wolves and talking like ravens; M.A.'s of the University, very superior and very voluble—all these people and more also you might find in the white room. (CW, 225)

Notably there is no hint in the story as to Lalun's own denominational community, her religiosity described only in terms of indistinguishable Indian ritualism and spirituality. What is presented here, of course, is a sort of ethnographic gallery of Indian "types" present in Lalun's salon, modern as well as premodern, a kind of condensed verbal equivalent of such visual projects of ethnographic classification as *The People of India*, the massive compilation of photographs of individuals conceived of as representing distinct types, published over a decade in the 1860s and 1870s.[47] Among these types are three to whom the reader's attention is individually drawn: the young narrator himself, a worldly and skeptical

English journalist, the stock narrator of numerous Kipling stories; a "fat gentleman wearing *pince-nez*," an instance of that familiar Victorian figure of ridicule, the anglicized Babu; and a "clean-bred" young man "with penciled eyebrows, small-cut nostrils, little feet and hands, and a very tired look in his eyes" (CW, 241, 222). And it is around the latter that the narrative quickly comes to circulate: "He was a young Mohammedan [we are told] who was suffering acutely from education of the English variety and knew it. His father had sent Wali Dad to a mission-school to get wisdom, and Wali Dad had absorbed more than even his father or the missionaries intended he should" (CW, 222). Having lost his faith as a result of his "educational mixture," his encounter with the culture of the modern West, Wali Dad appears to us a mournful figure, composing songs to the inimitable beauty of his Lalun, only too aware of his own anomalous situation, suspended as he is between two cultures (CW, 224): "Therefore . . . you are here to-day [he tells the narrator] instead of starving in your own country, and I am not a Muhammadan—I am a Product—a Demnition Product. That also I owe to you and yours; that I can not make an end to any sentence without quoting from your authors" (CW, 226).

The holy month of Muharrram arrives, a time during which Shia Muslims mourn the martyrdom of Husain, the Prophet Muhammad's grandson. As mourners march in public processions, the British administration and the narrator himself expect sectarian rioting between Hindus and Muslims with the certainty of a change of seasons. And when a riot does break out, those in the garrison throw themselves into the fray with great gusto, "unholily pleased, at the chance of what they called 'a little fun' " (CW, 238). The narrator and Wali Dad are out in the streets, the latter full of sarcasm at the religious enthusiasm on display. As the fighting becomes more vicious, however, they get separated, with Wali Dad showing "more heat than blank unbelief would be capable of" (CW, 236). Having found his way back to Lalun's apartment, the narrator is marshaled by the latter into safely delivering an old gentleman to one of the city gates. The narrator does not know, nor does the reader, that the old man is an old Sikh rebel prisoner of 1857, smuggled out of the fort while the soldiers are having their "little fun" in the town. Lalun and her accomplices, the fat gentleman and Wali Dad, wish to get him into the countryside, where, it is hoped, he will inspire a new generation of rebels. The British narrator now unknowingly performs the task that had been allotted to the young Muslim, a task he has failed in as a result of his own resurgent religious enthusiasm. As the narrator returns to Lalun's after delivering the old rebel into the Babu's hands, he stumbles over Wali Dad lying on the threshold:

> He was sobbing hysterically and his arms flapped like the wings of a goose. It was Wali Dad, Agnostic and Unbeliever, shoeless, turban-

> less, and frothing at the mouth, the flesh on his chest bruised and bleeding from the vehemence with which he had smitten himself. A broken torch-handle lay by his side and his quivering lips murmured, "*Ya Hasan! Ya Hussain!*" as I stooped over him. (CW, 241)

That Kipling would narrate the failure of an anti-British project as inevitable is hardly surprising. As Said noted with reference to *Kim*, "Kipling assumes a basically uncontested empire," although it is more accurate here to say that the story stages an attempted contestation of colonial rule in order to defuse it and demonstrate its ephemeral nature.[48] But still the narrative is interesting in a number of ways. First, Indian nationalism is forged in a courtesan's salon, a brothel, and finds its cathexes in the devotion or love of men for a whore, an unmistakable imperial comment on the nationalist worshiping of nation as Mother, to which I return at greater length in a later chapter. Second, it takes the form not of a social movement but an intrigue. In that apartment, away from the dust and heat of the bazaar, men can come to entertain strange fancies. The reality of India is still the streets of the old city, where there are no "Indians," only Hindus and Muslims, clashing with the predictability of seasonal events. As identities in conflict, therefore, "Hindu" and "Muslim" are almost facts of nature rather than social facts in history. The story's ethnographic perception of the Indian people is thus a contradictory one, for they appear in it simultaneously as one and as many. When, in response to his subaltern's question as to who should guard the old Sikh warrior, the captain in charge of the fort replies, " 'Sikhs, Pathans, Dogras—they're all alike, these black people,' " he is expressing, in racialized terms, a view that is negated elsewhere in the story in terms of the possibility of social collectivity and political action (CW, 232). Most important, nothing comes of the intrigue, as the old rebel finds himself out of place and forgotten in a country now subdued by the colonial rulers:

> He fled to those who knew him in the old days, but many of them were dead and more were changed, and all knew something of the Wrath of the Government. He went to the young men, but the glamour of his name had passed away, and they were entering native regiments or Government offices, and Khem Singh could give them neither pension, decorations, nor influence—nothing but a glorious death with their backs to the mouth of a gun . . . Moreover, Khem Singh was old, and anice-seed brandy was scarce, and he had left his silver cooking-pots in Fort Amara with his nice warm bedding, and the gentleman with the gold *pince-nez* was told by those [presumably foreign powers] who had employed him that Khem Singh as a popular leader was not worth the money paid. (CW, 242)

As Wali Dad himself puts it to the narrator, Khem Singh represents in the story a heroic India already past: "He was once a great man. There will never be any more great men in India. They will all, when they are boys, go whoring after strange gods, and they will become citizens—'fellow-citizens'—'illustrous fellow-citizens'" (CW, 229). The antithesis of the citizen, this characteristic form of modern subjectivity, is the "great man," capable of heroic action and able to inspire and lead legions of men into battle and sacrifice. The point Kipling is making here, through the characteristic note of mockery, is, of course, that while India is no longer capable of producing "great men," neither is it likely to produce "citizens," only individuals who are condemned to merely mimic the forms of public life—here forms of mutual address—that constitute citizenship. This is thus an early formulation of the literary figure of the colonial mimic man, which continues to be produced, to vastly divergent effect, in contemporary writers like V. S. Naipaul and Salman Rushdie.

As for the English themselves, in this story, as in so many of Kipling's works, in India even an ordinary Englishman, a mere "citizen" in his homeland, can become a "great man," like the soldiers rampaging through the streets of the city on horseback during the riot, whipping into shape the city's primordial and self-destructive energies. In India, far away from the drab and diminished life of an industrializing society, something like an epic and romantic life becomes once again possible. In this story, that is the meaning of India for its British rulers—in it they can be more than mere men, mere "fellow-citizens." As historians of the Raj have long noted, ideologies of British imperial rule in the nineteenth century were driven by the paradox of a society increasingly reorganized along national and liberal lines while becoming an empire in the process, since, as Thomas Metcalfe has pointed out, "the notion of a 'British' national community implied that the people of India were equally entitled to form their own national identity."[49] The liberal intelligentsia in the metropolis itself presents the intellectual historian with the "puzzling fact," as Uday Singh Mehta puts it, of having provided endorsement and philosophical justification for Britain's imperial expansion.[50] The invention of imperial selves is one of Kipling's characteristic preoccupations, elaborated, for instance, in the Mulvaney–Ortheris–Learoyd stories and "The Man Who Would Be King," but also in *Kim* and in numerous poems such as "The Road to Mandalay":

> Ship me somewheres east of Suez where the best is like the worst,
> Where there aren't no ten Commandments, an' a man can raise
> a thirst;
> For the temple-bells are callin', an' it's there that I would be—
> By the old Moulmein Pagoda, lookin' lazy at the sea—[51]

But especially striking in this account of the transition to post-1857 India is the role of the English narrator: it is he who (unwittingly) delivers their "heroic" past to the Indians, an unintended gift of which they prove incapable of making a national *history*. Thus we may read the function of the narrator within the plot, in both senses of that word, as a managing of the colonial anxiety that the natives' acquisition of Western knowledge, and their contact with the edifice of modern Western humanism in particular, both signs of the superiority of Europe over the East, will turn the tables on the rulers themselves, unsettling the antinomies of colonial knowledge.[52] As in so many of Kipling's stories, this anxiety finds expression in a final ironic turn, which here redefines the white man's relationship to Lalun, this flawed muse of Indian creativity: "But I was thinking how I had become Lalun's Vizier after all" (CW, 243). The old social order of India, heroic in its time and home to an epic imagination, had breathed its last in 1857 and become a picturesque (and safely confined) object of contemplation for India's foreign rulers; moreover, the new social classes to have emerged under colonial rule, despite their political fantasies, would ultimately prove incapable of posing a threat to the new colonial order. The British ruler of this vast Eastern world, worldly, skeptical, and possessed of an unclouded mind, could therefore nevertheless risk a fantasy of submission that is as much sexual—Lalun is a courtesan, after all—as it is political—"I had become Lalun's Vizier."

It is in this larger context of exploring the nature of Britain's supremacy in India, therefore, that the role the young Muslim comes to have in the failure of the plot becomes significant. The worldly Lalun should have known better than to trust such a youth with the important task, and the Babu's volubility, cowardice, and ineffectuality would have been immediately recognizable to Kipling's readers. Both these figures have their share of responsibility in the failure, above all in neglecting to understand their own historical situation and recognize that the time of Khem Singh is past. But the collapse of the intrigue hinges on the collapse of Wali Dad, which is a failure to sustain the modern and more specifically *secular* values he has supposedly acquired through his colonial education. In this failure of an "Indian" political community to cohere, it is the Muslim who bears this special blame—the inability to achieve "blank unbelief," that is, an authentically secular subjectivity—surrendering atavistically to a primordial consciousness and loyalty instead of refashioning himself within an emerging community of will which claims to be based on a secular and rational sense of oneself as an Indian. Thus, in this colonial fantasy of the necessary failure of an Indian experience of citizenship, the figure marked as Muslim bears a distinct representational burden, suspended between modern and premodern forms and becoming a stumbling block to the development of a secular and uniform citizen subjectivity.

Kipling's story is an unusual work of English literature in its time in the detail it brings to its treatment of the emerging experience of citizenship in India, its conflicts and contradictions. Here we see the beginnings of a concern with the nature of citizenship in a colonial society that emerges full-blown in a major work of English literature, as will become evident shortly, only in Forster's final novel. But the relationship of Kipling's story to the late imperial form of the Jewish Question, whose perhaps canonical elaboration is *Daniel Deronda*, is also complex and striking. The non-national subjectivity in question here is not Jewish but Indian and Muslim; empire is the name not of an impersonal global geography but of a personal, even intimate, tutelage and guardianship, and the nation in question is India itself, whose impossibility is the point of the story. If the Jews constitute, in Eliot's novel, an insurmountable problem for narratives of national existence so long as they remain a minority dispersed among the nations and do not themselves cohere as a nation, in Kipling's story the Muslims of India are an unmistakable sign of the impossibility of the transition from colony to nation, for they are a stumbling block for the emergence, to put it differently, of Enlightenment in the colony. Kipling is, of course, writing from within strident Anglo-Indian imperialism—the story was first collected in the book *In Black and White* in 1888 as part of the six-volume *Indian Railway Library*, travel reading for Anglo-India—as opposed to Eliot, whose literary credentials as a leading liberal voice in the metropolis were at the time unsurpassable.[53] There is first of all, therefore, an ideological difference at work here, the difference between varieties of liberalism and conservatism within late imperial culture. Eliot's account of empire as an impersonal geography, for instance, conforms fully to the instrumentalization of place that Mehta has identified as a distinct feature of the liberal philosophical tradition—to the extent that Palestine is the object of sentiment for some among the Jews of Europe, this is as a means to becoming more fully European.[54] As Mordechai puts it to The Philosophers, in a passage cited above: "let there be another great migration, another choosing of Israel to be a nationality whose members may still stretch to the ends of the earth, even as the sons of England and Germany, whom enterprise carries afar, but who still have a national hearth and a tribunal of national opinion" (*DD*, 457).

But beyond the differences of ideology in this sense, there is the significant difference of *site* or location. Kipling is writing, emphatically, from *within* the colony, with the possibilities and limits of colonial culture becoming realized in the very form of the writing. It is this difference of site, not simply that of politics and theme, that has something to do with both

Kipling's far from comfortable place within the canon of nineteenth-century British narrative as well as the basing of this reputation predominantly on his practice of the short story form. (In a later chapter I return to a more sustained assessment of the short story form in colonial India.) For the canonical realist novel in the nineteenth century assumes, to quote again from Said, a geographic structure "with England—socially, politically, morally charted and differentiated in immensely fine detail—at the center and a series of overseas territories connected to it at the peripheries."[55] In Kipling's early stories the "scene" of the narrative, not just of the action, is the colony itself. In other words, the canonical tradition of nineteenth-century narrative requires the sweep of imperial geography and historical time, a sweep, by definition, alien to the Anglo-Indian short story. Only in *Kim* (1901) is Kipling able to achieve that sweep within the novel form, even though the action of the plot remains limited to India itself. Hence Kipling's peculiar relationship to the canon of modern narrative—consummate practitioner of a "minor" narrative genre, strangely compelling to metropolitan literary culture and yet not quite an insider, brushed with the taint of being too provincial, too parochial, journalistic, primitive, even vulgar.[56]

If the place of *Kim* in the canonical tradition of the English novel is at least in part that it shows how Britain's imperial relationship to India could be inscribed in the novel form, Forster's *A Passage to India* is the direct beneficiary of that accomplishment. In that novel Forster brings to a climax and sums up the relationship of British liberalism to its Indian Empire. Voicing the unease with empire common to the writers and intellectuals of his generation, and Bloomsbury contempt for the closed-mindedness and tribalism of the Anglo-Indians in particular, Forster is nevertheless unable, as Said notes, to "recommend decolonization."[57] Instead, the novel ends, as Asha Varadharajan has argued, on a complex and unnerving note, namely, that "the relations of desire that bind Fielding and Aziz are, precisely and disconcertingly, the relations of power."[58]

A number of the themes and motifs of Forster's novel are prefigured in Kipling's story. The mutually agreed upon removal of women, or, to be more precise, wives, from the eroticized exchange of a masculine colonial encounter is one such motif—"you never speak to us about your women-folk," the narrator tells Wali Dad, "and we never speak about ours to you. That is the bar between us" (CW, 232)—and this motif is reproduced with a difference, as it were, in the encounter between Aziz and Fielding in which the former seals their friendship by showing the latter a picture of his late wife. The situating of Mohurrum as the seasonal eruption of Hindu-Muslim violence is another such motif,[59] as is the very device of "the Commissioner's tennis-parties, where the English stand on one side and the natives on the other, in order to promote social intercourse throughout the Empire" (CW, 233). Above all, like Kipling, Forster turns to distinctly "Muslim" figures, practices, and social imaginaries in order to elaborate a set of questions about the nature of India and of Britain's relationship to it.

As has often been noted, the India of Forster's novel is primarily (and perhaps predominantly) a Muslim India, with Fielding even explicitly registering the narrative's disdain for "the Hindus"—"I never really understood or liked them"[60]—and, to all the major "transactions" between the British and these Indian Muslims, as Parry has noted, "the Hindus are onlookers,"[61] often appearing somewhat apologetic about their intrusions into these interactions. In the evening isolation of the mosque in the early passage, what Aziz is said to have encountered is "Islam, his own country, more than a Faith, more than a battle-cry, more, much more . . . Islam, an attitude towards life both exquisite and durable, where his body and his thoughts found their home" (*PI*, 16). And Aziz is presented throughout the novel as a culturally homeless figure, trying but unable in the end to attach himself to the idea of India: "He was without natural affection for the land of his birth, but the Marabar Hills drove him to it. Half closing his eyes, he attempted to love India" (*PI*, 298). One of the chief vehicles and modalities of this distinctly "Muslim" sensibility in the novel is poetry—more precisely, the culture of Urdu poetic composition and reception, and its supposed antecedents in Persian and Arabic. Like Wali Dad, Aziz is a versifier in Persian and Urdu, and some of Forster's sharpest and most precise formulations about Indian politics and culture take place on this poetic terrain. It is through Aziz's recitation of poetry—"Persian, Urdu, a little Arabic" (*PI*, 12)—that Hamidullah and his guests are said, in the opening chapter, to have momentarily achieved a certain oneness with their environment: "India—a hundred Indias—whispered outside beneath the indifferent moon, but for the time India seemed one and their own, and they regarded their departed greatness by hearing its departure lamented, they felt young again because reminded that youth must fly" (*PI*, 12). And when, in the aftermath of the trial, Aziz is visited by the hapless judge, Mr. Das, who requests from him a nationalist poem for a relative's "new monthly magazine," a poem to project a "general Indian" into "existence," this request is accompanied by the caution, hesitatingly offered, to "not introduce too many Persian expressions into the poem, and not too much about the bulbul [nightingale]" (*PI*, 296–297). The Muslim's practice of the North Indian vernacular—the register called "Urdu"—produces a crisis for the nationalist project—the attempt to bring "the general Indian" into existence—a crisis concerning the non-indigenousness of established cultural forms, an entire complex of cultural alienization that is signified here by the terms "bulbul" and "Persian." Urdu and its literature are thus presented as uniquely Muslim practices and at odds with the (Hindu, majoritarian) nationalization of culture. It is not as though Forster appears unaware of the existence of anything beyond Islam and Muslims in India. On the contrary, the "hundred Indias" intrude constantly on the consciousness and interactions of the principal characters, like the riotous and formless celebration of "Gokul Ashtami" at Mau that frames Aziz's simultaneous rediscovery of his old friendship with the Englishman and his distancing himself from it, or, of course, the even more primal India, as Parry has described it, of the Marabar Hills and their caves. But the core of the novel's mental universe, the central threads in the unfolding of its plot, and the chief transactions it enacts between India and its foreign rulers all have a "Muslim" character or subtext, even as this latter is variously put under pressure from its "Indian" environment.

In the closing passage of the novel Forster sums up his exploration of the nature of Britain's Indian colony in a manner that makes visible the colonial impasse of late imperial liberal culture. I quote this densely packed and well-known passage in full:

> [Aziz] remembered that he had, or ought to have, a mother-land. Then he shouted: "India shall be a nation! No foreigners of any sort! Hindu and Muslim and Sikh and all shall be one! Hurrah! Hurrah for India! Hurrah! Hurrah!"
>
> India a nation! What an apotheosis! Last comer to the drab nineteenth-century sisterhood! Waddling in at this hour of the world to take her seat! She, whose only peer was the Holy Roman Empire, she shall rank with Guatemala and Belgium perhaps! Fielding mocked again. And Aziz in an awful rage danced this way and that, not knowing what to do, and cried: "Down with the English anyhow. That's certain. Clear out, you fellows, double quick, I say. We may hate one another, but we hate you most. If I don't make you go, Ahmed will, Karim will, if it's fifty-five hundred years we shall get rid of you, yes, we shall drive every blasted Englishman into the sea, and then"—he rode against him furiously—"and then," he concluded, half kissing him, "you and I shall be friends."
>
> "Why can't we be friends now?" said the other, holding him affectionately. "It's what I want. It's what you want."
>
> But the horses didn't want it—they swerved apart; the earth didn't want it, sending up rocks through which riders must pass single file; the temples, the tank, the jail, the palace, the birds, the carrion, the Guest House, that came into view as they issued from the gap and saw Mau beneath: they didn't want it, they said in their hundred voices, "No, not yet," and the sky said, "No, not there." (*PI*, 361–362)

Forster stages here an encounter between a white liberal and a colonial-turned-nationalist, a sort of primal scene of late imperial relations, in which the attempt to forge bonds of friendship has come squarely face to face with the intransigence of colonial society, represented here as almost a force of nature. In order for the liberal ideal of intimacy to be realized, the world itself would have to be different. Thus the purported ethical agency of the individual and the universalism of this ideal are brought up short in the face of the historical difference of colonial society, and liberal discourse is forced to carefully stage the nationalist critique of colonial relations, a critique whose truth it is able neither to accept nor fully to deny. Aware of the justice of the Indian sense of grievance, the novel nevertheless cannot view anticolonial nationalism as anything other than a species of sentimentality at best and tribalism at worst. Forced to admit that "we may hate one another," nationalism goes on to reveal for Forster its distinct *ressentiment*: "but we hate you most."

Fielding is, of course, a misfit in Anglo-India. Having "been caught by India late," and having already "seen too many cities and men," he is unable to function comfortably as a member of the Anglo-Indian "herd." Without "racial feeling" himself, he brings to the Indian phase of his career a real "belief in education": "He did not mind whom he taught; public schoolboys, mental defectives and policemen, had all come his way, and he had no objection to adding Indians." He becomes pegged in the culture of the Club as a "disruptive force, and rightly, for ideas are fatal to caste, and he used ideas by that most potent method—interchange." He believed, Forster writes, that the world "is a globe of men who are trying to reach one another and can best do so by the help of good will plus culture and intelligence" (*PI*, 63–65). Like that other colonial cosmopolitan, Joseph Conrad's Marlow, he represents a liberal and inclusive consciousness of the world. But this cosmopolitanism in Conrad and Forster stands in marked contrast to that of Eliot (and Deronda), a difference clearly visible, for instance, in Marlow's great ambivalence in *Heart of Darkness* toward Western projects in the colonies. The only factor that redeems modern colonial conquest and distinguishes it from plunder, he tells his audience on board the *Nellie*, is the "idea" of civilization and progress, but wherever he looks for signs of this ameliorative project, he finds, as much in the image of an African wearing trousers—"a dog in a parody of breeches"—as in the "excesses" of Kurtz, the idea in mockery of itself.[62] And Fielding, acutely alert to the distortions of colonial culture, for which awareness he has paid a dear social price in the course of Aziz's trial, ends by telling Aziz that he had " 'no further use for politeness' . . . meaning that the British Empire really can't be abolished because it's rude" (*PI*, 360).

In the essay of the late thirties, "What I Believe," widely received as a declaration of Bloomsbury values, Forster elaborates at length on the credo of friendship he ascribes to Fielding in the novel. Opposed in principle to all credos and to Belief and Faith, he is forced to formulate and announce his own beliefs, Forster writes, because he lives in "an Age of Faith." He is "an individualist and a liberal who has found liberalism crumbling beneath him." We are forced to admit that the world is based on "Force," and that civilized life, realization of liberal values and ideals, is possible only in the intervals when violence goes underground and is asleep. Constantly aware of the precariousness of this decent and creative life, we must nevertheless proceed "as if we were immortal and as if society was eternal." Where does one begin in "a world full of violence and cruelty"? The answer is simple: "With personal relationships." Modern "psychology"—that is, psychoanalysis—has, of course, unmasked the illusion "that the personality is solid, and the 'self' is an entity," but, for "the purpose of living," we must maintain precisely that illusion. The biggest threat to the integrity of this personal realm is "the idea of causes, and if I had to choose between betraying my country and betraying my friend I hope I should have the guts to betray my country."[63]

We may contextualize Forster's remarks in this essay and the friendship theme in the novel by reading into them the dilemmas of liberalism at a moment when the semantic space of "the modern" can no longer be considered coextensive with "the liberal" or with "democracy." The most visible threat to the liberal life that Forster has in mind is, of course, fascism—liberal values lie "battered beneath a jackboot"—but we may also add, with the novel in mind, anticolonial nationalism. The contrast with the late George Eliot could not be more striking. If the latter sought precisely the union of individual sensibility with a larger ameliorative project, achieved in *Deronda* through the imaginative geographies made available by empire, in Forster the retreat into the personal is nearly complete: "I hate the idea of causes." Even when the writer is forced to formulate a cause, as in this confession of the liberal faith, or through participating, as Forster did, in the anti-fascist cultural fronts of the thirties, it is in order to undermine the idea of cause itself. The fate of liberalism is tied no longer to the success of vast, world historical ideas, to a collective "change of heart." It rests now with ideas whose "action is no stronger than a flower."[64]

Which brings us back to the final passage of Forster's novel. Nationalism is an "apotheosis," a canonization of histories, cultures, and peoples. But given the epic magnitude and multifariousness of India's history and culture, this is a paltry resolution.[65] And the irony of this modern apotheosis in the colony is its *lateness*, condemning colonial society to a permanent delay, to living in the present in a time other than that of the present. This relationship to colonial modernity may help to explain the curious position of the Muslim characters in *A Passage to India*. Parry has read the sequence of sections and section titles in the novel in terms of a metaphysical exploration of the relation of West to East. I suggest an alternative, more historically inflected reading: beginning with "Mosque," the narrative goes through the colonial "muddle" (*PI*, 193) that is trial and "Caves," and ends with "Temple." In the course of the narrative Aziz undergoes a specific metamorphosis "from a racial into a nationalist entity," as Sara Suleri has noted.[66] It is this settling of identity that Fielding tries to preempt, and it is out of this temple where the nation is worshiped and canonized that he is trying to coax his friend. Aziz's cultural affiliations are "Muslim," Forster suggests, not nationalist-Indian:

> "Who do you want instead of the English? The Japanese?" jeered Fielding, drawing rein.
> "No, the Afghans. My own ancestors."
> "Oh, your Hindu friends will like that, won't they?" (*PI*, 361)

The preference for "Muslims" in this novel is therefore a preference for a non-national orientation to culture and history, a positing of the Muslim as stumbling block to a distinctly national modernity. It is not, in other words, primarily a *cultural* or *metaphysical* preference of the sort expressed by Forster elsewhere but rather a political one.[67] Secular nationalism—"Hindu and Muslim and Sikh and all shall be one"—is identified here as the claim and culture of the (Hindu) majority, to which the Muslims can be drawn only temporarily, in a momentary "entente" (*PI*, 296), out of a common sense of grievance against the British, because "we hate you most." If India is to be subjected to the modern apotheosis that is national history, the cultural trajectory of the Indian Muslim leads back not to the *Indic* origins imagined by nationalism—"temple"—but rather to the arrival of Muslim culture on the subcontinent—"Afghans" and "mosque." What Fielding is trying to tell Aziz is something like the following: the national apotheosis turns you, a Muslim, into someone who is marginal to the mainstream of social life. Aziz's numerous fits of historical musing and recollection in the novel, such as the flight of fancy at Fielding's tea party, imagining himself a Mughal ruler dispensing largesse to his subjects, are therefore expressions of a nostalgic affective mode, but this affective state—the melancholic remembering of a glorious "Muslim" past in India—is given the significant charge of exploding the contours of "India." His attempt to produce a poem in response to Das's request "generate[s] bulbuls at once," and the resulting product is "again about the decay of Islam and the brevity of love . . . and of no interest to these excellent Hindus" (*PI*, 298). In the course of his historical musings Aziz often turns to one of two Mughal emperors, Akbar or Aurangzeb, who come to represent polar opposite possibilities from the perspective of the question of Hindu-Muslim amity and coexistence in the subcontinent. His oscillation between these opposing possibilities suggests the contradictory impulses of the "Muslim" sensibility in the modern era that is so carefully elaborated in the novel—on the one hand, an ecumenical desire for a shared life with non-Muslims in India and, on the other, a retreat into the distinctness and impermeability of a Muslim self: " 'There is no God but God'; that symmetrical injunction melts in the mild airs of Mau; it belongs to pilgrimages and universities, not to feudalism and agriculture. When Aziz arrived, and found that even Islam is idolatrous, he grew scornful, and longed to purify the place, like Alamgir. But soon he didn't mind, like Akbar" (*PI*, 332). It is the *oscillation* between these two poles, rather than one of the poles itself ("Alamgir"), that constitutes the distinctness of "the Muslims" in the novel, and its conclusion is therefore simultaneously an excavation, prediction, and *endorsement* of Muslim separatism in the larger (rather than merely political) sense. In the larger view, then, we may read the entire narrative as staging the fitful and partial development of an Indian national secular and the troubled position of the (Muslim) minority within it.

The colonial impasse of late imperial liberal culture which Forster's novel marks and embodies is that it tries to incorporate colonial relations within its ideal of "personal relationships," while at the same time positing colonial difference as the impossibility of that assimilation. As for the prospects for Indian self-rule:

> "Away from us [Fielding tells Aziz] Indians go to seed at once. Look at the King-Emperor High School! Look at you, forgetting your medicine and going back to your charms." (*PI*, 360)

Again Kipling's story resonates here unmistakably:

> Year by year England sends out fresh drafts for the first fighting-line, which is officially called the Indian Civil Service. These die, or kill themselves by overwork, or are worried to death or broken in health and hope in order that the land may be protected from death and sickness, famine and war, and may eventually become capable of standing alone. It will never stand alone, but the idea is a pretty one, and men are willing to die for it, and yearly the work of pushing and coaxing and scolding and petting the country into good living goes forward. (CW, 296)

But the difference in tone is also striking: if for the Victorian Anglo-Indian the prospect of Indian nationhood and citizenship is occasion for a deployment of irony and high humor, in Forster it evokes a dogged response, marked by a simultaneous apprehension of the imperative for intimacy and friendship, the exigencies of "Force" in the world, and the pervasive feeling that "the world may well get worse."[68] And if Eliot turns to the Jewish minority in the metropolis in a last ditch effort to renew liberalism's global charter, Forster's search takes him to the colonial periphery itself, the universal appeal to intimacy and friendship now requiring that the colonial conflict is not reformulated as a struggle between nations. It is in these terms that we must read what Suleri calls his "revision of an imperial erotic": "In place of the Orientalist paradigm in which the colonizing presence is as irredeemably male as the colonized territory is female, *A Passage to India* presents an alternative colonial model: the most urgent cross-cultural invitations occur between male and male, with racial difference serving as a substitute for gender."[69] The practices of intimacy, friendship, and love in the salons and boudoirs of Bloomsbury are transferred in Forster's novel to the colonial periphery, to discover in this extension both their ultimate test and insurmountable limit. *A Passage to India* represents the most detailed and complex literary colonial elaboration of the crisis of nationalism at the moment of its enlargement into a mass movement, and it is to this conjuncture of nationalism on the verge, as it were, of attaining India that I now turn.

PART TWO

Displacements: On the Verge of India

CHAPTER THREE

Jawaharlal Nehru and Abul Kalam Azad

DISCOVERING INDIA

ON THE AFTERNOON OF 9 AUGUST 1942 a convoy of vehicles entered the main gate of Ahmednagar Fort in western India and deposited its passengers in front of a high-walled, enclosed compound that appeared to one of the arrivals to be about 200 feet long and 150 feet wide. Inside, the compound was lined on three sides by barracks-like structures, with verandahs running along the length of each line of rooms.[1] Most of those who arrived there on that afternoon were to spend almost three years within its confines, suspended in space and time as the world rushed from crisis to crisis outside those walls. When they first entered the compound the second great war in a quarter-century was raging at its peak. Hitler's military machine seemed unstoppable, its fateful thrust towards Stalingrad having only just begun. And, in India itself, British Indian troops had retreated back into the country, abandoning Burma to Japanese forces. There was widespread expectation of an invasion from across the border before the end of the year. When the inmates emerged from Ahmednagar Fort at various points in 1945, they entered what appeared to them a new world. The fascist onslaught had been definitively rolled back, and the end of the war was in sight. A new polarity of global power was emerging, and the full scale of the horrors of the genocide in Europe was becoming known. In India it was increasingly clear that the question was no longer whether but when the Raj would, as the inmates of the fort had put it the day before their arrests in Bombay, "quit India."

The internment of the members of the All-India Working Committee of the Indian National Congress after their passage of the so-called Quit India Resolution is the subject of legend in the culture of the nationalist movement. It was to be their last period of internment before the transfer of power from the final legatees of the East India Company and the British Raj to the nationalist elite.[2] The most famous intellectual product of this internment is Jawaharlal Nehru's *Discovery of India* (1946), written almost entirely in jail and one of the richest textual expressions of the modern nationalist imagination. Part historical interpretation, part autobiography, part prison diary, part allegory, and part polemic, *Discovery* is notoriously an embodiment of a self-assured and self-conscious nationalism, an account of the emergence of the modern, rationalist, and nationalist Indian consciousness out of the magisterial sweep of India's millennia-long history. It is a canonical expression of nationalism at the threshold of its realization in the nation-state, published the year before independence from British rule. Even for so partial a reader as Sarvepalli Gopal, however, who is Nehru's most extensive and sympathetic biographer, *Discovery* was "a great jumble of a book" and "lacking in analysis, elegance and clear thinking," its achievement instead residing in its portrayal of "an emotional comprehension of Indian nationalism."[3] Its momentous nature as testimonial was not lost on contemporary readers. In a characteristic reaction, Nehru's book was reviewed by D. D. Kosambi—mathematician, historian, archeologist, and Communist—under the title, "The Indian Bourgeoisie Comes of Age."[4] And in the ongoing, Subaltern Studies rethinking of the projects of nationalism, *Discovery* continues to be a central text: it is this work, for instance, to which Partha Chatterjee turns most often in the process of reconceptualizing the Nehruvian "moment" as nationalism writing "its own life-history."[5]

In this chapter my focus is not on *Discovery of India* itself but on its relationship to another, less well-known and less iconic product of this period of internment of the nationalist leadership at Ahmednagar Fort. I refer to *Ġhubār-e ḳhāṭir*, by Maulana Abul Kalam Azad, then president of the Congress and both the preeminent figure and leading interpreter of Muslim participation in Indian nationalism. Azad personally embodies, perhaps more acutely than any other individual, the larger historical paradox that among the leading religious leaders and institutions almost no one supported the cause of the Muslim League until fairly late in the game, and many even fought strenuously against the eventual partition of India. Here I suggest a number of ways to read these two works as giving expression and form to the question of selfhood and identity, as texts equally engaged, in other words, in the narrative and rhetorical exercise, with its own distinct history within the larger history of nationalism, that we may call "discovering India." In their mutual dissonances we may read signs of the process of minoritization within which the crisis of Muslim (and hence Indian) identity has historically unfolded. Azad's work, too, was written almost entirely at Ahmednagar Fort, in fact, on the other side of a wooden partition in the barracks he shared with Nehru, and this common yet distinct place and time of composition of each work provides a powerful image and a starting point for an attempt to comprehend their enormous thematic and formal differences, their intricately distinct inscriptions of the time and place of self and nation, but also their hugely divergent histories of reception over the last half century: one a widely read and canonized work of a self-assertive nationalism, the other a quiet and nearly forgotten book, just recently translated into English for the first time and remembered in the world of Urdu in India only as a brilliant exercise in belles lettres, an appendage to Azad's more "serious" and substantial work in Qur'anic exegesis and religious matters more generally. And in Pakistan, where, despite long-standing official hostility, Azad has not exactly been unknown, even this minimal sense of his entire oeuvre has been missing, and his religious writings are read in a disembodied manner as part of an Islamic tradition and discussion, without any sense of their place in a political and literary career that was, of course, in a strong sense, Indian. But although it is located firmly *in* Indian nationalism, Azad's text is nevertheless not fully *of* it. It is a careful, yet mediated and highly elusive exploration of the terrain of culture and identity in a colonial society. Replete with autobiographical recollections, extended bouts of self-doubt and self-analysis, accounts of daily prison life, reflections on political colleagues, warders, and fellow inmates, long and lyrical discourses on the author's musical tastes and love of flowers and Chinese tea, staggering displays of Farsi, Arabic, Urdu, and European erudition, prodigious displays of memory, transcultural imaginings, philological excurses, and historical musings, *Ghubār-e k̤hāṭir* is a rare and powerful work, achieving formal complexity and defying generic specification. I offer in the following pages a reading of this text but also of the life that is Azad's, which is itself treated here as a text of some complexity.

In this chapter I begin to explore certain aspects of the crisis of national identity in modern India in the middle decades of the twentieth century. I am concerned in particular with responses to this crisis as they are formulated in the work of three leading practitioners of Urdu writing. As I argue in this and the following two chapters, Urdu as a linguistic and literary complex—characteristic genres like the lyric *ġhazal* form, a historical basis in Mughal imperial culture and links to the Persianate world, a distinct higher vocabulary and script, and a privileged social status as the exclusive vernacular language of the colonial courts in its northern heartland from the 1830s to the end of the century, to name just a few of its features—constitutes the ground on which the contradictions of the nationalization of culture and society are played out. It is the literary and linguistic terrain in which the resolutions of Indianness are most clearly visible, with all their contradictions. In part 1 of this book I attempted to outline some of the ways in which, in the post–Enlightenment era in Western Europe, the effort to expound and enact the universals of liberal culture was repeatedly brought up short in the form of the continuing crisis concerning the identity of the Jews and their role in society. In the culture of late imperial Britain, I argued further, the narrative and rhetorical apparatus for the inscription of the Jews as minority is reinflected for a consideration of the place of Muslims in the social and cultural contradictions of Britain's Indian colony. In this second part I am concerned with the intersections of Indian nationalism with this colonial structure. The language and culture of nationalism, and also, of course, its constitutional imagination and efforts, in the end proved inadequate to the problematic of Indian Muslim identity, which remained in "excess," as it were, of the categorical structures and institutions in which it was sought to be contained. The ultimate moment of success for nationalism—its self-actualization in the postcolonial nation-state—is also the moment of the unmasking of its claim to represent society as a whole. The central question within this drama is whether the Muslims indeed constitute a *minority*. Although not always posed so starkly, this is certainly what is at stake in the separatist claim, so baffling and unmanageable not only to the nationalists but also to the apologia of separatism itself, that Muslims instead constitute a *nation*. In this and the following two chapters I explore the appearances of this question in literary and linguistic practice and the pressures it exerts on them. "Muslim" participation in Indian modernity, I argue at greater length in these chapters, has historically included what appears to be its opposite, namely, the claim (and experience) of being non-Indian. All progressive culture in Urdu, broadly conceived, has as one of its moments the attempt to reveal the Indian environment of this claim of not being Indian, and it is these various attempts that concern me in this part of the book.

Written in the form of twenty-four letters to a friend, Maulana Habibur Rahman Khan Shervani, the leading educator and publicist who had been the founding Vice Chancellor (Sheikh) of Osmania University and a prominent figure in the Mohammedan Educational Conference and in the Nadwat al-ʿUlamā (Association of Islamic Scholars), *Ġhubār-e k̲h̲āṭir* sustains throughout a sense of intimate encounters in the midst of the storms of public life. This insistence on the intimate and private is, in fact, the work's central formal conceit, which is explicitly addressed in the tenth letter, written before the end of Azad's first month of imprisonment: "In my art's emporium [dukkān-e suk̲h̲an], there are many types of goods, but when I take something out for you, I sift through it carefully, so that no political impurity [siyāsī milāvaṭ] is left in it" (*G*, 87). This is a remarkable posture for the prison writing of a nationalist leader to assume, and in itself marks the work's self-distancing from the kind of writing that is *The Discovery of India*, not just in thematic terms but also with respect to voice and form. To borrow from a characterization of Benjamin's correspondence with Scholem, Azad's text preserves "a dialectical tension between the private and the public nature of the utterance."[6] As insistently private texts that are nevertheless made available for public literary consumption—they were never actually sent to the person to whom they were nominally addressed—the letters represent a defiant stance toward the course of public events from their very midst. The title itself of Azad's work signals the firm intention to shy away from a monumental narrative of the nation. *Ġhubār* in Urdu can mean dust, dust clouds, or even debris, on the one hand, and fog or mist, on the other; and *ḳhāṭir* signifies something rather like interiority—interior spaces, states of mind, subjective thoughts and feelings. An *iẓāfat* construction such as *ġhubār-e ḳhāṭir*, and the more colloquial expression *dil kā ġhubār*, are thus metaphorical and move *ġhubār* in an inward direction, in order to signify a range of subjective states—vexation, grief, ill-feeling, and the piled-up memories of painful experiences. The title thus promises the exploration of a private rather than public life; yet questions about culture, history, and tradition arise repeatedly in the book, and concern with the contours of the modern self and of the "active" life are, as in Nehru's work, to be found throughout. Nehru's *Discovery* is, famously, a narrative of the emergence of nationalism out of the great sweep of India's history and an account of the constancy, throughout this process of historical development, of India's personality. The real subject of this narrative, however, is not "India" as such but rather the figure of "secular" nationalist. As I already argued earlier in the book, moreover, the emergence of this figure in the narrative is governed by a logic not of representation, strictly speaking, but of *exemplarity*. The "secular" nationalist can represent the nation, that is, speak for it, not because he is a representative figure, being of and like the people—which is Nehru's reading of Gandhi as a leader—but because he exemplifies the highest form of consciousness it is possible to attain in this colonial society. As I show in the following pages, *Ġhubār-e ḳhāṭir* interrupts this developmentalist narrative and this logic of exemplarity.

Repeatedly, the letters of *Ġhubār* display a gentle but wry and learned wit. The British officer assigned to supervise the imprisonment is always referred to by Azad as "Cheetah Khan"—the name, according to him, of a general under the legendary Chand Bibi, who betrayed his queen to Emperor Akbar's forces.[7] This little joke is profoundly anticolonial in nature, as it highlights the absurdity of this Englishman, a Major Sendak, supervising the imprisonment of these Indians in this medieval, earthen fortification in western India, literally a palimpsest of lives lived over the course of centuries, haunted by countless memories of inhabitants and invaders, victors and vanquished. The name, invented by Azad, quickly entered, he tells us, common usage, being routinely spoken even by the Indian warders, in a touching gesture of collusion with their prisoners. And when it comes to Nehru, humor becomes an even more meaningful force. The letters repeatedly return to the scene of their composition—they are always written before dawn, over cups of tea made in Azad's room. The only sound that disturbs the early morning silence, we are told at two points, is Jawaharlal's snoring, which Azad attributes to the latter's overly emotional personality—a subtle but devastating reframing of this supposed avatar of science and rationalism. And Nehru's snoring is usually followed, Azad tells us, by bouts of muttering in his sleep, mutterings that are always in English (*G*, 51)! These observations quietly hint at a critique of the Eurocentric cultural imaginary of the most "advanced" forms of nationalist thought and personality from a subject position that is marked as both vernacular and modern. And their delicacy stands in sharp contrast to Nehru's definitive and typical judgment on Azad—"He was a strange mixture of mediaeval scholasticism, eighteenth-century rationalism, and the modern outlook" (*DI*, 348). In this sense, Azad's is a work that engages repeatedly in the displacing of the antinomies of colonial culture—past and present, indigenous and alien, tradition and modernity—which, as Chatterjee has shown, structure the conceptual apparatus of Nehruvian thought, above all, in its approach to the life-world of the peasant masses but also, from my present perspective, in its attempts to comprehend and address the crisis of national culture centered on the question of the nature of the Muslims and their place in Indian life.

The Discovery of India and the Crisis of Muslim Identity

Repeatedly in the course of *Discovery*, Nehru turns to the perplexing problem of the political separatism of the Muslims. Although he attempts to give his readers a historical overview of the significance of Islam and Muslim culture on Indian soil—from the first arrival of Muslim conquerors, through the development of the Delhi Sultanate and the Mughal Empire, to the appearance of new social forces with the coming of British rule—at the heart of Nehru's reflections on the Muslims is the growing contemporary crisis about Muslim separatism and, above all, the (for him) perplexing figure of Muhammad Ali Jinnah and his Muslim League. Nehru's interpretations of the lives of some of the more significant Muslim individuals of the modern period—including Azad, Jinnah, Muhammad Ali, Syed Ahmed Khan, and Iqbal—are particularly revealing of his understanding of modern culture and society. The larger narrative movement of the work—its account of the emergence of a secular Indian consciousness out of the movement of the nation's history—is interrupted repeatedly by the intrusion of a problematic marked as Muslim. In the text the figure of the Muslim is situated in a classic structure of ambivalence—caught between the need to announce a uniform and universal citizenship, on the one hand, and, on the other, its heterogeneity to the figure of abstract citizen, a heterogeneity that is then displaced onto a narrative of social development: "There has been a difference of a generation or more in the development of the Hindu and Moslem middle classes, and the difference continues to show itself in many directions, political, economic, and other. It is this *lag* which produces a psychology of fear among the Moslems" (*DI*, 352; emphasis added). The problem of heterogeneity or *difference* in modern Indian life is thus translated into the problematic of Muslim *backwardness*—the failure of the "Muslim" bourgeoisie to catch up in social, economic, and cultural terms with its "Hindu" counterpart. It continues to trail "behind Hindus and others in science and industry," and this weakness is reflected politically in its inability to rally wholeheartedly to the Congress cause. Even those Muslim individuals, Like Azad and the Ali brothers, who had fully entered the national struggle, were marked by this underdevelopment, so that Azad was a "strange mixture of medieval scholasticism, eighteenth century rationalism, and the modern outlook" and Mohammad Ali "an odd mixture of Islamic tradition and an Oxford education" (*DI*, 348, 349). For Nehru, the only conclusion that could be drawn in the 1940s from a survey of Indian history in the modern era was that, "since British rule came to India, Moslems have produced few outstanding figures of the modern type" (*DI*, 390).

Some of the peculiar contradictions of Nehruvian thought become visible in remarks concerning Syed Ahmed Khan and his college at Aligarh. While deriding the latter's loyalism towards the colonial rulers, which Nehru explains in terms of his backwardness thesis concerning the Muslim elites, he cannot help but admire his advocacy of "modern" colonial education for Muslims as well as the fact that "Sir Syed had opposed [pan-Islamism] and written against Indians interesting themselves in Turkey and the Sultanate"—facets of the reformer's project that were, of course, indissolubly linked to his loyalism towards the British in the interests of the Muslim *ashrāf* in the aftermath of the cataclysm of 1857 (*DI*, 346). The colonial state—for instance, as in Hunter's *The Indian Musulmans* in the 1870s—and the nation-state of the future therefore both find the extraterritorial affiliations of "the Muslims" to be a problem, resulting from their attachment to tradition and their less than complete transition to modernity. By the turn of the century this peculiar cosmopolitanism of the culture of the *ashrāf* had become something to be utilized by the colonial state as a counter to nationalist claims to represent society, but with caution, given Britain's imperial designs on the territory of the collapsing Ottoman Empire and Caliphate. Nehru's scattered remarks on the Muslims in *Discovery* come at the end of nearly eight decades of nationalist involvement with the question of Muslim identity and its place in Indian life, and they project overall a sense of retrospective. If *Discovery* as a whole is, as Chatterjee so powerfully reinscribed it, "nationalism writing its own life-history," then its reflections on the Muslims may be read as the nationalist movement examining the social and cultural forces that repeatedly had thwarted its efforts to produce an inclusive national response to colonial subjugation.

Nehru had long spoken of the politics of Muslim separatism as a mere cloak for a "struggle for jobs" on the part of what he took to be these imperfectly formed Muslim elites, incapable of any form of politics beyond the manipulation "of the religious passions of the [Muslim] masses for their own [political and hence economic] ends."[8] It is within this social difference of the Muslim elites, that is, within their anomalous modernization, that he now places what he finds to be one of the most perplexing features of Muslim cultural life, namely, its extraterritorial cultural attachments and the drawing of cultural lineages that make havoc of any notion of a coherent and self-contained national culture, of the (Indian) national idea itself. Despite this search for "national roots" outside India's territory, in the splendors of medieval "Baghdad, Spain, Constantinople, central Asia, and elsewhere," their true cultural roots lie, of course in the classical culture of the Indic world, which, "with all its cultural variety and greatness, was a common heritage of all the Indian people, Hindu, Muslim, Christian, and others, and their ancestors had helped to build it. The fact of subsequent conversion to other faiths did not deprive them of this heritage" (*DI*, 344, 341). This stubborn feature of "Muslim" cultural and political imaginaries in the modern period can appear as nothing but perverse from the perspective of the nation and represents the site for perhaps the most often recurring critique of Muslim behavior from a range of nationalist positions. Despite his best efforts, Nehru could not always help being irritated by it; Nirad Chaudhuri reports encountering it in a remote village in East Bengal (in the form of a Muslim neighbor's stated preference for Iraqi dates!); and Suniti Kumar Chatterji, the renowned linguistics scholar of the nationalist era, saw it at work in the very existence of Urdu as a distinct literary register.[9] It is unquestionably the case that the Muslim elites who produced a public discourse on Muslim identity continued to see themselves in early colonial times as outsiders long settled in India, with individual families tracing their lineage to Afghanistan, Central Asia, Iran, Iraq, even Arabia. With the rise of Indian nationalism, that is, in the process of the *nationalization* of society, this *ashrāf* ideology of familial descent—in other words, this *kinship* ideology—is mapped onto the projected *political community* or *qaum* as a whole. Hence the allegorical dimension of Muslim narratives of personal or familial origins, as we shall see with respect to Azad. Nehruvian nationalism rejected the self-perception of

Muslim elites as naturalized foreigners—seeing them, instead, with few exceptions, as descendants of converts—but at the same time saw their cultural practices as not quite indigenous.

Nehru's own solution to the conundrum of Muslim identity in modern India is to offer it up to a solution in terms of the language of "minority rights" and state "protection": "There was no dispute about the usual provisions for minority protection, such as the League of Nations used to lay down. All those were agreed to and much more. Religion, culture, language, the fundamental rights of the individual and the group, were all to be protected and assured by basic constitutional provisions in a democratic constitution applying equally to all" (*DI*, 382). Nehru points here to the long history of constitutional negotiation—from the Lucknow Pact of 1916, which Jinnah helped to negotiate as an intermediary between the Congress and the Muslim League, to the controversial Motilal Nehru Report of 1928–29, the Round Table Conferences of the early 1930s, and beyond—through which the Congress leadership, and especially its Left-liberal factions, attempted to resolve the dispute over Muslim participation in the institutions of representative government in a (future) sovereign nation-state and to allay fears about the decline of *ashrāf* Muslim "influence," as it was called, over affairs of state and society. But from our present historical perspective, that is, from this side of the events at Ayodhya, to say nothing of those in Gujarat, this reference to the League of Nations and its system for the protection of minority rights can only appear in the light of historical irony: Nehru was writing these words in 1944, in the middle of the global catastrophe in whose outbreak the persecution of minorities in Europe—the Jews in particular—and the total collapse of the League system of nation-states had played such an enormous role. As Beni Prasad noted in 1946, the "failure of the guarantee system in central and eastern Europe [had] sapped the faith in its efficacy everywhere else."[10] The Minorities Treaties signed at the Paris Peace Conference had sought to guarantee the political and cultural rights of the groups turned overnight into minorities within the new nation-states that had emerged from the breakup of the multinational empires, in particular Austro-Hungary, and had established elaborate procedures for the League of Nations to adjudicate allegations of violations and the enforcement of treaty provisions. The Jews of Eastern and Central Europe emerged out of these tumultuous events in the role, as Hannah Arendt put it, of the "*minorité par excellence*," because they, of all the "nationalities" and "minorities" as defined in the treaties, formed a majority in none of the successor states.[11] For the first time in modern history, in other words, the Jews of Europe had been legally *defined* as a minority culture and people, and institutionalized as such, by international agreement. Thus, although the explicit purpose of the Minorities Treaties, as one contemporary observer noted, had been to ensure that "when the map of Central Europe was redrawn, every person should be left citizen of one state, and of one only,"[12] the result of the treaties over the next decade was a massive explosion in the population of stateless refugees. For Arendt, the stateless were not simply a sign of the failed efforts of the League of Nations but rather a necessary *product* of its normalization of "state peoples" and "minorities." Arendt's analysis of the European crisis during the interwar years highlights the radical destabilization and reinscription of the cultural and social totality at large that is inherent in the minoritization of any one social group or fragment of society. The history of the Congress's efforts to bring a resolution to the Hindu-Muslim conflict, *sincere* and strenuous as they were, repeatedly came up against this problem—the essential identity of minority "protection" with social vulnerability and marginalization. These efforts, moreover, move within a paradox, namely, they seek to bring to the question of Muslim existence and participation in Indian national life a language which had evolved in Europe alongside the nation-state form, amidst the recurring crises concerning Jewish-minority emancipation and assimilation.

As we have seen in the previous two chapters, emancipation—the granting of political rights in the form of uniform citizenship—and assimilation—a merging with the dominant culture and society—entered into a never-ending cycle in the nineteenth century, each appearing as a precondition of the other and insufficient in itself to put an end to "the Jewish Question." Zionism as a position within European culture was an attempt to break out of this cycle: it imagined an assimilation of the Jews into a Europe of nations by their normalization as a "national" (and thus, eventually, "state") people. While the Indian nationalists sought, sincerely, to solve the "communal" question through a minoritization of the problematic of Muslim identity, their opponents seem to have understood, more often implicitly, precisely what this "minoritization" would mean. The language of "minority rights" and state "protection" implies a social imaginary in which the history of the group in question appears as a passage from a (premodern) condition of confinement—"the ghetto"—to (modern) emancipation—uniform citizenship. It suggests a narrative of emancipation whose exemplary instance is the story of the breakdown of the ghetto. The modern, secular state, even though a "national" one, assumes the posture of a third and impartial force that embodies the emancipation and protection of the minority population. That this implied social imaginary fails to take hold in India is a sign that no such narrative was available to the (largely) North Indian Muslim elites who entered the political fray from the very first political expressions of the national idea in the mid-nineteenth century, who saw themselves instead as the descendants of the pre-British imperial elite, and of whom this shift in imagination was being required. In fact the Indian trajectory of the crisis of minority is a sort of mirror reflection of the European one, with ghettoization emerging at the *end* of the historical process, subsequent to the minoritization of the Muslims through the modality of Partition, rather than at its beginning. The vocabulary of the Jewish Question is ubiquitously present in Muslim citizenship in post-Ayodhya India: urban Muslim "ghettos," the "disloyal" Muslim, Muslim "separatism," minority "appeasement" by the liberal state, even Muslim "gangsterism"—these are some of the terms in which the Muslim question is posed and debated routinely in India today.

As I argued in the previous chapter, the process of modernization that the *ashrāf* underwent in the decades following 1857 took the form of a "reluctant embourgeoisement," a formulation I deploy in part as a critique of the teleological concept of Muslim "backwardness" or underdevelopment—one of whose canonical elaborations we have just seen in Nehru—while retaining a sense of the *ambivalence* of the *ashrāf*'s relationship to national modernity. It is an oft-repeated cliché in interpretations of Syed Ahmad Khan's public career, for instance, that he dragged the Muslims willy-nilly into the modern world, especially into the realm of modern education.[13] This cliché captures the *mood* of the modernization of *sharīf* society and culture in the late nineteenth and early twentieth centuries, a subjective element which had its objective equivalent in the *ashrāf*'s much commented upon preference for government service and professions such as medicine and higher education over entrepreneurship or financial speculation, portrayed with a touching forgiveness by Qurratulain Hyder in such novels as *My Temples, Too* (*Mērē bhī ṣanam-ḳhānē*, 1949), which chronicles the collapse of this culture in a corner of North India on the eve of independence and Partition. As Partha Chatterjee has noted, however, the lacuna of the social backwardness thesis as elaborated by Nehru to explain Muslim separatism is that it bases its explanation of communal division on the existence of such distinct social groups as "the Hindu bourgeoisie" and "the Muslim bourgeoisie"—assuming precisely what needs explaining—but, furthermore, that it cannot explain why it expects that "the Muslims" as a group would accept the political and cultural leadership of the Congress if they fully "developed" a bourgeoisie in its own normative terms.[14] Azad himself, as I show later on, repeatedly rejected the minoritization of Muslim history, and the Urdu language in particular, as patently absurd, and his utter rejection of the political separatism of the Muslim League must not be confused with submission to the dominant nationalist resolutions of the question of national identity.

Urdu, Hindi, Hindustani: The Dialectic of Dialect in Colonial India

Although Nehru himself gives scant attention to this dimension in *Discovery*, the Hindu-Muslim conflict in modern India from its beginnings, namely, from the 1860s onwards, came to be formulated increasingly in linguistic terms, that is, around the question of the status of Urdu and its problematic relationship to the emerging nationalist discourse of indigenousness.[15] Because of the particular significance of language in the functioning of the modernizing colonial state—in issues such as vernacular education, especially at the primary level, the language of the lower courts and therefore the question of the qualifications necessary for employment in the judicial system, and the need for vernacular linguistic knowledge at least at lower levels in almost all domains of governance—it is not an exaggeration to say that it is in the realm of language that a public discourse of communal conflict is most dramatically played out in the last four decades of the nineteenth century. Polarizing controversies concerning vernacular education, for instance, provided the impetus for separatist cultural projects like the Aligarh movement.[16] By the time a public discourse emerges in the 1860s in places like Allahabad and Benaras on the indigenousness of modern "Hindi"—that is, a newly standardized and Sanskritized version of the northern vernacular written in Devanagari script—and also on the foreignness of "Urdu"—that is, the vernacular written in Persian script and with an interweaving, at this point centuries old, of Persianate vocabulary and morphological forms (such as the *iẓāfat*)—this is a retrospective move, the split having already long occurred under the impact and even aegis of the modernizing colonial state, even if it is identifiable as partially or unequally evident in this or that place, at this or that time.

What we may call "official" histories of Urdu and Hindi literature, respectively—that is, histories of the language(s) written from the perspective of the rival historical claims of the one or the other—share a common link in that they are ultimately unable to reconcile their drive to establish linguistic and literary autonomy with the basic—linguistic, morphological, "objective"—fact that, at the spoken level at least, "Hindi" and "Urdu" designate the same linguistic stock or, at most, extremely slight dialectal variants of the same language complex, for which there is no encompassing name. In the terms of the ideology of Urdu speech practice itself, these differences cannot be said to be more than those of *lab o lahja*, that is, the hierarchy of social manners as it is encoded in speech. Typically, today, participants in the same conversation may diverge in how they identify the language they are speaking. Identification with "Urdu" or "Hindi" is therefore above all a self-positioning, however mediated or unconscious, within a language *polemic* rather than an unmediated identification of a language as such, whether defined in lexical, morphological, or orthographic terms. The history of this polemic begins, properly speaking, in the second half of the nineteenth century, although a prehistory of sorts may be traced to its first decade, in the literary and pedagogical practices of the College at Fort William, a conjuncture of vital significance for an understanding of the language and communal conflicts of which a serious critical history remains to be written.[17] The characteristic modern project of linguistic vernacularization—which we may characterize for our purposes here as the self-described attempt to make written and spoken language identical—that has historically been linked to the emergence of nation-states or, more precisely, to the nationalization of society is given a unique twist in northern India by the emergence of *rival* claims, from within the same language complex, to the authentic language of the people.[18] What critical scholarship must offer here, therefore, is not merely the history of a language (or two) as such but rather of a language *conflict* and its shifting rhetorical contours.

We might begin here by asking why the decisive language conflict in colonial times took place on the Hindi-Urdu terrain and not in Bengali, say, or Punjabi, let alone between the southern and northern language groups. In Punjab, in fact, other than the Sikh advocacy of Punjabi written in the Gurmukhi script, the language conflict took the same form as in Delhi and the North-Western Provinces, between the rival claims of modern High Hindi and Urdu conceived of in denominational terms. Further, the absence of a significant split in Bengal along such lines—that is, the continued existence of a single Bengali linguistic and literary tradition, despite debates about its "Sanskritization" or "Hinduization"—was so promiscuous a fact that it caused huge problems for protagonists of Urdu and Pakistani nationalists as they attempted to incorporate eastern Bengal into their claimed homeland, both before and after Partition, leading even to calls for Bengali to be eliminated altogether as an official language or to be written in the Persian-Urdu script.[19] Significantly the first major disturbances in the newly created East Pakistan in the early 1950s took place precisely around the issue of the status of Urdu as the dominant language of Pakistan. The answer to this question about the peculiarity of Hindi-Urdu takes us into the prehistory of this colonial conflict, for one facet of the historical expansion of the Mughal Empire from the early seventeenth century is that one form or another of the northern vernacular gradually became the lingua franca of large parts of the subcontinent. Thus only on this geographic and linguistic terrain could the question of *national* language have arisen, which speaks volumes about the continuities, despite the obvious disjunctures, between precolonial, colonial, and postcolonial society. In other words, when a question arose in colonial India over the meaning of national language and culture, both Indian nationalists and their Muslim opponents agreed that it was the northern belt and its language complex that could provide the answer. But instead of producing one standardized version of this language, the process of nationalization in fact produced two, although at different times in the course of the nineteenth century and under vastly unequal conditions. Furthermore, this linguistic split—between the dominant "Urdu" that was standardized (in journalism, in the new literary prose, in the colonial courts) during the century, a form of the premodern *khaṛī bōlī* ("upright speech") vernacular which was deeply imbricated in Indo-Persian culture, and a newly standardized and insurgent "Hindi" in the second half of the century that saw itself as the only modern descendant, and most developed form, of the medieval vernacular—was mapped simultaneously onto a denominational one.

That the "Muslim" identity produced by the *ashrāf* in the nineteenth century does not, properly speaking, constitute a minority identity, and that it was often the nationalists who acted as if from the position of minority, is made nowhere clearer than in the language debates, in the actions of those writers, teachers, and intellectuals who, in the latter half of the nineteenth century, invented the case for a Sanskritized vernacular, cleansed of all Persian influences and to be called Hindi, as the only legitimate language of the nation. For many decades this stance was a *minority* position in large parts of northern India, which was struggling to assert its claims against a dominant Urdu culture, in which many of these publicists of the new "Hindi" had themselves been formed. Thus, as late as the early 1920s, Tej Bahadur Sapru, one of the senior liberal figures in the nationalist movement, recalled this heritage plaintively, noting that it is "distressing to come across Hindu graduates and under-graduates in some parts of the U.P. [United Provinces] who think that their duty towards Hindi necessarily means and implies that they should exclude from their thought the language and literature in which their ancestors only a generation or two ago excelled."[20]

The larger historical question that needs answering, and whose detailed exploration is clearly beyond the scope of the present study, is when and how it came to be widely felt that "Muslims" and "Hindus" had different languages. A significant step has been taken in this direction by Shamsur Rahman Faruqi, in the early sections of *Early Urdu Literary Culture and History*.[21] Faruqi, a leading critic and literary historian of Urdu in India, removes this question from the *official* terrain, as I defined it above, of the Hindi-Urdu polemic, cutting through this dizzying maze in which not even the basic facts can be taken for granted, in order to attempt a precise historical understanding simply of the various names—Hindi, Urdu, Hindustani, Hindavi, Rekhta—by which aspects of the language, such as poetry or spoken forms, have historically been known. Faruqi's scrupulously stated purpose is to explode the assumption, introduced by early British Orientalists—administrators, lexicographers, historians, missionaries, philologists—and shared by nationalist publicists of Hindi since the late nineteenth century, that Urdu developed as a military language around the encampments of various foreign Muslim invaders and conquerors. In the eighteenth century, when the British first attempted to systematize their encounter with the language of North India, "the *urdū*" referred to the seat of Mughal power, Faruqi argues, namely, the city of Shahjahanabad, or Delhi. Hence the term *zabān-e urdū-e muʿallā* (shortened sometime to *urdū-e muʿallā* and even simply to *urdū*) meant "the language of the exalted royal city/court." To anyone fed a diet of the official histories of either Hindi or Urdu, it is startling to realize that, at least in some contemporary texts, this term clearly referred originally not to the forms of language practice that today we call Urdu but to *Persian*. The word *urdū* itself, Faruqi speculates, may have come to mean something like "royal city," "court," or "seat of imperial authority" from the late sixteenth century, when the emperor Akbar abandoned his seat at the newly built capital, Fatehpur Sikri, to create a sort of moving capital that carried the entire central administration with it. Only from the late eighteenth century can *zabān-e urdū-e muʿallā* and its abbreviations ever be said to refer to the vernacular. The earliest available instances are from the verse of Ghulam Hamadani Mushafi (to whom I return briefly in a later chapter). The term more commonly used by writers at this time, including Mushafi, for the language of their writing is *Hindi*, that is, the language of Hind, usually in order to distinguish it from Persian, with "Rekhta" often used as a designation for poetry written in this *rēḳhta*—"scattered" or "mixed"—language.[22] This remained the case well into the mid-nineteenth century, when writers like Syed Ahmed Khan, and even Ghalib, continued to use "Hindi," "Rekhta," and even "Hindavi" as the designation for their literary language. In Faruqi's convincing argument, only when "Hindi" is appropriated for the emergent Sanskritized High Hindi in the polemics of the 1860s onwards does this overlapping use of the terms begin to disappear. As Faruqi points out, even so iconic a poet of "Urdu" as Iqbal, when explaining, in the teens of the twentieth century, his turn to writing in Persian rather than the vernacular, used the term *Hindi* for the latter.[23] The new publicists of Urdu, and those of Hindi, progressively exacerbated the split—for instance, in the case of the former, by excising the enormous contribution of writers of Hindu origin to the history of the literature they claimed as their own, and by failing to examine in any serious way the links of literary Urdu to the variety of spoken and written forms of the vernacular, thereby further strengthening and establishing the conception of Urdu as a Muslim, alien, and elite practice. These publicists of Urdu in the late nineteenth and early twentieth centuries, one should note, were mostly not themselves writers considered to be significant for the development of its literature but instead were critics and scholars, and some were even bureaucrats and professional propagandists. In the next chapter I return to this question, and examine a paradox of Urdu literary culture in the 1930s and 1940s, namely, that this period of deepening cleavage in the public sphere in religio-linguistic terms is also the most progressive, the most secular, and the most integrated period in Urdu's modern literary history.

The notion of two languages, one Hindu, the other Muslim, undoubtedly owes its origin to British attempts to comprehend the structure of the populations coming under their purview from the late eighteenth century onwards. Here the entire history of British Orientalism and its encounters over the centuries with the Islamic world, as described by Edward Said in *Orientalism*, was decisive. These early observers of Indian society, and sometimes even late imperial writers like Hunter, viewed "the Muhamadans" in many ways as a uniform population dispersed over large regions of the Orient, including Western Asia, North Africa, Central Asia, and the Indian subcontinent, and described them by such terms as "nation" or "race." It was not unknown in the late eighteenth century, for instance, for British writers in India to refer to a Muslim there as a "Moor"; indeed, the term was used commonly enough as a designation for the language thought to be unique to the Muslims to require John Gilchrist to explicitly disapprove its use—"the Hindoostanee Language, Improperly Called Moors"—in the 1806 volume of *The British Indian Monitor*.[24] In sum, the British thought of Muslim existence as a whole in India as an *alien* presence, a perception reinforced by the self-perceptions of the *ashrāf* landed gentry with whom they came into contact in the waning decades of the Mughal Empire, whose families often traced their genealogies to the central Islamic lands. One of the iconic moments in this historical process is, of course, the project undertaken in the first few years of the nineteenth century under the supervision of Gilchrist at Fort William College, where he was Professor of Hindustani from 1800 to 1804.[25] Typically this moment has been understood as marking the birth of the modern vernacular languages of North India, not only by colonial historians but also by Indian protagonists of Urdu and of Hindi starting later in the century.[26] With the explicit purpose of producing texts in the spoken vernaculars for the use of young Englishmen being trained for a life of service to the empire in

India, Gilchrist sought out and commissioned a group of *munshīs*, *maulvīs*, and *paṇḍits* to produce versions of Persian, Arabic, Sanskrit, and Braj classics in the "Muhammadan" and "Hindoo" vernaculars of "Hindoostan." The products of this enterprise, above all Mir Amman's *Bāġh o bahār* (1804), revolutionized the writing of prose, producing for the first time, and *as a project of the colonial state*, a standard of prose writing in "Hindi" and "Oordoo" or "Hindoostanee." The history of modern literatures in these languages, traditions, or registers—however we may choose to think of them—is thus defined by the irony that, as Sadiq ur-Rahman Kidwai noted, "literary works that were not Indian in the sense that they were not addressed to the Indian readership have become the most cherished and well read classics of Urdu [and, we may add, Hindi] literature."[27] It is this thoroughly colonial situation of the "invention" of modern "Hindi" and "Urdu" prose, and thus the existence of the colonial effect, as it were, in the elaboration of literary histories for the two supposedly distinct traditions, which critical scholarship has so far failed to confront in any forceful or systematic manner. It is in this direction that Faruqi's recent work, and Rai's *Hindi Nationalism*, may be seen as taking an initial and important step.

In 1837 the colonial state made the vernacular written in Persian script the language of the lower courts in North India, a role that had been served until then by Persian itself. This established "Urdu" (or "Hindustani," as the British continued to call the language as well, despite the absence of any such usage among the speakers of the language) for the first time as *a language of the modern state*. Thus the process of rival standardizations that had already begun in the lexicography of the 1780s and 1790s, and further institutionalized in the Fort William practices of the 1800s, was now uniformly established as a feature of the structure of the colonial state. It was against this predominance of a distinct and standardized version of the vernacular and its relationship to the colonial state that a polemic began to emerge in the 1860s about the need for a purging of the language of all the "foreign" (that is, Persio-Arabic) influence of centuries—a classic linguistic project of modern nationalisms, as we have seen with respect to Fichte and German in a previous chapter.[28]

As already noted, the upheaval of 1857 marks a turning point in the history of the northern Hindi-Urdu belt in general, and of language and literature in particular. In the new, massively rearranged structure of society and the public sphere, the advocacy of the vernacular, for instance, in education, came to be split over the question, which *version* of the vernacular? The story of Syed Ahmed Khan's falling out, soon after his arrival in Aligarh in the mid-1860s, with his erstwhile comrades from among the Hindu *ashrāf*, such as Raja Jai Kishen Das, is an iconic one in this context.[29] In the 1870s and 1880s the polemic intensified, with the progressive emergence of two distinct and rival literary cultures, although the slow and always less than complete nature of this process of bifurcation is evident in the strange case of Munshi Premchand, who began writing in the first years of the twentieth century and, until his death in 1936, continued to see himself as both an Urdu and Hindi writer, and is claimed by both traditions as equally its own. In the final decade of the century the issue resurfaced, again as a matter of concern to the state, with the campaign to make the emergent Hindi written in Devanagari a language of the courts on a par with Urdu in the heartland North-Western Provinces, renamed the United Provinces (U.P.) of Agra and Oudh in 1902. The literature of this polemical conjuncture makes fascinating reading. In a pamphlet published in 1899, the anonymous author—in fact, Madan Mohan Malaviya, leader of the Hindu Mahasabha and luminary of the religious wing of the Congress—lays out the case for Hindi/Devanagari in the courts on two main counts: the *foreign* nature of Urdu (and the indigenousness of Hindi) and also its *inherent defects* (and thus the inherent advantages of Hindi). On the one hand, Urdu "characters" and Urdu vocabulary are of Persian origin and therefore unintelligible to the great mass of the people, all except a small number of elite educated Muslims and Kayastha Hindus; on the other, the irrationality of the script, and especially of the short-hand *shikasta* form used in court documents, makes it notoriously open to willful misinterpretation and manipulation. Overall, the result is an esoteric system of writing, alien and mysterious to the people. The only authentic alternative can be Hindi, that is, the vernacular written in Devanagari, a script of Sanskritic origin. Of primary concern to the author is mass vernacular education and that the Urdu form of the vernacular continues to predominate over the "true vernacular" in this domain, owing, the argument goes, to the government's patronage of "the fashionable official dialect Urdu" by making it the language of the courts, at the cost of the "homely indigenous style" of the people.[30]

A response to Malaviya's argument against Urdu came in the form of another anonymous pamphlet, published from Allahabad in 1900. That a good amount of this large polemical literature is published anonymously is telling in itself: it marks a discretion that suggests the continued existence of an encompassing public sphere and of forms of sociality across denominational difference. The respondent in this instance replies to the charge of the alienness of Urdu by arguing that there is no such thing as a purely indigenous vernacular in North India, these having been formed by repeated interactions with, and subjugation by, invading peoples and their speech forms and traditions, including Sanskrit, the language of the Aryan invaders who entered the subcontinent from Iran. The ancient spoken vernaculars, termed Prakrit or "vulgar" by the Aryan literate elites, "were anterior to Sanskrit, contemporary with it, and they eventually survived it," so that "[the modern vernacular] cannot appropriately be called a lineal descendant of any single one of these" foreign linguistic influences, such as Sanskrit, Old Persian, Greek, or Scythian. Furthermore, Persian is closely linked historically with Sanskrit—both are Aryan languages with their origins in Iran—so that the more recent Persian influences on the vernacular were in the nature of a return to the origin.[31] Both participants in this debate clearly assume a scientific perspective, claiming verifiable evidence for their cause, and yet at the same time the most fantastic notions are mobilized in the most off-handed manner. Every aspect of the entire history of the vernacular and its relationship to the classical antecedents is put into question once again in this second pamphlet and the terms of the argument of the first inverted on almost every count. This felt need, in each intervention, for a complete, historical accounting of the language(s) from the very beginnings is among the most characteristic features of the contributions to the Hindi-Urdu polemic—evident in books, articles, pamphlets, even speeches—not only in this period but even in our own time. Any intervention into the language polemic invites a reopening of the most basic ideas about the historic origins and development of the language, dialects, script, speech forms, and poetic and prose literature that constitute the entire Hindi-Urdu complex.

The sense that the version of the vernacular in which one has been intellectually formed is not truly one's own, which we encountered in Malaviya's text, is a recurring motif of the birth of modern Hindi, and here the modalities of the Hindi-Urdu conflict converge with wider historical processes in the nationalization of culture and society in the modern world, also visible in the denigration of Yiddish, another "mixed" (although, unlike Urdu, hardly "high" cultural) language and one often formed by precisely those who spoke most fervently of a dispersed but single Jewish *Volk* and a Jewish nation.[32] The birth of modern Sanskritized Hindi and of modern Hebrew, two instances of language invention linked to the nationalization and minoritization of linguistic and cultural practices, impels us to reexamine some notions about the process of vernacularization and the rise of national cultures that have become conventional in recent years. I especially have in mind Benedict Anderson's influential essay, which laid out for the first time a theoretical basis for thinking about the nation as a cultural form or, rather, as a sociopolitical form whose basic modalities are elaborated most compellingly in the realm of language and culture, broadly conceived. For Anderson, vernacularization arises out of the concatenation of a host of semi-autonomous historical factors, above all the internal logic of what he calls "print-capitalism," but its dominant *social* logic is provided by the need of an emergent middle-class intelligentsia to "invite the masses into history," an invitation that must be written "in a language they understood."[33] But "vernacularization" cannot simply be conceived of as making a formerly elite discourse available to the masses (in their already existing language). That is the *ideological* form it can assume in a number of European societies in the process of their nationalization, which Anderson takes as the historical norm. In the context of Hindi and Hebrew, however, it is much more patently clear that vernacularization linked to the rise of national cultures requires the *invention* (by elites) of essentially new forms of spoken and written language as the language of the people-nation, based though they are on some past morphological and orthographical complex or textual traditions or both. From the perspective of those late-nineteenth- and early-twentieth-century developments that Anderson has consigned to a copycat role regarding established "models" of nationalism, vernacularization, rather than being viewed as a people-nation coming into possession of its own speech and writing, may be seen as the *putting into practice* by aspiring state elites the "possessive" theory of language that we have seen at work before in the emergent "nation-thinking" of the early nineteenth century in Fichte and Scott but whose first systematic elaborations date back at least to the writings of Herder of the 1760s and 1770s—*this* language in *this* place for *this* people. Urdu as a linguistic and literary register, with its distinct hierarchies of "purified" (*shusta*) and "rustic" (*gañvār*) forms of the vernacular, therefore proved vulnerable to a modern politics of linguistic vernacularization, carried out in the *name* of the people and their language—even though it was nothing other than one of the particular forms of the northern vernacular, and even though, as Rai has so compellingly argued, the Hindi that emerged in rejection of it is no less suppressing of the linguistic diversity of the North and no less distant from genuinely popular linguistic forms.[34] The charge of elitism against Urdu cannot settle the case in favor of Hindi as the sole possible linguistic instrument of a project of nationalization on Indian soil. In the end, it proved possible to establish Urdu within a national project in one part of India—the part now known as Pakistan. The contradiction was not between elite linguistic practices and those of the masses, but within the modernizing elite itself, between its *ashrāf* and *savarna* segments, between their rival conceptions of how to attempt a "national" project vis-à-vis the people which nevertheless shared a sense of Indian society as consisting of "Hindu" and "Muslim" masses.

When the Hindi-Urdu question resurfaced again in the mid-1930s, its focus was not so much the colonial state but the national state of the future. At the center of the controversy was Gandhi himself, and the result once again was political polarization, with erstwhile admirers of the Mahatma finding themselves in the opposite camp. This was perhaps most notably the case with Maulvi Abdul Haq, the most prominent publicist of Urdu in the first half of the twentieth century, who broke publicly with Gandhi at the 1936 meeting of the Akhil Bharatiya Sahitya Parishad in Nagpur.[35] It has become routine scholarly practice to view Gandhi, in contradistinction to Nehru, as an anti-modernist critic of the modernizing state. There is a great deal of truth to this view, of course, although, as I noted in the prologue, it cannot explain the mutual imbrication of the Gandhian and Nehruvian projects. The Gandhi that emerges from the language debates of the mid-1930s, however, is a rather different figure, a fierce proponent of the linguistic remapping of society along classically nation-state lines. His writings and speeches of this period clearly reveal that, for Gandhi, the goal of the nationalist movement could only be one national language and one script, even if political circumstances required the postponement of that goal to some undetermined future time. He spoke of Urdu—the vernacular "written in Persian script, and with a preponderance of Persian or Arabic words"—as exclusively the language of the Muslims and called for a recognition of "the right of Musulmans" to practice the vernacular in that way. As for the Hindus who are also formed in this version of the vernacular, Gandhi leaves no doubt: "The propagation of the Devanagari script among the Hindus of the Punjab, as elsewhere, will still continue." The proper national language for Hindus, despite their cultural and linguistic formation, can only be Hindi/Devanagari, and Muslims must be allowed for the time being to "write the language . . . as they have done hitherto."[36] Gandhi leaves no doubt that he sees this linguistic and orthographic variation as a *problem* for the nationalist movement, and even throws his weight behind the proposal current in some Hindi circles to make Devanagari the universal and sole script for *all* the languages of India, northern and southern included. In his writings and speeches of 1935–1937 on the subject, Gandhi identifies two different kinds of obstacle confronting the project of universalizing—that is, nationalizing—Hindi/Devanagri: one is along the national-provincial axis, and the other the Hindu-Muslim axis. His understanding of the difference between these two kinds of language problem is of interest for us here:

> Different languages descended from or intimately connected with Sanskrit *ought* to have one script, and that is surely Devanagri. Different scripts are an unnecessary hindrance to the learning by the people of one province the language of other provinces. Even Europe, which is not one nation, has generally adopted one script. Why should India,

> which claims to be and is one nation, not have one script? I know *I am inconsistent when I tolerate both Devanagri and Urdu scripts* for the same language. But my inconsistency is not quite foolish. *There is Hindu-Muslim friction at the present moment.* It is wise and necessary for the educated Hindus and Muslims to show mutual respect and toleration to the utmost extent possible. Hence, the option for Devanagri or Urdu scripts. *Happily, there is no friction between provinces.* Hence, the desirability of advocating a reform which means a closer knitting together of provinces in more ways than one.[37]

The Hindi-Urdu question is thus fundamentally different from the question of the relationship of the provincial languages to one single national language, the vernacular of the North, for in this case the very identity and nature of this vernacular are at stake, not just its role as the language of the nation. Gandhi's proposed solution, elaborated repeatedly in his writings of this period and in his speeches (also published almost immediately in the various organs of the Gandhian movement), is "tolerance" of the heterogeneity represented by Urdu as a formation distinct from the Hindi that emerged since the 1860s, until such time as "the hearts of the two [that is, Hindus and Muslims] meet, [and] the two forms of the same language will be fused together, and we shall have a resultant of the two, containing as many Sanskrit, Persian, Arabic or other words as may be necessary for its full growth and full expression."[38] Gandhi seems to have made no sustained attempt in these widely disseminated interventions to imagine the linguistic, literary, and cultural heterogeneity represented by Urdu as a permanent and legitimate feature of the "national" culture of India.

The polemics of this period sometimes make strange reading, as much of the energy seems to have been spent on what this national language in the making ought to be called. This period in the history of the polemic is the heyday of the term "Hindustani," which the British alone had introduced and used, as a term that overlapped with "Urdu" but was now revived in an effort to designate the shared linguistic stock of the rival forms of the vernacular. Such a move received quite a lot of support on the Urdu side of the divide. Manifestos were published, speeches made, and literary journals launched to propagate the use of the term among self-described Urdu speakers.[39] In 1935 Gandhi persuaded the Hindi Sahitya Sammelan to include the version written in Persian script, that is, "Urdu," *within* its definition of "Hindi." Then, in 1936 in Nagpur at the Akhil Bharatiya Sahitya Parishad, an offshoot of the Sammelan, he proposed the composite name "Hindi-Hindustani." The Urdu-*vālē* who were present, "especially Abdul Haq Sahab," Gandhi wrote, "stoutly opposed me there," and would not accept the inclusion of the word "Hindi" in what was meant to be an inclusive and composite designation, and the Hindi activists rejected any use of "Urdu," even in conjunction with "Hindi." So while it is true that "Hindi nationalists" like Purushottam Das Tandon complained in the mid- to late 1930s of what they saw as Gandhi's repeated concessions to the forces of Urdu, as Francesca Orsini has demonstrated in great detail, it is also the case that Gandhi seems never to have veered significantly from a basic framework that he shared with them, in which linguistic heterogeneity and plurality poses an insurmountable problem for the idea of a single people and a single nation.[40]

While I am not suggesting that this was a uniquely decisive moment on the twisting road to Partition, it is interesting nevertheless to imagine what form the language politics may have taken in the 1940s had Gandhi managed in Nagpur to win over the widely influential Abdul Haq and his Anjuman-e Taraqqī-e Urdū (Association for the Promotion of Urdu), a person and an organization with impeccable credentials in the public proselytization of the cause of Urdu. In the event, Abdul Haq began publicly declaring, in response to his experience there, that "Nagpur" had become "Wake-up-pur," as before another audience in Nagpur in 1940: "main isē ab Nāgpūr nahīñ, jagpūr kahtā hūñ" ("I now call it not Nagpur, but Wake-up-pur"), and sympathetic interpreters of his career speak of the occasion as a decisive turning point in his life, much in the way that those of Jinnah speak of the failed All-Parties Convention and the Motilal Nehru Report of 1928 as his parting of ways with his erstwhile comrades in the Congress.[41] At the time of Partition, although he went to Karachi to set up a central office for the Anjuman in Pakistan, Abdul Haq in fact tried to stay on in Delhi himself, insisting on his Indian nationality, despite the looting of the Anjuman's office and priceless library and the appropriation of its building, but opted ultimately for Karachi in the face of widespread hostility to his work and presence in official circles in India.[42] Nehru, meanwhile, in 1937, in his characteristic fashion, offered a "rational" and "scientific" solution of his own to "the language problem": the national language was to be a "Basic Hindustani" on the model of "Basic English"; both scripts would be recognized at the local and national levels, and individuals would choose which script to learn; furthermore, Bengali, Devanagari, Marathi, and Gujarati scripts would be "unified," as would the Urdu and Sindhi (since both were derived from Persian), and a common script would be devised for the languages of the South, if Devanagari was found to be unacceptable there.[43] Typically, Nehru's was not a proposal substantially different from Gandhi's but appeared more secular in its approach to the linguistic question as it made no direct reference to the denominational or communal one.

The complexity of this failed encounter in the mid-1930s may be understood, in part, by recalling that the emergence of Urdu as a standardized and secular written vernacular and language of state in the nineteenth century was also accompanied, paradoxically, by a process of at least a partial *sacralization* of it—experienced, above all, through the perceived proximity of Urdu script to the Arabic but also through a myriad of lexical and morphological associations.[44] Thus modern High Hindi written in Devanagari, from the perspective of this sacralized element in Urdu, appears not just as a secular rival to the claim of national vernacular but also as *the religious other*, as so many concrete signs of the polytheism constantly lurking below the surface and threatening the dissolution of (Indian) Islam. Proponents of Urdu from the late nineteenth century were thus caught in a contradictory set of positions—arguing, on the one hand, that Urdu was already the lingua franca of the northern belt, and therefore already in a national position with respect to the other languages of India, and, on the other, seeing any threatened depreciation in the status of Urdu as an attack on Muslims in particular and even on Islam. This contradiction—but also the mutual reliance—between the secular and sacral lives of Urdu was made apparent in a tragicomic way almost immediately following Partition, when impassioned advocates and defenders of Urdu such as Abdul Haq and Syed Sulaiman Nadvi, after leaving their ancestral homes in their setting years in life at least partly because of what they thought Pakistan would mean for Urdu, and for the *ashrāf* classes formed in Urdu, found themselves having to defend its status as the exclusive national language against the claims of Bengali, the first language of a majority of the citizens of the new "Muslim" state, a language written in a single script of Sanskritic origin and without a developed controversy about distinct linguistic variants marked by denominational difference. Abdul Haq produced another mountain of polemic in his remaining years in Urdu's cause, and a sense of bafflement, even panic, is patent in them. But perhaps a remark of Nadvi's from 1951 is most revealing about the levels of bitterness and the lowering of discourse produced by the growing realization of this possibility of a renewed homelessness of Urdu in its new supposed homeland: "the majority of Bengalis [that is, in Pakistan] cannot be delivered from enslavement to Hindu culture, Hindu mythology, and Hindu literature, until such time as they free their language from Sanskritic Bangla and Sanskritic script."[45]

Thus something like Gershom Scholem's understanding of the repression of the sacral in Zionism's secular "actualization" of Hebrew as a national language in Palestine, quietly expressed in the famous open letter to Franz Rosenzweig in 1926, written long after the onset of the latter's debilitating illness and loss of speech, is apposite to the cognate history of the question of the national vernacular in India and Pakistan. More precisely, it is a sort of *mirror reflection* of Scholem's formulation that is relevant to us here. For Scholem, the generation (his own) that sought to revive the ancient and sacred language as a language of everyday life, and "delivered the ancient names and seals to the youth," did so "blindly," with a naïve and unwarranted belief "that language has been secularized," and never feared "the uprising of a sacred language." But in "a language where he is invoked back a thousand times, God will not stay silent," so will not "the religious violence of this language one day break out against the ones who speak it?"[46] Scholem, himself one of the great proponents of Zionism among the European Jewish intelligentsia of his generation, nevertheless appears here to have feared the religious millenarianism lurking within the secular redemptionism of the Zionist project and to foresee the apocalyptic forms of violence it could produce when it resurfaced.[47] The letter thus represents a certain concession, in the light of his close encounter with the Yishuv, to German-Jewish critics of Zionism like Rosenzweig. In the case of Urdu in the late nineteenth and early twentieth centuries, the process by which a certain standardized version of the North Indian vernacular became cast progressively as the communal (or "national") language of "the Muslims," a religious minority, did not so much repress but indeed unleashed a parallel sacralization. The premodern language complex out of which it emerged had never been a sacred language in the usual sense, although a great deal of religious writing, mostly verse, had been produced in it over the centuries. It is this sacral element in the politics of language and of community as such that the secular-liberal leadership of the separatist movement, Jinnah included, could never control or even precisely manipulate.[48] The parallels between early Jewish nationalism and Indian Muslim separatism lie in the fact that although, in either case, a secular state was demanded in the name of a minority identified at least in part by its attachment to a distinct religious tradition, the secularization of the tradition into "culture" and "identity" that the national option assumed was never sufficient to its own claims. In the South Asian instance, some of this complex process is visible in a somewhat simple form in the curious history of the name itself that the movement and later the country acquired. The name had been concocted in the 1930s in Cambridge by Chaudhari Rahmat Ali, a famous Punjabi crackpot, as an anagram of the names of the provinces the new state was meant to incorporate. But never has the name been thought of as such, invoking, instead, the concept of being *pāk* or ritually pure—hence the "Land of the Pure." The irony, of course, is that this particular notion of ritual purity is not imaginable as an element of Islamic culture anywhere outside the Indian environment, outside, that is, the caste structure of Indian society.[49]

Out of Place and Out of Time: Self and Society in the Colonial World

Within the epistolary, and therefore fragmentary, occasional, and episodic form of *Ġhubār* emerges a narrative of a disjointed life and formation which may be read as an allegory of the trajectories and crises of the culture of the *ashrāf* elites of North India in the course of the nineteenth century, of their social self-perceptions and narratives of origins in the central Islamic lands. This narrative stresses its author's upbringing in a religious environment, in a family of hereditary divines hailing from the Delhi region. Azad was born in Mecca, he tells us, where his father had studied, settled, and married a woman from a distinguished religious family—Arab, according to Azad, but, by some biographical accounts, from a family of Indian origin—and at some point in the first decade of his life the family returned to India and settled in Calcutta. But the events of his early years are a matter of considerable confusion and controversy, and his own autobiographical statements from different periods of life—beside *Ġhubār* and *Tażkira* (Memoir, written in 1916), these include the "dictated" texts *Abū al-Kālām kī kahānī ḳhud un kī zabānī* (The story of Abul Kalam, in his own voice), dictated in prison presumably in the early 1920s, and *India Wins Freedom* (dictated by Azad in Urdu and supposedly approved in English transcript in the years before his death in 1958), and a number of essays, lectures, and letters—contradict one another on a large number of counts: the year of his family's return to India, his mother tongue and first language, his travels outside India and his possible relationship to al-Azhar University, his involvement (or not) with the Bengali revolutionaries, and even his date of birth and original given name all seem open to uncertainty and debate.[50] In *Ġhubār*, Azad makes his complex origins the basis for exploring the plurality of the colonial world and the possibilities of emergence of selves in tension with its cultural and temporal hierarchies. It is in late Victorian Calcutta, the metropolis of Britain's Indian Empire, and the birthplace of middle-class Indian nationalism, that the "strange mixture" that is Azad begins to take form. It is a fitful and fragmented narrative of emergence from the world of tradition. This world is figured in the form of the religious and cultural world of the family home, the center of the devotional cult surrounding the father. Azad is educated entirely at home, first by his father, and then by a succession of *maulvīs*, in the *dars-e niẓāmī*, the eighteenth-century curriculum associated with the Farangi Mahall *madrasa* and the basis of Indo-Muslim education in the early nineteenth century. As Azad himself puts it, "by this measure, I was, as it were, living the life of a hundred years earlier in India" (*G*, 95). This formation is singular not only in its complete bypassing of the colonial educational regime, and of English, but also of the system of Islamic seminaries then in place in North India, including Farangi Mahall and Deoband, a fact that repeatedly hobbled Azad's later efforts to assert his authority over the formally trained *ʿulamā*, for instance, during the Khilafat agitation of the early 1920s, which remained dominated by Farangi Mahallis led by Abdul Bari and his followers, the Ali brothers.[51]

One of the recurring preoccupations of Azad's text is the nature of time, and temporal figures such as "anachronistic" (nā-vaqt) and "high speed" (tēz raftārī) dominate this narrative of early life, producing the sense of a life out of place and out of time (*G*, 91, 93). Repeatedly Azad testifies to a sense of living at a different, faster pace compared to those around him and to being ahead of his time. This sense is in tension, however, with the opposing perception, that of living the life of a century earlier. The colonial hierarchy implicit in the feeling of living in the past is confronted here with a different temporality, so that in the end it is not at all clear whether "anachronistic" means being ahead of or behind the present. The linear and transparent passage of time—past, present, future—is itself rendered discontinuous and opaque by this life that is in the present but not of it, and it is out of this series of temporal displacements that the narrative stages something like a non-historicist history of the modern self. In a brief letter towards the end of the book, reflecting on the nature of time itself, Azad notes the impossibility of living in the present, which is either a recollection of the past or an imagining of the future (*G*, 248–249). What appeared to Nehru, from the other side of the wooden barrier in Ahmednagar Fort, as a "strange mixture" of past and present, as the anachronistic *survival* of the past in the present, becomes, in Azad's self-fashioning, a reconfiguration of the relationship of the alien to the indigenous, of past to present, and of tradition to modernity. The adjective Azad uses most often to describe the religious and cultural atmosphere of his childhood home is *taqlīdī*—customary, conventional, or received, carrying with it the sense of unthinking and uncritical imitation and acceptance of authority. He rebelled against this conventional religious life roughly at the age of fifteen, he tells us, but is unable to understand where the seeds of "doubt" (shak) and rebellion could have come from (*G*, 100–102). However, this critique of *taqlīd*, which is also an element in almost every single "reform" effort directed at Muslims since the eighteenth century—for instance, the movement associated with Shah Waliullah in the late eighteenth century, the *jihād* of Syed Ahmed Barelvi in the 1820s and 1830s, the Deoband seminary and Syed Ahmed Khan's Aligarh movement in the second half of the nineteenth century, and even, to an extent, the Farangi Mahallis—places Azad's personal rebellion squarely within the larger trajectory of Islam in India while at the same time insisting on its own modernity. To extrapolate from this distinct formation that is Azad's a "traditional" personality rather than one of "the modern type" (Nehru) is, first of all, to adopt a particularly *colonial view of education*, taking curriculum itself as the determinant of personality. Azad started his public life as a journalist, a religious and literary figure, while still in his teens. As a young adult he founded political and religious organizations, participated in public campaigns and political struggles, and spent years in colonial jails. While barely in his thirties, he rose to the top of the organizational structure of the nationalist movement and, late in life, spent more than a decade as the minister of education in the postcolonial state. How else do we conceive of participation in modern social and political life? What else would personality of "the modern type" look like? What Nehru means by the latter phrase is, of course, *assimilation into the Anglophone middle class*—"English" education, English as the primary language of communication, public and private, and formation in a cultural hierarchy in which English functions as the pristine sign of modernity. The vernacular languages and their textual traditions, and "classical" education of one or the other sort, are here unequivocal signs of underdevelopment and inimical to the modern temperament, personality, or "type."

This linguistic and cultural hierarchy, which had informed not only the so-called Anglicist thread in colonial educational policy, such as expressed in Macaulay's famous Minute in 1835, but also such Orientalist projects as Sanskrit College (in Beneras) and Delhi College, which were supposed to emphasize and support the literatures of Sanskrit, and Arabic and Farsi, respectively.[52] The entailed structural disadvantage had marked the rise of the modern vernaculars themselves. As Gauri Viswanathan has painstakingly demonstrated, the rise of English studies in India in the mid-nineteenth century was linked to the government's reluctance, which was of constant concern to the missionaries, to interfere directly in native religious life for fear of "inflaming" native sentiments, and education in English language and literature, reinscribed as a secular body of writing, eventually came to be seen as the more effective way to erode the authority of the traditional learned classes.[53] That the products of this education—the new middle classes—ultimately drove the British themselves to distraction with their "talkativeness" in English and were violently ridiculed by them, as we have seen in Kipling, is another story. But that middle-class culture did not permanently succeed in undoing the terms of this hierarchy despite a number of attempts to indigenize education—Tagore's Shantiniketan and Osmania University in the Muslim princely state of Hyderabad are two very different but obvious early-twentieth-century examples—will have to be the starting point for a critical history of colonial education yet to be written. Nehru's own education—home tutoring in Allahabad mostly by British tutors until the age of fifteen, followed by two years at Harrow, three at Cambridge, and two at the Inner Temple—embodies this structure perhaps to an extreme degree. And his interpretations of the lives of the leading Muslim personages are inscribed throughout with this hierarchy—thus Azad and Muhammad Ali are "strange" and "odd" mixtures of the archaic and the modern, and Jinnah, who is perhaps even more Anglicized than Nehru, and therefore meets the official requirements of the "modern" personality in this colonial society, is even more baffling as the self-proclaimed representative of Muslim separatism. Azad's account in *Ġhubār* suggests another possibility of reading his own particular trajectory: a "traditional" educational regime in the midst of the "modern" social conditions of the colonial metropolis, producing a distinct formation and "type" that is visibly "modern" in significant ways and yet not entirely subsumable under the hierarchies of colonial culture. Azad is therefore, in the end, an indeterminate figure in this social world—not a member of the traditional *ʿulamā*, properly speaking, and yet able to marshal religious authority of some significance; a militant journalist and writer, and yet, given his education and childhood formation, not entirely assimilable to the category of modern intellectual; a politician, clearly, and yet neither a sanctified populist (like Gandhi) nor a statesman of the *dirigiste* type (like Nehru). Thus his observation about Nehru muttering in English in his sleep, mischievous though it is, is far from casual and is, in fact, overcoded with significations. It contains the perception that the dreamworld of the most "advanced" forms of nationalist thought continues to be lived in "English," that is, in the Eurocentric imaginary of colonial culture, revealed here to the "vernacular" ear in an unselfconscious moment. Suggested here, ever so gently, and with an ironic sense of its vulnerabilities in colonial culture, is the possibility of a *vernacular* modernity, out of joint with the colonial world. What "vernacular" or "indigenous" might mean with reference to Azad is, of course, a question with its own significance, and I return to it later.

Critical at every stage in Azad's life is the relationship to the intellectual and political legacy of Syed Ahmed Khan's reformist Aligarh movement, as noted by Aijaz Ahmad in his long essay on Azad, which is one of the first important attempts to lay down systematically the basic problems of interpretation involved in an examination of the latter's long and, in many ways, perplexing and paradoxical career. The precise doctrinal position Azad's religious and political writings ultimately imply is itself an unresolved question, filled with ambiguities. In this, however, they reflect to varying degrees, perhaps more than any other oeuvre from the first half of the century, the entire *field* in which distinctly "Muslim" positions—pan-Islamism, British loyalism, Aligarh rationalism, scripturalist orthodoxy, Sufi mysticism of various sorts, Indian nationalism, Muslim separatism—are staked and produced. Azad's first expository writings—the journalism of *Lisān al-ṣidq* (The language of truth), for instance, which appeared in 1903, when Azad was about fifteen years old—are largely in tune with Aligarh rationalism and religious reform, in opposition, we may add, to the "customary" religiosity of the paternal home, but are also pan-Islamic, roughly along the lines of the Rashid Rida-Shibli Naumani axis. (As I have already noted, Syed Ahmed Khan spent much of his public career in the late nineteenth century convincing his British patrons that Indian Muslims rejected pan-Islamism, and hence loyalty to the Ottoman Sultan and Caliph, and wanted nothing more than to be *Indian* Muslims loyal to the colonial state.) The famous essay from 1910 on Sarmad the Martyr—the seventeenth-century Sufi saint, possibly of Jewish (and Irani or Armenian) origin, who was executed on the orders of the emperor Aurangzeb for heresy—is bathed, on the contrary, in ecstatic religiosity and the celebration of mystical Sufi transgression. Here Azad links himself explicitly to this other Islamic tradition, that of Sarmad and al-Hallaj, which takes rebellion to the borders of apostasy. (Three years earlier in Baghdad, the city of al-Hallaj's tenth-century execution on charges of heresy, Azad had met, as a fellow student of a *shaiḳh* associated with the shrine of the martyr, the Orientalist Louis Massignon, who was to become the leading modern interpreter of the life of al-Hallaj. Azad is buried a few yards away from Sarmad's mausoleum, near the foot of the main steps of the Jāmaʿ Masjid in Old Delhi.)[54] The writings of the *al-Hilāl* (The crescent) and *al-Balāġh* (The communiqué) period—that is, of the World War I years—mark another reversal, orthodox in religious terms and politically anti-Aligarh, rejecting the latter's political quietism and closeness to colonial officialdom. As before, pan-Islamism appears as an anti-British position, but now, as an extraterritorial, non-Indian affiliation it is in tension with Azad's explicit nationalism. The writings of the 1920s and 1930s, above all *Tarjumān al-Qur'ān* (Interpretation of the Qur'an), the monumental and unfinished translation and commentary—written fitfully during the 1920s and published in the early 1930s—begin an exploration of the basis for an *Islamic* argument for participation in Indian nationalism, which reaches an apogee of sorts in the Ramgarh address in 1940.[55] And in *Ġhubār-e ḳhāṭir*, Azad approaches a deism that Syed Ahmed Khan could never have imagined in his most *nēcharī* (naturistic) moments, to use the term of abuse flung at him by his Muslim critics, above all al-Afghani.[56] Furthermore, while the "political" is presumably "sifted" out from this work in order to stake out a private or interior space, this individual history of belief and taste is marked by a cultural cosmopolitanism that is inflected simultaneously in several civilizational registers—"Indian," "Islamic," even "Asian"—and has its own definite political implications.

The Unprovable Creed of India

In three of the letters in *Ġhubār* (nos. 6, 12, and 13), Azad describes his attempt to reconstruct "certainty" of belief ("yaqīn") out of the morass of doubt and despondency (*G*, 101). As a defense of the existence of God, it is no more, but also no less, interesting than any such attempt can be and represents an effort to bring this question out of the realm of *taqlīd* or customary belief and into that of *taḥqīq* or rational inquiry (*G*, 39). But I read this exploration of "certainty" not simply in religious terms but as an account of the possibilities of certainty and belief in social life as a whole and, more concretely, in the midst of the crisis in modern Indian life surrounding the question of the particularity of the Muslims. Azad points in two, at least seemingly contradictory directions: on the one hand, he approaches something like a conception of the godhead as the ultimate cause of the universe, and, on the other, points to the *human* need for belief in the existence of the supreme being as the ultimate goal of all human strivings (*G*, 116–117). What these conceptions evidently share is a sort of deistic belief in an absentee God, a natural religion at least on the verge of rejecting the legitimacy of revelation, and Azad is clearly influenced in his argument for the existence of God by his understanding of Victorian debates, his formulations recalling, for instance, the atheism debates between George Jacob Holyoake and his critics.[57] Azad, of course, does not take the final deistic step, in *Ġhubār-e ḳhāṭir* or elsewhere, and remained evasive whenever confronted with this possibility by orthodox Muslim interlocutors. However, the resolutions he offers to these contradictions in *Ġhubār* are significant from the perspective of the question of Islam's relationship to Hinduism as well as the problem of the relationship of the Muslims to Indian national identity.

Azad offers in a few pages in *Ġhubār* speculations on the history of religion that have as their basis a concept of the human need for a "personal" God of attributes which militates against all attempts to conceive of God in impersonal terms. Even Islam, which perhaps goes furthest in the depersonalization of God and forbids all comparison and representation, reverts repeatedly, in the Qur'an itself, to an accommodation with this human need, and "in some places even had to open windows of metaphor" as a means of approaching that which cannot be made subject to substitution (*G*, 122). In other words, Islam achieves for Azad a delicate balance between the affirmation of transcendence (*tanzīh*) and comparison (*tashbīh*) and thus immanence. The ultimate source of this formulation for Azad is Ibn al-Arabi, the twelfth- and thirteenth-century Andalusian Sufi master and one of the ultimate theosophical authorities in South Asian Islam.[58] In one remarkable passage, Azad not only compares but equates *waḥdat al-wujūd* ("the oneness of being," or "the oneness of that which is found"),[59] the most famous and influential concept of Ibn al-Arabi's theosophical system, with the philosophy of the Upanishads, an equation that is itself part of the history of Sufism in India: "India is the oldest source of the concept of *waḥdat al-wujūd* in the world" (*G*, 120). First of all, this specifically Islamic concept, that is, *waḥdat al-wujūd*, which is canonical to the development of Sufi thought and practice in the Middle Ages in the central Islamic lands as in India, is removed from that context per se, becoming a *general* term for theological monism. More specifically, in being equated with the philosophy of *advaita* (non-dualism), it marks an *opening up of the Islamic tradition to its Indian environment* and represents an attempt to move "Islam" (in India) towards an encounter with its supposed polytheistic other. Azad thus takes this concept from the early history of Sufism in India—that is, "*waḥdat al-wujūd* equals *advaita*"—which had emerged as a form of accommodation and mediation between Islamic and indigenous traditions in the medieval era, and attempts to make it available, in the mid-twentieth century, for an examination of the question of the identity of the Muslims in Indian modernity.[60] Nowhere is Azad in doubt about the existence of an "Islamic" textual tradition that crosses modern geopolitical borders, and that he takes as a given. But here he deploys the Islamic tradition and its concepts in a manner that facilitates the crossing of its own boundaries. Islamic neo-orthodoxy in late colonial India had repeatedly experienced its encounters with modern Hinduism—for instance, in the Arya Samaj's campaign for *shuddhī*, or reconversion to Hinduism, in the 1920s, or in recurring local conflicts that centered on the playing of Hindu devotional music in the vicinity of mosques[61]—as a fundamental crisis, in terms that sought to recall the founding narratives of Islam's emergence out of, and struggle with, seventh-century Arabian polytheism. Azad, who had himself been a significant contributor to the emergence of this neo-orthodoxy since the first decade of the century, never surrendered to that sense of panic, and in these pages in *Ġhubār*, he stages, with immeasurable delicacy and grace, the possibility of reframing that encounter. It is a gesture of putting the self in dialogue with the other and calls for and performs a crossing of the boundaries of tradition. Unlike with the most "advanced" forms of secularist thought, however, Azad's formulation views the "enlightened" crossing of the received boundaries of communal life as a trajectory that does not require an erasure from memory of its own point of origin.

It is significant to recall some of the debates about culture that dominated public life in the years immediately preceding Azad's imprisonment with his colleagues at Ahmednagar. As noted earlier, Gandhi played a major role in the mid- to late 1930s in reigniting the question of national language and the nature of Hindi and Urdu, causing a flurry of cultural activity and advocacy of Hindi both within and outside the Congress. And, in this same period, leaders of the Left in the party, Nehru among them, began to argue publicly that there was no such thing as Hindu or Muslim culture, only Indian. This was the case, for instance, with Kanwar Muhammad Ashraf, hand-picked by Nehru in 1937 to lead the ill-fated "mass contacts" program that was meant to bypass the Muslim League and directly mobilize the Muslim masses for the cause of the Congress.[62] Such public remarks received wide coverage in the Urdu press and inadvertently fueled the Muslim League's fire, its claim that the rule of the Congress in a sovereign, democratic, and centralized India would mean the ultimate dissolution of Muslim particularity. A distance separates Azad's conception, which does not seek to suppress the distinctness of cultural and religious affiliations in India even as it opens them up to a mutual articulation, from the Nehruvian resolution, in which, despite all the talk of unity in diversity, culture cannot but appear in the end as a single space marked by its *Indic* origins.

In his address to the Congress in Ramgarh in 1940, Azad was to insist on the composite and intersecting nature of the space of national culture:

> I am a Muslim, and feel it with pride that I am a Muslim. The glorious, thirteen-hundred-year-old traditions of Islam are part of my inheritance. I am not ready to allow even its smallest part to be wasted. Islamic education, Islamic history, Islamic arts and sciences, Islamic civilization, these constitute my wealth. And it is my duty to protect it. As a Muslim, I have a particular existence in the religious and cultural sphere. And I cannot tolerate that anyone interfere in it. But alongside all these feelings [iḥsāsāt], I have another feeling also, which has been produced by the realities of my life. The spirit of Islam does not stop me from it; it guides me in this direction. I feel it with pride that I am Indian [Hindustānī]. I am an element in the composite [*muttaḥida*], indivisible nationality of India. I am a significant element of its composite nationality, without which the figure of its greatness remains incomplete.[63]

To be an Indian Muslim was therefore to exist at the intersection of two great circles, neither one reducible to the other. Islam arrived in India as only the last of the numerous "caravans" whose destination India had been "fated" to become, and this arrival represented the "coming together of the streams of two different nations and civilizations." And while these streams, "like the Ganges and the Jamna," at first flowed apart, with time "they had to flow into each other." On the very day of that confluence, a "new India" began to be formed in place of the "old India," and after eleven hundred years, Islam had "the same claim on this land as Hinduism" (*G*, 298). The ways in which this narrative of the arrival of Islam in India differs from that provided by Nehru in *Discovery* are notable. The story of this "arrival" is told in the Ramgarh address from the perspective of the entity that "arrived." Also noteworthy is that conversion, the cornerstone of the Nehruvian account, is missing here entirely, with the Muslims as a whole figured as outsiders who settled on Indian soil and became naturalized. And instead of a narrative of the growing communalization of an originally syncretic and indistinguishable collective life, we are given an account of previously distinct entities gradually unmolding into one another. He thus speaks of the history of Islam and of Muslims in India in essentially the same terms, for instance, as those used in 1939 by Nadvi, who surely represented the opposite end of the spectrum regarding the question of Muslim identity and Indian nationalism: "Muslims, whether they came to this country from Arabia, or Turkistan and Khurasan, or Iran, or Afghanistan, on arriving here remained neither Arab, nor Turkish, nor Irani, nor Afghani, but became pure Hindustani."[64] Azad's historical narrative, in other words, is told from the perspective of the North Indian Muslim *ashrāf*, rather than from a generic nationalist position, and represents an argument for the "composite" and "unified" nature of Indian nationality from *within* the terms of *sharīf* culture, which proved so troublesome to the elaboration of nationalist claims to representation—assuming, contrary to Nehru, the integrity and autonomy of a distinct set of "Muslim" cultural claims, which form a necessary element in the composite that is "the new India."

In a letter in *Ġhubār* in which he discusses autobiographical and confessional narrative—what he calls "egotistic literature" (*G*, 179)—Azad speaks of the difficulties of the construction of the self in writing, placing his own text in distinguished and mixed company: Augustine, Rousseau, Strindberg, Anatole France, and Gide, on the one hand, and al-Ghazzali, ibn Khaldun, the Mughal emperors Babar and Jahangir, and Mulla Abdul Qadir Badayuni, on the other. What we encounter in these authors' confessional writings, he argues, is not unmediated access to the historical personage in question but rather a self produced in writing. What gains our attention is not the "spontaneous" self itself but rather the *composition* of the spontaneity of the self (*G*, 186). Such an understanding of representation, of course, brings into question the ontological status of the nationalist self itself, and the subject that emerges in and through the pages of *Ġhubār-e ḳhāṭir*—in its scholarly discourses, its little stories, and its faulty and fragmented recollections—is culturally and historically a complex figure that is not fully assimilable to what it means, in nationalist thought, to be an Indian in the normative sense.

Addressing the annual gathering of the All-India Congress Committee as its president in 1940, Azad had begun with an analysis of the political situation in India, and the world at large, in the aftermath of the declaration of India's entry into the war by the Viceroy on 3 September 1939. The question of the moment, he tells his audience, is whether India as a nation will participate fully in the global struggle against the fascist powers on the side of the Allies, including, of course, India's colonial rulers in Britain. It is a remarkable piece of political analysis that lays bare the contradictions of a war being fought in the name of "democracy, freedom, and world peace" that nevertheless assumes the *colonial* relation of Britain to India as a given (*K*, 276). Azad briefly summarizes the reasoning and internal debates that led the Congress to demand that the government clarify its reasons for going to war and its intentions regarding the political future of India. Its replies, he goes on, dashed any hope that the "old era" of domination was over. The viceroy's response, "the most comrehensive example of the exhausting prolixity of the official literature of the Government of India," made it clear that India's rulers, while calling upon Indians to throw themselves into the global war on the side of Britain under the banners of "democracy and freedom," had no intention of rethinking their own autocratic rule over India (*K*, 278). For four years the world had resonated with these cries: "But as soon as India raised this question [of national self-determination], the truth had to emerge unveiled. Now we are told that the freedom of nations is without doubt the goal of this fight, but its moves cannot extend beyond the geographical boundaries of Europe. The inhabitants of Asia and Africa should not have the courage to raise their eyes in hope" (*K*, 280). Furthermore, this "racial" limitation of the supposedly universal liberal principles was not British per se but European, and existed both outside and within European society: "[The British response] is representative of that face of the European continent that has been in front of the world for nearly two centuries. All the principles of individual and collective freedom that came to be recognized in the nineteenth and twentieth centuries—the right to claim them remained limited to the European nations alone, and even among the European nations, was never extended beyond the narrow circle of Christian Europe" (*K*, 281). The unmarked category in this remarkable last sentence, of course, is that of the Jews, with Azad linking the racism of colonial rule to the failure to grant full equality and emancipation to the Jews. Delivered in 1940, this speech can thus be linked to critiques of the liberal Enlightenment roughly contemporary to it in which the legacies of the eighteenth century are reexamined in the light of the twentieth-century catastrophe surrounding the Jewish minorities of the European nation-states.

But the main concern of the address was the "sectarian problem" in India itself and its relationship to India's political future (*K*, 286). The surest sign that British imperialism had not changed its old ways was that it was now using the Hindu-Muslim conflict—which its own policies had encouraged and exacerbated over the decades—as a roadblock to Indian self-determination. This second half of the address is a brief but remarkable testament of Muslim participation in the national struggle, laying out with stunning clarity the complexity of the relationship of Azad's thought to Indian nationalism—the discursive universe in which it moves but to which it does not fully belong. While Azad repeatedly speaks, in the settled lingua franca of the Congress, of "shared" (*mushtarika*), and "composite" or "unified" (*muttaḥida*) nationality, this is not his most significant contribution here to the discourse on national identity (*K*, 291, 297, passim). For, unlike Nehru—to whom, despite his sincere attention to the problem of Muslim separatism, it cannot but appear as spurious and a form of false consciousness—Azad not only does not deny the fundamental reality of the conflict but, instead, makes its resolution "the primary condition for the realization of India's national goal," that is, independence from colonial rule (*K*, 288). To the question whether the Muslims of India constitute a minority Azad offers a complex answer: "Nothing in India's political problems has been misunderstood to such a degree as that the status of Muslims in India is that of a political minority, and that therefore they should be fearful concerning their rights and interests in a democratic India. This one foundational error has opened the door to numerous other errors. And walls have begun to be raised on top of these faulty foundations" (*K*, 291). Muslim separatism is a house built on the faulty foundations of *fear*, namely, the apprehension that Muslims in a free and democratic India would be a vulnerable minority and that *svarāj* (self-rule, the call of the nationalist movement), as the Muslim Leaguers never tired of repeating, would mean "Hindu raj." For Azad, a politics based on fear could not possibly lead to anything constructive and would only result in the most profound degradation of that—a collective Muslim life in India—whose dissolution had been feared.

Underlying this "fear," for Azad, is the very meaning and usage of the term "minority," and having rehearsed the principles underlying the Congress's constitutional efforts for the resolution of the minorities question, Azad raises this more fundamental issue:

> In political speech, when the word "minority" [*aqalliyat*] is used, it does not mean that any group of human individuals that, according to a

> simple arithmetical formula, is fewer in number than another such group is necessarily a "minority" and ought to be concerned about its security. Rather, what is meant by the term is a *weaker* group [*kamzōr jamāʿat*] that, in terms both of number and ability, does not find itself able to live alongside a larger and powerful group and feel confident in its own ability to defend itself.... Alongside quantity [*taʿdād*], it is also a question of *quality* [*nauʾīyyat*]... Therefore, in order for there to be a minority, together with the relative difference of number, the presence of other factors is also required. (*K*, 292; emphases added)

The "quality" of the social and political situation of the Muslims in India utterly precludes the non-quantitative "factors" that define a social group as a minority; they constitute instead a "vast," or "great," social group ("*ʿaẓīm gurōh*") about which it cannot even be imagined that it suffers from those social disabilities or "weaknesses" that we associate with the experience of minorities (*K*, 292). The Muslims are, first of all, a significant presence in all the regions of the country and constitute a majority in four—five, if the territory of Baluchistan is counted—of the eleven provinces of British India, with the non-Muslim populations within them in the position of minority. For Azad, the politics of the Muslim League, motivated as it is by the fear of minoritization, ignores the social *strength* of Muslim polity on an all-India scale. The larger significance of Azad's elaboration of the Muslim question here is the implicit recognition that, no matter how much the nation-state—the sovereign and democratic, future India of the Congress's constitutional imagination—attempts to reduce the heterogeneity of the polity to the supposedly disinterested, number principle of democratic society, the terms "minority" and "majority" designate *relative alignments of force structuring the social imaginary* rather than merely the logic of relative quantities. In sum, instead of merely repeating the nationalist claim to represent, in the full sense, all of society, Azad seems to be calling upon "the Muslims" for a *willed suspension of disbelief* in this claim. As in his discourse on the existence of God, where, after a point, reasoned arguments reach their limit and all that remains is the mystical light of "illumination and enlightenment" ("*kashf o mushāhida*"), here, too, he calls for a leap of faith in an ultimately unprovable creed (*G*, 129). *This* leap of faith marks the *secularism* of Azad's public life, conducted though it is in the terms of the *doxa*, the debates, and the tensions and contradictions of a single religious tradition.

In the immediate aftermath of India's Partition, which, of all the leading Congress leaders, he alone had courageously refused to go along with, Azad returned in another address to this theme of what it meant to be minoritized, this time not in abstract or even political terms but rather in terms of the phenomenology, the concrete experience, of the event of Partition. The address was delivered in Delhi on 24 October 1947, and its location itself is significant and places the address within a frame of historical meanings: it was delivered as a *khuṭba* or sermon to a Friday congregation at Shahjahan's Jāmaʿ Masjid in the old city, a particularly resonant symbol of the spiritual and intellectual life of the Muslim *ashrāf* of North India, surrounded by a thousand landmarks of Indo-Muslim history from the course of centuries, a history capped by the Partition massacres and the desperate flight of thousands from their ancestral homes. It is this atmosphere in which Azad's text explicitly places itself and takes as its starting point to look back at the entire history of Islam in India. These five or six pages of transcribed speech constitute one of the most remarkable texts of India's Partition, on a par in literary terms with the greatest works of Partition literature and utterly different in style and voice from anything Azad himself had ever written. Azad establishes the voice and relation of addressor to addressee early on. The elaborately staged, formal politesse of his usual oratorical style is abandoned, as he addresses his audience in the second-person singular/informal "tum" rather than the plural/formal "āp," thus assuming an informal and personal tone, as if a family elder were admonishing its younger and wayward members for the destruction their own actions have wrought on themselves, and on the family as a whole. This alone marks a complete departure from the tone of the Ramgarh address:

> Today, when I see the agitation in your eyes and the desolation of your hearts, I suddenly recall all the forgotten stories of the last few years. Do you remember? I had called out to you, and you cut my tongue off; I raised my pen [*qalam*], and you cut off [*qalam*] my hands; I tried to walk ahead, but you chopped off my feet; I tried to turn around and you broke my back; when the bitter politics of the past seven years, which have now abandoned you, were still in their infancy, I shook you on the road to peril, but you not only ignored my call, you renewed all the traditions [*sunnatēñ*, as in "traditions of the Prophet"] of forgetfulness [*ġhaflat*] and denial [*inkār*]. The result is well known, that today those very dangers have surrounded you whose fear had led you far away from the Straight Path [*ṣirāṭ-e mustaqīm*]. (*K*, 337)

The last sentences bring an Islamic vocabulary to the critique of the politics of Muslim separatism, which are reframed here as the forgetting and even outright rejection of the righteous "message" or call. This (Indian Muslim) failure to answer, and take up, the call is itself part of a *sunnah*, a counter-tradition of sorts, in a line of descent from those who had denied the prophethood of Muhammad. The righteous call here is, of course, to national struggle, the invitation to reconstitute society in the act of opposing colonial rule, and those who denied or rejected it have renewed that older tradition of imperviousness to the righteous call. The denier or *munkir* is a stock figure of the everyday pedagogy of Islam in South Asia, a sign of the perverse recalcitrance of the human substance when presented with the means to its own salvation, and therefore the sign of a kind of transcendental failure of humanity. Azad's formulation historicizes that figure and redefines precisely those Indian Muslims who claim to have acted in the political realm in the name of their Muslimness as those who cannot recognize the Truth. The sermon appears to level this charge at the Indian Muslim community as a whole, which failed repeatedly to answer the speaker's call, fashioning for itself, instead, "idols" to follow and worship, but by which they have now been abandoned (*K*, 338).

In other words, the context as well as the subject of Azad's sermon is the devastating failure of Muslim politics in the modern era, the failed participation of the Muslims as a community in India's political modernity. The history of that effort, which may be said to have begun in the aftermath of the uprisings of 1857, is evoked here in strangely condensed form:

> There was a time . . . when I called out to you and said . . . that political revolution has been written into India's fate and its chains of enslavement are about to fall off in the air of freedom in the twentieth century; [that] if you fail to march in step with the times and continue to make this present life of delay your practice and your mark, the historian of the future will write that your community, which was a mass of seventy million human beings, adopted an attitude towards the country's independence that is the mark of nations about to be erased from history. (*K*, 338–339)

The politics of Muslim separatism, which had emerged first in those early decades as a divisive force in Indian politics and culture, had led to the catastrophic division of the country, including the division of the Muslim population itself, to a massive outbreak of fear and violence, and the uprooting of millions of human beings. It was precisely the politics that had insisted on the Muslims being a nation and not a minority that had acquiesced in the minoritization of the Muslims in India. Only a few years ago, Azad tells his audience, he had told them that the "two nation theory" would prove "fatal" for "the meaningful life." But the "supports" they had instead relied upon had now abandoned them to fate, like so many "orphans" (*K*, 338). It was fear that had driven this politics, and fear that was now driving them to abandon their ancestral homes for a supposed homeland across the border. For Azad, therefore, Muslim separatism was *a politics of fear* and thus doomed from the start to fail to produce creative possibilities for collective Muslim participation in modern life. As in the Ramgarh address, Azad counters this fear with a call to *himmat* (determination, strength of will), a common enough word in Urdu with secular and everyday significations but resonant nevertheless with religious meanings, especially pertaining to the Sufi disciplines and the "high spiritual ambition" or "power" that protects the true believers on the road to oneness with God.[65] But whereas at Ramgarh Azad had called for *himmat* in a willed suspension of disbelief in the nationalist claim to representation, a suspension that was possible, he had noted, because the Muslims did not constitute a vulnerable minority in Indian polity, the term now pertained to facing the fear and vulnerability inherent in the new minoritization in India: "Look, the tall minarets of the mosque are eagerly asking, where have you misplaced the pages of your history? It was only yesterday that your caravans performed their ablutions on the bank of the Jamuna. And today here you are, afraid of remaining in Delhi, although it has long been irrigated [*sēñchī ga'ī*] with your blood" (*K*, 340). If the divisive politics of the Muslim League had been a form of escape from the changed political realities of modern India, that escapism was now being concretized in the flight of Muslims from their homes. Azad offers a scathing critique of the so-called exchange of populations, refusing to attribute religious motives to the supposedly voluntary departure of Muslims to Pakistan, and mocks the use of the term *hijrat*—"the sacred name of *hijrat*" (*K*, 340)—to describe this migration, movement, or displacement. This invocation of *hijrat*, one of the most resonant political concepts in Islam, with its more specific history in Indian Muslim culture since the nineteenth century is a complex set of significations, and marks a kind of departure from Azad's own earlier stand on *hijrat* from British India, therefore deserving a closer look at this point.

The word *hijrat* (usually transliterated *hijrah* from the Arabic), which may be translated as "departure," "exit," "emigration," or "exodus," and which is the term used to designate the emigration of Muhammad and his followers in 622 CE from Mecca, where they had constituted an oppressed sect, to Medina (then Yathrib), where they became an established religious community, was appropriated in Urdu at the Partition of India for the mass movement of populations that accompanied it, specifically the displacement of Muslims from the Urdu-Hindi heartland to the territories that became Pakistan. In purely semantic terms, therefore, it would not be incorrect to say that this usage sought to lend to the latter historical experience an epic, even sacred, quality. This is not, historically, a unique appropriation, as the same word and concept is used in Turkish, for example, for the displacement of ethnic Turks and Muslims from the Ottoman lands that became part of Greece in the years following the Turkish defeat in World War I.[66] It is also part of a longer history of usage in modern Indian history itself, a distinctly colonial history extending back at least to the *fatāwā* or legal judgments of Shah Abdul Aziz of the first years of the nineteenth century declaring British India to be *dār al-ḥarb* ("abode of war").[67] In the *jihādī* movements that emerged in North India in the subsequent decades—Syed Ahmed Barelvi's followers in the northwestern regions and the Farā'izī movement in Bengal—the possibility of *hijrat* with a view to returning some day to do battle against the infidel rulers (Hindus, Sikhs, or British Christians) played a distinct and important role. As a concept in Islamic disputation, *hijrah*—the injunction to physical movement away from a zone of non-belief in which Islam is under threat—is closely related to the concept of *jihād*—the injunction to do battle, even with physical means, against a power that is a threat to Islam. It is thus a legal, *sharīʿa*-related concept, although Sufi thought has sometimes spoken of internal or spiritual emigration, a withdrawal into the self. Still, it remains a nebulous and largely contingent concept open to widely divergent interpretations in specific historical conjunctures, and, as Muhammad Khalid Masud has noted, although discussions of *hijrah* are "frequent in *fatāwā* literature, which consists of responses to particular situations, they are scattered throughout the regular books of Islamic law rather then grouped together under the heading of emigration."[68] The legal judgments concerning emigration typically consider such questions as whether it is voluntary or obligatory and under what conditions is it one or the other, and, above all, what conditions in the world bring it into play at all. According to the model provided by the original *hijrah* of Islam, to undertake such displacement is to break all bonds with one's community of origin, including kinship ties, in order to create a new social order in which an Islamic communal life becomes (perhaps once again) possible.[69] This notion of a new beginning unburdened by the past, inherent as a defining element in the discourse of *hijrah*, became subject in the Partition "*hijrat*," as I attempt to demonstrate in a later chapter regarding the poetry of Faiz Ahmed Faiz, to an entire dialectic of memory and forgetting that constitutes one of the modalities of Partition into our own times.

The charged political atmosphere in which the Khilafat movement emerged was rife with talk of *hijrat* and *jihād*, with the emigration to Afghanistan of Ubaid Allah Sindhi and his small group of followers in 1915 providing a concrete example for Muslims to follow. The long and slow death of the Ottoman Empire and Caliphate in the second decade of the twentieth century, including such events as the Libyan campaign and the Balkan wars, produced in India an explosive political situation, which led eventually to the campaign for the defense of the Caliphate ("ḳhilāfat" in Urdu), the first mass political campaign against the British in India, which also led directly to the first mass mobilization of the Congress under Gandhi in the movement for "Non-Cooperation." During the Khilafat agitation itself, the option of *hijrat* was openly discussed by the leadership, with the Ali brothers taking an early lead in this regard.[70] Azad himself repeatedly explored these inter-related themes—*dār al-ḥarb* and *dār al-Islām*, *jihād* and *hijrat*—declaring in front of a Khilafat gathering in Agra in 1921, for instance, that the British had become, in Islamic legal terms (*az rū'-e sharī'at*) an "enemy at war" (*farīq-e muḥārib*) to the Muslims of India and, in fact, of the world (*K*, 48–49). In April or May 1920 he even went so far as to issue a *fatwā* calling for consideration of the *hijrat* option, while stressing that it would not be incumbent on *all* Muslims in British India to migrate. (What would that have looked like?) In the summer of 1920 events took an unexpected turn with the explosion onto the scene of a popular movement for emigration to Afghanistan, which took the Khilafat leadership by surprise. This campaign was emboldened by Azad's *fatwā* and by official Afghan encouragement, whose real function seems to have been as a bargaining chip in negotiations with the British following the Third Anglo-Afghan War of 1919. In the chaos of the ensuing events, thousands perished in the course of the arduous journey, attempted for the most part on foot, and tens of thousands more were reduced to penury, having disposed of their worldly belongings before undertaking the *hijrat*.[71] It was among the more bizarre episodes of the Khilafat agitation, a movement not exactly short on bizarre episodes.

Even in the midst of the *hijrat* fever in the early 1920s, Azad had spoken of the possibility of Hindu-Muslim unity as an *Islamic* duty, citing the precedent of the Prophet's alliances and establishment of peace with "the residents of Medina and idol worshipers" ("ahl-e Madīna aur but-parast lōgōñ sē muṣāliḥat") (*K*, 51). Over the next two decades he developed and refined this strategy, above all in the commentary on the first chapter of the Qur'an in his *Tarjumān*. Now, in 1947, he spoke against the turn of events that had made Indian *independence* the occasion for a mass exodus of Muslims. To *this* search for a homeland outside the home, Azad opposed his own life, which had always been one of "exile" ("*ġharīb al-vaṭanī*"), he wrote, even when "living in the homeland" ("*vaṭan*") (*K*, 338). It is a deeply revealing formulation, one that describes many aspects of Azad's life and career: his, as it were, eighteenth-century upbringing in late-nineteenth- and early-twentieth-century Calcutta; his relationship to mainstream "Muslim" politics in the decades following the collapse of the Khilafat movement in the early 1920s; his place within Indian nationalism itself as the field of politics became increasingly polarized along communal lines; and the very notion of tradition that is assumed in his elaboration of the "Muslim" element in a composite or shared Indian nationality. The peculiarity of political development of the *ashrāf* as a distinct class in modern Indian society—their historic refusal as a numerical minority to accept minority status in society—has stamped, perhaps irrevocably, their image in history. Large numbers of these *ashrāf* of "Hindustan"—that is, principally the regions now consisting of Delhi, Uttar Pradesh, Bihar, Rajasthan, and Madhya Pradesh—whose survivors and descendants comprise a majority of the urban population of Sind in Pakistan—moved at Partition from one part of India to another, where it became possible to belong to a newly emerging polity where they would not be constituted as a minority. I am speaking here not of motives, desires, and external compulsions as they applied to individual persons and families, for which there can be no generalization, but of the larger narrative within which this historic upheaval has come to be placed and comprehended. What we glimpse so powerfully in the life and work of Azad, however, is that there always were counter-possibilities within *sharīf* culture itself. Azad's work took shape within, and was addressed to, this very class and its culture—in its conception of an Islamic tradition and a global Islamic *'umma*, its elaboration of the cosmopolitan and essentially non-national cultural affiliations of the Indian Muslims, and its narratives of the "arrival" and naturalization of Muslims in India—and was effectively an appeal to it to have the *dignity* to not be afraid of becoming a minority.

In what are perhaps the most moving passages in *Ġhubār-e k͟hāṭir*, spread out over two letters, Azad describes his developing relationship with a group of sparrows that had taken up residence in the nooks and crannies between the ceiling and beams of his barracks room. Here Azad creates an elaborate allegory of conflict and coexistence, developing in detail, by their displacement onto his interactions with these birds, such themes as overcoming fear of the other, the fitful and piecemeal nature of all such endeavors, and the imperative and possibilities for adjusting to the presence of the other and sharing an existence with it. These passages represent nothing short of a distillation of the ethics implicit in Azad's great and complex political career, and here the possibility of coexistence is elaborated in fully secular terms, without recourse to an explicitly religious vocabulary. They are perhaps the purest instance of the strategies of displacement that characterize Azad's exploration of "political" issues in *Ġhubār*. Read allegorically—and Azad refers to the tale at one point as "this 'Conference of the Birds,'" recalling the twelfth-century Sufi allegory by the great Persian poet and mystic, Fariduddin Attar (Farīd al-Din ʿAṭṭār)—they reveal the utter human poverty of the politics of separatism and communalism, and constitute perhaps one of the most far-reaching critiques of these corrosive tendencies in

India's modern life (*G*, 222).[72] At the same time, I would argue, they also contain the elements of a critique of the *implicit majoritarianism* of "secular" nationalism itself and its failure ultimately to produce a convincing *ethico*-political practice of coexistence in an undivided India.

A "Conference of the Birds": Towards an Ethics of Coexistence

Azad begins his tale with an account of the unexpected "invasion" of the sparrows into his room one day and their infringement on the patterns of his daily life—his bed and "washing table," as well as the floor of the room, are covered with the debris of their "constructions" overhead. The language here is entirely that of human warfare, with a mock-heroic tone produced by the highly Persianate terminology—the birds, for instance, are spoken of as "my adversary" (*mērā ḥarīf*) "the enemy" (*dushman*), and "the enemies' forces" (*dushman kī fauj*). Faced with this unprovoked invasion by the strangers, the person whose home has been invaded tries to tolerate the intrusion and is "patient for a few days," but finally his "tolerance" gives way, and he is "forced to conclude that there was no alternative to a fight." There is something enormously touching about the images evoked here—this venerable *maulānā* in his mid-fifties, a figure clad in his characteristic *kurtā-pājāma* and long-coat or *achkan*, chasing after the flock of birds, first with an umbrella and then with a tall bamboo staff: "Please do not ask what manner of engagement ensued in the field of battle [*maidān-e kārzār*]. All around the room, the adversary was in circumambulation [*ṭavāf*] and I, bamboo in hand, was running madly behind it." The immediate result of this counterattack is an apparent victory, with the birds chased out, and the room reclaimed, but shortly after the cessation of hostilities, and while the victor has become engrossed once again in his writing, the defeated return and reestablish themselves in every cranny of the ceiling. The result is a renewed engagement, and this time the birds are chased "far beyond the border" (*sarhad*), out of the verandah where their "forces" had begun to "regroup" anew. This time the victory seems decisive, but when the chronicler of these events, "not entirely free from anxieties for the future," returns from lunch a little later, the gains of battle have been entirely reversed, and the adversary is found to be "in occupation of the entire room." On being confronted in this way with the fate of his "illusory victories," the supposed victor is forced finally to realize that, "while it is easy to bring the adversary low momentarily, it is not easy to defeat its passionate desire to continue to remain in place" (*jōsh-e istiqāmat*). The only way left for him is therefore to "adopt such behaviors [*rasm o rāh*] that it becomes possible to live in one home with these uninvited guests" (*G*, 212, 213).

The rest of the letter is a detailed allegory of these movements and adjustments, a series of suggestions about how to adjust to the other's presence once the option of outright "war," of wiping out the other, has been ruled out. From a condition of conflict and warfare, it is possible, we are gradually led to understand, to achieve not only truce, but coexistence, even "love." The first change that occurs once the paradigm has shifted from war to the possibility of coexistence is at the level of language itself—the other is now referred to not as "enemy" or "adversary" but instead as "neighbor," even "guest." Azad is commenting here on the importance of generosity *in language*, on language as a terrain for the accommodation of a possible approach to, and of, the other. He began, Azad writes, by moving the furniture around so as to minimize the disruption of his life by the birds' activities, even though this meant aesthetic disfigurement of the room, and the small objects of his toilette that were exposed to the falling debris were covered up with new dust-cloths purchased for him in town by the prison authorities. These adjustments having been made, the next stage in the process of reconciliation is reached when, one day, "it occurred [to me] that if a truce has been reached, it should be a complete truce. It is not right to be living in the same home, but like strangers" (*G*, 214). A complex dance thus begins that centers around the offering of food—grains of uncooked rice—to the birds. At first Azad scatters the grains randomly over the floor, but subsequent offerings are placed in the lid of a tin can and brought progressively closer to the physical presence of the "host." It is a gradual and fitful process, consisting of discrete and distinct steps or stages, each one representing a partial overcoming of fears and distances that marked the previous one. This narrative of discrete steps recalls, first of all, the Sufi conception of the stations (*maqāmāt*) on "the Path" to *tauḥīd*, or confession, of the oneness of God. But a more interesting feature of this mutual dance between the "birds" and the narrator of the tale is the way this mutual approach and disarming is made possible by indirectness and dissembling, with the man feigning disinterest in the approach of the birds, and the birds, it seems to him, feigning disinterest in his offerings of food, as they circle, re-circle, and bypass it many times before their final approach. Repeatedly Azad speaks of turning himself to "stone" to facilitate this approach, until the birds come to treat him at least partly as an inevitable and inert feature of their environment, occasionally resting on his knees and shoulders but hurriedly flying away at the slightest movement or sound he makes, saying to themselves, as he imagines it, that "there is a piece of stone lying on this sofa, but from time to time it becomes a man" (*G*, 221). Thus the way to facilitate the approach of a distant, unexpected, and unknown other is to undertake a series of self-adjustments, to transform oneself, even to the point of turning oneself to "stone," that is, suppressing one's subjectivity in order to present oneself to the other as *object* of *its* projects and desires. But this self-presentation is, of course, a form of dissembling and therefore represents only a partial and momentary surrender of subjectivity, and one that has the positive result of making possible a passage from "remoteness to nearness" (*buʿd sē qarb*) and hence the possibility genuinely of sharing a social space with the other (*G*, 219). Second, this is a gradual and fitful process that moves in a series of discrete stages. Thus the remoteness of the other cannot be canceled out in a single moment or action, once and for all, in advance of the painstaking process of building forms of communication but rather only through this interaction itself. That the communication does not necessarily lead to transparency and a complete understanding of the other, moreover, does not mean that it cannot facilitate a form of coexistence.

That these allegorical elements resonate with something like an ethical critique of separatism should be clear. In order to live "in the same house," it will not do to demand that one's fear of the other, of its strength and intentions, be put to rest once and for all and before one agrees to enter the (social) process of sharing that space. Only by entering the social process can the fear be addressed—gradually, piecemeal, and with patience. There is no transcendental resolution here, only the prospect of the gradual emergence of trust and the managing of fear. On the other hand, however, the allegory may be read as an account of the measures that *the larger, more powerful being* must undertake in order to allay the fears of that smaller, less powerful creature which it can momentarily force to flee but whose existence it cannot suppress forever. In other words, the allegory is about the relative alignment of force that structures the life of society into majority and minority domains, and the adjustments called for from the majority in order to achieve an ethical practice of coexistence.

It might appear at first that there are some convergences here with the ethics that Emmanuel Levinas would begin to develop in the years following the Second World War. As in Levinas, the ethics implicit in the allegory of the birds implies an initial act of generosity, of opening to the other, as a precondition for the emergence of the social, for the possibility of "living in the same house," as the tale has it. In both instances, furthermore, the bridging of the distance separating the two beings does not imply or require their mutual surrender of autonomy. Hence, in the bird allegory, the "man" who has turned to "stone" is free to return to his normal impulses, letting a sigh of pleasure escape on recalling an apposite verse of poetry (*G*, 221), and the birds, now uncertain about the nature of that which they have approached, can momentarily fly away. As with Levinas, the possibility of sharing a social space here is not predicated on the sublation of their discrete locations in a global perspective. That global vantage for nationalist thought is, of course, the nation itself, with its "Indic" genealogy, and we have already seen the manner in which Azad seeks to displace its cultural, temporal, and historical categories. In Azad's text, contrary to Levinas, the political is not emptied out into the ethical. Ethical thinking is elaborated not in metaphysical terms, but on the ground of history, in terms of the process of the nationalization of society. If Levinasian thought emerges as an *ethical* critique of totalization and its moral failures in the wake of the European genocide, Azad's allegory, composed four years before the communal holocaust that was to shake the subcontinent, is a *politico*-ethical critique of the escalations and political failures that were hurtling society toward its own disintegration. But these striking parallels—despite vast distances of politics, culture, history, and philosophical tradition and vocabulary—raise the question of the *contemporaneity*, in a sense other than the merely chronological, of the conclusion of the Jewish Question on the continent of Europe—genocidal annihilation followed by "national" resettlement in Palestine—and the supposed resolution of the crisis of Muslim identity on the Indian subcontinent—massive uprooting of populations and the partition of territory, accomplished in the midst, and through the modality, of a social cataclysm of holocaust proportions. The history of Zionism and Indian Muslim separatism unfolded over almost precisely the same period of time, that is, the first half of the twentieth century, and of course the establishment of the (European) Jewish state and the creation of the (Indian) Muslim state occurred less than a year apart in its fifth decade, both through massive transfers of population and the partitioning of territories in the process of their abandonment by the British Empire. But these are contemporaneous developments in another, more important sense as well. They are both signs of a crisis in the nation-state system at a specific moment in its history. They mark the inability of the modern system of nation-states to complete the nationalization of society except through its violent reorganization: breakdown of communities, massacres and transfer of populations, in the one instance, and, in the other, dispersal and industrialized genocide followed by resettlement in a distant and violently appropriated land and the displacement of its own indigenous inhabitants.

Azad's formulation of the Muslim question in his writings of the last years before the end of colonial rule—their narratives of Indo-Muslim history, their performance of extraterritorial, extra-Indic cultural affiliations, their elaboration of an Urdu idiom at odds with notions of the national-popular, their conception of a distinctly Muslim presence in Indian society, and their very resistance to the minoritization of Muslim identity—must be seen as having emerged, as I argue, from within the terms of the culture of the *ashrāf*. The difference between Azad's position here and the position taken by the Muslim League and Jinnah in his final years does not reside in accepting the nationalist equation of Muslims with minority. Both Azad's formulation and Jinnah's two-nation theory, which attempted to resolve and give political form to the historical ambivalence, the reluctant embourgoisement, of *ashrāf* culture, represent attempts to find a basis other than minority for the participation of Muslims in the life of modern India. The difference between them lies in Azad's assertion that if the Muslims did not constitute a minority in Indian society, they could and ought to take the risk of suspending disbelief in the national idea. This introduction of the thematics of power, fear, and uncertain action, that is, of an *ethics* of coexistence, into the *political* domain, even more than his distinctly Islamic polemics for a nationalist politics, marks the originality of Azad as a public and political figure and constitutes the *secularism* of the life's work of this devout and religiously learned person. The significance that Mushirul Hasan perceived in the contrast between Azad's forgotten little mausoleum amidst the decaying monuments of Old Delhi and that of Jinnah in Karachi, itself an enormous and triumphalist monument to the life history of the Muslim nation-state, may now be spelled out more precisely: this difference marks the fragility of the ethical demand when confronted with the political language of nation-statehood. It is Azad's accomplishment to have placed this ethico-political question, with all its complexity and vulnerability, before a society precisely in the decades of its most violent rearrangement into a system of nation-states.

CHAPTER FOUR

Saadat Hasan Manto

A GREATER STORY WRITER THAN GOD

When Saadat Hasan Manto died in 1955 at the age of forty-three, from liver ailments caused by years of excessive drinking, he reportedly left behind an epitaph he had written for himself: "Here lies Saadat Hasan Manto. With him lie buried all the arts and mysteries of short story writing. Under tons of earth he lies, wondering if he is a greater short story writer than God."[1] At the time he was firmly established as one of the greatest practitioners of the Urdu *afsāna* or short story form, but was also considered an *enfant terrible*, with a reputation for zealous drinking and carousing in the urban demi-monde. He was widely criticized within the literary world and beyond for relatively explicit handling of sex in his stories and had been tried several times, by both colonial and post-colonial governments, for violating obscenity laws. And he had been hounded out of the All-India Progressive Writers' Association (AIPWA), the umbrella organization of nationalist writers founded in 1936, which had initially welcomed him as a patriotic and committed writer. At the time of his death his connections to the association had long been severed, his erstwhile friends now accusing him of having abandoned realism, of being obsessed with abnormal personality and the morbid.[2] He had barely survived the Partition of India in 1947, both physically and artistically, suffering a paralyzing breakdown on his arrival in the now Pakistani city of Lahore from Bombay, where he had spent much of his artistic life associated in one way or another with the Hindustani film industry. The Partition and its aftermath became an obsessive theme in his later writing, and his stories of this period are widely considered among the most forceful accounts of the trauma of India's national fragmentation. It is often for these that he is most remembered.

Given this enormous historical density to Manto's life and career, how may we begin to unpack the semantic baggage of his self-chosen epitaph in a register other than the biographical? What are the arts and mysteries of short story writing? What is this debris under which they lie buried? Who is Manto? Who or what is God? To mock God and his Creation is, of course, to invoke the powers of the demonic. Irony itself, as Lukács once noted, is inherently demonic. For the novel form, which Lukács considered "the epic of a world that has been abandoned by God," irony consists in "the freedom of the writer in his relationship to God, the transcendental condition of the objectivity of form-giving." In turning to irony, modern subjectivity achieves, Lukács writes, the highest freedom that one can achieve in a Godless world. To be possessed of a demon is to "overreach [oneself] in ways that have no reason and cannot be explained by reason, challenging all the psychological or sociological foundations of [one's] existence."[3] Manto's ironic epitaph is first a commentary on the type of form-giving that is the Urdu *afsāna* or short story, this concrete modern bid to give subjective "freedom" a form. It is an invitation to consider the nature of the "transcendental condition of the objectivity of [this] form-giving" and of the specific freedom to which it gives form. But Manto's epitaph gives this modern bid at freedom a further twist. For it is directed not so much at the existence of God as at God's epic ambitions: the possibility that Manto's stories might well be "greater" than God's also implies that the stories of which God is author are indeed "short" ones. It is not a disavowal of the "transcendental conditions" that "God" represents but rather their immanent interrogation.

I suggest that we read in the epitaph Manto's ironic relationship to the culture of Indian nationalism, particularly the bourgeois universalism of its "moment of arrival," which Partha Chatterjee has associated with the figure and the influence of Jawaharlal Nehru. This chapter is concerned in part with Manto's relationship to the "Progressive" literary culture of this Nehruvian moment. I argued at some length in earlier chapters that the figure of the Muslim poses unique problems for the Nehruvian discourse concerning the emergence of a secular Indian consciousness. It seeks to contain the crisis of cultural difference at the heart of the national community by translating the problem of "Muslim" difference into the problematic of a minority culture and history. I suggest here that we read Manto's entire oeuvre as a series of literary attempts to dislodge, from within, the terms of the attempted nationalist resolution of the question of collective selfhood and belonging. Manto's ironic epitaph makes explicit what is already implicit in his practice of the short story form: an immanent critique of nationalism's divine ambitions, of its claim to a God-like perch above society. Manto turns the Urdu short story—itself a "minor" genre that is made to do the work in Urdu, as I argue shortly, of a "major" one—into a means of dislodging the resolutions of that nationalism from within and renders an account of national modernity inscribed not with affirmations of identity and subjectivity but with displacement and difference.

It is as part of such a move, I argue later, that we should read the proliferation in Manto's fiction of a figure that has been at the center of the controversies surrounding his work: the subaltern urban figure of prostitute. I read this figure as Manto's reinscription of what, to borrow Sandhya Shetty's words, is a conventional and tenacious "moment in the Indian nationalist discourse's production of woman: the allegorical figuration of the nation as mother."[4] "Motherness," Salman Rushdie writes in his characteristic fashion in *The Moor's Last Sigh*, "is a big idea in India, maybe our biggest: the land as mother, the mother as land, as the firm ground beneath our feet.... I'm talking *major* mother country."[5] Manto's stories offer an ironic rewriting of this pervasive familial (and atemporal) semiotic of nationalism that makes it available for a historical interrogation. At the same time Manto's impoverished and exploited prostitutes displace the high cultural figure of the courtesan (*ṭavā'if*) through which narratives of a distinct "Muslim" cultural experience have so often been mediated in modern Indian culture. At least since the publication and progressively pan-Indian reception and success of Mirza Muhammad Hadi Rusva's novel *Umrā'ō Jān Adā* (1899), the figure of the Muslim courtesan has been a stock figure of the Indian national imaginary, a means to signifying the distinctness of a "Muslim" presence within the space of national culture. If nationalism's mobilization of motherhood as a metaphor for national belonging has a history as long as nationalism itself—from its early canonization in Bankimchandra Chatterjee's novel *Ānandamaṭh* (1882), through the utilization of the mother as sign in such national mobilizations as cow protection campaigns, in the massive public discourse produced in response to Katherine Mayo's *Mother India* (1927), and Nehru's invocation in *Discovery of India* of the sign "Bharat Mata" as the means through which the rationalist and secular nationalist intellectual may communicate with the peasant masses, to such moments of post-independence nationalist culture as Mehboob's classic film "Mother India" (1955) and Congress politics under Indira Gandhi[6]—then the relation of Muslim as minority to national culture is posed in terms of an organization of affect whose characteristic figure is that classic figure of duplicity, the courtesan. (In postcolonial popular culture, the so-called Muslim social genre of Bombay cinema is perhaps the most familiar instance of this articulation.)[7] A number of important studies in recent years have critically examined the gendered semiotics and sociology of the formation of nationalist identity in colonial India, but these have largely confined themselves to an analysis of the instability of the mother signifier itself. The almost exclusive focus on a narrowly defined nationalist discourse has obscured from view the larger field of significations in which a range of different and often rival and conflicting representations of the nation were produced. I attempt here to move this exploration in a somewhat different direction and argue that locating the mother within the larger field of contested and conflictual significations of the nation-space must lead necessarily to those other projections that mediate between the economy of sex and gender identifications and the vicissitudes of collective selfhood: the courtesan and prostitute.[8] In order to understand the nature of the home that stands under the sign of the mother, we must examine closely the inhabitants of that other gendered space, the brothel. If the domesticated and desexualized figure of the mother becomes a critical moment in the interpellation of the (male) subject as *national* subject, then the trouble that "Muslim" represents for nationalist discourse is enunciated through the excessive and improperly sexual figure of the courtesan or prostitute. In Manto's stories the brothel and its inhabitants come to acquire a critical energy that makes visible the representational work of the nation and suggest possibilities of national belonging in terms of forms of "love" not subsumable under the discourse of filial piety and devotion.

Urdu and the Writing of India

My larger concern here is to suggest some ways of thinking about the relationship of Urdu literature in the two decades before the Partition of India to the canonical forms of nationalism. Any reading of Urdu literary production during the period in question must confront the paradox that the era of modern Indian history that saw the most decisive bifurcation of national politics along religio-communal lines is perhaps the most secularist period in the history of modern Urdu literature. Thus none of the writers who came to prominence in this period—Manto, Ismat Chughtai, Miraji, Faiz Ahmed Faiz, to name only a few—could see themselves as addressing a primarily Muslim audience, as Iqbal, for instance, had been able to do in at least some of his major works a mere two decades earlier. This aggressively "national" stance came to be marked in Urdu literary culture in a number of ways. Urdu writers took the lead in the formation of the AIPWA in 1935–36 and continued to have a disproportionate influence on its affairs at the national level up to and even beyond Partition. The rapid success of this organization in its early years is itself deserving of more rigorous literary-historical attention than it has so far received: founded in London by a group of Indian students who had played a role of sorts on the margins of the emerging anti-fascist cultural fronts in Europe, with the Urdu writer Sajjad Zaheer assuming the lead among them, within a year it had held its first all-India meeting in Lucknow, gathering together an astonishing range of the country's most distinguished writers, with the doyen of Hindi-Urdu narrative, Munshi Premchand, as its president.[9] Urdu writers also filled, in disproportionate numbers, the ranks of such newly emerging sites of national cultural production as All-India Radio and the Bombay film industry. Furthermore, as even a cursory perusal of literary journals from the period reveals, the personnel of Urdu literary culture cut across communal lines with regard to origin. This is especially true of the Punjab but also of the heartland of the Hindi-Urdu conflict, Delhi and the United Provinces (UP). But, above all, this national rather than separatist or communal posture must be read in the literature itself, for instance, in the development of what was taken to be a "realist" practice in fiction—by such writers as Manto, Rajinder Singh Bedi, Chughtai, Krishan Chander, Muhammad Hasan Askari, Ahmad Naseem Qasmi, Upendra Nath Ashk, Akhtar Husain Raipuri, among numerous others[10]—with narrative becoming the staging ground for a vision of national life as secular social landscape: the life of India's "eternal" villages under the onslaughts of modernity, the psycho-sexual tensions and crises of the middle-class home, the multilayered energy and movement of the modern cities, each with its range of social types and problematics. (In poetry, as I argue in the next chapter, these changes are signaled by the transformation of the protocols of the classical Urdu lyric, in particular the *ġhazal* form, a genre and tradition that came under increasing criticism in modern times—in the cultures of both Indian nationalism and Muslim separatism—for its inwardness and imperviousness to Indian nature and reality.)[11]

These young men and women, largely in their twenties and thirties in 1936, many of whom were ridiculed unfairly and erroneously by some contemporaries then and later as naïve propagandists of the vision of the AIPWA, produced a double revolution in their time in Urdu literary culture. At a moment when even many intellectuals among the nationalists, such as Suniti Kumar Chatterji, were deriding Urdu literature for its supposedly ethereal postures and preoccupations, and even Gandhi spoke of Urdu as an exclusively Muslim tradition, they forced, on the one hand, an encounter between this literary tradition and the most significant social forces in India in the early twentieth century, and, on the other, demonstrated that Urdu could be and was the terrain for truly national social imaginings. It was their critics, such as Askari and Saleem Ahmed in the 1950s and 1960s, who proved naïve in this regard when they spoke of a poet such as Faiz as a mere sloganeer—a colossal and unforgivable failure of critical ability, given the complexity of their other literary judgments. Something of this failure must have been felt by these critics themselves, and near the end of his life Ahmed even conceded to an interviewer that, despite everything, he considered "Faiz to be Pakistan's greatest poet, the best poet."[12] I argue here, however, that we read these developments of the 1930s and 1940s against the grain, that despite this secularist and "national" posture of Urdu literary culture, the relationship of Urdu to nationalism ultimately remains an ambivalent one. What characterizes the distinctness of Urdu linguistic practices and literary production is precisely that its forms cannot be canonized within the discourse of national culture, as indexed, for instance, in Gandhi's controversial identification of Urdu as an exclusively Muslim register and style.

The paradoxical posture of Urdu during the period in question, in which Urdu literary production seems to be staking national-secular claims despite its increasing public identification by nationalists as a "minority" culture and problematic, is further complicated by the fact that this period also sees the near-disappearance of what is widely held to be the national form par excellence, namely, the novel, and sees, instead, the appearance of a new and self-confident short story in the work of a new generation of writers.[13] Urdu is perhaps unique among the major literatures of South Asia in its emphasis on the short story as the primary genre of narrative fiction, even in the decades since Partition. In Urdu the hierarchical relationship of novel to short story that one would expect of any major narrative tradition is reversed. This is particularly striking in that some of the kinds of transition associated with the move from epic to novel and modern narrative—picaresque, didactic, and historical fictions, for instance—began to take place in Urdu much earlier than in the other major North Indian languages.[14] The commissioned narratives produced at Fort William College for the linguistic training of colonial officials in the first decade of the nineteenth century—collections of original fairy tales in the classical Persian style such as Mirza Rajab Ali Beg's *Fasāna-e ʿajā'ib* (probably written in 1824–25), the standardization and translation of pre-modern epic cycles like *Dāstān-e Amīr Ḥamza* (published by the Naval Kishore house of Lucknow from the 1860s onwards), the reformist and didactic works of Nazir Ahmad (also 1860s onwards), the immensely popular picaresque narratives of Ratan Nath Sarshar written under the influence of Cervantes (*Fasāna-e Āzād* first serialized in the *Avadh akhbār* beginning in 1778), and the historical romances of Abdul Haleem Sharar (1890s onwards)—these milestones in the development of modern narrative forms in Urdu should have presaged a prominent place for the novel form in twentieth-century literary culture. It is a source of constant concern and speculation in Urdu criticism that this, in fact, has not turned out to be the case, that despite the appearance of some accomplished practitioners—for instance, Rusva and Premchand in the early decades of this century, Qurratulain Hyder in the decades after 1947, and Abdullah Husain in more recent years—the development of the novel form has not constituted anything like the sort of coherent and canonical tradition that we associate with the major languages of Western Europe, with Arabic and

Japanese, or even with other Indian languages like Bengali. More important, the novel has undergone nothing like the elaboration that the short story has been subject to in Urdu itself, to say nothing of lyric poetry.

My contention here is that the two processes I have just outlined are not unrelated, that this particular distribution of genres—this foregrounding of the short story at the cost of the novel—may be understood in terms of the ambivalent relationship of Urdu literary culture to the discourse of Indian nationhood, in terms of the particular *location* of Urdu within the larger space of Indian literature(s). The privileging of the short story in modern Urdu literature is a function of this problematic of minoritization. The absence of a canonical novel form in Urdu may be understood as an inscription, at the level of literary form and institution, of the dialectic of selfhood in Indian modernity. For an enunciation of the "major" claims of nationhood as the exclusive way of being in the world, Urdu turns to a "minor" epic form, thereby lending to those claims an air of contingency. Lukács argued in *The Theory of the Novel* that what distinguishes the nineteenth-century novel as a genre, what makes it the epic of the modern world, is its capacity to narrate the socialization of the individual, its inscription at the level of form of the claim that life is ethically meaningful. Although clearly a work that precedes the explicitly Marxist turn, properly speaking, in Lukács's writings, *Theory* cannot entirely be detached from it and may be spoken of as a proto-materialist work in its concern with the relationship between form, the individual, and society. For the nationalist narrative in late colonial India—and this applies as much to Nehru's nonfictional works *An Autobiography* and *The Discovery of India* as it does to such contemporary novels as Mulk Raj Anand's *Untouchable* (1935) or Premchand's *Gōdān* (1936)—the representative self that is the object of the narrative has a secular nationalist consciousness as its defining characteristic. For the Nehruvian, "Progressive" aesthetics that emerged in the 1930s under the influence of Popular Front conceptions of artwork and society, telling the truth of society in fiction—"realism"—amounted to narrating the emergence of this consciousness—the abstract and secular citizen subject—as the highest form of consciousness possible in a colonial society.[15] The protocols of social realism, first formulated as a program at the Soviet Writers' Congress in 1934 and adopted as official Popular Front policy in 1935, undergo a transformation in being transplanted to a colonial setting.[16] What the language of realist aesthetics now seeks to define is a specific relationship between writing and the nation so that it is more accurate to speak of *national realism* in this context. A revealing document in this connection is the speech that Anand, a founding member of the AIPWA from its London phase, delivered at the association's convention at Calcutta in 1938. Anand argued that the goal of social realism is as much the "portrayal . . . of all those tragedies in the obscure lanes and alleys of our towns and villages" as it is the imperative to "release the dormant potentialities of our people buried in an animal biology and make them the creative will which may take us from the infancy of our six thousand years to milleniums [*sic*] of a less elemental struggle for individual perfection."[17] "Realism" here is therefore only as much a matter of mimesis in the present as it is of narrating the (national) passage from primitivism to modernity. The degraded life of India's peasant masses is barely above the level of "animal biology," and it is the task of the committed writer to narrate the conditions of possibility of the passage from this limited state of existence to the universal consciousness of the citizen subject—"individual perfection." And in Anand's novel *Untouchable*, the totality that is the nation is concretized as the formal tension between the universalist and secular consciousness of the narrator and the subaltern protagonist Bakha, a consciousness whose limits are defined by, and in struggle against, the socioreligious institutions of caste society.

Lukács argued of the modern short story that it, along with the other "minor epic forms," focuses on a *fragment* of social life rather than its totality, letting the whole enter "only as the thoughts and feelings of [the] hero," thereby presenting "completeness" in entirely subjective terms. Lukács considered the short story to be "the narrative form which pinpoints the strangeness and ambiguity of life": "It sees absurdity in all its undisguised and unadorned nakedness, and the exorcising power of this view, without fear or hope, gives it the consecration of form."[18] The Urdu short story takes such an exorcising stance with respect to the narrative of Indian selfhood. Its staging of that selfhood remains an ironic one. The fragments it isolates from the stream of life and elevates into form do not merely point toward a totality, however subjective, of which they are a part. It puts the terms of this totality in question and holds at bay the resolutions whose "end" is the form of consciousness that is the abstract citizen subject. In the work of the generation of writers who followed in Manto's wake, this ambivalence of the Urdu short story—the formal possibilities of a "minor" genre directed to "major" ends—is perhaps nowhere better expressed than in the story "Iḥsān Manzil" (Ihsan Mansion) by Intizar Husain, in which the genre of expansive family saga as postcolonial national allegory—one need only think here of the Cairo Trilogy, of *One Hundred Years of Solitude*, or of *Midnight's Children*—is compacted and thus made ironic in the tale of an *ashrāf* Muslim family over four generations, each generation's adolescent rebellion against its parents taking on the content of the major cultural movements of Indo-Muslim life from the 1860s to the 1940s, from Aligarh rationalism to the socio-sexual iconoclasm of the 1930s associated with the short story collection *Añgārē*. This brutally funny and yet affectionate parody of modern Indo-Muslim history highlights the fragility of the nation-community's claim to a continuous history. In smiling at the touching naïveté of the adolescent rebels and their complete innocence of the cyclical and generational inversion of conformism and rebellion, orthodoxy and its heterodox interrogation, we perceive that the very act of bringing the epic down to earth is itself epic in a way but that perception is treated ironically in the story, and epic ambition is revealed to be fragmentary, occasional, and ultimately ephemeral.

This characteristic feature of the Urdu short story, its ambivalent and ironic relationship to the narrative forms of national culture, is exemplified in Manto's practice of the form. Manto himself once attempted to identify this character by describing the short story as a "sañgīn" genre—grave, serious, or severe but also dangerous. More than any of his contemporaries, Manto explores the possibilities of writing itself as a national institution. His post-Partition writings, to which I return at the end of this chapter, represent a complex and multifaceted exploration of the cultural reinscriptions and rearrangements out of which the fiction of two autonomous nationalities was being produced. But his earlier writings are also obsessed with the representational structure of national belonging, with the meaning of national culture, and with the ethical and aesthetic dilemmas of a writer in a colonial society on the verge of gaining at least formal independence. Above all, Manto raises these questions as an *Urdu* writer, a writer of a language itself embroiled in the crisis of national culture, from within a literary culture imputed with a minority orientation and consciousness in the discourse of the nation. That is the ambition and larger distinctness of his oeuvre and his place in the literary history of not only Urdu but of India itself.

Mother India: Woman and National Modernity

In a number of mostly early, pre-Partition stories, Manto develops a set of themes around the national-allegorical possibilities of woman as signifier but simultaneously explodes such possibilities by turning to sexually and morally displaced figures that are central to the controversies concerning obscenity that his stories created. (The meaning of "obscenity" in this connection is of interest itself, and I return to this subject later.) In such stories as "Ḳhushiyā," "Insult" ("Hatak"), "Shārdā," "Bābū Gōpīnāth," "My Name Is Radha" ("Mērā nām Rādhā hai"), "Jānakī," "Mummy" ("Mammī"), and, above all, "Black Trousers" ("Kālī shalvār"), some of which I discuss at length below, Manto pays almost obsessive attention to such figures—in both senses—and especially to the figure of prostitute, returning to it again and again, examining in ever more detail and from various angles and perspectives the world of the brothel, the characters who inhabit it, and the light he insists it throws on the world outside. The myriad little dramas of desire, lust, and yearning that emerge within these stories contain within them elements of a purposeful social imaginary and are not, as his detractors would have it, merely exercises in iconoclasm for its own sake. The figure of prostitute stands in Manto's stories not simply in opposition to the virtuous wife and mother of nationalist imagination but rather as a means of exploring the complexities of the latter itself as signifier.

The uncanny mirrorings of brothel and home are the subject of "Insult," for instance, in which the prostitute Saugandhi maintains a curious fiction with her lover, Madho, who visits her in Bombay from time to time and always manages to extract money from her despite the repeated cautionings of her pimp, Ram Lal, always promising to return it by money order as soon as he returns home to Poona (now Pune) and even to send her more money for her upkeep. Madho keeps insisting volubly that she give up her profession and let him support her, even as they both know it is she and her trade that support him. He exaggeratedly threatens to leave her if she does not clear her room of the paraphernalia of her trade—bottles of cheap perfume and makeup, garish clothing, pornographic prints on the wall. Madho's feigned interest in her life, his formulaic insistence that she turn her brothel into a home, draws Saugandhi to him and strengthens her love. In fact, Manto tells us, she is a person with an almost infinite capacity for loving, quite capable of willing herself into believing that each encounter with a client is an act of falling in love. Often, we are told, she is overwhelmed by a desire to take the man's head in her lap and sing to him until he falls sleep. Both Madho and Saugandhi are liars, Manto tells us, living a counterfeit life, like cheap costume jewelry with shiny gold or silver plating. But Saugandhi is happy, because "those who cannot afford to own real gold can satisfy themselves with such trinkets."[19] It is Saugandhi's ability to find the basis of love in an untruth that interests us here. Her pretense with Madho, her lover, that he visits her not in a brothel but a home, and her ability to imagine her anonymous clients as lovers, both suggest a form of love whose truth is based in an untruth.

The precarious stability of this world comes crashing down abruptly with a brief encounter between Saugandhi and a bourgeois client (*sēṭh*), an event hinted at in the story's title, "Insult." One night Saugandhi is standing on a dimly lit street corner trying to peer into the rolled up window of a car. As the window is rolled down, someone inside the car shines a flashlight in her face for a brief blinding moment. As the light is turned off Saugandhi hears a grunt of displeasure—"Unh!"—and the window is rolled back up; suddenly the car drives off into the night. Ram Lal walks away, remarking, matter-of-factly, "Didn't like you, I suppose," and Saugandhi is left standing alone on the street, the memory of that grunt of distaste unleashing a storm in her mind (*MR*, 907/*AV*, 251). The following passages are superbly crafted, an early Manto exercise in modernist prose which would be fully developed only later in such stories as "Phundnē" (Tassles)—onomatopoeia abound, familiar words take on unfamiliar meanings, an almost mantric repetition of words and sounds prevails, and narrative voice is overwhelmed by interior monologue. The language here mirrors the crisis of self that the encounter has precipitated. As her head reels from the rejection, the "insult," Saugandhi begins to wonder why it so wounded her:

> She wondered why she suddenly longed for someone to sing her praises. Never had she wanted it so much before. Why did she now look even at the inanimate things around her in a way that begged for approval? Why was every fragment of her being becoming "mother"? Why was she ready to gather all the things of the earth [*dhartī kī har shai*] into her lap like a mother? Why did she want to embrace the lamppost in front of her, to place her warm cheek against the cold metal and absorb all its chill? (*MR*, 911/*AV*, 254)

The language of this passage begins to render indistinct the opposition of mother to prostitute. The signs of motherhood and domesticity appear, uncannily, within the world of the brothel. But, furthermore, the fantasy of motherly love and nurture elaborated here renders the "mother" allegory itself visible as a fantasy whose ultimate object is to encompass and contain "the earth" itself. Manto's use of *dhartī* is significant, for it refers not just to the living earth but to a particular portion of it, that which is known and meaningful, a bit of the earth that is *ours*. In other words, *dhartī* points to the territorial body of the nation, and the story draws attention here to the national-allegorical possibilities of the woman's body. By juxtaposing the sexualized and commodified body of the prostitute to the desexualized and idealized body of the mother-nation—which appears here, moreover, as fantasy—the text produces a multiplicity of meanings: the desexualized mother is revealed to be the icon of a particular sexual—but also communal and national—politics, the exploitation of the prostitute is presented as the truth of the idealization of the mother, and the prostitute herself is held up as an ethical figure, a tenuous and temporary icon of an alternative conception of human community and attachments.

Lying and the possibilities of love are also the theme of "Babu Gopi Nath," another Bombay story, written in the mid-1940s.[20] The story is about the narrator Manto's encounter with, and moral education at the hands of, Babu Gopi Nath, a middle-aged man who has come from Lahore, bringing with him a prostitute named Zeenat, a beautiful and hopelessly naïve young woman whose marriage he wishes to arrange with a suitably wealthy man before retiring himself to a hermit's life. On the day of the wedding, when Manto sees Zeenat in the bridal chamber, looking for all intents and purposes like a demure bride, he cannot resist shattering the illusion. "What is this farce?" he asks Zeenat, reducing her to tears (*MN*, 291/*KE*, 148). From the position of the middle-class intellectual—Manto the narrator is a writer and journalist—such a configuration of human relations appears farcical, a mixing of categories and crossing of boundaries. But, in the end, it is Manto who is reduced to regret and embarrassment, as Babu Gopi Nath, now visible in his full complexity as father, mother, lover, pimp, and saint, turns to him with tears in his eyes and reproaches him for having so thoughtlessly ridiculed Zeenat. Thus both these stories present the brothel as a tenuous world constantly under threat from the outside. The delicate fiction that sustains this world is destroyed in each case by a member of the outside world who represents bourgeois respectability—in Saugandhi's case, by a wealthy client; in Zeenat's, by a middle-class intellectual. Some have argued that, despite his oft-stated intention to write about women who are (sexually) transgressive, even rebellious, Manto most often produces characters whose rebelliousness is at best ambivalent, even superficial, that this intention is inscribed at one level in the narrative and undermined at others.[21] The desire for a normalization of her (sexual) self that we have seen in Saugandhi, for instance, or Zeenat's attempt to become the demure bride, might lead us to agree with this characterization of Manto's women. While I do not take this reading to be incorrect as such, I feel it misses the more important point that this "make-believe" is itself a figure for the politics of (nationalist) representation.[22] It marks a refusal to romanticize as autonomous those locations in society whose resources of culture and affect provide the means for an ethical critique of nationalism—and, more precisely, what I have called "national realism." It points to the subordinate and dependent position of these locations, even as they are held up as models of human relations and emerge from the narrative in their complexity as possible resources for the representation of collective cultural practices made unimaginable in the pious projection of the middle-class family as microcosm of the nation.

Manto's most ironic comment on the solemnities of motherhood as signifier perhaps come in "Mummy," which recounts a series of encounters in Poona between the narrator, again named Manto, and an older English woman, a widow named Stella Jackson, whom everyone addresses as "Mummy." Manto, the narrator, meets Stella through some of his friends in the film industry who belong to her circle of devoted young men and women. The very idea of family is turned on its head by this loose and voluntary association of individuals brought together by their love of Mummy's company, and motherhood itself is made ironic in this figure's excessiveness—she is foreign, garishly made up, often drunk, and sexually permissive. The foreign word by which she is addressed, and which stands as the title of the story, itself marks a rejection of the purity of the (Indian) family as produced in the icon of the desexualized and virtuous mother. It is "explosive" in the sense Adorno ascribes to unassimilated "foreign words" (*Fremdwörter*) in general: it points to the inadequacy of the category of the indigenous and militates against the stultification produced by the claim to closure of a "native" (*eigen*) discourse.[23] But at the climactic moment of the story, at a moment of crisis for this family, Stella is able, paradoxically, to act as the mother of her brood of young bohemians and misfits, her adopted children, and manages to prevent the seduction of a young girl of fifteen in her charge by one of Manto's raucous friends. This paradox is a characteristic Manto gesture, put here in the service of unsettling and rearranging the qualities collected under the sign of the mother in the representative practices of nationalist culture.

In an essay written in early 1947 as a response to the public pillorying of his work as obscene, Manto addresses the question of sexual morality and the possibilities of narrative, and explains the significance of his female characterizations:

> If in my neighbourhood a woman is daily abused by her husband and then polishes his shoes, I feel no sympathy for her whatsoever. But when a woman fights with her husband, threatens to kill herself, and then goes off to the movies, and I see the husband for two hours in a state of great worry and agitation, I develop a strange sympathy for them both . . . The hard working woman who grinds grain all day and sleeps peacefully at night cannot be the heroine of my stories. My heroine can only be the prostitute who stays up all night and sleeps all day but wakes up suddenly sometimes from a nightmare in which old age is knocking at her door . . . Her filth, her illnesses, her irritation, her bad language—these appeal to me. I write about these and completely ignore the pure locution, the good health, and the finesse of respectable women.[24]

Here Manto ties the possibility of writing to the forms of displacement of the (sexual) morality of the (nationalist) middle class that the prostitute represents. But Manto's most complex exploration of the brothel and its inhabitants in relation to the crisis of national culture and belonging comes in the story "Black Trousers," written most likely in 1940, to which I now turn in some detail. The story begins with a description of the life of Sultana, who has recently moved to Delhi from the military cantonment town of Ambala in the Punjab. In Ambala, we are told, most of her customers were British soldiers, and she had learned a few English sentences from them. Business there was good, and Sultana considered these Englishmen to be better than Indian clients. Although they spoke a language she did not understand, even this had proved an advantage of sorts, for she could curse them in her own language if they bothered her too much or grew too rowdy, smiling all the time and suggesting by her tone that she was speaking lovingly to them. Since she had moved to Delhi, however, her business had collapsed. Where previously she could make up to twenty rupees a day after a few hours' work, in Delhi she had made barely that much in three months. It was next to having no income at all, and slowly her meager jewelry had had to be pawned off piece by piece.

I suggest that we read Sultana's move from Ambala to Delhi, from the provinces to the colonial capital, and her aspirations for success there, as a reorientation of life expectations along national lines. She moved there not out of a desire on her own part—such concerns seem beyond her horizon, and she is portrayed as someone with strictly local interests. It was not she but her lover and pimp, Khuda Bakhsh, who, Manto writes, was taken by a sudden and inexplicable desire to move to Delhi. She willingly followed him because, as her business had picked up after she met him in Ambala, she, being a superstitious person (*ẓaʿīf al-iʿtiqād*), considered him a source of good luck (*MN*, 660). (Manto uses the forms *mubārak* and *bhāgvān*, the first of clearly Arabic lineage, the second a *tadbhava* derivative of the Sanskritic *bhāgyavān*. His very name, Khuda Bakhsh, meaning "God-given" or "gift of God," suggests this aspect of their relationship.) He is a man of the world, a former truck driver, now with a small business as a pavement photographer outside the train station. He has some education, and although he is constantly chasing after one holy man or another, and is a devotee of Nizamuddin Auliya, the renowned medieval Sufi saint of Delhi, his relationship to technology is carefully contrasted to that of Sultana's, who screams in terror when she accidentally pulls on the flush chain in the bathroom, and the water rushes out below her. The main reference point for her concerning modern technology are the railways, and she wonders, when she first sees the flushing chain, why the bathroom should have a chain like a passenger compartment in a train. It is also significant in this regard that Khuda Bakhsh's profession entails taking photographs of English soldiers stationed in Ambala cantonment, that is, creating images of the colonial rulers. His predicament hints at the dilemma of the native artist: he is busy domesticating a foreign technology and form, and relies for personal success alternately on the (modern, rational) ethic of "hard work" and the (pre-modern, indigenous, "irrational") hopes of saintly intervention. The photographic images he creates of English clients themselves hint at a recurring artistic threat for the native artist, namely, the endless reproduction of colonial culture. At the behest of this man, functioning partly within an indigenous idiom but literate also in the use of Western forms and technology, Sultana moves to Delhi and exchanges English clients for Indian ones.

Sultana at first is lost in Delhi, literally, as she is unable to find her way back to her apartment. She lives in a quarter built by city authorities specifically for prostitutes, and all the buildings appear to her to be "of the same design" (*MN*, 661/*AV*, 209). She eventually learns to recognize her building by the laundry on the ground floor. Sultana's initial inability to find her home, her bearings, in this place called "Delhi," suggests the uniform space of nation and citizenship, seemingly without the landmarks of status, difference, and belonging that allow her to navigate within the regime of colonial sovereignty which in this story is given the name "Ambala." In other words, if Ambala signifies the militarily enforced relationship of a tributary colonial state to its subaltern subjects, Delhi represents the modern regime of power that Foucault called governmentality, which proceeds through the ability "to structure the possible field of action of others," and which relies not so much on external supervision or discipline as on suggesting the possibility of freedom of action for those who are to be governed.[25] It is to this place where colonial subjects are to become citizens that Sultana is brought by her lover-pimp. That transformation, however, does not proceed in the manner promised. When Sultana does gain a foothold in this space, it is only a tentative one, and secured by external, artificial means, for example, the laundry on the ground floor becomes a means of recognizing the apartment above it. It is a containment of terror rather than its final disappearance, like her eventual understanding of the chain in the bathroom: by pulling on it, she can make human refuse disappear into the ground.

The incident in the toilet hints, first of all, at the nationalist cult of technology. It also highlights those distances and discrepancies between the subaltern and elite domains of the colonial world whose political dimension Ranajit Guha described as "dominance without hegemony." For Guha, as noted in an earlier chapter, the defining characteristic of the native bourgeoisie in a colonial setting is its lack of heroic ambition to re-create society in its own image. Like the foreign elite at the helm of the colonial state, it is content to rule the subaltern masses by coercion rather than through their conversion to the universalism of its projects and values. In "The New Law" ("Nayā qānūn"), another Manto story from the early 1940s, the bourgeois project in question is not technological modernization but the politics of constitutionalism. The story centers around a horse-cart driver in Lahore named Mangu, humorously and gently portrayed, who is generally respected in the community of cart drivers as a man with a certain knowledge of the world. One day Mangu picks up two passengers at the High Court, native (*Mārwāṛī*) businessmen, and comes to understand from their excited conversation that a *nayā qānūn* (new law, or constitution) is about to be implemented which will make Indians free to be Indians in their own country and protect them from the arbitrary insults and oppressions of the English.[26] Thrilled by this prospect, Mangu announces the news to his audience at the horse-cart stand and anxiously begins to count the days till the auspicious occasion. The day finally comes, and Mangu learns a lesson in the discrepancy between subaltern hopes and bourgeois aspirations. As he is taking a break from his work and thinking about when and where he will see the new constitution, an Englishman, whom the former recognizes as the passenger who had abused him one day the year before, hails Mangu rudely. The man asks to be driven to Hira Mandi, the ancient prostitution district of Lahore's walled city. Mangu asks for an arbitrarily high fare, they get into an argument, and when the Englishman raises his cane at him, Mangu gives him a memorable thrashing, enlightening him in the process that the English would have to change their old ways now that the "new law" was here. The police then arrive, and Mangu himself is thrashed and dragged off to the police station, uncomprehending and shouting all the way, "the new law, the new law" (*MR*, 719/*KE*, 92). In "The New Law," Manto highlights the differing relationships of the subaltern and the bourgeois nationalists to colonial political "reform." Half understanding the nationalist interpretation of the law, the subaltern is willing to act and claim the new dignity and status ("citizen") he thinks it is promising him, only to be roundly disabused of that illusion. In "Black Trousers," Sultana is similarly baffled by the workings of modernity, in her case the mysteries of planned urbanization and the introduction of sewage technology.[27]

Manto tells us that in Delhi Sultana languishes. Clients do not come, not even for a fraction of what she would have charged the English soldiers in Ambala. Khuda Bakhsh disappears sometimes for days, chasing after holy men in the shadow of Purana Qila, the ruined Old Fort of Sultanate and Mughal Delhi—holy men who, he hopes, will change his luck and make business boom. Sultana repeatedly tells him that she hasn't taken to Delhi, but he always turns down her suggestions that they move back to Ambala, saying that they are in the capital to stay and that things are bound to improve. Alone all day, Sultana finds herself drifting to the balcony of her flat, increasingly engrossed in watching the comings and goings of engines and freight carriages in the railway yard across the street.

If the incident in the toilet already hints at the nationalist cult of technology, the railway yard dramatizes more explicitly the workings of national modernity, the modernization of the nation, watched this time by Sultana, as it were, from afar. This function of the railways as a pristine sign of colonial modernity is well established in modern Indian fiction. But the real interest of these passages lies not so much in that signification itself as in the attention the story repeatedly draws to the uncanny resemblance between the two spaces described: the goings-on of the railway yard, on the one hand, and, on the other, the world of the brothel. The effect is not so much allegorical as meta-allegorical. For instance, observing the railway lines glinting in the twilight, Sultana finds her gaze turning to her own arms, where her veins seem to her to be marking her body as the lines mark the ground, the territorial body of the nation. The clouds of smoke rising up from the engines appear to her to take on the shapes of heavyset men. Sometimes it seems to her as if this world of criss-crossing tracks, of billowing clouds of smoke and steam, is itself like a brothel: a crowd of numberless carriages being driven this way or that by a few bloated and self-important steam engines. Sometimes the engines appear to be like the prosperous merchants who visited her in Ambala and she herself like a solitary carriage, pushed down a track by some unknown person towards an unknown destination, as others throw the switches that determine her direction.

There is much of contemporary critical interest in these passages. Manto himself cites them, in an essay responding to the charge of obscenity, only to argue that his prostitute stories are realistic and not obscene, a question to which I shall return.[28] Of concern here in the railway yard passages, however, is the way in which they make visible the representational practices of the nation. For Sultana's perception that the worlds of national modernization and of the brothel are reflections of each other, that moment of allegory and counter-allegory, is made possible only in this place called "Delhi." Even in the Ambala cantonment, Manto tells us, she lived near the railway station, but such thoughts never entered her mind there. Only within a *national* orientation, in other words, do these allegorical connections between the body of the woman and the body politic become possible. Manto's text, moreover, draws attention to and comments on the national allegory itself. The effect of the passage as a whole, that is, is meta-allegorical. Thus Manto's text reproduces the classic tropic structure of the nationalist text, namely, the figuring of nation as woman, but ironically displaces its locus from mother to prostitute, commenting in the process on the allegories inherent in the nation as a representational form.

These meta-allegorical possibilities of the prostitute as a figure of displacement and mediation are fully elaborated in the concluding incident, hinted at in the title. As Sultana languishes on Delhi's G. B. Road, the holy month of Muharram approaches, and she realizes that she does not have a full suit of the traditional black clothes that she would need to mark this month of ritual mourning. She has a white tunic and scarf, which Khuda Bakhsh gave her for Diwali, and she can dye these black. But she does not have a pair of black trousers (*shalvār*). Her two neighborhood friends, also prostitutes, have shiny new black clothes made of satin and georgette. One of them, Mukhtar, has new satin trousers which Sultana eyes with particular envy. As Muharram draws near, Sultana's panic mounts. She begs Khuda Bakhsh to somehow raise the money for a new pair of trousers, but he leaves her with no illusions. Finally, she approaches Shankar, whom she had befriended one day when, standing on the balcony looking across at the railway yard, she had noticed a young man in the street looking up at her, and, on her signal, he had come up to her apartment. But Shankar had quickly disabused her of any hope that he would prove to be a client. Insisting that *she* had summoned him and so should pay for his company, with sexual services, he had left her stunned at the sudden reversal of the roles of professional and client. At first she was angry, but they had quickly become friends and he was a frequent visitor to Sultana's home. Anxiously stressing that she is not asking that he pay for her services, Sultana finally tells Shankar her problem and asks not that he give her the money for the trousers but that he give her the trousers themselves—in other words, a gift. Shankar tells her he has no money but nevertheless promises to present her with a black *shalvār* by the first of Muharram. He then points to Sultana's cheap costume earrings and asks if he can have them. Wondering what he could possibly want with such worthless jewelry, she hands them over to him. Sultana is not at all certain that Shankar will keep his promise, but early on the morning of the first there is a knock on her door, and it is Shankar, looking dishevelled, as though he just stumbled out of bed nearby. He hands Sultana a bundle and leaves: it is a new black *shalvār*, one rather resembling her friend Mukhtar's. Thrilled by the prospect of a complete suit of clothes, but even more thrilled because Shankar kept his promise, Sultana changes into her new clothes. Just then there is a knock on the door, and it is Mukhtar. As the two women meet at the door, something stops them in their tracks, as Mukhtar eyes Sultana's new trousers and the latter recognizes Mukhtar's new earrings. The women lie to each other about their new acquisitions, and the story ends with the intimation that the two then remained silent for a brief moment. In their silence, in their mutual recognition of love and betrayal, we may read Manto's relationship to that orientation of the nationalist subject which comes to us coded as love for the Mother-nation. For Shankar's betrayal of Sultana (and of Mukhtar) does not imply an *absence* of "love." On the contrary, it is precisely the simultaneity of faithfulness and betrayal that constitutes for Manto the variety of love he places in the brothel.

Although he appears near the end of the story, Shankar is an instrumental figure and, through him, the story approaches most explicitly the problematic of political and cultural identity. When, on first meeting Sultana, he makes fun of Khuda Bakhsh for chasing after holy men, she responds that he is making fun of "our holy men" because he himself is a Hindu. Shankar's response is a typical Manto exercise in inversion: "In places such as these [that is, brothels], Hindu-Muslim questions do not arise. Even great *paṇḍits* and *maulvīs*, were they to come here, would become *sharīf*" (*MR*, 668/*KE*, 215). It is a remarkable passage, dense with cultural, social, and political significations. At its center is the notion of *sharāfat*, one of the most overcoded words in the glossary of modern North Indian history. As discussed in previous chapters, *sharāfat* is at once decency, nobility of character, social respectability, and the fact of belonging to the diffuse and overlapping set of elite Muslim castes, subcastes and other social groupings known as the *shurafā* or *ashrāf*. As the meaning of *sharāfat* is transformed in the nineteenth century to incorporate the emerging experience of bourgeois respectability, it is rendered ironic in the figure of the *ṭavāif*, who is now simultaneously fallen woman and guardian of at least some high cultural forms—as *salonière*, arbiter of literary and musical taste, and instructor in elite social manners. The courtesan belonged in very concrete ways to the precolonial social elites of cities like Lahore and Lucknow.[29] So if by the end of the nineteenth century she provided a compelling representation of the problematic of being Muslim in the emergence of the Indian modern—most famously, as I have noted, in Rusva's novel—this is owing at least in part to her ability to stand in metonymically for the culture of the pre-modern elites of North India. In other words, the figure of courtesan is an elaboration of the *ambivalent* relationship of the emergent complex of elite Muslim identity to the cultural practices of the nation, an ambivalence typically misrecognized in secular nationalist discourse, as we have seen with respect to Nehru, as the sign simply of a lag in the development of a modernizing elite among the Muslims. Thus of significance here is the courtesan's function as a figure of duplicity, of the equivocal allegiance of "the Muslim" to the emerging Indian national narrative. The anxiety about the treacherousness of the Muslim, whose history is inseparable from and as old as the history of national sentiment itself, is given here the shape of the cultivated and capricious courtesan, a sign of the continued Muslim domination of the elite cultural domains in North India within which the contest over the practices of a national language and culture was taking place and, at the same time, an indication of the unassimilability of these elite cultural practices marked as Muslim to the emerging narratives of India's national existence. Thus in the transition from Rusva to Manto, from the semiotics of the courtesan to those of the "common" prostitute, we may read the lineaments of a larger history, the trajectory of the development of national experience that Partha Chatterjee has spoken of as the movement from "the moment of departure" of nationalist thought to its "moment of arrival." If the courtesan in *Umrā'ō Jān Adā* is to be read as a supplement to the nation-Mother at nationalism's moment of departure, in Manto's bedraggled prostitutes we encounter its reinscription at its moment of arrival. Rusva's elite courtesan encodes the relationship of the *ashrāf* to nationalism's attempted reorientation of the subject towards a veneration of the nation-Mother, a reorientation whose most influential literary representation, as already noted, is often held to be Mahendra's conversion at the hands of the *sanyāsīs* in Bankim's *Ānandamaṭh*.[30] In the elite program of religious reform envisioned by nationalism at its moment of departure, the figuring of nation as mother therefore performs a central function: it seeks to fix the (elite) subject's orientation towards the nation as the love of the (male) child for its mother. In the courtly gatherings in Umrao Jan's salon we see another model of human relations: here the extraction of her patrons' tribute by a culturally accomplished courtesan, rather than filial piety, governs the possibility of "love," that is, of human attachment. The stylized figure of the courtesan thus points to "the Muslim" as a distinct problematic, history, and community, while at the same time marking this community as ambivalently modern—a tributary and at the same time "voluntary" or nonorganic form of coherence of the collective.[31]

In Manto's stories the elevated figure of courtesan is stripped of the appurtenances of style, a move sometimes figured, as it were, literally, in the figure of a naked woman—as we have seen in "Black Trousers," but also in "Khushiya"—and is reduced to an "ordinary" prostitute. Manto's prostitutes eke out a tawdry and miserable existence in the back lanes of Bombay, in small cantonment towns, in the planned prostitutes' quarters of colonial Delhi. Thus we may read these stories, in a literary historical register, as accounts of the transformation of the representational practices of nationalist culture, as embodiments of a fragmentary history of the (gendered) sign in the life of the nation. The meaning of "Mother India" at nationalism's moment of arrival is considerably altered from its significance at its moment of departure. For the secular nationalist, it is a symbol that emerges spontaneously in the realm of subaltern life, as made dramatically clear in the section of *Discovery of India* titled

"Bharat Mata," discussed at some length earlier in the book, and is the means not to the interpellation of the elite male subject himself but of his interaction with the masses. This frankly instrumental mobilization of a desexualized motherhood is translated in Manto's fiction into the sexual exploitation of the prostitute. Thus such figures as Ram Lal and Madho in "Insult" and Khuda Bakhsh in "Black Trousers," who put female sexuality in circulation, occupy the position of the nationalist in Manto's meta-allegorical displacement from mother to prostitute.

This is the position that Shankar, in his first meeting with Sultana, refuses to occupy. His reply to Sultana, as I noted, hinges around an interrogation of the meaning of *sharāfat*, and, in the first instance, uncouples the latter term's moral and sociological significations. But here *sharāfat* is also given a specifically political meaning. Were they to be made subject to the rules of "places such as these," that is, brothels, even "*paṇḍits*" and "*maulvīs*" would become "*sharīf*," that is, "decent" or "respectable." Elaborated here are the terms of (political and cultural) "decency" regarding the crisis of Muslim, and hence national, identity. The term *paṇḍit* in this context also evokes the figure of Nehru, who was universally referred to in the public domain as "Paṇḍit Nehru," and thus is part of an interrogation of Nehruvian secularism's claim to be above religious identification and difference. As with secular nationalism, "decency" here means a rejection of communal separatism, but this rejection does not take the form of a mere disavowal of difference. To the realm of (national-) bourgeois respectability and its familial elaborations of national belonging, Manto counters the brothel, with its own unique resources of affect, attachment, and freedom.

The prostitute, of course, has long been a paradigmatic figure for modern literature, especially for the literature of the modern West, and around her have circulated a number of anxieties about chaos and social disruption. According to Susan Buck-Morss's reading of Benjamin's arcades project, for instance, in the Paris of the Second Empire she represents the feminization of *flânerie*; she is the female equivalent of the *flâneur* par excellence.[32] What makes the prostitute threatening for the regulation of space in the industrial metropolis is her ability to circulate within social space across the internal dividers of bourgeois society: from private to public domains, across class boundaries, in violation of the distinction between seller and commodity. Hence the need for her social regulation, a process Charles Bernheimer has compared to her regulated appearance in the modernist work of art, with the (male) artist turning the prostitute into the paradigm of female sexuality.[33] In the colonial city, as Claire Wills has noted, she also traverses the boundaries of race and nation.[34] We may thus read Sultana's exchanging of British Tommy clients, at the behest of her pimp, for Indian bourgeois patrons as Manto's inscription of nationalism's masculinist anxieties about the treacherousness of undomesticated female sexuality. But in Manto's Delhi, unlike Joyce's Dublin, to which Wills alludes here, the threat the prostitute poses is not one linked to her as a figure of *flânerie*. On the contrary, as we have seen, she is at first literally lost in this uniform modern space characterized by anonymity and the chance encounter—both conditions for the activity of the *flâneur*—and if finally she is able to maneuver through it with some success, this proficiency is of a tentative, external, and artificial nature. What she highlights is the alterity of the subaltern, not its subsumability within a narrative of ethical development, and therefore she marks the ambivalent universalism of the projects of colonial and nationalist modernity.[35] But the larger threat the prostitute poses in Manto's story is to the domesticated female sexuality that provides the idiom of national belonging. The prostitute, the characteristic figure of deceitfulness and duplicity, provides Manto with a way to reinscribe the workings of faithfulness and loyalty in the narrative of national modernity. She and her environment—the brothel—hint at the possibility of another form of "love" for the nation. It is a form of love we may speak of as improper, in that it is both transgressive and not true to its own name—one that is less singular and totalizing, outside the discourse of filial nature, more open to doubt and betrayal. In this sense we may read Shankar as a figure for the Urdu writer himself. The latter's ambivalent relationship to the canonical protocols of the nation as they are produced in the culture of nationalism, the *betrayal* inherent in his demystification of those protocols, and the paradoxical act of cultural and political fidelity of which he ultimately proves capable—these features of Urdu literary culture find an appropriate representation in the relationship of Shankar to Sultana and Mukhtar in Manto's story. And if at nationalism's moment of departure, the literary language and tradition could be figured as the mannered, stylized, and elite courtesan—not just by Urdu's Hindi antagonists, as Alok Rai has shown, but in the period's most significant Urdu novel itself—Manto reinscribes it as a common prostitute, thus freeing the language from the mannered and limited existence of the Avadh *ashrāf*.[36]

I emphasize here that, in arguing that we read the sexual circulation of women in Manto's stories as a representation of bourgeois nationalism's instrumental relation to the gendered sign in the public domain, I do not suggest that we view the prostitute as simply a figure for capitalist modernity in its colonial-nationalist version. In "Insult," for instance, it is the brothel that makes possible at least a semblance of "love," of human attachment, as against the impersonal forces of the market, and the possibility of this semblance is destroyed by the relentless logic of the market, whose agent in the story is the bourgeois client—the client's grunt of disapproval is his judgment on the woman as commodity. It is interesting, therefore, that neither the bourgeois nor the prostitute can truly traverse the distance between these two worlds of home and brothel—for the latter, this traversal can only be the object of an unfulfilled desire—and they must meet in the street, the proper site to negotiate an exchange. As in "Black Trousers," the brothel here, for Manto, is not simply synonymous with the logic of commodity exchange that regulates urban public space. The brothel is that which makes unstable the opposition of public and private, highlighting the gendered metaphor of domesticity that governs the "public" domain of national belonging. It is also significant in this regard that Sultana's new trousers do not come as payment for sexual services, from within the regime of commodity exchange in which she is administered by Khuda Bakhsh, but rather as a gift. It is a remarkable conclusion to the story, one that carries an implicit critique of bourgeois modernity, of the exchangeability of values, but which in no way relies upon a gesture of recuperation or return to some uncomplicated past of presence and propriety. Here the (bourgeois) home is itself contaminated by the logic of exchange as it is put in circulation as a sign by an instrumental nationalist rationality. And the gift itself is improper, an unknowing exchange between two women with their common lover as the mediating term. By thus opening up the opposing terms "gift" and "commodity" to a mutual influence, the text complicates the opposition of tradition to modernity, past to present. If, through Shankar, Manto is able to produce a critique of religio-communalist sentiment, this is achieved neither through a narrative of ethical development whose actual or projected end point is the abstract and "secular" citizen subject, "bare and blank," as Lessing has it, nor by reference to an eternal and undifferentiated India, but rather in the "brothel," in the contingent and unreliable give and take of human interaction. Shankar is the figure for an indigenous and vernacular modernity whose rejection of communalism rests on the assumption that it is *possible* to live otherwise, rather than inevitable.

The inhabitants of Manto's brothels are therefore meaningful figures in the contested field of significations that is national belonging. They allow us to see more fully the workings of gender in the crisis of national identity. The language of motherhood and veneration is indeed implicated in the history of the Hindu-Muslim conflict in colonial India, but not because the figure of the venerated Mother is derived from religious practices that are exclusively of the "Hindu" majority, as is sometimes argued even by critics of Muslim separatism, and even from "nationalist Muslim" positions.[37] Such arguments are metalepses, a confusing of cause and effect, for the figuring of nation as Mother is itself instrumental in the division of the field of national experience into "major" and "minor" realms marked by religious difference. The function of this figure is to insert the subject within an economy of filial "love" towards the nation-object, to produce the subject precisely as national subject. The male subject marked by "Muslim" difference, even when offered a place in this tableau of familial love, cannot be figured as the *son* of the nation-Mother. The singularity of affect or "love" implied in the veneration of the nation-Mother would, in other words, place "the Muslims" in the position of minority, distinct from the sons of the Mother even if allied with them. It is this solution of the crisis of identity in colonial India, the creation of "sons" and "others," that is always at least *implicit* in the categories of nationalist thought, whose critique Manto's stories make possible by suggesting that one may imagine social cohesion and cultural belonging in terms other than that of filial love. Manto's prostitutes shatter the familial tableau of national culture and hint at possibilities of "love" unimagined in the affective economy of nationalized culture.

Exploited, abused, and exhausted, the women in Manto's stories nevertheless continue to manufacture within their lives the signs of ordinary existence—religious-ritual observances, the pangs of human attachment, even love and marriage. Confined by colonial law and indigenous custom to the margins of society, defined by ascendant bourgeois morality as those who live by the sale of their "virtue," they somehow manage, perversely, to lead virtuous lives. Manto himself speculates about this inversion in one of his essays on the prostitute:

> I find strange talk of the repeated sale of virtue. . . . Virtue, to the extent that I understand it, is sold only once. And that only if we equate it with the purity of character of the woman of the purely domestic sort. . . . Because it is quite possible that, among prostitutes, that woman is considered virtuous who is true to the principles of her trade, who doesn't hand over her body for free.[38]

The significance of the prostitute figure for Manto is that she unsettles and puts in motion the antinomies of national-bourgeois respectability. Her ambiguous status as seller and commodity makes visible the exploitation of domesticated female sexuality in the bourgeois home. But once inscribed in the gendered troping of nation and national belonging, she also highlights this exploitation of woman as metaphor and stands as a rebuke to the frank instrumentalism with which bourgeois nationalism mobilizes the image of Mother. I am not suggesting here that we read Manto's reinscription of this figure as a proto-feminist critique of nationalist neo-patriarchy. As with the prostitute in Benjamin's reading of the Paris arcades, she does not represent an unambiguous affirmation of an autonomous female sexuality.[39] The gendered subject that emerges in Manto's stories is not, properly speaking, a feminist subject. But Manto's lack of sentimentalism in this regard is itself salutory, avoiding any easy, and ultimately masculinist, gestures of representability. What these stories do make possible is a denaturalization of the work of gender in the representative practices of national culture. Furthermore—and this is the larger point of my readings so far in this chapter—for Manto, the form of improper and non-totalizing love of which she is the figure makes available possibilities of selfhood and human attachment which are denied and suppressed by nationalism. She exposes the claim of purity of the "national family," of the "chaste maternity" of the nation, and for this reason can become a site for opening up the question of identity precisely where nationalism would attempt to bring it to closure and conclusion.[40]

Parting Words: Society and the Violence of Literature

For the remainder of this chapter I turn to the question of Partition in Manto's later writings and to their transfiguration of the earlier concerns we have seen in the stories above. Manto's master text of Partition is, of course, "Ṭōba Ṭēk Siñgh." This relatively brief story both provides an overview of the historical event, mercilessly taking apart the larger territorial logic of the Partition, and is fastidiously detailed in its examination of the shifting borders of madness and insanity in a world that has come unhinged. A masterful exercise in the use of irony and inversion, the story is an essentially humanist text, making visible the resources of affect and feeling that are required in order to imagine the human in fundamentally inhuman times. And Bishen Singh, the deranged Punjabi peasant who, in a real sense, *chooses* not to decide and to die in the no-man's land separating the two newly divided countries, is a figure for all those, like Manto himself, who are unable to make the decision required of them, and we might well say that Manto the writer died on that piece of earth that belongs to no nation-state. The confused and seemingly insane queries of this inmate of a lunatic asylum as he tries to figure out the new location of his native village, after which the story is named, are the sanest and most pertinent questions it is possible to ask in this moment. At one level, then, Bishan Singh is a figure for the writer, and his constantly repeated, not quite nonsensical statement—"opaṛ dī guṛguṛ dī anēksi dī bē-dhyānā dī mung dī dāl āf dī lālṭain"—is a sort of Punjabi Jabberwocky, and nothing if not itself a piece of verbal art. On the verge of being deported to India along with all the other Hindu and Sikh inmates of the asylum, Bishen Singh gives his signature utterance a final permutation—"opaṛ dī guṛguṛ dī anēksi dī bē-dhyānā dī mung dī dāl āf dī Pākistān aiñḍ Hindustān āf dī dar fṭṭē mūñh"—turning it into a curse, a performative statement rather than a failed descriptive one, a sort of non-constative "plague on both your houses."[41] The question posed by Manto's Partition writing as a whole concerns the adequacy of language, and the language of fiction in particular, to the almost sublime appearance of society at the moment of its fragmentation. One of Manto's responses to the enormity of the task, as I argue shortly, is to reduce the language of narrative to a sort of bare minimum. His great achievement is to have asked how language itself is partitioned.

At the time of Partition, Manto was in Bombay, with a successful though not entirely happy career at Filmistan Studios as a staff screenwriter. Soon after, he defected with the matinee idol Ashok Kumar and others to the then defunct Bombay Talkies. The raging fires of communal strife that accompanied the division of the country, including continuous threats to the Muslim employees of Bombay Talkies, finally drove him from the city that had been his home for almost a decade, and he joined his wife and children across the new border in Lahore, a city he had never lived in before. On arriving in Lahore, he suffered, by all accounts, a complete breakdown. It was a devastated city, emptied of half its original population and teeming with refugees. He himself has written extensively about this period, in essays extremely rich in material for an understanding of his later stories. For three months, he writes, he found himself in a state of complete confusion, unable to connect in any way with his surroundings and unable to write: "Despite great effort, I couldn't separate India from Pakistan. Repeatedly I was troubled by the same question: will the literature of Pakistan be a literature apart? If so, what will it be like? All that was written in undivided India, who is now its owner? Will that, too, be partitioned?"[42] Manto's first writings in Lahore were short sketches, almost parabolic in nature, which he wrote for *Imrōz*, the newspaper then edited by Faiz. Collected later into two thin volumes, these writings, some of them literally a few words long, represent an implosion of language, as if, in attempting to find its way around in the dust and darkness of the partition of the country, narrative is reduced to its barest minimum. Many of these pieces are centered around the ironic use of specific words, the new vocabulary of Partition and independent statehood. One, called "Fireworks," adopts a mock journalistic tone, reporting that "Pakistani parents" have asked the government to fix an annual quota for the deaths of Pakistani children in incidents connected with fireworks. The real absurdity is not so much the demand for quotas as the pretention that there might be such things as "Pakistani" parents or children.[43] But most of the pieces, especially those collected in *Siyāh Hāshīyē* (Black silhouettes), are depictions of communal violence, individual acts, even fragments of individual actions, in which macropolitical assumptions about nation and community stand exposed.[44]

In Pakistan, Manto writes in the essay cited just above, at first he could not take up the short story. The reason he gives, cited earlier in the chapter, is worth repeating: he considers that genre, he says, to be a *sañgīn* form. The adjective *sañgīn* has a range of meanings. Etymologically pointing to something made of, or in, stone (*sañg*), it can refer, for instance, to the great magnitude of a crime or punishment, or the seriousness of a situation. A rough English equivalent might be "grave" or "severe." I suggest that we read in this word the density of relations I have tried to outline between Manto's short stories and the canonical forms of national narrative. The partition of the national formation is then that moment which brings these relations to crisis and leaves their future uncertain. When he finally returned to the short story, Manto produced, in a few hours over two consecutive days, two of his best-known Partition stories, "Open It" ("Khōl Dō") and "Cold Meat" ("Ṭhañḍā Gōsht"). The publication of the first led to a temporary banning of the journal in which it appeared, and that of the second produced obscenity charges and two lengthy trials.

In the remaining pages, I turn to these two stories, perhaps Manto's most notorious, in order to pursue some of the themes that are central to this chapter. As with the earlier stories discussed above, these also revolve around an exploration of the social meanings of the gendered sign, with the figure of the female victim of "communal" sexual violence now as their focus. In such stories as "Gormukh Singh's Last Wish" ("Gōrmukh Siñgh kī vaṣīyat"), "Mozail," "Cold Meat," and "Open It," to which I return at some length below, Manto turns to an examination of the meaning of sexual violence within the violence of Partition as a whole, and its significance for the rearranging and reinscription of identities at this historical moment. Manto places the violence directed at women at the heart of his Partition narratives, insisting that it is in this experience that the real meaning of Partition becomes visible. Some of the more powerful of these stories concern the partitioning not only of consciousness or subjectivity but also of bodies, exploring the manner in which Partition is inscribed, and enacted through this inscription, on human bodies. In "Cold Meat," for instance, it is not just the body of the woman victim and its place in the social world that is transformed forever by a rape but the body of the perpetrator himself, who becomes impotent in the aftermath of the act, and is stabbed to death by his lover in a fit of jealousy when she learns what he has done.

"Open It" begins with an old man slowly regaining consciousness in a refugee camp on the Pakistani side of the new border. Unable to remember where he is and why, he is even more confused to find himself in the midst of this sea of humanity. "His entire being," writes Manto, "was in a state of suspension."[45] Slowly he starts to remember the events of the last few days—riots, arson, looting, narrow escapes, gunfire, railway stations. Suddenly Sirajuddin remembers his daughter, Sakina, who is nowhere in sight. All he finds is her *dōpaṭṭa*, or scarf, bunched up in his coat pocket. He cannot recall if he managed to get her to the station or if she survived the ride on the train, which traversed twenty miles in more than eight hours and was repeatedly stopped and attacked by rioters. For six days Sirajuddin remains in this suspended state. We may read Sirajuddin's disorientation in the refugee camp as an account of the condition of the Urdu writer, and of writing in general, in the midst of the dust and darkness of Partition. Here we may recall Manto's own description of the effect his first writings, the parabolic pieces spoken of earlier, had on his own state of confusion: "I sensed that my pen had gropingly found a way in the fog that surrounded me."[46] Slowly Sirajuddin learns to grope his way around in that darkness and finds a group of young Muslim men, volunteers making daring trips across the border to retrieve lost Muslim women. He describes his daughter to the young men—"she has light skin, and she's very beautiful, takes not after me but her mother; she's seventeen, has large eyes and a beauty mark on her right cheek" (*MK*, 12/*MD*, 12). The young men assure him that if she is alive they will find her. Many days and many border crossings later the men find Sakina by the side of the road. She is terrified of them, but they convince her that they only want to rescue her and return her to her father. Many more days pass, and Sirajuddin receives no news of his daughter. One day he runs into the same young men in the camp. "Did you find my daughter?" he asks. "We will, we will," they reply in unison (*MK*, 13/*MD*, 13). That evening the father is sitting in the camp when a girl is carried in and taken to the clinic. She was found lying unconscious by the railway lines. Sirajuddin slowly enters the room and sees a corpse lying on a stretcher. Suddenly the lights are turned on, and Sirajuddin, noticing the mark on the corpse's face, screams out his daughter's name. The doctor who had entered the room checks for a pulse on the prostrate body and says to Sirajuddin: "The window—open it." The final lines of the story are horrifying in their impact: "There was a movement in Sakina's dead body [murda jism]. With lifeless [bējān] hands she untied the drawstring of her pants and slipped them down her legs. The old man screamed out with joy: 'She's alive, my daughter is alive!' The doctor broke out from head to toe in a cold sweat" (*MK*, 14/*MD*, 14).

Narratives of the Partition of India, from literary works to political discourse, journalism and oral traditions, have long been dominated by the figure of the "violated" woman, sexually assaulted, kidnapped, even killed. Manto's fictions may again be regarded as exemplary in this regard, giving literary substance and form to this figure ubiquitously present in the culture of Partition. In recent years a growing body of feminist historical scholarship on the Partition has clarified the nature and scope of the forms of violence marked by gender and communal identity, the role of the apparatus of the emerging nation-states, and the crisis of community and national identity around the question of the "disposal" of these abducted women. Owing to the pioneering work of Urvashi Butalia, Ritu Menon, Kamla Bhasin, Veena Das, and others, we have begun to comprehend the impact of Partition on the lives of displaced women and the complicit efforts of the two states to appropriate the violence done to them within an ideology of community and nation.[47] In her analysis of the efforts of the Indian and Pakistani states to "repatriate" what they considered "abducted" women, Butalia has demonstrated that the nation-state became ideologically complicit with patriarchal kinship structures to define women as the property of one community or another, and therefore as necessarily belonging to one or the other state.[48] Thus abducted women identifiable as Muslim were transferred to Pakistan, and those as Hindu and Sikh to India, regardless of the location of their original homes, regardless of their present identities or homes, regardless of the willingness of their original families to take them back or their present ones to let them go, and regardless, of course, of what the women themselves wanted. It became the state's *right* and duty to take possession of these women based entirely on a determination of identity, defined as belonging to one religious community or another. Butalia draws our attention to the telling fact that the agreements over the exchange of women were among the very first agreements between the two independent states.

It is this complicity between the two states that emerged out of Partition, this strategy of normalization through which they mutually define themselves by taking possession of women, that Manto's story seeks to expose and undermine. For what shocks the expectations of the reader in "Open It" is that this act of communalized rape is not *cross*-communal but rather is perpetrated by men of the *same* community as the victim's. The communal identity of the perpetrators is as significant in this instance as it would have been in the other. If in this historical moment the state abrogates to itself the memories of primordiality that gather around the modern social grouping we call "community," Manto's story unhinges those claims, makes the national home unhomely, and reveals the fabricated nature of those memories. The ubiquitous presence of the woman victim in Manto's Partition stories is not simply an account, in a realistic register, of the horrific scale of sexual violence that engulfed northern India during Partition. Or, rather, if it *is* an account of this violence, it is so only in a mediated form. In the first instance, it suggests that Partition itself is a kind of *abduction* of collective life, an attempt to uproot, displace, appropriate, and resettle people but also the narratives of communal and national identity. It forces the recognition that the woman victim is not merely a metaphor for the partitioned nation. It is precisely through this form of violence, through its numbing repetition on a subcontinental scale, that the partition of a society is enacted. But this figure also marks a moment of self-recognition for the form itself: Manto's *afsāna* form, in its ironic relationship to national narrative, comes to recognize its own gendered tropology *as* tropology, the instrumentality of its own use of woman. In orienting itself towards this fact in an ironic mode, Manto's short story encounters the limit of its own line of development. Manto's Partition narratives are indeed epic in their ambition, inscribed with the formal intention to tell the tale of the social totality itself. But this epos of an entire subcontinent is told as a series of fragments, from the interstitial points of the social imaginary, from minor locations within it.

Finally, in a number of narratives, including the short story "Sahā'ē" and "Murlī kī dhun" (The melody of Krishna's flute) a narrative memoir of his friendship with the film actor Shyam, Manto explodes the myth of neutrality of the secularist standpoint, in which the act of communal violence is displaced onto some other social actor, usually subaltern. The theme here is friendship, and, more precisely, friendship between men across the boundaries of denominational difference. A scene occurs in both these narratives in which two friends, about to be parted forever, curse each other for belonging to the other religious community as they fall sobbing into each other's arms. In another scene in the latter text, Manto recalls going with Shyam to meet some Sikh refugees from the Punjab where he hears the horrifying tales of the violence perpetrated against them by Muslims: "When we left, I said to Shyam, 'I am a Muslim. Do you not feel like killing me?' In a very serious manner, Shyam replied, 'not now, but when I was listening to the story of the Muslims' outrages [maẕālim], I could have killed you then.' On hearing this from Shyam's mouth, I was shaken to the core [dil kō zabardast dhakkā lagā]. At that moment perhaps I, too, could have killed him."[49] A version of this episode also appeared in the short story (*MR*, 21). Thus the most distinct feature of Manto's Partition writing may be its *proximity* to the violence on which it refuses to pass serene judgment from above or afar. Manto refuses to follow the unspoken convention in Partition literature that requires, as Muhammad Hasan Askari once noted in a remarkable essay on the former's Partition writings, and exaggerating only slightly, that "if at the beginning of the story five Hindus have been killed, then before the story is concluded five Muslims must also be accounted for."[50] The social experience itself has been so extreme, Askari wrote, that,

> "a mere list of the depredations [ẓulmōñ kī fahrist] now has no effect on [the reader]. . . . extreme acts of injustice [ẓulm] have become so mundane now that extraordinary things no longer startle people. . . . If [these] short stories of Partition were not great literature, that would be one thing. But they cannot even fulfill their social purpose successfully. Because the things these stories present [to the reader] are not even news anymore. . . . If anything can startle us in an extraordinary circumstance, it is not extraordinary facts or actions but the most mundane and everyday things.[51]

Thus, for Askari, merely cataloguing barbarism in the realist mode fails not only as literature but also fails the social mission it seems to want to uphold—to clarify the moral issues and inculcate a desire to end the violence. While the monolithic formulation, "short stories of Partition," may be a bit of a straw man here, nevertheless Askari correctly identifies a constant pressure, tendency, and *temptation* in Partition literature in general, and sometimes in Manto's writings as well, to display a posture of detachment and distance from the violence, to build a cordon sanitaire around the language of literature. At its best Manto's writing does not hesitate to expose the language of fiction to the violence of Partition, taking us ever closer to the interiority of the victim, but above all of the perpetrator, affirming the existence of the human in all its mundaneness even in the midst of the most extreme moment.

Nation, Fragment, Totality

As noted earlier, initially Manto had been hailed by Progressive critics as a realist and patriotic writer but then eventually was condemned by them as having an exaggerated and unhealthy interest in the abnormal and the prurient. In 1944 Zaheer described Manto's story "Odor" ("Bū") at the All-India Urdu Congress as escapist, even reactionary, marking the beginnings of the break between Manto and the Urdu section of the AIPWA.[52] The charge of obscenity to which his stories became subject from a wide range of literary quarters obviously refers at one level to content, to Manto's relatively explicit treatment of sexuality, both in the stories concerned with domestic or commercialized sexuality as well as in those that risk the representation of rape as collective violence. But it also contains a larger resonance, pointing to their transgression of the protocols of what I have termed "national realism." The insistent irony of Manto's stories, his characteristic irreverence for all cultural and political pieties and solemnities, and his elevation of doubt and "betrayal" to something like the imperatives of an ethical life—all these factors taken together indeed cannot but translate within a national realist aesthetics as *obscenity*. Perhaps the most revealing condemnation of his work from the Left came a few years after Partition from Ali Sardar Jafri, the leading Progressive poet and critic. Comparing Manto's stories unfavorably with those of Krishan Chander, who was by then producing boilerplate and utterly forgettable narratives of rural life and Partition violence, Jafri wrote: "The difference between Krishan's and Manto's stories is this, that Manto's heroes are mutilated men; therefore they cannot be representative, because they cannot represent the evolution of life. Krishan's heroes are courageous and conscious builders of life. They express evolution; therefore they are representative."[53] What is "obscene" about Manto's stories, therefore, is that they undermine the narrative resolutions through which the representative—that is, national—self is produced. The real point of the debate about Manto's work is the cavalier attitude of his stories not towards sex itself but rather towards the nation or, more precisely, towards the gendered narratives of national belonging. In the end it is difficult to say unequivocally why the leading Progressive writers turned so suddenly on Manto and with such ferocity, although clearly a formulaic attachment to the requirement of "normality" and rejection of all affect and behavior deemed "obscene" played a great role in it. On the other hand, it must be said that Manto allowed this critique from the officials of an organization to drive him into an equally ideological rejection of the ideas and affinities which only recently had seen him celebrated, to his satisfaction, as a leading writer in a Progressive mold. The ease of this slippage must not be glossed over, and perhaps reveals the limits of his own ability to contemplate and welcome the possibilities for wide and deep social transformations. Yet it does not take away from his literary achievement; it merely helps us to map its boundaries and limitations.

Earlier I argued, following Lukács, that what is distinct about the short story as a "minor epic form" is that it "singles out a fragment from the immeasurable infinity of the events of life," thereby making possible a relation of subject to totality which is distinct from that of the realist novel.[54] As a possibility of writing, the short story, perhaps, is rather like the phenomenon of "exile"—a ubiquitous literary phenomenon, somewhat inchoately felt to be fundamental in an unspecified way to the modern enterprise of literature itself, and yet not quite amenable to a grand theoretical synthesis, unlike, for instance, the novel or national belonging as a cultural form. Urdu's emphasis on the short story, I suggested, should be read in terms of this formal ambiguity. Urdu literary culture in late colonial India is located ambivalently at the cusp of "nation" and "minority," resisting precisely the resolutions the Partition attempted to implement, that is, minoritization in India and nationalization in Pakistan. In the next chapter I argue that these resolutions remain incomplete, that at its best Urdu literature continues to be the site for recovering forms of selfhood, community, and collective memory at odds with the categories of the nation-state system. In Urdu, we might say, aesthetic value itself is inextricably linked, in however mediated a form, to the question of the wound of Partition and how in literary terms we might come to terms with it. The situation of Urdu therefore allows us to comprehend the categories of minority experience in a more complex manner than has often been the case in recent discussions of "minority literature." Minority is an ongoing process and pressure, necessarily incomplete, rather than a thing, simply a *type* of writing distinguished by its demographic and sociological situation. It is thus akin to what the school of Durkheimian sociology used to call a "total social fact," in which the nature and identity of the social totality itself is at stake. The standpoint of Urdu, the history of its minoritization that is inherent in the history of the emergence of national experience in India, provides a unique vantage point on this nexus of relations between minority and social and cultural totality.

But of more immediate concern to us here is Manto's relationship as a writer to this wider literary and cultural problematic. It is not my contention that the nature of Manto's short stories is *typically* "obscene," in the over-coded sense outlined above, or that, in the two decades leading up to Partition, longer narratives were not produced in Urdu—the work of Premchand and Krishan Chander, for instance, provides counter-evidence on both these counts. I suggest, instead, that Manto is not so much a representative as an *exemplary* Urdu writer in his relationship to the discourse of nationhood. His work exemplifies in a unique manner the tensions that constitute Urdu as a literary formation at this key moment in its modern history. In his practice of the short story form, Manto inscribes this tension as the paradox of a "minor" narrative form mobilized for "major" literary and cultural aims. The (gendered) "fragment of life" that is the brothel appears with great frequency in Manto's stories, especially in the stories of the first decade of his career, the decade before Partition. But this fragment does not simply affirm the totality of the modern life of the nation. Rather, it disturbs the serenity of the manner in which that totality is produced, pointing always to the possibility of collective ways of life that are less singular and more hospitable to individual and collective freedom.

CHAPTER FIVE

Faiz Ahmed Faiz

TOWARDS A LYRIC HISTORY OF INDIA

At its best, the Urdu lyric verse of Faiz Ahmed Faiz (1911–1984) can make available to the reader a disconcerting form of ecstasy, a sense of elation at the self being put in question, giving even the thoroughly secular reader the taste of an affective utopia not entirely distinguishable from religious feeling. It is, at the very least, a paradoxical structure of feeling, given the explicitly Marxist and anti-clerical affiliations of his poetry, which displays a marked interest in the secularization of culture and language. Faiz, who, like Manto, began his writing career in the 1930s, is widely (though certainly not universally) regarded as the most significant Urdu poet of the postcolonial period. His poetry exemplifies some of the central dilemmas of Urdu writing in the aftermath of India's Partition at the moment of independence from British rule. It represents a profound attempt to unhitch literary production from the cultural projects of either postcolonial state in order to make visible meanings that have still not been entirely reified and subsumed within the cultural logic of the nation-state system. Despite his stature as the uncrowned poet laureate of Pakistan during the first several decades of its existence, his is notoriously an oeuvre with vast audiences across what was once North India—the map of its reception seemingly erasing the national boundaries that are the territorial legacy of Partition. Against much of Faiz criticism, I argue here that the foremost theme of Faiz's poetry, which defines it as a body of writing, is the meaning and legacy of Partition. If, as I argued in the previous chapter, the problematic of minoritization came to be inscribed in Urdu narrative at the level of genre in a foregrounding of the short story as the primary genre of narrative fiction, in poetry it translated into debates about the meaning and nature, the very possibility, of lyric verse in modernity. In the decades following the 1857 Revolt, for instance, the classical tradition of lyric poetry, and in particular the *ġhazal* form, became the site of fierce contention about the prospects of a distinct "Muslim" experience in Indian modernity and came to be singled out as the genre par excellence of Muslim decline and decadence, as too decorative, subjective, and impervious to nature and (Indian) reality, incapable of the sober intellectual effort and didactic purpose called for in the "new" world.[1] The poetry of Faiz exemplifies, for the postcolonial period, the unique relationship of Urdu literary production to the crisis of Indian national culture that is marked by the figure of the Muslim.

The lyric element in Faiz's poetry—its intensely personal contemplation of love and of the sensuous—poses a notorious problem of interpretation: he is a self-avowedly political poet—laureled in the Soviet Union, repeatedly persecuted by reactionary postcolonial regimes—whose most intense poetic accomplishments are examinations of subjective states. The orthodox solution—shared by critics of many different political persuasions—has been to argue that Faiz merely turns a "traditional" poetic vocabulary to radical political ends, that we should read the figure of the distant beloved, for instance, as a figuring of the anticipated revolution.[2] I suggest a somewhat different direction here and argue, first of all, that the *political* element in Faiz's work cannot be read without the mediation of the *social.* Faiz's exploration of the affects of separation and union with the beloved enables us to examine the subject, the "I," of Urdu writing. It would be incorrect to assume that Faiz's "Progressiveness"—his association with the literary culture that carries the imprimatur of the AIPWA—implies a dismissal of the question of identity. The central drama of his poetry is the dialectic of a collective selfhood at the disjunctures of language, culture, nation, and community. In his well-known argument about the relationship of lyric poetry to society, Theodor Adorno suggested that it is precisely the apparent distance of lyric poetry from social determinations that constitutes its social meaning. He held out the paradoxical possibility that its distance from the social actually made lyric poetry an exemplary site for the inscription of social meanings. The more the lyric reduces itself to the pure subjectivity of the "I," Adorno argued, the more complete the precipitation of the social within its content will be. The more it immerses itself in that which takes individual form, the more it is elevated to the level of universality but one that is "social in nature."[3] In this chapter I elucidate the place of lyric in Faiz's work and its relationship to the social horizon that is brought to a crisis in Partition. It is precisely in those poems that are closest to being "pure" lyric, that is, those in which the inward turn is most complete, rather than in such explicitly Partition poems as "Freedom's Dawn," ("Ṣubḥ-e āzādī"), that we may glimpse these social meanings in their fullest elaboration.

I wish to explore the possibility that Faiz's love lyrics give expression to a self in partition, that they make visible a dialectic of self and other in which the subject and object of desire do not so much become one as simultaneously come near and become distant, exchange places, are rendered uncertain. The desire for *viṣāl*, or union, takes the form of this dialectic itself. In the years following India's Partition, the problematic of national fragmentation comes to imbue the lyric world of Faiz's verse in profound and explicit ways. But the broader problematic of a partitioned self is already present in the poems of the pre-Partition years, at least as potential, something these poems point to and anticipate. The social truth embodied in Faiz's lyric poetry is that the emergence of the (modern) self is also its self-division. The truth of the self is its contradictory, tense, and antagonistic reality. Faiz makes it possible to think about identity in post-Partition South Asia in terms other than those normalized within the shared vocabulary of the postcolonial states. The purportedly autonomous national selves that emerged from Partition are revealed to be what they are—moments within the dialectic of Indian modernity. And "Partition" comes to acquire meanings very different from its usual significations, now referring not merely to the events of 1947 (or even of 1946–48) but to a history of social ("communal") identifications co-extensive with the history of the Indian modern itself. The immense popularity of Faiz's poetry in the Urdu-Hindi regions, its almost iconic status as a pan–South Asian oeuvre, is a vague but nevertheless conclusive measure of its success in making available an experience of self that is Indian in the encompassing sense, across the boundaries of the "communal" and nation-state divides. But this is a staging of selfhood that takes division seriously, refusing to treat it as merely epiphenomenal, as in the unity-in-diversity formula of Indian nationalism. It suggests, in fact, that division, the indefinitely extended separation from the beloved, constitutes the very ground from which union can be contemplated. It is commonplace in Faiz criticism to invoke love of country or nation as an essential feature of his poetry.[4] Faiz himself thematizes this on several occasions, as in the early poem "Two Loves" ("Dō ʿishq"): "In the same fashion I have loved my darling country, / In the same manner my heart has throbbed with devotion to her" (*PF*, 166–167).[5] But it is not accidental that neither the criticism nor the poetry itself is unequivocal about what the term "country" (*vaṭan*) signifies. It might even be said that to speak of *vaṭan* and *qaum* (nation or people) in the context of Faiz is to remain meaningfully silent about the objects towards which they point: does love of country or patriotism of Faiz's poetry attach itself to any *one* of the postcolonial states of South Asia? Does it represent, on the contrary, a hope for the dissolution of these states? What is its stance on Partition, their moment of coming into being? Does it imply a "civilizational" referent? If so, which civilization—Indic, Indo-Persian, or Islamic? Where exactly, in other words, is the poet's home?

The symbolic vocabulary of Faiz's poetry draws on the stock of traditional, Persio-Arabic images available to the classical Urdu *ġhazal*—*barbat o nai* (lyre and flute), *lauḥ o qalam* (tablet and pen), *ṭauq o salāsil* (neck-irons and chain), *kākul o lab* (lock of hair and lip), *dasht o gulzār* (wilderness and garden)—resisting the "plain" language that had already become more common with some of his contemporaries and is more so with the generation of poets who have followed in his wake. In this sense Faiz's poetry is a living rebuke to the ideal of a neutral "Hindustani" idiom from which both Arabo-Persian and Sanskritic influences have been excised, an ideal to which the secularist, "anti-communalist" imagination in South Asia has been repeatedly drawn. Victor Kiernan, his translator and lifelong friend, notes that Faiz "was repelled by the prospect held up by Gandhi of a united 'Hindostani' language, a nondescript neither Hindi nor Urdu."[6] The mytho-poetic universe of his work is replete with references to Persian, Arabic, and "Islamic" sources, although, as Kiernan has noted, "a fondness for allusion to things Hindu, even religious, has not left him," an important question to which I shall return.[7] My contention here is that the question of collective selfhood—the meaning of "nation," "people," "culture," "community"—is at the heart of Faiz's poetry, and not merely in the sense of his political devotion to "the people" and contempt for their exploitation by neofeudalism and colonial and postcolonial capital. Faiz problematizes the very notion of nation or people, raising fundamental questions about identity and subjectivity and their historical determinations. More precisely, in Faiz's poetry both the degradation of human life in colonial and postcolonial modernity—exploitation—and the withholding of a collective selfhood at peace with itself—what I am calling Partition—find common expression in the suffering of the lyric subject.

Love and Its Discontents: The Lyric Poet in the World

In a small number of early poems, one or two of which have something like a programmatic status in his oeuvre, Faiz stages the aesthetic dilemmas of the modern poet. They are meta-poetic texts, for in them Faiz explores the nature and meaning of lyric poetry in modern life. In such poems from the late 1930s as "The Subject of Poetry" ("Mauẓūʿ-e suḳhan") and "My Fellow, My Friend" ("Mirē hamdam, mirē dōst"), but, above all, in "Love Do Not Ask for That Old Love Again" ("Mujh sē pahlī sī maḥabbat mērī maḥbūb na māṅg"), we find the poetic persona torn between the exquisite demands of unrequited love, on the one hand, and the demands of the larger world and its oppressions, on the other. Faiz himself has spoken of these poems as turning points in his aesthetic development, marking a growing sense of dissatisfaction with the dominant, "romantic" literary ethos of the times.[8] Thus, in the last poem mentioned above, the dominant mood is set by the speaker's request of the beloved not to ask for the kind of love formerly given—"pahlī sī maḥabbat"—a singular love, alert to nothing but the beloved's charms and cruelties. The speaker lists the efficacies of this love in which he had formerly believed and concludes the first section of the poem with the confession that "It was not true all this but only wishing" ("Yūñ na thā maiñ nē faqaṭ chāhā thā yūñ hō jā'ē"). After noting the cruelties of the outer world—its injustice, inequality, and alienation—with which the beloved must compete for the speaker/lover's attention, the poem ends on the note on which it began: "Love do not ask for that old love again." In "The Subject of Poetry," the same tension between the alternative demands on the speaker's senses is maintained, but this tension is approached, as it were, from the other direction. Alternating between the mysteries of the beloved and those of the larger world, the poem ends by affirming that the poet cannot expect to overcome the former as his true theme:

> —These too are subjects; more there are;—but oh,
> Those limbs that curve so fatally ravishingly!
> Oh that sweet wretch, those lips parting so slow—
> Tell me where else such witchery could be!
> No other theme [lit., subject] will ever fit my rhyme;
> Nowhere but here is poetry's native clime [lit., homeland].
>
> [Yeh bhī haiñ aisē ka'ī aur bhī maẓmūñ hōñgē
> Lēkin us shōḳh kē āhista sē khultē hū'ē hoñṭ
> Hā'ē us jism kē kambaḳht dil-āvēz ḳhuṭūt
> Āp hī kahīyyē kahīñ aisē bhī afsūñ hōñgē?
> Apnā mauẓū'-e suḳhan inkē sivā aur nahīñ
> Ṭab'-e shā'ir kā vaṭan inkē sivā aur nahīñ][9]

These early poems have most often been read as signs of a young poet's political awakening but a politicization that does not lead to an abandonment of concern with the integrity of literary language. Faiz himself has contributed to the authority of this reading.[10] While I do not take this to be an incorrect interpretation, I read the apparent dualism of these poems—interiority (*andarūnīyat* in Urdu poetics) and affect versus externality (*ḳhārijīyat*) and the outer world, lyric poetry versus society—somewhat differently, as demonstrating an interest in the relationship between the lyric self of Urdu poetry and the "wider" world of contradiction and conflict over the meaning of nation and community. I argue that these poems enact, *in a literary-historical register*, the dilemmas and complexities of a "Muslim" selfhood in Indian modernity. The phrase "pahlī sī maḥabbat" points to the problematic of love in the classical Urdu lyric, and the poem comments on the relationship of the modern poet, located in the national-cultural space that is (late colonial)

India, to that classical tradition. In Pakistan Faiz has long been spoken of as a "national" poet, as *the* national poet during the first forty years of the country's life. I contend that this cannot mean what it usually is thought to mean, that in part the accomplishment, the grandeur and ambition, of his work is precisely that it raises serious doubts about whether the nation-state form can account for the complexities of culture and identity in modern South Asia.

Born early in the second decade of this century in the now Pakistani city of Sialkot, Faiz received an education that was becoming increasingly typical for young men of his regional, religious, and class background—the rudiments of Quranic instruction, Persian and Arabic with the local *maulvī*, modern schooling of the colonial (in his case, missionary) sort, and degrees in (in his case, English and Arabic) literature.[11] According to his own account, Faiz's early reading consisted of a diet of Urdu poetry of the classical period, in particular Mir (1723?–1810) and Ghalib (1795?–1869), and the major nineteenth-century works of Urdu narrative. After finishing his studies at the Government and Oriental Colleges, Lahore—those bastions of modern higher learning for northwestern colonial India—Faiz took up a teaching position at Amritsar, where he was first exposed to Indian Marxism and to nationalist political culture generally, primarily through two colleagues, the writers Dr. Rashid Jahan and her husband, Mahmuduzzafar (Maḥmūd al-Ẓafar), who had already become notorious for their publications in *Añgārē* ("Burning Coals," 1932), the anthology of short stories by four young radical writers that created an uproar for its iconoclastic treatment of sexuality, religious orthodoxy, and other "social" themes and was finally banned by the colonial government.[12] Faiz's first collection of poetry appeared in 1941, and the last to be published in his lifetime, in 1981.[13] Occasionally Faiz also published widely read volumes of critical essays, letters, and memoirs. In Amritsar, Faiz was drawn into the literary circles that proved to be the core group in the establishment of the AIPWA in 1936, and he subsequently came to be identified as the leading "Progressive" voice in Urdu poetry while also maintaining his autonomy from that organization and from the Communist Party, never assuming the role of spokesman with respect to either in quite the same way as did a number of his contemporaries, such as Sajjad Zaheer and Ali Sardar Jafry. Jafry once even accused Faiz of equivocating about the goals of Progressive poetry and of "drawing such curtains of metaphor" ("istiʿārīyat") around one of his poems—"Freedom's Dawn"—that "one cannot tell who is sitting behind them."[14] He joined the colonial Indian army after the collapse of the Hitler-Stalin Pact, at a time when the official policy of the Indian National Congress was non-cooperation with the war effort, rose to the rank of lieutenant colonel, and returned to civilian life in 1946 with a MBE (Member of the British Empire). A few years after independence, during which time he rose to prominence in Pakistan as a newspaper editor and labor unionist, he was arrested in 1951 with a number of other radical writers, political activists, and military officers—including Zaheer, one of the *Añgārē* writers who was the leading founder of the AIPWA and, after Partition, became secretary general of the newly founded Communist Party of Pakistan—and senior military officers charged with conspiring against the state.[15] The arrests, part of a general crackdown on the Pakistani Left, had a chilling effect on political and cultural life, and marked the beginnings of Pakistan's realignment as a front-line U.S. satellite in the Cold War and as a reliable regional client after the rise of Mohammad Mossadegh in Iran, a role whose price the country continues to pay to this day. After a trial during which the shadow of a death sentence hung over him, Faiz was sentenced to imprisonment and was finally released after spending more than four years in various prisons in Pakistan. In the late 1950s, with the implementation of martial law in Pakistan, Faiz was again in jail, this time only for a few months. Already by the late 1950s he had developed an increasingly international reputation, especially in the socialist countries and many parts of the Third World. In 1962 he was awarded the Lenin Peace Prize, and at the end of his life, in self-imposed exile from Zia's Pakistan, served for several years as editor of *Lotus*, the journal of the Permanent Bureau of Afro-Asian Writers, which he edited from Beirut, living there for some of the years of that city's devastation, including the months of the Israeli siege and bombardment. In Beirut he composed a small body of what is the most exquisite exile poetry in modern Urdu literature, "an enactment of a homecoming expressed through defiance and loss," in the words of Edward Said, who met him in Beirut during those exile years.[16] I turn to this poetry at the end of the chapter and argue that it represents an attempt to introduce exile and homelessness into the vocabulary of Urdu verse as a constitutive experience. Read together with the early "meta-poetic" poems, this later exile poetry demonstrates that, for Faiz, Urdu is, in a strong sense, a homeless literature and culture, that he sees its entire modern history as a series of uprootings and displacements.

The appropriateness of using the term "lyric poetry" in anything more than a loose and descriptive sense with respect to Urdu writing in general and Faiz in particular is not self-evident and requires some justification. Although Urdu has a number of terms, such as the adjectives *bazmīya* and *ġhinā'īya*, that provide only partial equivalents of the corresponding English term, Urdu poetics makes no extensive theoretical use of such an umbrella concept and proceeds largely in generic terms—and especially in terms of the mutual opposition of the *ġhazal* and the *naẓm*. It is certainly part of the specificity of Faiz's work that, unlike some of his contemporaries, he does not turn his back on the "classical" poetic genres, the *ġhazal* in particular, with its rigid meter and rhyme schemes, and its set themes centered around the experience of separation from the beloved. He could arguably be credited with having resuscitated this form after half a century of neglect and disdain. As I argued at some length in earlier chapters, in the decades following the suppression of the uprisings of 1857–58, with the collapse of the tottering social structure that had been the basis of the Urdu literary culture of the *ashrāf* elites in northern India, "reform"—religious, social, cultural, political, and educational—became something like a slogan among these social groupings of what I have termed a process not so much of incomplete as reluctant embourgoisement, the Aligarh movement of Syed Ahmed Khan being only the most famous and influential of these reform efforts directed at Muslims.[17] Classical Urdu poetry, and the *ġhazal* in particular, became subject, as already noted, to a fierce critique and project of reform within this new literary culture. What is remarkable in the judgment about the *ġhazal*, however, is that it was held, in only slightly different form, both by the nationalist "Hindi" opponents of the dominance of Urdu literary culture and by its Aligarh-connected protagonists and defenders, like Muhammad Husain Azad and Altaf Husain Hali. At issue was therefore a certain language of poetry that, although "popular," as Hali admitted, was now considered far removed from the everyday reality, including linguistic reality, of the people.[18] This charge against Urdu, which, as we have seen, was at the heart of the early Hindi critique of Urdu, and was vehemently denied by the publicists of Urdu in their defensive moments, was thus not absent from the new poetics being developed in Urdu itself.[19] But for nationalist writers, beginning in the late nineteenth century, the *ġhazal* became something like an icon of the vast distances separating the Muslim *ashrāf* from the space of the genuinely popular. (As we have seen in a previous chapter, Forster gives room in his novel of India to this nationalist objection.) Such distrust of the *ġhazal* survived into the twentieth century, and indeed into our own times, among both the literary movements committed to the social purposiveness of poetry, including the Marxists of the AIPWA who were Faiz's contemporaries and comrades, as well as their critics and opponents whose commitment to the intellectual demands of modern poetry is in the name of art for art's sake.[20] The Urdu *ġhazal* and the constellation surrounding it—metrical structures, histories of composition and reception, Persianate vocabulary and thematic conventions, and the image associated with it of an imperial culture in decline—retain a distinct place in the postcolonial Indian cultural imaginary, from popular "Hindi" cinema to such a work of Indo-English fiction as Anita Desai's *In Custody*, despite the massive effort in recent decades to denaturalize and alienate Urdu to contemporary Indian culture and society. Perhaps like no other poetic form in northern India, the history of this lyric genre is inextricably linked with the emergence and development of national culture, and in no other form is the question (and the contradictions) of society-as-nation so deeply inscribed, not even in the *gīt*, or "song," in North Indian languages like Bengali and Hindi that is sometimes said to be the national-popular poetic genre par excellence, most famously in the poetic practice of Rabindranath Tagore.

Even in his practice of the diffuse *naẓm* form—whose only possible definition is apparently that it is a non-narrative and "continuous" poem that is not a *ġhazal*—Faiz bridges the divide between these varieties of poetic writing and imbues the lyric world of the former with the non-national forms of affectivity characteristic of the latter. In this chapter I look most closely at a number of poems that are not strictly *ġhazals* but apply the concept of lyric to Faiz's oeuvre as a whole, irrespective of genre in the narrow sense. In treating Faiz as a modern lyric poet, however, I am not suggesting that we engage in a search for qualities in modern Urdu verse that are characteristic of the lyric in modern Western poetry. On the contrary, my analysis of a number of Faiz's poems is intended precisely to enable us to explore the specificities of modern lyric in a colonial and postcolonial society. Above all, what the concept of lyric makes possible is the *translation*, the passage, of Faiz's poetry from a literary history that is specifically Urdu into a critical space for the discussion of *Indian* literary modernity as a whole. To the extent that Faiz's poetry itself pushes towards ending the inwardness of the Urdu poetic tradition, as I later argue, his work itself implies and requires this critical move.

The Past of the Self Is Another Country: Lyric Subject and Memory

I now turn to the theme of separation and union in Faiz's love poetry by working through its elaboration in one of his best-known lyric poems, "Yād" ("Memory"). The poem appears in the collection *Dast-e ṣabā* (1952) and has been made hugely popular by the singer Iqbal Bano as "Dasht-e tanhā'ī":

> In the desert of solitude, my love, quiver (1)
> the shadows of your voice, your lips' mirage.
> In the desert of solitude, under the dust of distance,
> the flowers of your presence bloom.

From somewhere nearby rises the flame of your breathing, (5)
burning slowly in its own perfume.
Afar, beyond the horizon, glistening, drop by drop,
falls the dew from your heart-consoling eyes.

So lovingly, O my love, has placed (9)
your memory its hand this moment on my heart,
it seems, though this distance is young,
The day of separation is ended, the night of union
has arrived.

[Dasht-e tanhā'ī mēñ, ai jān-e jahāñ, larzāñ haiñ (1)
Tērī āvāz kē sā'ē, tērē hōñṭōñ kē sarāb
Dasht-e tanhā'ī mēñ, dūrī kē ḳhas o ḳhāk tālē
Khil rahē haiñ, tērē pahlū kē saman aur gulāb

Uṭh rahī hai kahīñ qurbat sē tērī sāñs kī āñch (5)
Apnī ḳhushbū mēñ sulagtī hū'ī, maddham maddham
Dūr—ufaq pār, chamaktī hū'ī qat̤ra qat̤ra
Gir rahī hai tērī dildār naz̤ar kī shabnam

Is qadar pyār sē, ai jān-e jahāñ, rakkhā hai (9)
Dil kē ruḳhsār pē is vaqt tērī yād nē hāth
Yūñ gumāñ hōtā hai, garche hai abhī ṣubḥ-e firāq
Ḍhal gayā hijr kā din, ā bhī ga'ī vaṣl kī rāt] (*NV*, 184–185)[21]

Dominant in the first stanza is the image of solitude as expanse of desert or wilderness, expressed in the string "Dasht-e tanhā'ī" (the desert/wilderness of solitude/loneliness) which opens lines 1 and 3. The metaphor also governs the second stanza, as the spatial language of line 5—"From somewhere nearby rises the flame of your breathing"—acquires a geographical register in line 7: "Afar, beyond the horizon..." The dominance of this desert metaphor is sustained in the treatment of the beloved, at least in the first stanza. There, the solitary subject is confronted with the "mirage"-like presence of the object of its desire—"the shadows of your voice, your lips' mirage." For the subject, the shadows and mirage are both signs of the beloved. But whereas a mirage points to an absent, illusory object, the shadow of an object, although immaterial in itself, is a sign of the object's physical presence. Placed in combination with each other, however, each is infused with new meanings. The mirage becomes something more than illusion, more than a mere projection of a desire intensely felt, like a vision of water in a parched land; and the shadow becomes something less than the sign of a physical presence. The geographical metaphor is fused here with a visual one, and together they come to signify the manner of the beloved's becoming-present. What exactly this manner is becomes clearer in the next two lines (3–4), for here "the flowers [lit., jasmine and rose] of your presence" are said to bloom "under the dust [lit., the withered bushes and dust] of distance." In other words, the nearness or presence of the beloved does not cancel out its distance. And the reverse is also true: the distance of the beloved is also the mode of its coming near. This theme is developed in the second stanza. In lines 5–6, the "flame" ("āñch") of the beloved's breathing is said to be rising from somewhere near the speaking subject—"kahīñ qurbat sē"—and yet, simultaneously, the "consoling eyes" of the beloved are placed by the speaker "Afar, beyond the horizon."

In the third and final stanza, the geographical metaphor is abandoned, and we are within an internal, purely subjective space. This intimate space is signified here by "heart" ("dil") or, more precisely, by its "cheek" ("rukhsār"), which is traditionally a sign of the beloved's beauty and of (the lover's) intimacy with the beloved but here expresses the tenderness of the lover's own heart (l. 10). The inexpressible beauty of this image—a human heart gently caressed by an other's hand, as a lover's cheek is touched by the beloved—is an expression of the desire for an end to suffering, for union, for reconciliation of subject and object. It expresses a desire for the form of reconciliation that Adorno has called "peace": "Peace is the state of distinctness without domination, with the distinct participating in each other."[22] The presence of the beloved continues in this stanza also to be its distance. For the beloved enters this interior realm only as image or "memory." In the last two lines (11–12), the poem turns to the intensity of this caress of memory, to its *effect* upon the subject: the "gumāñ" (appearance/feeling/illusion) that the "day of separation has ended, the night of union has arrived."

Like the first two stanzas, therefore, the third stanza also enacts the dialectic of separation and union, in which separation is indefinitely extended, and union, intensely desired and felt, does not cancel out the distance between the subject and the object of desire. It renders uncertain the distinction between them but not in order to appropriate the life of the object in the interest of the subject. The object is also revealed to be a subject and the (desiring) subject an object of (the other's) desire. The beloved is at the same time distant, and hence other, and intimately present to the self as itself. In other words, the self that emerges in the course of "Yād" is a divided one, not at home with itself, desiring reconciliation and wholeness and yet cognizant that its own distance from itself is the very source of its movement and life. It is an uncanny interplay of nearness and distance precisely summed up in a four-line poem titled "Marsīa" ("Elegy") that appears in *Sar-e Vādī-e Sīnā* (1971):

Having gone afar you are near to me,
When were you so close to me?
You will not come now, nor leave,
Meeting and parting [hijrāñ] are now the same to me.

[Dūr jā kar qarīb hō jitnē
ham sē kab tum qarīb thē itnē
Ab na ā'ōgē tum na jā'ōgē
vaṣl o hijrāñ baham hū'ē kitnē] (*NV*, 438)[23]

We may begin to outline the social meanings of this lyric self by noting the resonances of the word "hijr" (separation) in the final stanza of "Yād" (and of its derivative *hijrāñ* in "Marsīa"). A transformation of the Arabic *hajr*, the word is the most frequently used term in classical Urdu poetry for separation or parting from the beloved. As is well known, the meanings of this word and those of its paired opposite, *viṣāl* (union), constitute one of the central and most familiar problems in Urdu poetics. These meanings vary not only from poet to poet or era to era but also from one poetic genre to another, among the works of the same poet, and often within the same poem itself. Thus, for instance, depending on the poemic context, the words may signify the dynamics of romantic or erotic love or of religious devotion. In the Sufi traditions of Urdu (and Persian) poetry in particular, *viṣāl* is a sign for mystic union with the divine, for the desire of the self to become extinct (*fanā*) in a realization of its *ʿishq-e ḥaqīqī* or "true" love of God, compared to which the love of man for man is only *ʿishq-e majāzī*, inauthentic or "metaphorical" love. Most typically a verse may be interpreted at several different levels, in several different registers, simultaneously.[24] The problematic of "love" is thus constituted around an oscillation or productive tension between other-worldly and this-worldly significations. In latter times this poetic language is very far indeed from any concrete practice of Sufism. In Faiz, paradoxically, this religious substratum is again brought close to the surface in order to be secularized anew.

The secularization of *hijr* in Faiz's poetry is part of the general secularization of poetic language and purpose which he and his contemporaries undertake. One aspect of this secularization has been that the Sufistic eroticism of the vocabulary of the traditional poetic genres, and the *ġhazal* in particular, has acquired political meanings, most explicitly in militant poets such as Habib Jalib, who was associated with the world of radical student politics in the 1960s, but also in more serious poets like Faiz himself. Thus, for instance, *vafā* (loyalty or devotion) and *junūn* (madness or intoxication) come to mean political steadfastness and selfless abandon, the rational and irrational components, respectively, of commitment. Faiz's most programmatic announcement of the secularizing impulse of his poetry comes perhaps in "Prayer" ("Duʿā"), a poem written in the mid-1960s:

Come, let us too lift our hands
We for whom prayer is a custom forgotten,
We who except for love's flame
Remember neither idol nor god—

[Ā'īyē hāth uṭhā'ēñ ham bhī
Ham jinhēñ rasm-e duʿā yād nahīñ
Ham jinhēñ sōz-e maḥabbat kē sivā
Kō'ī but kō'ī ḵhudā yād nahīñ.][25]

Prayer may be a "forgotten" custom for the lyric subject, but its very knowledge of this fact belies a memory of a living connection to it. The secular subject contains within itself traces of the life-world signified here by "idol" and "god." Thus the problematic of an uncannily present other, which we have seen in "Memory," is also an account here of the relationship to the non-modern and the manner in which it becomes present to the modern subject. Secularism and even atheism live in the South Asian world in great proximity to the religious, in marked contrast with the structure of relations within which they have evolved in the West at least since the eighteenth century. A great deal of Faiz's poetry performs this proximity, and in this poem, too, secularization is not a mere rejection of religious experience but rather a wrestling with it. This is not an expression of a positivistic atheism that wants simply to abolish the religious impulse in a rationalized culture of struggle and action—"love" in the sense of political commitment. Instead, what is performed in Faiz's poetry is the recognition of the immense power of religious thought and experience for the modern subject. More specifically, the unorthodox and transgressive energies that are always at least implicit in the mystical Sufi tradition are turned in Faiz's verse against religious orthodoxy and its alliance with oppressive worldly authority. A Marxist and internationalist poet, Faiz is nevertheless immersed in the religious language of mystical Indian Islam, both in its high cultural elaboration in the Urdu poetic tradition and as a kind of cultural lingua franca in South Asia. Faiz's poetry reveals a deep respect and *love* for this culture and a recognition of the poet's very complex relationship to it. It represents an agonistic embracing of a particular religious tradition—the Indo-Muslim and Urdu poetic elaborations of Sufi expression—in order to produce out of it the resources for modernity; at the same time, therefore, it also points to the worldly basis of religious experience itself. As we have seen with Azad and even Manto, for Faiz, too, the elaboration of a secular social imaginary entails an encounter with the world of Sufi Islam at one level or another (Sarmad the Martyr, the popular cult of Sufi saints, al-Hallaj, and the very vocabulary of classical Urdu poetry). At no point, however, is this merely a nostalgic embracing of a supposedly syncretic religious life as the authentic indigenous idiom of coexistence, and (poetic) modernity appears as a kind of dialectic of the religious and the secular or worldly.

The problematic of *hijr* in the work of Faiz therefore cannot fail to evoke that other narrative-mythological constellation, designated by the related word *hijrat*, which has been discussed with respect to Partition in chapter 3: the appropriation in Urdu for the dislocations and emigrations that accompanied Partition, especially from the Hindi-Urdu heartland to the territory of Pakistan, of the foundational narrative of Islamic community. It lends to the Partition experience an epic quality and seeks to contain it within a narrative of departure or leave-taking. Faiz explores (and exploits) this historical density of *hijr* as a signifier of relation to place, community, uprooting, and the paradoxes of restoration and return. Although, of course, he himself was not strictly a *muhājir* or Partition migrant—having been born and raised within the territorial limits later claimed for Pakistan—*hijr-hijrat* becomes in his poetry a metonym for the displacements of Partition as a whole, the massive fissure it requires of people, language, culture, and memory coming to be figured as the experience of prolonged separation from the beloved. The *political* impulse in Faiz's poetry can thus only be understood through the mediation of the *social*. For the desire for justice, the steadfastness in face of suffering and oppression, and the belief in a new dawn, are complicated by the "partitioned" nature of the collective subject. In other words, the significance of Faiz's repeated use of *hijr* and its derivatives is that it imbues the lyric experience of separation from the beloved with a concrete historical meaning—the parting of ways or leave-taking that is Partition. If, in Sufi traditions, to speak simultaneously of the pain and joy of *hijr* is to point to a future consummation of love in death or self-extinction, then in Faiz this prolongation of separation from the beloved becomes the modality of collective selfhood, its very mode of being in history and the world.[26] It is significant in this connection that, within Pakistan, critics have sometimes complained about the seeming masochism of such prolongation of *hijr* in Faiz's poetry, in marked contrast to the work of his contemporary Miraji, for instance, where the attempt to project an authentic selfhood not only takes the form of an actualization of union but often is made literal in sexual release. This complaint is significant, for, from within a framework that affirms the terms of Partition, this refusal to grant autonomy to the self (from the whims of the beloved) can indeed only appear masochistic. The lyric subject in Faiz's poetry is located at those borderlands of self and world where autonomy and heteronomy lose their distinctness, where the self is confronted with the uncanny presence of an other that is also self. For Faiz, the end of *hijr* is not a literal union. The sadness of *hijr* echoes the finality of *hijrat*, of leaving your home forever, but it also inverts the implied religious sanction for Partition by reinscribing the self's taking leave of the (antagonistic) other as a separation from the beloved.

When Faiz speaks of lost companions and almost forgotten friendships, as he does in a number of poems from the 1950s onwards, he is echoing an experience that is common in the entire northern belt that was affected by Partition. Take, for instance, the opening lines of "Pā'ūñ sē lahū kō dhō ḍālō" ("Wash the Blood Off Your Feet"):

> What could I [lit., we] have done, gone where?
> My feet were bare
> and every road was scattered with thorns—
> of ruined friendships, of loves left behind,
> of eras of loyalty that finished, one by one.
>
> [Ham kyā kartē kis rāh chaltē
> Har rāh mēñ kāñṭē bikhrē thē
> Un rishtōñ kē jō chhūṭ ga'ē
> Un ṣadyōñ kē yārānōñ kē
> Jō ik ik kar kē ṭūṭ ga'ē.][27]

I suggest that we read "eras" (lit., centuries) here as a sign of historical time and "friendships" (lit., relations or connections) and "loves" (lit., friendships, companionships, or loves) as pointing towards the fabric, the *text* of culture, difference, and identity in history. The modes and forms in which memories of the pre-Partition past are popularly kept alive pose questions of immense importance and interest for scholarship and have only begun to be explored. In Pakistani cities like Lahore, Karachi, Hyderabad, and Rawalpindi, which were cleared of their large Hindu and Sikh populations within months of August 1947, the signs of these erstwhile residents are ubiquitously present—in the sight of sealed-off temples, in street and neighborhood names that continue in use despite municipal attempts to erase them, in the signs of the "other's" tongue above doorways in the old quarter of any city. The memories and stories of older eyewitnesses, the tales travelers tell of revisiting long abandoned homes, the enormous font of verbal genres—folk songs, nursery rhymes, proverbs, and popular tales about characters like Birbal and Mulla Dopiaza—are among the many everyday means of unsettling the finality of Partition, of disconcerting the self with its own uncertainty. The paradox at the heart of Faiz reception is that while he writes poetry that is "difficult" in some obvious ways and true to the subjective demands of lyric, it is this enormous font of popular memory that it seeks to mobilize. We can say of him, as Adorno does of Brecht, that in his poetry "linguistic integrity" does not result in poetic elitism or "esotericism."[28] The suffering of the subject in Faiz's poetry, or rather its pleasure *and* suffering at being separated from the beloved, echoes in lyric terms what is already present everywhere in popular experience, even if in ways that are muted, less than conscious, and fragmentary.

If *hijr* and its derivatives point us in the direction of dislocations and separations that are collective, such a historical reading of Faiz's lyric poems is also made possible in other ways. Since *Dast-e ṣabā* (1952), an increasing number of poems in successive collections appear dated by month and year or by exact date, and many are also marked by place of composition, which in the case of the poems of *Dast-e ṣabā* and *Zindāñ-nāma* (1956) is most often a Pakistani prison. This dating and "placing" of the poems is almost always significant. I suggest that we read the date (or the place name, where it exists, or both) as an extra-poemic, *historical text* requiring interpretation, in interaction with which the poem reveals its meaning. The date functions with respect to the text of the poem in the manner that Gérard Genette has ascribed to "paratexts."[29] "Elegy," for instance, is dated "August 1968," and "Prayer" is accompanied by "Independence Day, 14 August 1967." In fact, the month of August, during which Pakistan and India celebrate their independence from colonial rule, and Pakistan its separation from India, appears frequently over the years as the date of composition of numerous poems. The extra-poemic, "historical" reference here is to the complex text of *national* independence-Partition, lending to these poems a quality of national stocktaking. The pronouns *ham* (we) and *tum* (you, [singular/familiar]) acquire in this context a collective resonance, even as the lyric quality of the poems, their uncompromising subjectivity, produces a sense of deep intimacy, of meetings and partings at the very core of the self, which define its very existence.

Let us take, for instance, "Black-Out" ("Blaik-Ā'ūṭ"), which appears in *Sar-e Vādī-e Sīnā* and is dated "September 1965." The historical reference in the date is to the Indo-Pakistani War of that month, the first full-scale war between the two postcolonial nation-states, which is a watershed in their histories. As C. M. Naim has argued, for Urdu literary culture, in particular, the war proved a turning point, for, with the ensuing suspension of communications between the countries, Urdu literary production and reception began to take place within national spheres in increasingly less contact with each other.[30] The availability of books and journals from the other side of the border, visits of writers and critics, and simultaneuous publication of works in both countries, all common in the period leading up to the war, fell sharply in the following years, and indeed has been almost extinct for decades. The year marks the entrenchment of ideological polarization between "Indian" and "Pakistani" writers, with increasing self-consciousness about hitching literary production to the cultural fortunes of either the one state or the other. In the wider cultural milieu as well, the war led to a suspension of contacts between the two societies, which had been common and routine earlier, ranging from frequent family visits within divided families to the public availability from across the border of cultural commodities, such as magazines and films. The English loan-word that is the title of Faiz's poem makes reference to the introduction of a new vocabulary of war into Urdu, which, like its technology, is of foreign and Western origin. The poem itself remains faithful to the subjective demands of lyric poetry, with the collective and historical reference made explicit through the title and date of composition:

> Since the lamps have been without light, (1)
> I am seeking, moving about, in the dust: I do not know where
> Both my eyes have been lost;
> You who are familiar with me, give me some sign of myself.
> It is as if into every vein has descended,
> Wave on wave, the murderous river of some poison, (6)
> Carrying longing for you, memory of you, my love;
> How to know where, in what wave, my heart is swallowed?
> Wait one moment, till from some world beyond
> Lightning comes towards me with bright hand. (10)
> And the lost pearls of my eyes,
> As luminous pearls of new eyes drunk with the cup of darkness,
> Restores.
> Wait one moment till somewhere the breadth of the river is found,
> And, renewed, my heart, (15)
> Having been washed in poison and annihilated, finds some landing-place
> Then let me come bringing, by way of offering, new sight and heart,
> Let me make the praise of beauty, let me write of the theme of love.[31]

[Jab sē bēnūr hū'ī haiñ sham'ēñ
Ḳhāk mēñ ḍhūñḍtā phirtā hūñ, na jānē kis jā
Khō ga'ī haiñ mērī dōnōñ āñkhēñ
Tum jō vāqif hō batā'ō kō'ī pahchāñ mērī
Is ṭaraḥ hai kih har ik rag mēñ utar āyā hai
Mauj dar mauj kisī zahr kā qātil daryā
Tērā armān, tērī yād līyē jān mērī
Jānē kis mauj mēñ ġhalṭāñ hai kahāñ dil mērā
Ēk pal ṭhahrō kih us pār kisī dunyā sē
Barq a'ē mērī jānib, yad-e baiẓa lē kar
Aur mērī āñkhōñ kē gum-gashta guhar
Jām-e ẓulmat sē siyāhmast na'ī āñkhōñ kē shabtāb guhar,
Lauṭā dē
Ēk pal ṭhahrō kih daryā kā kahīñ pāṭ lagē
Aur nayā dil mērā
Zahr mēñ dhul kē, fanā hō kē kisī ghāṭ lagē
Phir pa'-ē naẓr na'ē dīda o dil lē kē chalūñ
Ḥusn kī madh karūñ, shauq kā maẓmūñ likkhūñ]

The poem opens in darkness, in a state of lightlessness that is external—"Since the lamps have been without light." But this absence of light is, as it were, reflected internally, and the speaker finds himself lost, in search of himself. The first three lines of the poem are an elaboration of this metaphor of darkness—darkness as metaphor for forgetting, for losing oneself. In line 4 the speaker addresses an other being, asking to be recognized and hence restored to his own (lost) identity. But this other is also an intimate, who is familiar ("vāqif") with the latter's identity ("pahchāñ"). In lines 5–8 there is a shift of metaphors, and the crisis of the self is likened to the infusion of an unknown poison—"the murderous river of some poison" (l. 6)—into the veins, a deluge into which the self—"my life" (l. 7) and "my heart" (l. 8)—struggling to keep from drowning, carries its memories of, and longing for, the beloved (ll. 7–8). In the elaboration of this second metaphor as well, therefore, we get a shift of emphasis from externality and the physical to interiority.

In lines 9–13 the poem returns to the metaphor of light or, rather, returns to the darkness metaphor of lines 1–4 by reversing it into the image of light as deliverance from the darkness of the self. This section of the poem opens with the gentle injunction to wait, to be patient—"Ēk pal ṭhahrō" ("Wait one moment")—which is repeated at the beginning of the next section, lines 14–16. Clearly lines 9–10 contain a primary allusion—"from some world beyond" and the "bright hand" of lightning—to the (here Qur'anic) story of Moses on Mount Sinai, an allusion made explicit in the title poem in this collection, "Sar-e Vādī-e Sīnā," written on the occasion of the 1967 Arab-Israeli War. But here I again stress the manner in which this image is secularized: "us pār," unlike "beyond" in English, is more suggestive of a horizontal gesture, directed towards the horizon, than a vertical one, towards the heavens, which the strictly religious image would require. The light that restores comes, in other words, from beyond the horizon—an orientation we have already seen in the poem "Memory." The feeling produced by the phrase "from some world beyond" is of a neighboring world that should be unknown, and yet is half-familiar and vaguely remembered.

The spatial register in which these images, and indeed the use of space in "Memory," become meaningful is the very opposite of state territoriality or of a geography whose scale is larger than human. There is something small-scale and intimate about it. It suggests distances that are traversable by human beings. It is a register to which Faiz repeatedly turns in order to convey a sense of a place both not so far away and yet not so close as to be indistinguishable from *here.* I suggest that we read this complex spatial imagery as a means of exploring, within the terms of lyric poetry, the connections between culture and geography or, more precisely, the process through which the nation-state converts its territory into a *national* geography. Here Faiz is able to render a human geography that traverses the boundaries, and escapes the territorial logic, of the nation-state. In a number of essays and lectures from the 1960s, to which I return below, Faiz raises the basic geographical conundrum faced by Urdu writing in Pakistan: the historical "home" of Urdu—Delhi, Uttar Pradesh, Hyderabad—lies beyond the territorial confines of the country. In his lyric poems this question is echoed by the predicament of a dislocated, displaced lover, often depicted as imagining union with a beloved left behind in a world—nearly but not completely forgotten—somewhere beyond the horizon.

In lines 14–16 of "Black-Out," the metaphors shift again, and the dominant image is once more that of a river, a broad and mighty river, and the struggle of the self to keep from drowning. But this river, which could consume the self, is also the means to its restoration, to the healing of its wounds. In fact, in order to be restored to itself, in order to find a riverbank ("ghāṭ"), the self must be bathed in this poison and become extinct ("fanā"). Having come to know annihilation, it is born anew. That Faiz uses reaching a *ghāṭ* as an image of restoration and healing is not insignificant. It is an Indic (rather than Persio-Arabic) word and image, with a clear reference both to the Hindu sacralization of bathing in river waters as a means to purification and to the ritual cremation of the dead. Furthermore, "fanā" points to the Sufi goal of extinguishing the self in the (divine) object of the self's desire. But in its secularization here it has a utopian impulse, signifying an end to the self's suffering. This combination of these images—the one clearly of "Muslim" origin, the other "Hindu"—is an attempt, in this poem occasioned by the war of 1965, to keep open possibilities of collective selfhood which that event was closing off. Nothing is more natural to a nation-state than going to war, and it may be argued that this particular war was a key moment in the realization of the nation-state form in postcolonial South Asia. That is certainly how it was perceived in contemporary Urdu writing, and, aside from Faiz's own poems of that moment, Ahmad Faraz's "Maiñ kyūñ udās nahīñ" is among the more famous literary responses to the dilemmas it posed. But even in Faraz's poem, there is a slipping into the terms provided by the structure of national citizenship, as the speaker singles out and names the Pakistani cities of Sialkot and Lahore, both on the border with India and both threatened with occupation, and bemoans their suffering.[32] In Faiz's work, on the contrary, the insight about the war as interpellative event is held onto steadfastly, and, above all, suffering never becomes an alibi for a reification of the self. The functioning of lyric in Faiz's writing as a whole is as an abrupt flash of memory—not a fully formed recollection but rather an instantaneous sensation, of the self in motion, in dialogue with an other that is, uncannily, also self.

The final two lines of "Black-Out" offer a glimpse of reconciliation and restoration. Having been washed in poison and made anew, armed with "new sight and heart," the self becomes capable once again of "praise of beauty" and of writing of "the subject of love." This resolution is highly significant, for it comments on the seemingly dualistic movement of programmatic poems like "Love Do Not Ask for My Old Love Again" and "The Subject of Poetry," discussed earlier in the chapter, and opens it up to the influence of a third term.[33] If those early, pre-Partition poems suggest an internal tension or, as it were, poemic indecision between the aesthetic autonomy of love and lyric, on the one hand, and the material predications of the (lyric) subject, on the other, these closing lines suggest that the earlier duality was not simply the opposition of lyric self and society but rather that the identity of the social was at stake *all along* in each of its terms. Thus it is not simply the material environment of the lyric self that poses the problem of the social; the interior world of affect itself raises questions about collective identity. The closure of that lyric world is a figure for the illusion of autonomy of Urdu literary culture and identity as a whole. And the coherence of that world is disturbed by the uncanny appearance of the other. To suggest that the lyric self in modern Urdu can no longer be contained within the world defined by love's intoxications is to insist, in historical retrospect, that the claim to autonomy of that world is itself socially determined, that it is a moment within the contradictory movement of a larger whole. Thus in neither of the two early poems is the lyric sensibility simply canceled and overcome by a higher sensibility. The two are held in an indefinite, dialectical tension, with the result that while the first term is forced to open itself up to the second, larger term, it does not simply submerge its identity within it. The poems announce an end to the isolation of the lyric subject or, rather, an end to the illusion of its isolation. But they do not cancel out the distance between the interior world of subjectivity (*dāḵhilīyat*) and the outer world of objectification (*ḵhārijīyat*). To the extent that these poems are programmatic works, therefore, this is not simply in the sense that they announce an aesthetic of commitment. They are essays, in the etymological sense, in literary and cultural history. They explore the relationship of the lyric in Urdu to the larger history of social and "communal" contradictions that is the history of the Indian modern itself, raising questions about the "subject" of Urdu writing in the double sense of the word, a duality that the word *mauẓūʿ* shares with its English equivalent. What these poems make visible is the social life of the lyric subject—the subject as it appears in classical Urdu lyric—its isolation now appearing as its mode of being in the (Indian) world.[34] In the closing lines of "Black-Out," the impossibility of sustaining the purely lyric sensibility is finally explicitly linked to the vicissitudes of collective and national selfhood. What forces the lyric self to look beyond itself, to other pleasures and sufferings than those of love, is therefore a recognition of its own fragmented reality. The lyric as an aesthetic mode will become possible once again only when the wounds of the self are healed and it is whole again. In other words, the lyric, and the "purely" aesthetic in general, are held up as a utopian possibility linked to the end of the antagonisms, and hence suffering, of the collective subject.

In "Sipāhī kā marṡīa" ("Soldier's Elegy"), another poem from this period and dated "October 1965"—that is, marking the end of the war—this refusal to reify self and other is given a novel turn. The poem, in the voice of a parent (perhaps mother) addressing the parent's dead son, abandons "high" Urdu vocabulary altogether, and turns to an idiom whose resonances are, I would argue, "Hindavi," in a generalization of the function that *ghāṭ* performs in "Black-Out":

Uṭhō ab māṭī sē uṭhō
Jāgō mērē lāl,
Ab jāgō mērē lāl
Tumrī sēj sajāvan kāran
Dēkhō ā'ī rain andhyāran . . . (*NV*, 412–414)

[Stand up, get up from the dust
Wake up, my son
You wake up now, my son
Look, to make your bed
Dark night has arrived . . .]

The linguistic effect here is untranslatable into English. (A very partial parallel would be a poem about World War II written in Middle English.) It is as if, in this moment of crisis for collective selfhood, modern Urdu becomes inadequate as a vehicle for grief. Made possible here by the linguistic displacement is an exploration of the communal and nation-state conflict in terms of the dissonances of language and language history. "Hindavi" is, of course, a term with a complex history of usage as a name for spoken or poetic language over the centuries, and, as Shamsur Rahman Faruqi has noted, among its overlapping and sometimes contradictory references are those to the poetic tradition of the late seventeenth and eighteenth centuries that today is exclusively referred to as Urdu.[35] I use it here, however, in the more familiar contemporary sense of the wide range of vernacular poetic practices that are often excised from official histories of Urdu as too vernacular, that is, not Persianized enough, to be considered an antecedent for the "classical" literary Urdu that emerged in the seventeenth and eighteenth centuries but is embraced within modern Hindi literary culture as the medieval font from which modern, *shudh*, or "pure," Hindi has evolved.[36] This dissonance of literary histories, in which perhaps the most emblematic name is that of Amir Khusro (1258–1325), poet and follower of the Chishti Sufi saint Nizamuddin Auliya of Delhi, is one of the more fraught issues in the history of the Hindi-Urdu conflict over the last century and a half. The poem opens up a window on the vast linguistic-literary vista—Braj, Avadhi, Bhojpuri, Dakhni, Maithli, Rajasthani, to name just a handful of the vernacular language forms that the northern region (and its southern outposts) have produced over the centuries—that has been occluded from view in the standardization of rival "Hindi" and "Urdu" registers, each of which has its own distinct place *within* this range of language and literary practices, despite disavowals of filiation and descent in the one instance (that is, in modern Urdu) and claims to being the encompassing linguistic and literary form in the other (that is, in modern Hindi). Faiz therefore undermines here, within a linguistic register, the claims for an autonomous Muslim (and hence Pakistani) selfhood, on the one hand, and an autonomous Hindu-Indian self, on the other. He places the language that is conspicuously absent from the poem, namely, modern "high" Urdu, in a line of descent from the lingua franca of fourteenth-century northern India. Or, rather, the surface of modern language is peeled off to reveal submerged sounds and meanings. To turn to "Hindavi" in order to articulate the grieving voice of the modern self is to reveal affinities beneath the surface of modern Urdu that are disavowed in its official history. If *this* poem can belong to the canon of Urdu, and of Pakistani, literature, then the linguistic and cultural configurations of self and other are not what the postcolonial nation-states, in this moment of self-definition through war, require them to be. This linguistic displacement makes it impossible for the poem to be canonized as an elegy for a *Pakistani* soldier alone. But it does this not through disavowals of difference—"we are all the same"—but rather precisely through a careful elaboration of the text of linguistic, cultural, and historical discontinuities.

Faiz returns to the themes and motifs of "Soldier's Elegy" in a poem dated "September 1975"—pointing to the tenth anniversary of the war of 1965. The poem, "Mōrī araj sunō" (Hear my plaint), is accompanied by a dedication to Amir Khusro and opens with a series of citations from the Hindavi verses attributed to the latter, each in a plaintive mode, asking for recognition, for the attention of the other, for deliverance and restoration. In other words, Faiz provides a clue here about how we may read that earlier poem as well. Unlike in the former poem, however, here modern Urdu provides the dominant discourse, with the Hindavi in the subordinate position of citation, a mode appropriate to *remembering* the war and the crisis of self it had precipitated a decade earlier. The language of the rest of the poem, following the lines in Hindavi, is the "normal" language of Faiz's poetry, with words and phrases from the citations inserted. The overall effect of the poem is therefore again to resist a reification of self and other, to disconcert the self with a recognition of the sameness of the other, without collapsing the distinction between them. The poemic present, signified by "ab" ("now"), points to the moment of the modern, specified by the self's apperception of itself in the other. As in so many of Faiz's poems, modernity *is* the putting into motion of self and other.

Impossible Narratives of the Nation

In the 1960s, as he became established, despite official distrust and harassment, in the role of something like a national poet in Pakistan, Faiz became a key figure in a wide-ranging public debate about the problem of "culture" in Pakistan, among other leading participants such as Muhammad Hasan Askari, Saleem Ahmed, and Jamil Jalibi. The question of the distinctness or identity (*tashaḳhḳhus*) of Indian Muslim culture had, in fact, informed a large number of his writings on Urdu literary history as early as the 1930s. But now, in a number of essays and lectures, Faiz turned to the post-Partition situation and developed a theory of the three-dimensionality of national culture, sometimes using the English "culture" but more often the Urdu *tahzīb*.[37] The latter word, unlike *s̤aqāfat*, is closer to "civilization" than to "culture" in the sense of the arts, or even of "folk" culture. In fact, in defending his choice of terms, he made it clear that what he has in mind is precisely the sense of collective selfhood, essence, and destiny that is implied by "national culture." The three dimensions of the culture of a people or nation—the word he most often uses is *qaum*—are its length (*ṭūl*), breadth (*arz*), and depth (*gahrā'ī*). The first of these terms refers to the historical expanse of the culture of a nation, the question of when historically a nation locates its beginnings; the second refers to its geographical extension, that is, to the geographical home of the national culture; and the third is a measure of the extent to which the given cultural complex penetrates society as a whole—the problem, in other words, of hegemony. Each of these "dimensions" poses a set of problems for Pakistan, all of them interconnected, but while the problem of "depth"—differences of culture by class, region, and the rural-urban divide—is one the country shares with numerous other nations in the world, the first two imply unique problems with no clear solutions. Faiz's contributions to this debate assume that if Pakistan is to continue to exist as a separate state—these writings predate the breakup of Pakistan and the creation of Bangladesh—these solutions must be found. He insists upon the importance of culture in the work of nation building and proposes a vast project of *national* cultural production, distribution, and exposition, constantly clarified and informed by historical, linguistic, and literary research into the history and mutual relations of each of the linguistic and literary formations in the country, always with an emphasis on what is common to them and unifies them rather than what is distinct and therefore divisive. But it is his formulation of the historical and geographical "dimensions" of Pakistani "culture" that is of most interest to us here.

The question of national culture in Pakistan is characterized, first of all, according to Faiz, by a problem that arises as soon as one tries to specify the point of origin of the culture to which Pakistan as a nation-state is heir. If this beginning is located in the earliest settled culture known to have inhabited the territory that is now Pakistan, namely, the Indus Valley or Harappan civilization, then all the intervening stages and influences—from the Vedic-Aryan to the Buddhist and Greek—must also be included in "our" cultural heritage. This means, of course, Faiz told his readers and audiences, that the cultural prehistory of Pakistan, a state created in the name of the cultural distinctness of Indian Muslims—is not distinguishable from that of post-Partition India. All Muslim countries, Faiz points out, trace their history to some pre-Islamic culture: Egypt to Pharaonic times, Iraq to Babylon, even Arabia to the so-called *jāhilīyya* (Age of Ignorance). But if pre-Islamic, Indic culture is also our own, does that not negate the very basis of the demand for Pakistan? If, on the other hand, "our" history begins with the arrival of Islam on the Indian subcontinent, that is, if we see as our ancestors the Muslim conquerors, traders, and divines who brought Islam to India, then are we not faced with the problem that the cultures of these various Muslim invaders—who include Iranians, Afghans, Arabs, and Central Asian Turks—must also be considered "our" heritage, surely a notion that confounds the very idea of nation?

Similar difficulties arise if we approach the problem of national culture along the "dimension" of geography. If the culture of Pakistan is simply the culture or succession of cultures that have been produced within the territory that is now Pakistan, then aside from the problem of "regional" differences—and, of course, Pakistan consisted then of two segments separated by a thousand miles—what becomes of the culture that was produced, as Faiz puts it, "over there" (*vahāñ*): "[the] national language of West Pakistan, it has been decided, is Urdu, whose real homeland [*aṣlī dēs*] is not this side of Wagha but that side of the Jamna, and its most venerable [*buzurg-tarīn*] poets and writers are asleep [*mahv-e ḳhvāb*] far from our borders. Similarly, the preparation and development of our music, painting, architecture, and other arts also took place in centers that Mr. Radcliffe did not include within our boundaries [*ḥudūd*]."[38] In this passage we see, first of all, the geographical register we have already identified in Faiz's poetry: the border post of Wagha, here coming to stand in for the border between the two countries as a whole, is on the site of an old village on the outskirts of Lahore, the city where Faiz lived for much of his life both before and after Partition. (During the war of 1965 Indian troops crossed the border at Wagha and threatened to enter Lahore.) Second, Faiz highlights the arbitrariness of the nation-state boundaries in question, and hence the discontinuities of national history, by referring to the English barrister who produced the eponymous "Award" that marked the territories of the two newly partitioned countries. If the territorial basis of a nation-state is so clearly the result of an arbitrary colonial decision, can an effort to answer the question of national culture within the confines of territory produce anything but arbitrary results? If, on the other hand, we loosen the territorial requirement and look beyond the borders of Pakistan for the sources of its culture, then on what basis can this extension be made? The "Indic" basis leads to the problem already identified; the "Islamic" basis threatens to extend the search indefinitely and make the notion of a distinct Pakistani nationality ("Pākistānīyat") meaningless.

The solutions Faiz proposes to this conundrum vary from writing to writing and often contradict one another. On one occasion he says that Pakistan's cultural history extends five thousand years, four thousand of which "we" share with "them"—he alternates between "Hindus," "Hindustan," and "Bharat"—and the last one thousand "we" do not; another time he claims that every cultural accomplishment of any Muslim culture is, by virtue of "our" being Muslims, also our own. And sometimes he steadfastly refuses to offer answers, saying that they can be provided only in the future. Faiz's confused and contradictory answers to the questions he himself raised are in themselves meaningful. They highlight a number of *narrative* difficulties that Pakistan as nation-state poses. The underlying question that Faiz's efforts all seem to point towards is this: What kind of national narrative can Pakistan produce? He argues repeatedly that national culture ("qaumī tahzīb") is not "a natural characteristic or something one is born into" ("fiṭrī aur paidā'ishī ṣifat") but rather a "willful and creative act" ("irādī aur takhlīqī ʿamal"), a set of meanings produced in narration.[39] This creative effort was not undertaken, he notes, when the demand for Pakistan was raised and now has become unavoidable.

The confusions and contradictions Faiz points to, together with his clear-sighted perception that national belonging is a "creative" act, already hint at what is made clear in his poetic works: that Pakistan cannot become the site for the elaboration of a narrative that is strictly national—in other words, a narrative that posits the existence of an autonomous subject marked by the attribute of "Pakistaniness." Put differently, it cannot deliver what Etienne Balibar has called "the two symmetrical figures of the illusion of national identity," namely, the sense of a collective destiny, whose contours, furthermore, are already visible, however imperfectly, at the moment of origin.[40] Such a narrative would assume the continuous and autonomous existence of a "Muslim" self finally realized in the form of the Pakistani nation-state. There were, of course, numerous attempts at producing such a synthesis in the decades after Partition; among the better-known scholarly works in English are Aziz Ahmed's *Studies in Islamic Culture in the Indian Environment* and Ishtiaq Husain Qureshi's *The Muslim Community of the Indo-Pakistan Subcontinent*.[41] As an essayist, Faiz demonstrates concisely the confusions and contradictions into which such a framework falls. As a poet, he allows the perception that not only can a "Muslim" or "Pakistani" self not be attributed with an autonomous development, that its very meaning is incomprehensible without reference to the self whose development is the theme of the *Indian* national narrative, but that this meaning consists precisely in undermining the resolutions and syntheses, the narrative twists and turns, through which that "Indian" self is produced.

Towards a Lyric History of India

As we have seen, the poetic program Faiz announced early in his career envisioned orienting the lyric subject towards the larger world. I have argued that some of his most ambitious and effective poems are a series of exercises precisely in ending the isolation of the lyric subject or, rather, in ending its illusion of isolation. They take the form of imbuing it with the recognition that what it takes as object, as the larger world of things, is itself subject and in dialogue with it. This dialectic of inner and outer worlds, I have argued further, carries collective and historical resonances; it is an enactment of the relationship of "Muslim" culture and identity to the emergence of a wider "Indian" modernity. The self-absorption of the lyric subject in classical Urdu poetry, so widely and repeatedly condemned since the nineteenth century, becomes for Faiz a *social* fact. And if that lyric subject—and its locus classicus is the *ġhazal*—appeared to be, as Azad and Hali had argued, addicted to fantasy and impervious to reality and nature, that judgment could itself be explained in terms of the emergence of the horizon of "nature" and "reality" that we call the nation. Hali had been very clear in his *Muqaddama-e shiʿr o shāʿirī* (Introduction to Poetry and Poetics, 1893) about what he had in mind when he recommended "naichral shāʿirī" (natural poetry): "By 'natural poetry' is meant that poetry which, in terms of both words and meanings, is in accord with nature and habit . . . [in accord with] the everyday form of the language, because this everyday speech carries for the inhabitants of the country where it is spoken, the weight of nature [*nēchar*] or second nature [*saikinḍ nēchar*]."[42] Therein lies the *modernity* of his and Azad's critique of classical lyric: it seeks to reorient writing within an emerging *national* experience organized around such terms as the indigenous and the vernacular, with the fatally necessary corollary that it enter the field of contest and conflict over the meaning of community and nation. In this sense, Faiz is indeed a descendant of these nineteenth-century reformers—and we should recall that his early formation took place in a milieu where the writings of *na'ī raushnī* (the New Light) had acquired canonical status—with the crucial difference that for him this project is to be carried out not through didactic poetry, as it is for Hali, but in terms of the lyric itself.[43] What is the nature of the modern (Indian) self? That is the question underlying the reorientation of the Urdu lyric subject in Faiz's poetry, and it is this same question that informs his periodic essayistic forays into the realm of "Pakistani culture."

The enormous paradox of Partition for Faiz is that it requires a rewriting of the self in the name of whose preservation it had been demanded. It is a paradox that he sometimes figures as the collision of different, inner and outer languages of self, as in this couplet from a *ġhazal* dated "1953":

> The heart as such
> had settled its every doubt
> when I [lit., we] set out to see her
>   But on seeing her

the lips spoke love's unrehearsed words
and everything changed everything changed[44]

[Dil sē to har muʿāmla kar kē chalē thē ṣaf ham
Kahnē mēñ un kē sāmnē bāt badal badal ga'ī]

I suggest that we read the pathos of this couplet, this sense of the impossibility of saying what you mean, as a response to "public" languages of selfhood and identity. Here Faiz points to the excess that cannot be contained within the categorical structure of the nation-state, within which "Muslim" is placed at the cusp of a fatal dilemma: it can signify *either* "a separate nation" *or* "an Indian minority." Faiz's entire lyric oeuvre is a refusal to accept the terms of this fixing of identity and an attempt to put the self in motion. The narrative element in this couplet—the self setting out with confessional intent to encounter an other but finding its own words becoming alien, producing meanings other than those intended—must be read in a collective and historical register as an interpretation of the history of conflict over the meaning of nation and communal identity and, in particular, as an interpretation of the history of Muslim cultural separatism. Faiz is indeed a descendant of the writers and intellectuals of the New Light who, a century earlier, postulated for the first time the distinctness of a "Muslim" experience in Indian modernity. But, with historical retrospection, he bathes that assertion itself in the subdued light of pathos, pointing to the twists and turns, the re-routings and misfirings that mark the passage from that moment to our own. This *ġhazal*, composed in 1953, is a comment on India's Partition from this side of the cataclysmic event, filled with infinite sadness at what Indian Muslim "nationhood" has finally been revealed, in the cold light of statehood and "sovereignty," to mean. Faiz distills that historical pathos into the subjective language of the *ġhazal*, giving it the form of the lover's sadness at the impossibility of saying, when face to face with the beloved, exactly what you mean.

The recurring image in Faiz's poetry of an ever elusive totality that is no less real for its elusiveness shares something of the melancholy of Adorno's concept of a contradictory whole whose "movements" are visible only in the "changes" of the fragments: "The whole cannot be put together by adding the separated halves, but in both there appear, however distantly, the changes of the whole, which only moves in contradiction."[45] This concept of the dialectic is an attempt to comprehend totality in late modernity, once "the attempt to change the world," as Adorno put it, has been missed.[46] The "lateness" of the contemporary world for Adorno thus resides in the fact that it is the aftermath of a disappointment, a kind of dénouement once the utopian hopes generated by modern European history have suffered a catastrophic defeat. Hence the series of questions that Adorno directs at contemporary culture: Is it possible to write poetry after Auschwitz? Is philosophy possible once the chance to realize it in a transformation of human existence has been missed? Is it possible, or even desirable, to defend the subject in an age when it is besieged on all sides by the forces of mass culture and mass destruction? Postcolonial culture is, of course, itself constituted by an aftermath and marked by the "late" acquisition of the cultural artifacts of the European nineteenth century: national sovereignty, the popular will, the demand for democracy. In postcolonial South Asia, this moment is also that which follows the partitioning of northern Indian society. As noted in the prologue, Frantz Fanon argued long ago that in order to be transplanted to the colonial setting, "Marxist analysis should always be slightly stretched."[47] The "lateness" of postcolonial culture itself requires a stretching of the concept of late modernity, its uncoupling from the narrative of economic over-development and over-consumption and its opening up instead to a comprehension of the aftermath of decolonization. Faiz is certainly not an "Adornian" poet in the sense in which Celan, Becket, or even Mann might be spoken of as Adornian writers.[48] But my purpose here is to rethink and expand what it means to write in and of the vistas of "lateness" that Said and others have identified in the constellations of Adorno's thought. Faiz is the poet of a late *postcolonial* modernity, a poet who directs the energies of negative thinking—the heterodox mystical gesture of *inkār* (refusal) to which his poetry repeatedly returns—at the congealed cultural and social forms that constitute the postcolonial present. For Adorno, the concept of lyric poetry has a referent that is "completely modern," and "the manifestations in earlier periods of the specifically lyric spirit familiar to us are only isolated flashes."[49] Faiz, however, turns to the traditional Urdu lyric itself and extracts from it a vocabulary for the elaboration of the relation of self to world, individual to totality. He elaborates an experience of modern Indian selfhood that seeks to escape the cultural logic of the nation-state system inaugurated at Partition, that paradoxical moment of realization through reinscription, of success through failure. He does this, furthermore, by immersion in the Indo-Islamic poetic tradition, with its deep relationship to Sufi thought and practice, and its long involvement in the crisis of culture and identity on the subcontinent. This is the larger meaning of Faiz as an Urdu poet with an immense audience across the political and cultural boundaries implemented by Partition. His is not an appropriation of the fragment from the position of totality, but neither is it an attempt to reconceive the fragment itself as a totality. His is the oeuvre of an aftermath once the chance to achieve India, to "change the world," as it were, has been missed. He confronts the fragment itself with its fragmentary nature, making perceptible to it its own objective situation as an element in a contradictory whole. To put it differently and more explicitly in historical terms, we might say that "Faiz" is another name for the perception, shadowy and subterranean for the most part but abruptly and momentarily bursting through the surface of language and experience from time to time, that the disavowal of Indianness is an irreducible feature of Indianness itself.

Words Out of Place: Urdu as a Literature of Exile

Towards the end of his life, Faiz returned to a number of these themes and motifs—the search for a definition of the self, the other who comes bearing the meaning of self, the meaning of place and home, the relation of modern poetry to the classical antecedents—and combined them into a multifaceted image of exile. In conclusion, I turn to one of these late poems, written during the period of his own exile from Zia's Pakistan. Much of the work contained in the collection *Mirē dil mirē musāfir*, the last to be published in his lifetime, dates from this period and was composed in London, the Soviet Union, and Beirut. The book itself is dedicated to Yasser Arafat, and a number of poems in it invoke the figure of the Palestinian as a quintessential figure of exile. I concentrate here on "Dil-e man musāfir-e man," the opening poem in the collection, from whose first line the latter takes its title. The title of the poem is difficult to render into English, but perhaps "My Heart, My Fellow Traveler" might be an adequate working translation.

A recurring poetic structure in Faiz's work is literary citation, as in "Hear my plaint" above, namely, the insertion into poems of phrases and even entire lines from one or another of the classical masters, often from the *ġhazals* of Ghalib. More often the citations are not the exact replication of a literary precedent but rather recall an original in some specific way.[50] It is a technique that poses unique problems of rhyme scheme and meter, since the *ġhazal* in particular follows one or another from a relatively small set of strictly defined metrical schemes and an absolutely inflexible rhyme scheme (aa–ba–ca).[51] Among Hali's critiques of the genre is exactly the charge that what unifies it is rhyme and meter rather than the elaboration of a single continuous (*musalsal*) theme. Hence its popularity and its institutionalized reception in the form of the *mushāʿira*, where an audience can enthusiastically and loudly anticipate the end of a verse before the poet has finished reciting it—all features of Urdu poetry and poetic reception that Hali considered inimical to modernity.[52] In the present poem Faiz turns this seeming limitation—the mnemonic quality lent to the *ġhazal* by meter and rhyme—to his advantage by replicating, towards the end of the poem, the meter and rhyme scheme of one of Ghalib's most famous *ġhazals*.[53] This formal citation is accompanied by citation at the level of content: lines 14–15 and 18–19 are slightly amended versions of the first and second hemistich, respectively, of the eighth couplet of Ghalib's *ġhazal*; furthermore, lines 10–13 also echo a couplet from a *ġhazal* by Ghulam Hamadani Mushafi (1750–1824).[54] The exact parallels with Mushafi and with Ghalib are as follows:

Faiz	Mushafi
10. Sar-e kū'-e na-āshnāyāñ 11. Hamēñ din sē rāt karnā	1. Tērē kūchē is bahānē, mujhē din kō rāt karnā
12. Kabhī is sē bāt karnā 13. Kabhī us sē bāt karnā	2. Kabhī is sē bāt karnā, kabhī us sē bāt karnā

Faiz	Ghalib
14. Tumhēñ kyā kahūñ kih kyā hai 15. Shab-e gham burī balā hai . . .	1. Kahūñ kis sē main kih kyā hai, shab-e gham burī balā hai
18. Hamēñ kyā burā thā marnā 19. Agar ēk bār hōtā (*NV*, 613–614)	2. Mujhē kyā burā thā marnā agar ēk bār hōtā

The dominant affect of this poem is the pathos of recollection. Faiz produces an image of exile as a constant effort to remember, expressed in the latter half of the poem in the effort to "remember" literary antecedents. Lines 1–9 constitute the first section of the poem, in which the idea of exile is introduced and elaborated upon. The idea itself is introduced in lines 1–4, as the speaker addresses his own self—"my heart" ("mirē dil")—with the intimation that it is "again" ordained that "we" leave home ("vaṭan"—country/homeland). The word "phir " here is significant, for it introduces the idea of repetition, establishing this as only the *latest* in a long series of exiles. And its relationship to "vaṭan" suggests that we are concerned with repetitions in *historical* time. Lines 5–9 offer an elaboration of the idea of exile: to be in exile is to wander in search of some "yār-e nāma bar" ("friend bearing a missive") and to ask "every stranger" "(har ik ajnabī") for the way back to the home one has left behind. "Yār" could simply mean someone who is known or familiar, the opposite of stranger, but it is also a conventional poetic term for the beloved; and "ajnabī" signifies both stranger and foreigner. Thus to be in exile is both to be in constant search of the familiar/beloved who comes bearing a letter ("nāma"), a message, from home, and to interrogate strangers about the identity of the place that is one's own. To be in exile is to engage in a constant effort to remember, to rediscover, a self that is at home.

If the first half of the poem introduces and elaborates the theme of exile as remembrance or recollection, the rest of the poem is an *enactment* of that exile. This enactment takes the form, as I have already noted, of the textual effort to "remember" classical literary antecedents. Let us consider the Mushafi parallels first. Lines 10–11 echo the first hemistich of Mushafi's couplet. Line 10 shares nothing lexically with the first half of the hemistich, but it recalls it metrically and semantically. "Kūcha" and "kū" are both "street." But if in Mushafi it is the beloved's street ("your street"), in Faiz it is a street inhabited by "strangers." Line 11 is nearly identical with the second half of the hemistich, except that the first-person singular pronoun "mujhē" is replaced by the plural form, "hamēñ"—a substitution in line with Faiz's preference for the first-person plural, a preference that, as I have argued, lends to the language of selfhood a collective resonance. Lines 12–13 are identical with the second hemistich. If in Mushafi's couplet the dominant image is that of the speaker-lover lingering in the street of the beloved in the hope of catching sight of her, randomly engaging passers-by in conversation, in Faiz's poem the speaker finds himself in an unfamiliar street, searching for his own identity, for *himself*, among strangers. One of the relationships with the classical lyric that this poem enacts, therefore, centers around the identity of the self: the specificity of the modern in this poem is to *open up* the question of selfhood, to display the self in motion, searching for itself in and through "some" other.

The "Mushafi" segment of the poem (lines 10–13) is followed immediately by two lines that echo the first hemistich from Ghalib's couplet. The difference between the two rests in that Faiz replaces the openness of the quest for the other—"kahūñ kis sē main" ("to whom should I say")—with a definite addressee—"tumhēñ kyā kahūñ" ("what should I say to *you*?"). Lines 16–17 are, lexically speaking, original, but they echo the Ghalib couplet, and the *ġhazal* from which it is taken, in terms of rhyme and meter. Their function is therefore to interrupt the expectations of the reader, or rather to fulfill them only in part, by postponing the second hemistich, or its echo, until lines 18–19. And here the only displacement of the original is in the substitution of the first-person singular "mujhe" with the plural form, "hamēñ," a substitution that lends a collective resonance to the language of selfhood, as we saw in "Black-Out." The last six lines of the poem therefore give the impression of a run-on "Ghalib" *ġhazal* couplet (ab–b), with an extra "second" hemistich. Alternatively the last four lines together suggest the first couplet of a *ġhazal* (aa).

The choice of poets to "echo" here is significant. Mushafi is among the important poets of the late eighteenth and early nineteenth centuries, who spent much of his creative life in Lucknow, although whether he belongs to the "Lucknow School" of poets is open to question in a way that it is not with respect to such later Lucknow-resident poets as Shaikh

Imam Bakhsh Nasikh (1771–1838) or Khwaja Haider Ali Atish (1778–1847), the latter a student of Mushafi's.[55] He was credited, by the British Orientalist scholar of Urdu Grahame Bailey, with being the first poet to use the word "Urdu" as the name of the language of his poetry.[56] Ghalib's poetry, of course, represents the culmination of the rival "Delhi School." He is the final eminence of the period in Urdu literary history that ends with the uprising of 1857, and a transitional figure between the "classical" tradition and the "moderns," like Azad and Hali. Between them, therefore, these two poets signify in Faiz's poem the classical heritage of the modern lyric poet. Together they constitute an image of "home" for the poet in exile. But they are both literary ancestors who lie "asleep," to borrow the image Faiz uses in the essay I cited, "that side of the Jamna," rather than "this side of Wagha." In this imaginative home-coming, in other words, the poetic consciousness in exile finds that home itself is a form of displacement, figured here in the disorientations of inter-textual echo.

Thus the subject of Urdu (lyric) writing is for Faiz, in a strong sense, a homeless one. Faiz's poetic intent here is to confront the subject with its own displacements and, in the larger context of his oeuvre, to propose that its reorientation towards the "larger" world, which constitutes its modernity, also means a critique of forms of existence premised upon notions of being, as it were, at home. To adopt a secular relationship to the world is to renounce the possibility of such an existence. Urdu for Faiz cannot be normalized as the language, literature, and culture of a (Muslim) nation-state. But nor is it assimilable to the contours of a "minority" (Indian) literature. The gesture that properly expresses the ambivalence of this position at the cusp of nation and minority is the look always directed elsewhere and, as in so many of Faiz's poems, towards the horizon, which serves as a figure for the limits of normalized perception. For it is there, just beyond the limits of what it is permissible to perceive, that the self encounters its own incompleteness and manages to capture the fleeting perception that what it had taken to be its outer boundary is a line of internal division, that its own truth, its wholeness, takes the form of an unresolved contradiction. Partition appears in Faiz as a defining feature of the self itself, the manner in which a collective self has been produced in modernity. The collectivity-in-antagonism pointed to here is therefore both nation and not nation. For although it is the project of the nation-state in South Asia to normalize its emergence from colonial rule as the realization of autonomous national selves, a project against which Faiz's entire oeuvre is directed, it is by working through, rather than simply disavowing, the partitioned national experiences of postcolonial South Asia that this larger self-in-contradiction can now ever even be perceived.

In this sense, then, for Faiz, modern Urdu writing can only be a writing of exile, a writing that seeks constantly to displace the relationship of language and self to place. The selfhood that it takes as its subject, in both senses of that word, is not a self at home. Furthermore, Faiz's poetic practice insists, and demonstrates, that that is precisely Urdu's vocation, its special meaning and place in the panorama of Indian cultures. The powerful tradition of lyric poetry in Urdu, long accused of its indifference to properly Indian realities, is revived and given a new lease on life in Faiz and his contemporaries not because they infuse old words with new meanings, as the intentionalist cliché in Faiz criticism would have it, but because in their practice it becomes a site for the elaboration of a selfhood at odds with the geometry of selves put into place by Partition. In his lyric poetry, Faiz pushes the terms of identity and selfhood to their limits, to the point where they turn upon themselves and reveal the partial nature of postcolonial "national" experience. In this sense, Faiz may be said to be situated somewhere very close to Manto and Azad, even though he is quite distant from them, and they from each other, on an ideological spectrum, with vastly different tastes in politics, religion, and even literature and culture. In this and the previous two chapters I have attempted to show that what these major writers from the middle decades of the century bring to Urdu literary history, from very different directions and points of origin, is the essentially exilic thrust of their writing, or, more precisely, that their oeuvres consist of forms of elaboration that do not consecrate the nation-state as the natural horizon of culture and community. The ongoing process of the partition of Indian culture and society becomes the occasion and means in their writing for an exploration of the mediated production of selves and the fissures and displacements out of which their sense of wholeness is produced. These are, we should note, *vernacular* forms of displacement, by which I mean that they do not simply replicate the antinomies of colonial culture—local versus cosmopolitan, indigenous versus modern—and view the great indigenizing machinery of nation and nation-state as itself a product of the colonial world. One aim of these chapters has therefore been to attempt to rescue the problematic of exilic consciousness—"ġharīb al-vaṭanī," as Azad so beautifully called it for his Friday audience in Delhi in 1947—from the stultifying contemporary debates between what we may term, on the one hand, postmodern globalists and, on the other, national localists, a debate in which neither side seems capable of recognizing and comprehending these exercises in vernacular modernity.

Epilogue

IN MY BEGINNING IS MY END: JEWISH EXILE AND THE LANGUAGE OF ENGLISH INDIA

In the second part of this book I have explored the involvement of Indian national culture with the crisis of Muslim identity, the question of whether the Muslims constitute a minority. In my reading the Partition of India was an attempt to bring about not only the establishment of a Muslim nation-state but also the minoritization of "the Muslims," and through it the nationalization of Indian culture and polity, by means of a massive rearrangement of populations, identities, desires, and memories that sought to turn roughly two-thirds of the Muslims of the Indian subcontinent into non-Indians. For a critical project that seeks to place cultural and political realities in contemporary South Asia in such a frame, the significance of Urdu literary culture is an enormous and complex one. For, as I have tried to show in part 2 of this work, a defining feature of Urdu literary history is the resistance it offers to canonization, its tense, agonistic, and *negative* relationship to the nation-state as a frame for the formation of cultures and selves. If the entire history of the Hindi-Urdu conflict in colonial India highlights this unassimilability of Urdu within a national canon, then this problem is not simply resolved once and for all at and through Partition. Despite the institutionalization of Urdu as the official language of the nation-state of Pakistan, and its opposite but not equal minoritization in postcolonial India, Urdu literary production at its most ambitious—in the post-Partition work of such writers as Faiz, Manto, Qurratulain Hyder, Intizar Husain, Fehmida Riaz, and Nayyar Masud—continues to recall and make available to the reader forms of consciousness and possibilities of selfhood disavowed by the nation-state, constantly driven to look across a purportedly uncrossable border. Urdu remains, fundamentally, a homeless literature, its history an exemplary embodiment of some of the central processes and dilemmas of modern culture: nation formation, canonization, minority consciousness, "partitioning" of cultures, exile and displacement, crossing of borders, and anxious and agonistic formation of selves. In my account the literature of Urdu emerges as the site par excellence for questioning the inevitability of the historical outcome we signify as "Partition" and for staging so many interruptions of this dialectical process of the mutual determinations of nationality and minority.

Having explored in the previous section of this book certain aspects of Urdu as a literary configuration in the middle decades of the twentieth century, I turn in these remaining pages, by way of a final elaboration, to another literary terrain—contemporary Anglophone narrative literature with links to India or of Indian origin—which, in the late twentieth century, has sought to return us to the cultural frames of exile, diaspora, displacement, and the critique of the "settled" forms of thinking and social imagination associated with nationalism and the nation-state. As is well known, exiles, émigrés, refugees, migrant workers, displaced persons, and minority figures of various sorts figure prominently in this narrative literature and constitute one of its dominant preoccupations—here one need only think of any number of the works of, for instance, V. S. Naipaul, Salman Rushdie, Bharati Mukherjee, Anita Desai, Amitav Ghosh, and Hanif Koreishi, but especially *The Bend in the River* (1979), *The Satanic Verses* (1987), *The Moor's Last Sigh* (1995), *Jasmine* (1989), *Baumgartner's Bombay* (1988), *In an Antique Land* (1992), *In Custody* (1984), and *Sammy and Rosie Get Laid* (1988). In a number of these important works of "cosmopolitical" fiction, as Bishnupriya Ghosh has so accurately described them recently—among them *The Moor's Last Sigh*, *In an Antique Land*, and *Baumgartner's Bombay* (to which I turn at some length below)—this preoccupation has taken the explicit form of a turn to a narrative exploration of the metaphorical possibilities of Jewishness.[1] The emergence of the metaphorics of Jewishness, in its links to exile and minority, in the midst of this particular, globally disseminated form of postcolonial culture is significant for an interpretation of the meanings of minority in the postcolonial present. In it, the form—the Indo-English novel—and the culture reveal at least a partial awareness of their own genealogy, a recognition that an exploration of the problematic of exilic consciousness resonates with the history of European Jews in the modern era. Some years ago Meenakshi Mukherjee spoke of the Indo-English fictional narrative tradition as "twice born fiction." It is a profound formulation that captures, on the one hand, the elite location and elite-making function of English, language and literature, as a formation in Indian society since colonial times and, on the other, the fact that it is "a product of two parent traditions," that is, the essentially nonlinear and displaced nature of its emergence.[2] This book has been in part an attempt at a genealogy of the present, of the minority problematic as it precipitates a series of crises in contemporary culture, and has sought to provide an outline of the subterranean route by which that nineteenth-century question in Europe traveled to colonial India. I seek now to examine more explicitly the possibilities of affiliation between two seemingly distinct intellectual trajectories within contemporary culture—on one side, the critique of colonial and postcolonial culture as a global formation, a critique that is at least a century old in its modern form but has been given a new shape and new turn in the last quarter-century, and, on the other, the critique of European modernity from the perspective of the question of Jewish existence, inextricable at this point from the history of philosophy, theory, and criticism in the twentieth century.

The Location of Exile and the Postcolonial Imagination

In *The Moor's Last Sigh*, Rushdie seeks to displace the grand events of India's modern history, which had provided so much fodder for the characteristic parodic rewriting of history in his earlier works, to the margins of the page as he tells the story of a family of Catholics and Jews far removed from the mainstream clash of culture and identity in colonial and postcolonial India—"Are not my personages Indian, every one? Well, then: this too is an Indian yarn."[3] The protagonist-narrator is Moraes "Moor" Zogoiby, last remaining heir of the Da Gama-Zogoiby spice and nut dynasty of Cochin, half-Jew and half-Catholic—a "cathjew" nut, as he puts it—writing in distant Spanish exile the history of his family that is also the history of the nation as viewed from his particular location of, as it were, a minority of one. "Moorish Spain" and "Bombay" serve in the novel as the names for social imaginaries that allow for the coexistence of diverse and plural elements, with the collapse of the former in the late fifteenth century providing a host of metaphors for the collapse of the latter in the pogroms and bombings, the mob and Mob violence, that followed in the aftermath of December 6, 1992:

> Just as the fanatical "Catholic Kings" had besieged Granada and awaited the Alhambra's fall, so now barbarism was standing at our gates. O Bombay! *Prima in Indis! Gateway to India! Star of the East with her face to the West.* Like Granada—al-Gharnatah of the Arabs—you were the glory of the time. But a darker time came upon you, and just as Boabdil, the last Nasrid Sultan, was too weak to defend his great treasure, so we too, were proved wanting. (*MLS*, 372)

The political rise of violent Hindu nationalism in Bombay and Maharashtra in the form of the Shiv Sena, which appears here as "Mumbai's Axis" or the M.A., is thus figured as a sort of *Reconquista*, with the "mongrel" Bombay of the Nehruvian decades consumed by the violent religious, ethnic, and linguistic rigidities of "Maharashtra for Maharashtrans." The novel thus continues the idealization of the Bombay of the 1950s and 1960s—that is, of the immediate decades following the partition—as a cosmopolitan space that has been a recurrent feature of Rushdie's writings from *Midnight's Children* onwards, a Bombay produced out of encounters between the seemingly distinct and incompatible histories of Jews, Catholics, Portuguese, Hindus, Muslims, Anglo-Indians, Goans, Gujaratis, Maharashtrans, South Indians, Parsis, and numerous others. This nostalgic reconstruction, versions of which exist with reference to most major urban centers in South Asia—Karachi, Calcutta, Delhi, Madras—is a familiar modality of culture of the contemporary diaspora. But Rushdie's "Bombay" makes possible very specific possibilities of narration and representation. Rushdie's explicitly stated purpose as storyteller is to make sure that "Majority, that mighty elephant, and her sidekick, Major-Minority, will not crush my tale beneath her feet" (*MLS*, 87). It is not just a clever wordplay but a formulation that is deeply perceptive about the nature of the so-called Hindu-Muslim conflict in the modern era and the crisis of Muslim identity, which has teetered historically, as I have tried to show in part 2 of the book, on the brink of this distinction between *major* and *minor* domains and possibilities. For a retelling of this larger story of the nation, Rushdie proposes an irreducibly minor (Jew, Catholic, Portuguese, Indian, orphaned, deformed) and exilic (in Benengeli, recalling Cide Hamete [Sidi Hamid] Benengeli, the Moorish author whose amanuensis Cervantes feigns to be) location. Even the "Jewish" line in Moor's genealogy is part "Arab," rumored to be descended from an illegitimate encounter with "Boabdil," that is, Abu Abdallah, the last Moorish ruler of Granada. Boabdil on the verge of being forced into exile provides the master motif of the novel, as it does of the series of paintings by Aurora Zogoiby and Vasco Miranda whose title provides the title of the novel as well. This identification of the Arab—Jewish as well as Muslim—ghosts that haunt Catholic Spain provides the center of a series of swirling perceptions about the violence inherent in any attempt at settling and fixing culture and identity. Against "Majority" and "Major-Minority" as (rival but essentially identical) forms of social identification, the novel proposes a community of minor and exilic formations and groupings under constant threat of erasure from those dominant forms.

Amitav Ghosh's *In an Antique Land* also draws on the history of Jewish migrancy, but in this case the transnational possibilities inherent in the commercial functions fulfilled by Jewish populations in medieval society become the means to an exploration of forms of cosmopolitanism that predate the coming of the European navies to the Indian Ocean world. In the medieval sections of Ghosh's narrative, it is Jewish traders, in possession of multiple economic, linguistic, and cultural literacies, familiar with commercial centers and ports of call in southern Asia, Arabia, and Africa, and one with an Indian household slave in tow, who provide the links between India and Egypt and North Africa. It is a world that disappears with the coming of the Europeans and their enforcement of zones of influence, religion, culture, and identity, but its traces remain hidden in the Geniza, the document chamber of the ancient Ben Ezra Synagogue in Fustat, from where they are dispersed to numerous Western libraries and archives beginning in the late nineteenth century, to be "discovered" by the narrator, himself a cosmopolitan and displaced figure—Indian citizen, Anglophone writer, Oxford-trained anthropologist—in the published writings of an Orientalist scholar. Here Marx's much maligned observation about capitalism and the Jews seems to have been stood on its head: it is in the past, the book seems to suggest, that we were all a little bit more like the Jews. In the sections of the narrative situated in the historical present, broadly conceived, on the contrary, Egyptians and Indians meet each other as total strangers, unaware of the vanished world to which they once equally belonged. In a nicely written passage, an encounter with a village mulla—the narrator is engaged in anthropological fieldwork nearby and hopes to gain knowledge of indigenous medicinal practice—degenerates quickly into misunderstandings and a shouting match about which country produces better "guns and tanks and bombs." In his ensuing depression, the narrator is forced to conclude that "[we] were both travelling, he and I: we were travelling in the West." Where once Indians and Egyptians could have met as members of their respective civilizations, they could now communicate only in this shared language of the West—"science and tanks and guns and bombs."[4] And the refashioning of Egypt as a national society in the course of the twentieth century required a foundational forgetting of key aspects of its own past—not only the now lost Indian Ocean world but also the presence of a vital Jewish culture within it, as evidenced, for instance, in the once ancient Ben Ezra community or the shrine of the saint Sidi Abu-Hasira, visited unself-consciously by Egyptian Muslims but whose Jewish origin had been forgotten both from popular and official memory.[5]

Whereas Ghosh, in *In an Antique Land*, seeks to re-imagine the Jews as the agents of a vernacular, non-Eurocentric cosmopolitanism in the Afro-Asian world and Rushdie, in *The Moor's Last Sigh*, attempts to turn exile into the condition of oppositional culture, Desai, in *Baumgartner's Bombay*, seeks to disconcert our expectations of the trajectories implied in narratives of Jewish exile. And she does so, in particular, by taking as her protagonist, if such an essential non-actor may be spoken of as a protagonist, Hugo Baumgartner, a young Jewish man from Berlin who escapes to India from possible annihilation at the hands of the Nazis and ends up spending the rest of his life there, only to have Germany catch up with him in the end, as he is murdered in his filthy Bombay apartment, which reeks from the countless cats he shares it with, by a half-starved young German, a counter-cultural denizen of Khatmandu temples and Benaras cremation *ghāṭs*. Naturalized as a citizen but, to the end, an alien in any of India's seeming plethora of cultures, Hugo somehow manages in the half-century of his life that he spends in the country to make for himself, as the title of the book suggests, something like a home. He is, like the language he fashions for himself on arriving in India out of bits of English and the indistinguishable Indian vernaculars, "not Indian, but India's."[6] Much of Desai's narrative is an exploration of what kind of belonging this is, of what it can tell us about belonging itself, the sense that a human experience is of *this* place and of *this* people. Displaced persons of various sorts—exiles, refugees, "enemy aliens," impoverished rural migrants—are to be found everywhere in this novel. Hugo himself is the ultimate outsider, embarrassed even at the possibility of belonging to anyone or anything, however fleeting or tentative such a connection may be, the eternal exile shunned even by his fellow refugees, whose "natural condition" is "silence" (*BB*, 117). The novel may be seen as performing a double insistence—its implicit claim, on the one hand, that the situation of the truly "homeless" in modern culture is not merely incidental to that culture and, on the other, that its postcolonial location, in the sense that its specificity is the experience of an imperial aftermath by a formerly colonized society, provides a unique vantage point on that modernity. Desai's novel seeks to excavate a subterranean history—not simply of Europe, as in Arendt's well-known argument about the rise of Nazism[7]—but of the modern world, a network of subterranean and uncanny linkages that connect "Europe" to the world's "peripheries."

The novel is structured as a weaving together of two narratives, both centered on Hugo. The first, spread out in chapters 1, 3, 5, and 7, follows him from the morning to the late evening of a single day in Bombay, the last of his life. The second, which unfolds across chapters 2, 4, and 6, is a narrative of his life, starting with his childhood in an affluent and cultivated Jewish home in Berlin and ending with a summation of his life in Bombay five decades after his first arrival in that city from Europe. And this larger interweaving of narratives is framed by brief opening and closing sections whose present is the afternoon following Hugo's last day, both centered around Lotte, his longtime friend and lover. The novel opens with her fleeing in grief and terror from the bloody scene of Hugo's murder and closes with her in her own apartment, with mementos of Hugo's life spread out on the table before her. In this configuration of time, therefore, the novel forces an ironic articulation between two distinct narrative forms, namely, the classic *Bildungsroman* and the modernist narrative whose chronology spans a single day. By the end of the penultimate chapter of the book (the sixth), the second narrative has caught up with the first. Life has caught up with death.

The moment of Hugo's death and the manner in which it occurs form a powerful framing device for the novel's staggered and zigzagging narrative. His end comes at the hands of Kurt, a young German countercultural tourist, impoverished and malnourished, at once ascetic and seeker of Tantric pleasure and vice. Hugo had rescued him from the street and brought him back to his own cluttered and filthy home for a reason he did not quite understand. He is first drawn to the boy as he lies passed out at a table in a restaurant that Hugo frequents, because Hugo knows instinctively that he is German: "He had sensed, he had *smelt* the German in him like a cat might smell another and know its history, its territory" (*BB*, 21). But this chance encounter brought an uncontrollable stream of memories, a terrifying flood of recollections that took him further and further back, to childhood and to death:

> That fair hair, that peeled flesh and the flash on the wrist—it was a certain type that Baumgartner had escaped, forgotten. Then why had this boy to come after him, in lederhosen, in marching boots, striding over the mountains to the sound of the *Wandervogels Lied*? The *Lieder* and the campfire. The campfire and the beer. The beer and the yodelling. The yodelling and the marching. The marching and the shooting. The shooting and the killing. The killing and the killing and the killing. (*BB*, 21)

This series connecting the slumped over blonde body in Bombay to Auschwitz and Treblinka is a metonymic one; the connections between its terms are substantive and not merely metaphorical. They point, in other words, to a continuity between contemporary Europe and that earlier genocide. It is significant that, whereas for Baumgartner their encounter is determined, and, in fact, overdetermined, by the history of their common society of origin, Kurt betrays not the slightest comprehension of this history that has deposited the other on these distant shores. The Europe of post-sixties generational conflict, in which one generation of Europeans rejects the Eurocentric legacy of the previous one—a rejection here embodied in Kurt's countercultural relationship to India—is subjected to a sharp critique here for failing to confront and comprehend its own history. Desai inscribes this imperviousness of Europe to its own history on the very bodies of the German and the Jew, the former "tall and well-built, with the heavy square bones of an ox or a sportsman," and the latter the very picture of decrepitude and decay, all flab and sweat and effort. Thus Baumgartner's body is itself the record of a history that cannot be contained in a classically proportioned form, and common to the efficiency of the killers and the countercultural discipline and asceticism of Kurt is an intolerance for the mess, the untidiness, the uncontainability that is Baumgartner. And that this young German killer of the old Jew escapes detection and capture is itself a telling comment on the claim to progress in postwar Europe and the evasion of historical responsibility that is implicit in this countercultural rejection of classical European culture. The manner of Hugo's demise thus provides a seemingly pessimistic ending to Desai's novel, but, as this ending is also the beginning of the narrative, the overall effect is that of a circular motion, a condition that has not yet been worked through and therefore has not yet been overcome, rather than a linear one fated inexorably toward decline.

As a young child, Hugo is already confronted repeatedly with the sensation of being someone or something that stands apart and cannot assimilate. One year in an episode at school, just before the Christmas holidays, he has the first of many such experiences, in which he finds himself firmly shutting off the possibility of belonging to a group or community. It happens at their Christmas party, where the children of Hugo's class are lined up to receive gifts from their teacher that their parents have left for them, and the teacher realizes that Hugo is without a gift. Although egged on by the teacher and by his classmates, Hugo is unable to move and accept the makeshift gift she offers him, refusing this small gesture of inclusion, sensing instinctively what kind of inclusion it is:

> Then the agony was over and he could collapse into the dark ditch of his shame. What was the shame? The sense that he did not belong to the picture-book world of the fir tree, the gifts and the celebration? But no one had said that. Was it just that he sensed he did not belong to the radiant, the triumphant of the world? A strange sensation, surely, for a child. He could not understand it himself, or explain it. It baffled him, and frightened him even—even if he realized that at that moment he had willfully chosen to turn from the step up to the step down. (*BB*, 36–37)

This Christmas episode is, of course, a classic, even stereotypical tale of a Jewish childhood in a gentile society. But this notion that human beings *belong* in the world in fundamentally different ways is one Desai repeats creatively throughout the novel. When the Nazi expropriations and oppression have begun, and his father, once the proud bourgeois businessman, commits suicide after a short internment in Dachau, the family business and even home are gradually taken over by the father's junior partner, identified only as "the gentleman from Hamburg." Hugo's mother silences her son's protests with "the old saying, 'Stepchildren must behave doubly well.' "[8] (The father's self-inflicted death by gassing is both a prefiguring and an inversion of what is to be actualized in the camps, the fate that, unbeknownst to the family, awaits his wife.) And when, in wartime India, Hugo, in a bizarre and horrific irony, is interned by the British authorities along with all other "Germans" as an enemy alien, he immediately senses that the British soldier, who imposes barracks-room discipline on them, and the self-appointed leaders of the German internees "were of a kind—the ruling kind" (*BB*, 51, 104). The "ruling kind", the "triumphant", the "true children"—terms such as these circulate throughout Desai's narrative as a way of generating a perception of the maldistribution, as Said has put it, of "power and powerlessness" in society, a perception of the unequal possibilities of relating self to world and collectivity.[9]

Significant to Desai's purpose in the novel is that both mother and son spend the war in a camp—the routine solution in the twentieth century to the crisis of statelessness and displacement—the former for being a Jew in Germany and the latter for being a German outside it.[10] It is part of the decency of the novel that it does not seek to "represent" the Holocaust. But the presence of the violence is felt throughout the novel, from the opening pages to the very last words, and its most powerful trace in the novel is the bundle of postcards, each stamped with the number "J 673/1," that Lotte rescues from Baumgartner's bloodied apartment—cards from his mother, the last of them dating back to February 1941, a few months before the first mass deportations from the Reich. I return later to the cards and the elaboration of the text of culture and violence they make possible but here turn to Baumgartner's internment in India and the questions it raises about culture and violence, about the relationship of Europe to the colonies, and about the meaning of German and Jew. It is through *this* internment, through this *displacement* of the German-Jewish problematic to (colonial) Indian soil, that Desai approaches the question of the meaning of the genocide for modernity. The irony informing Hugo's internment is that it represents a handing over of the Jewish refugee outside Europe to precisely the forms of authority that his exile enabled him to escape from in Europe. The camp begins to resemble Nazi Germany, with the Jewish internees at the mercy of the group—"a certain kind of German" (*BB*, 115)—who naturally come to occupy positions of power and authority: a ritualized physical regime is quickly established, displays of loyalty are coerced out of the Jewish inmates, and their mail, both incoming and outgoing, disappears. As the embarrassed British commandant withdraws from the detailed exercise of authority, "empty spaces [are] allowed into which others could step in" (*BB*, 108). The regime that emerges is ruthlessly efficient and utilitarian:

> But with it went an authoritarianism that really came into its own, really triumphed on that hellish parade-ground under the summer sun. Whereas the British commandant had only half-heartedly carried out what was a mere formality, almost a mockery of a true ceremony, the Nazis seized upon it with an authority that was awesome. To Baumgartner, at least, awesome. In no time, the men were lined up, the lines straightened, the men straightened, mouths opened, and a sound drawn out of them that seemed to answer the force of the summer sun, the force of the dust winds, with an equal force. (*BB*, 115)

This may not be a Nazi concentration camp, but the social psychology represented here is recognizable as that of fascism. This characteristic mixture of bullying, scapegoating, collaboration, and muted rebellion is the psychology of the boys' schoolyard that Adorno had in mind when he declared aphoristically that "in Fascism the nightmare of childhood has come true."[11] When some of the Jews, the younger ones in particular, finally rebel against this coercion and refuse to yell "Heil Hitler!" at the turnout in the morning and are beaten by the "Aryans," the British commandant is nonplussed: "Why is everyone so excited? This happens all the time in our public schools—it doesn't mean much, just a thrashing" (*BB*, 117).

One consequence of this displacing of German fascism to colonial soil is the insertion of the British into its problematic, therefore removing the former from within the confines of a single nation-state and restoring to it the horizon of (European) modernity as a whole. The camp commandant is a decent figure, embarrassed at this military internment of civilians, and the soldiers with whom Baumgartner pleads to reconsider his internment as "hostile alien" are also impartial, in the bureaucratic manner, in their attempts to determine his "status." But here Desai is pointing to the implicit "collaboration" between the language and apparatus of liberal nation-statehood and the treatment of its Jewish minority by the Third Reich (*BB*, 117). At stake is the meaning of citizenship, explored here through its opposite, the quality of being an "alien." The judgment of the English soldier, when looking over Baumgartner's papers, that he is "German, born in Germany," is revealed to be of one with the hiss "*Jude, hin*!" which Baumgartner thinks he hears from a German inmate when the news on the radio is of the Russian stand at Stalingrad. Here the British state and the Third Reich are in the positions, respectively, of "democrat" and "anti-Semite" in Sartre's famous account of their mutual dialectic: "The [latter] wishes to destroy him as a man and leave nothing in him but the Jew, the pariah, the untouchable; the [former] wishes to destroy him as a Jew and leave nothing in him but the man, the abstract and universal subject of the rights of man and the rights of the citizen."[12] Although seemingly made from mutually opposing systems for the determination of citizenship—the liberal and the totalitarian—between them they leave no room for the victim's plea: "Yes, but of Jewish origin, therefore a refugee" (*BB*, 105, 116).

Into that connective "therefore" Desai distills the entire crisis of citizenship, of selfhood in a Europe of nations, in the first half of the twentieth century. Desai's narrative here highlights Jewishness as a crisis for the narratives of European culture and community. It underlines the link between "Jewish origin" and the possibility of becoming a "refugee," and forces an engagement with that political drama staged, as it were, "elsewhere" (*BB*, 89). The ubiquitous figure in this crisis in Europe is that of the stateless refugee, a figure more symptomatic of the conditions of modern politics, as Arendt argued in *The Origins of Totalitarianism*, than even the citizen, long considered the chief political accomplishment of Enlightenment and emancipation. For Arendt, the paradox the stateless pose for modernity is that, through loss of a specific, concrete relationship to a state, they lose their *abstract* and supposedly inalienable rights as human beings. Civil rights "were supposed to embody and spell out in the form of tangible laws the eternal Rights of Man, which by themselves were supposed to be independent of citizenship and nationality." And yet they "proved to be unenforceable—even in the countries whose constitutions were based upon them—whenever people appeared who were no longer citizens of any sovereign state." It is not so much specific human rights, moreover, that are lost in this condition, as the *right to have rights*, the most abstract right of all. In Desai's novel, it is through the device of the internment camp that these contradictions of statehood and statelessness, belonging and not belonging, are explored, with the camp becoming the site for a substitute repatriation, a restoration to a *patria* or homeland. According to Arendt, the significance of the internment camp, the *routine* solution in the twentieth century to the plight of the displaced, was that it became the "substitute for a nonexistent homeland."[13] In *Baumgartner's Bombay*, this problematic of "repatriation" is given a further twist: here it is the British (colonial) authorities that "repatriate" the Jewish refugee to, as it were, "Germany." Liberalism, as embodied in the British authorities' assumptions about citizenship and the political identities of Europeans, calls for the dissolution of "Jew" into "citizen" and delivers him up to the fate reserved for him by totalitarianism. This "monstrous mistake," this tussle between liberalism and fascism over the meaning of Jew and citizen, awaits for its clarification some "magic word" that does not exist (*BB*, 106).

This muddle, this constitutive confusion over the identity of self and other, citizen and alien, militarist and refugee, is given a further twist for Hugo when, on emerging from the camp after the war, he is baffled to see Calcutta itself in flames. His friend, Habibullah, soon flees to the newly created East Pakistan, for reasons Baumgartner cannot understand, while Habibullah does not comprehend why Baumgartner cannot return to his own homeland. And when the latter finally receives the packet of postcards that had arrived from his mother, dated from late 1939 to early 1941, and begins to understand what has happened, he realizes that "the Calcutta he lived in now—the Calcutta that had seen the famine of 1943, that had prepared for a Japanese attack, that had been used and drained by the war and war profiteers and now prepared for the great partition—was the proper setting for his mourning" (*BB*, 165–166). This assertion, that the Indian holocaust is a *proper* setting for mourning the European genocide, is perhaps one of the central claims of Desai's novel, established through a delicately elaborated and haunting perception of an uncanny and subterranean link between that crisis of minority and statelessness "elsewhere" and *this* partitioning of self and society. Jewish homelessness becomes in this novel not a quintessentially European experience; rather, its uncanny mirrorings may be seen elsewhere, and in India itself on the verge of independence.

Desai's most compelling exploration of the paradoxes of self and belonging may be in the terrain of language, precisely, the language of childhood, from nursery rhymes and children's songs, which appear in the original German in the text, to the endearments with which the mother addresses her long separated son. For Hugo, the language of childhood, that is, German, is also the language of death, and the novel carefully elaborates this dual nature of the survivor's language. We read early in the novel that, for the child, the sound of his mother's singing is "like spun sugar, like sugar being drawn out of him in glossy threads," but it is a sweetness that is strangely "precarious" (*BB*, 28). These songs stand in marked contrast with other songs, the nationalistic and militaristic ones sung by the authoritarian Germans in the camp. But this image of sweetness and sugar is significant and recurs frequently in the novel, often associated with the mother's speech, that is, with the mother tongue; in fact, the novel opens and closes with this very image. It is repeated in the language of the postcards, which, once deciphered by Lotte, crystallizes the meaning of German sounds for the Jewish exile. Lotte had picked the postcards off the bloodied floor of Hugo's apartment in desperation, simply to have something to remember him by. Only when she stumbles back into her own apartment does their significance slowly begin to dawn on her. The "antiquated baby-language," the mother's solicitous words directed to a child in a distant land—"*Meine kleine Maus*, *mein*

Hugo, Geliebter, I am well and do not worry"—make her "bunch her fingers, clutch her neck, as if she were choking" (*BB*, 3):

> Lotte pressed her fingers to her lips, to her eyes, to her ears, trying to prevent those words, that language, from entering her, invading her. Its sweetness, the assault of sweetness, cramming her mouth, her eyes, her ears, drowning her in its sugar. The language she wanted not to hear or speak. It was pummelling her, pushing against her and into her, and with her mouth stuffed she moaned, "*Nein, nein, nein*, Hugo, no." Her teeth bit on the crystals and her nerves screamed at their sweetness. All the marzipan, all the barley sugar, the chocolates and toffees of childhood descended on her with their soft, sticking, suffocating sweetness. Enough to embrace her, enough to stifle her, enough to obliterate her. Sugary, treacly, warm, oozing love, childhood love, little mice and bunny rabbits of love—sweet, warm, choking, childish love. Lotte wept and drowned. (*BB*, 4–5)

But the sounds of German in the mouth of the exile are simultaneously like crystals of sugar and shards of glass: "Do not worry, do not worry, Lotte mocked, spitting out those pieces of sugar as if they were glass and cut her" (*BB*, 3). This image of broken glass is then repeated later in the novel, but earlier in time, when Hugo and his family are hiding in their apartment as the business is ransacked below: "The next night the noise increased—glass splintered, crashed, slid all over the floor in slanting, shining heaps" (*BB*, 42).[14] The image of broken glass thus mediates between sugar as an image of mother tongue, of childhood, of home, and the possibility of genocidal violence implicit in the relation of "Jew" to "German." Childhood is not quite the memory exclusively of innocent pleasures, and home is now revealed in this jarring moment of exile to have been itself a form of displacement.

The thematics of migrancy and exile in the postcolonial Anglophone novel, and in the bogey man "postcolonial criticism," have been subjected to severe critique in recent years. This critique was first mounted at length by Aijaz Ahmad more than a decade ago in his book *In Theory: Classes, Nations, Literatures* and is still limited to the terms he set:

> The ideological ambiguity in these rhetorics of migrancy resides in the key fact that the migrant in question comes from a *nation* which is subordinated in the imperialist system of intra-state [*sic*] relationships, but, simultaneously, from the *class*, more often than not, which is the dominant class within that nation—this, in turn, makes it possible for that migrant to arrive in the metropolitan country to join not the working classes but the professional middle strata, hence to forge a

> kind of rhetoric which submerges the class question and speaks of migrancy as an ontological condition, more or less.[15]

This is not an inaccurate description of a certain contemporary elite configuration—of some ideological elements in Rushdie's work, for instance, which are most often expressed in editorial remarks about migrancy that take the form of essays as well as narratorial digressions in the novels themselves. More broadly, however, this critique has failed to provide any compelling understanding of the *non*-privileged forms of mass displacement and uprooting that have characterized politics and society in the modern era, nor, of course, to explore the bearing they have on culture and critique in general.[16] The call for exilic thinking is a recommendation not about *where* to live—North or South, in Ahmed's stark formulation—but rather *how* to live wherever one happens to be, given the unmistakable reality that for almost a century the marginalization and uprooting of entire populations on a massive scale has been the norm rather than the exception to the rule of local and global politics around the world. Claims of unmediated attachment to place and tradition must be confronted not only with their mediated and fabricated nature, as has become a kind of norm since *Imagined Communities*, but also with the price they exact daily on our ability to think critically about the contemporary world. The work of critique in this historical conjuncture—and, as Said might have said, of the intellectual vocation as such—is to not surrender to the deep nationalization of thought and sentiment, of culture and solidarity, that continues to be an important element of the cultural logic of late capitalist society, even and especially in the midst of the escalation of the globalization of its forms.

But to attempt to respond to Ahmed in this manner is perhaps already to read his text as a work of theory or criticism, as a critique of theory and criticism, which I do not take it primarily to be. More productively, it may and should be read as a certain kind of narrative and, to be precise, *a postcolonial allegory of return*, its writing having coincided with the author's "return" in middle age from a tenured job at a U.S. university to India, the country of his birth, from which his family had emigrated in his youth to Pakistan, the country from which he himself in his turn had later emigrated to the United States as a young man. It is, of course, as a critique of this broader movement of postcolonial middle-class migrancy to the West, of which his own individual journey many years earlier was an instance, that the thrust of the book had been launched. This agonized substratum of self-examination, self-reproach, and self-reinvention, displaced in the book largely onto Said, and without reference to which the particular mood and location of the book cannot be understood, has been missed almost entirely in its reception, especially by some progressives in the West who took it up as an authentically Third World cudgel with which to beat upon "multicultural" tendencies in the culture where they had previously felt silenced. And in response to a critic who pointed out the fabricated nature of this account of (a newly found) Indianness (from which his Pakistani background, as well as his long residence in the West, had initially at least been erased entirely), Ahmad could only speak apologetically and cryptically of "my wanderings."[17] In this sense, *In Theory* could be read fruitfully alongside Rushdie's *Satanic Verses*, another postcolonial narrative of "return" in which the cosmopolitan and deracinated migrant, Saladin Chamcha, is reinserted into national belonging and political meaningfulness by his literal return "home" to India. His very name—*chamcha*, literally spoon, used metaphorically in the North Indian languages to designate a sidekick or sycophant—suggests a sycophantic aping of the (former) colonial masters. Facilitating the completion of this transformation is Zeeny Vakil, the Marxist intellectual and activist he falls in love with on his return. This migrant's longing for a place in the sun which has always been one's own is as much present in Rushdie's novel as in Ahmad's narrative. The latter, in spite of itself, therefore reveals the powerful functioning of a postcolonial mythology across the supposedly impregnable boundaries of political disputation.

Baumgartner's Bombay represents a relentless unraveling of this mythology of hearth and home by its refraction through the figure of the Jewish refugee, the quintessential figure of exile for the narratives of Europe's modernity. Here, not only is the European crisis concretized in the Holocaust examined from an Indian location, but the constitution of "India" itself is observed from the place in the world inhabited by a refugee from the European genocide. We come to see in Desai's novel that the Jewish refugee is a figure of rebuke (or at least caution) not only to the Europe of nations whose emergence required its marginalization and then extermination but to all those places and moments in the modern era—Western, non-Western, metropolitan, colonial, postcolonial—in which such dramas of the consolidation of national societies through the marginalization and uprooting of "other" peoples have been played out. And the "question of class," far from being "submerged" in the novel in an "ontology" of migrancy, as Ahmad's blanket account would have it, is placed in a tense articulation with the problematic of exile and minority: the comfortable bourgeois background of the Baumgartner family in Germany—signified as much by the father's secure status as a successful businessman as by the mother's immersion in German literature—cannot prevent their being swept up in the racial reorganization of society by the Nazis. And, in Bombay, Hugo's wanderings through the city are always brought to an anxious conclusion as he approaches his apartment building and is forced to encounter Jagu, the drunk and violent rural migrant whose "famine-struck" family ekes out the barest existence on the filth of the pavement and open sewer outside (*BB*, 7). Jagu is himself a displaced person of a certain sort with little or no access to the "postcolonial" India of sovereignty and citizenship. Desai creates a distinct and strange bond between these two men: each recognizes in the other a trace, a shadow, or a whisper of his own degradation. What Baumgartner feels daily at the sight of this man, who had once beaten him up in a drunken state, is, we are told, not fear "but unease, an apprehension" (*BB*, 7). And when he is murdered, it is Jagu who is immediately cornered by the residents of the building and dragged off by the police, even though it was he who had discovered the body and alerted the neighbors. Jagu inhabits the interstices, the "pavement" and "gutter," of this postcolonial citizenship, his consciousness—resentful, irrational, explosive—posing a constant danger to the seemingly tranquil tableau of citizen subjectivity (*BB*, 6).

Baumgartner's Bombay is thus an attempt to examine the consequences of linking one cultural site on the globe to another, of affiliating the one with the other, and thus may be spoken of to that extent as a "cosmopolitical" work. The novel represents an effort to affiliate postcolonial writer and writing in English to the European history of displacement that is the history of Jewishness as minority. But such a judgment immediately raises questions about the kind of cosmopolitanism, the kind of affiliation, this is. The novel insists that we place this history at the center of our narratives of modernity, that we make it the prism through which to refract our understanding of the dialectic of selfhood in the modern world. The cosmopolitanism that it proposes for postcolonial writing is, in other words, a cosmopolitanism of "stepchildren" rather than of the "ruling kind" or the "triumphant of the world." The authentic affiliations for this Anglophone literature are with those cultural positions at which language is an ambivalent experience, simultaneously like crystals of sugar in the mouth and shards of glass. It is with these marginal, exilic, and fragmented perspectives on "Europe," rather than with the triumphant narratives of the emergence of national cultures and canons, that Desai attempts to forge her narrative links, and inscribes the difficulties of these affiliations in the very form of the novel. For Desai, postcolonial culture—that is, the culture of critique, on the one hand, of Western liberalism's involvement with the processes of colonial rule and racialization of the world, and, on the other, of the continuing legacies of this involvement in the present—finds natural affinities in the history of Europe's other victims.

These operations, this continuous displacement and inversion of what constitutes outside and inside, local and cosmopolitan, universal and particular, are similar to the operations that this book itself has attempted to put in play. My effort here was to provide the outline of a contemporary critical practice that draws upon that earlier "Jewish" tradition ("the other Jewish tradition," as Arendt called it in contradistinction to both mainstream Zionism and "*parvenu*" assmilation) and to make available for discussions of our modern selfhood in postcolonial South Asia the history of the crisis over the meaning of Jewishness in Western modernity. Liberal secularism in the post-Enlightenment era, I have argued in these pages, repeatedly encounters the stumbling block of minority as both the object of its projects and the sign of its own impossibility. The categories of minority experience, within which liberal culture attempts to contain the crisis of minority, are inseparable from the history of the Jewish Question, of which they are the cultural and political sediment. A postcolonial secularism that seeks to move beyond the contemporary liberal impasse must learn to recognize the presence of this history in its own concepts and categories, and this book has been an attempt to take a few initial and tentative steps in that direction.

Futures Past

Towards the middle of 1998 the crisis of Muslim identity in modern Indian history entered the nuclear age. The process of normalization of Muslim (and Indian) identity that began in colonial times, and that translated into a new, postcolonial configuration with the Partition of India, thus entered a more intensive and catastrophic phase. This ongoing conflict between the sovereign states of India and Pakistan, and the possibilities for a solution to the conflict, continue to be understood in terms of the imperatives of *raison d'état.* The thrust of the argument in this book would suggest an alternative approach. The nation-state conflict in contemporary South Asia must itself be understood within the larger problematic of Indian modernity and the normalization of identities it implies. This is an *inter-state* conflict of a particular sort, for it is played out on the stage of a single *national* problematic. Pakistani nationalism, in other words, continues also to be an Indian communalism, just as Indian nationalism—as much of the "secular" variety as the more recent and resurgent "Hindu" one—continues to be an attempt to normalize a normative Indian experience and identity through an ongoing effort to minoritize "the Muslim." The challenge of criticism is to avoid the temptation to affirm the terms of this normalization and therefore resist the cultural projects of the nation-state. I use "*the* nation-state" deliberately here, for I wish to point to the implicit collaboration between these postcolonial states, that is, to the common language of national selfhood that they deploy. The task of critical scholarship is to make visible this collaboration between them, to highlight the manner in which they seek to normalize modern South Asian existence in terms of the autonomy of national cultures. My attempt in this book has been to produce a critique of the positivism of the nation-state, and to show that social experience does not enter the national concept within which it is sought to be contained without leaving an excess and remainder.

Adorno's aphoristic statement that "even the steps which society takes to exterminate itself are at the same time absurd acts of unleashed self-preservation" offers a fruitful way of thinking about the very meaning of "society" within the drama of self-destruction that has been performed in South Asia over the last quarter-century.[18] Adorno's claim that such destructive acts are "forms of unconscious social action against suffering" is open to the charge, as he anticipated in the preface to *Negative Dialectics*, of being metaphysical, that is, of being based on a metaphysics of human suffering.[19] But the meaning of suffering for Adorno is an utterly historical one. For although suffering is "objectivity that weighs upon the subject," the "objective" realm for him is the congealed forms of society itself.[20] I argued in the previous chapter that the relationship of subject and object in Faiz's verse problematizes the very identity of the social, that it reveals the social to be non-identical with its own concept. The suffering of the subject lies in its distance from the object but is also constitutive of the subject itself, rather than merely external to it. If this dialectic of subject and object in Faiz's poetry is an expression of the constitution of self and other in Indian modernity, as I have argued, what it makes apparent is the suffering of purportedly autonomous selves that are fragmented or incomplete. The self-destructiveness of "society" in contemporary southern Asia, given only its most graphic expression and an apocalyptic means to its ends in the form of inter-state nuclear competition and conflict, is not only the cause but also, simply, a sign of untold human suffering. Any attempt to understand the political and cultural realities of the contemporary moment, as of the modern period as a whole, is faced with the challenge, to paraphrase Adorno only slightly, to lend a voice to this suffering.[21] As I have suggested a number of times in this book, this political and ethical demand on intellectual life can be met only if we renounce the certainties of "home," if we resist the apotheosis of the nation-state as the only proper dwelling place of culture and self.

The history of intensification of the Hindu-Muslim conflict as a nation-state conflict since 1947 has been paralleled since 1948 in the Middle East with an increasingly greater intensification of the struggle over the nature of society and community in the so-called Holy Land. More than a century and a half after Marx's attempt to theoretically comprehend and critique the emergence of "the Jewish Question," therefore, and six decades after its double "solution" in genocide and statehood, the crisis of Jewish identity produced by the modernization of Western societies in the late eighteenth and nineteenth centuries continues to precipitate political crises, now on a global scale. A fuller discussion of these matters—the dramatic historic shift in the condition of statelessness from European populations to Third World ones, the significance of the disappearance of Palestine for the culture of decolonization on a world scale and the globalization of the so-called Jewish Question of post-Enlightenment European society—must of necessity be postponed for another occasion. But we should note here once again the decisive difference in the ways in which the crisis of minority has played itself out in the two instances I have considered in this book—the European, metropolitan crisis is offered up to a colonial solution, by postponing indefinitely the decolonization of a non-European society, while the Indian trajectory leads simply to the fragmentation of a colonial society at the very moment of its emergence from colonial rule. By linking the emergence of the crisis of Muslim identity in late colonial India to the earlier crisis around the Jews, I have attempted an introductory ground clearing, a sort of conceptual and historical propaedeutics, for a wider examination of the crisis of minority in its global diffusion and its link to political partitions in the twentieth century and into our own times. If this book's engagement with the literary output of these two historical trajectories comes to be seen as an attempt to develop a critical practice that situates, critiques, and tries to unravel the assumption of inevitability that attaches to these phenomena and trajectories in the modern era—an exercise in secular criticism, to return again to Said—the long labor of its composition will have been worth it.

Notes

Prologue

1. For an extended, empirically grounded argument for the existence of a system of "riot production" in North India in which political parties, volunteer organizations, the police and other security forces, local and state bureaucracies, and the media play a role, see Paul R. Brass, *The Production of Hindu-Muslim Violence in Contemporary India* (Delhi: Oxford University Press, 2003).

2. For the concept of "citizen subject," see Etienne Balibar, "Citizen Subject," in *Who Comes After the Subject?* ed. Eduardo Cadava, Peter Connor, and Jean-Luc Nancy (New York: Routledge, 1991). The scholarship produced in the aftermath of Ayodhya, and in response to it, is now enormous. For a small selection, see *Making India Hindu: Religion, Community, and the Politics of Democracy in India*, ed. David Ludden, 2nd ed. (Delhi: Oxford University Press, 2005 [1995]); Mushirul Hasan, *Legacy of a Divided Nation: India's Muslims since Independence* (Delhi: Oxford University Press, 1997); *Hindus and Others: The Question of Identity in India Today*, ed. Gyanendra Pandey (Delhi: Oxford University Press, 1993); and Tapan Basu, Pradit Datta, and Sumit Sarkar et al., *Khaki Shorts and Saffron Flags* (New Delhi: Orient Longman, 1993).

3. See Max Horkheimer and Theodor W. Adorno, *Dialectic of Enlightenment: Philosophical Fragments*, ed. Gunzelin Schmid Noerr, trans. Edmund Jephcott (Stanford: Stanford University Press, 2002), 4.

4. One of the most influential accounts in recent decades has been Partha Chatterjee's *Nationalist Thought and the Colonial World: A Derivative Discourse* (Minnesota: University of Minnesota Press, 1993).

5. See, for instance, Sander L. Gilman, *The Jew's Body* (New York: Routledge, 1991); Bryan Cheyette, *Constructions of "the Jew" in English Literature and Society: Racial Representations, 1875–1945* (Cambridge: Cambridge University Press, 1993); James Shapiro, *Shakespeare and the Jews* (New York: Columbia University Press, 1996); Ira B. Nadel, *James Joyce and the Jews: Culture and Texts* (Houndmills, Basingstoke, Hampshire: Macmillan, 1989); Jonathan Freedman, *The Temple of Culture: Assimilation and Anti-Semitism in Literary Anglo-America* (New York: Oxford University Press, 2000); and Irene Tucker, *A Probable State: The Novel, the Contract, and the Jews* (Chicago: University of Chicago Press, 2002).

6. Chatterjee, *Nationalist Thought and the Colonial World*, 168.

7. See Hannah Arendt, *The Origins of Totalitarianism*, new ed. (New York: Harcourt Brace, 1979), esp. 302; Horkheimer and Adorno, *Dialectic of Enlightenment*, 86; Jawaharlal Nehru, *The Discovery of India* (Delhi: Oxford University Press, 1989 [1946]), 326, but see also 18; Aimé Césaire, *Discourse on Colonialism* (New York: Monthly Review Press, 1972), 14; and Amilcar Cabral, *Return to the Source: Selected Speeches* (New York: Monthly Review Press, 1974), 39.

8. See Jonathan Boyarin and Daniel Boyarin, "Introduction: So What's New?" in *Jews and Other Differences: The New Jewish Cultural Studies*, ed. Jonathan Boyarin and Daniel Boyarin (Minneapolis: University of Minnesota Press, 1997), ix; and Daniel Boyarin and Jonathan Boyarin, "Generation: Diaspora and the Ground of Jewish Identity," *Critical Inquiry* 19, no. 4 (summer 1993): 693–725. See also Jonathan Boyarin, *Storm from Paradise: The Politics of Jewish Memory* (Minneapolis: University of Minnesota Press, 1992), esp. 77–115; and idem, *Palestine and Jewish History: Criticism at the Borders of Ethnography* (Minneapolis: University of Minnesota Press, 1996). This is also an organizing premise of the collection *Modernity, Culture, and "the Jew,"* ed. Bryan Cheyette and Laura Marcus (Cambridge: Polity, 1998).

9. The phrase is Jonathan Boyarin's, although he uses it in the context of European Jewry alone, not postcolonial migrancy. See Boyarin, *Storm from Paradise*, 77.

10. See Jean-Paul Sartre, *Anti-Semite and Jew*, trans. George J. Becker (New York: Schocken, 1976), 66–69; Jean François Lyotard, *Heidegger and "the jews,"* trans. Andreas Michel and Mark Roberts (Minneapolis: University of Minnesota Press, 1990), 3; Arendt, *The Origins of Totalitarianism*, xv; Richard J. Bernstein, *Hannah Arendt and the Jewish Question* (Cambridge, Mass.: MIT Press, 1996), 47–48; and Boyarin and Boyarin, "Diaspora: Generation and the Ground of Jewish Identity," 700–701.

11. See, among their numerous other writings, Boyarin and Boyarin, "Diaspora: Generation and the Ground of Jewish Identity," 721.

12. See Hannah Arendt, "The Jew as Pariah: A Hidden Tradition," in idem, *The Jew as Pariah: Jewish Identity and Politics in the Modern Age*, ed. Ron H. Feldman (New York: Grove, 1978), 68; and Max Weber, *Ancient Judaism* (Glencoe, Ill.: Free Press, 1952).

13. It is perhaps with these affinities in mind that Said described himself to an Israeli journalist, not a touch ironically, as "the last Jewish intellectual." See Edward W. Said, *Power, Politics, and Culture: Interviews with Edward W. Said*, ed. Gauri Viswanathan (New York: Pantheon, 2001), 458.

14. Edward W. Said, *Beginnings: Intention and Method* (New York: Columbia University Press, 1975), 372–373. Also see Michel Foucault, "Nietzsche, Genealogy, History," *Language, Counter-Memory, Practice: Selected Essays and Interviews*, ed. Donald F. Bouchard (Ithaca: Cornell University Press, 1977), 139–164.

15. I am grateful to Jim Chandler for this suggestion.

16. Wlad Godzich, *The Culture of Literacy* (Cambridge, Mass.: Harvard University Press, 1994), 277. Also see Tucker, *A Probable State*, 7–12.

17. For a critique of primordialism in the comparative study of social conflict, see Arjun Appadurai, *Modernity at Large* (Minneapolis: University of Minnesota Press, 1998).

18. Gilles Deleuze and Félix Guattari, *Kafka: Toward a Minor Literature*, trans. Dana Polan (Minneapolis: University of Minnesota Press, 1986), 16.

19. See David Lloyd, *Nationalism and Minor Literature: James Clarence Mangan and the Emergence of Irish Cultural Nationalism* (Berkeley: University

of California Press, 1987); idem, "Genet's Genealogy: European Minorities and the Ends of the Canon," *Cultural Critique* 6 (spring 1987): 161–186; idem, *Anomalous States: Irish Writing and the Post-Colonial Moment* (Durham: Duke University Press, 1993); and idem, with Paul Thomas, *Culture and the State* (New York: Routledge, 1998).

20. Arendt, *The Origins of Totalitarianism*, 277, 293.

21. *Les Lieux de Mémoire*, ed. Pierre Nora, 7 vols. (Paris: Editions Gallimard, 1984–92). An abridged translation under the direction of Pierre Nora, is now available as *Realms of Memory: The Construction of the French Past*, 3 vols. (New York: Columbia University Press, 1996–98).

22. For fuller elaborations of such critical practices of secularism, see Aamir R. Mufti, "Auerbach in Istanbul: Edward Said, Secular Criticism, and the Question of Minority Culture," *Critical Inquiry*, 25.1 (autumn 1998): 95–124; and idem, "Critical Secularism: A Reintroduction for Perilous Times," *boundary 2*, 31, no. 2 (summer 2004): 1–11.

23. Fanon's most extended discussion of psychoanalysis in the colonial context is, of course, in *Black Skins, White Masks* (New York: Grove, 1967); but see also idem "Colonial War and Mental Disorders," in *The Wretched of the Earth*, trans. Constance Farrington (New York: Grove, 1979), 249–310. For the comment on Marxism, see Fanon, *The Wretched of the Earth*, 40.

24. Fanon, *The Wretched of the Earth*, 250.

25. Ranajit Guha, "A Conquest Foretold," *Social Text* 54 (spring 1998): 85.

26. I am grateful to Gayatri Spivak for this suggestion.

27. G. N. Devy, *After Amnesia: Tradition and Change in Indian Literary Criticism* (Hyderabad: Orient Longman, 1995), 59, 10.

28. In what follows I have been influenced greatly by conversations with Professor C. M. Naim, to whom I am grateful for sharing his knowledge and understanding of Askari's work with me, and for his generosity and patience with my own interpretations. Responsibility for the views offered here is, of course, my own.

29. Muhammad Hasan Askari, *Majmūʿa* (Lahore: Sang-e Mīl, 1994), 580–581; emphasis added.

30. Askari, *Majmūʿa*, 584–85. This equation has a complex significance in the cultural history of Muslim India in the modern era. Its earlier appearance in the Indian nationalist formulations of Abul Kalam Azad is discussed in chapter 3.

31. Askari, *Majmūʿa*, 639.

32. See ibid., 1171–1268.

33. See Ashis Nandy, *The Intimate Enemy: Loss and Recovery of Self under Colonialism* (Delhi: Oxford University Press, 1991); and "The Politics of Secularism and the Recovery of Religious Tolerance, in *Mirrors of Violence: Communities, Riots and Survivors in South Asia*, ed. Veena Das (Delhi: Oxford University Press, 1992), 69–93. For a critique of Nandy's indigenism, see Mufti, "Auerbach in Istanbul," 113–119.

34. Arendt, "The Jew as Pariah," 67.

35. Abdallah Laroui, *L'idéologie arabe contemporaine: essai critique*, preface by Maxime Rodinson (Paris: François Maspero, 1967), 68.

36. The term "vernacular modernities," as I use it here, owes some of its impulse and substance to Homi Bhabha's deployment of the term "vernacular" in "Editor's Introduction: Minority Maneuvers and Unsettled Negotiations," *Critical Inquiry* 23 (spring 1997): 431–459.

37. "Die Wilden sind nicht bessere Menschen." See Theodor W. Adorno, *Minima Moralia: Reflexionen aus dem beschädigten Leben* (Berlin: Suhrkampf Verlag, 1951), 84. For a translation, see Theodor Adorno, *Minima Moralia: Reflections from Damaged Life*, trans. E. F. N. Jephcott (London: Verso, 1989), 52–53.

38. See Adorno, *Minima Moralia: Reflections from Damaged Life*, 18.

39. Ibid., 50.

40. Ibid., 52.

41. Jean-Paul Sartre, preface to Fanon, *The Wretched of the Earth*, 7, 24, 21, 24, 27, 31.

42. Fanon, *The Wretched of the Earth*, 315.

43. "Carnapverehrern in Indien." See Adorno, *Minima Moralia: Reflexionen aus dem beschädigten Leben*, 85.

44. Adorno, *Minima Moralia: Reflections from Damaged Life*, 53.

45. See, for instance, "Perennial Fashion—Jazz," in Theodor W. Adorno, *Prisms* (Cambridge, Mass.: MIT Press, 1988), 119–132.

46. "Überdruß"—literally, weariness. See Adorno, *Minima Moralia: Reflexionen aus dem beschädigten Leben*, 85; and *Minima Moralia: Reflections from Damaged Life*, 52.

47. Horkheimer and Adorno, *Dialectic of Enlightenment*, 1. This edition is henceforth cited within parentheses as *DE*. The opening essay, which since the 1947 edition has been known as "The Concept of Enlightenment," was, in the original, mimeographed internal release by the Institute for Social Research in Los Angeles (1944), simply titled, "The Dialectic of Enlightenment." See Gunzelin Schmid Noerr, "Editor's Afterword," in Horkheimer and Adorno, *Dialectic of Enlightenment*, 221.

48. This is not wholly dissimilar from Lévi-Strauss's defamiliarizing of the question regarding the Western provenance of industrial civilization through comparison with the social and technological inventions of the Neolithic revolution, whose origins in particular human populations, he points out, ceased to matter to their subsequent history. See Claude Lévi-Strauss, "Race and History," in *Structural Anthropology*, vol. 2, trans. Monique Layton (Harmondsworth, UK: Penguin Books, 1978) 351–352.

49. See Ranajit Guha, *Dominance without Hegemony* (Cambridge, Mass.: Harvard University Press, 1997).

50. See, in particular, Ranajit Guha, "On Some Aspects of the Historiography of Colonial India," in *Selected Subaltern Studies*, ed. Ranajit Guha and Gayatri Chakravorty Spivak (New York: Oxford University Press, 1988), 37–44; idem, "The Prose of Counter-Insurgency," in Guha and Spivak, *Selected Subaltern Studies*, 45–88; and idem, *Elementary Aspects of Peasant Insurgency in Colonial India* (Delhi: Oxford University Press, 1986).

51. Adorno, *Minima Moralia: Reflections from Damaged Life*, 151. For a reading of this passage and its significance for the larger concerns of Adorno's

work, see Keya Ganguly, "Adorno, Authenticity, Critique," in *Marxism, Modernity, and Postcolonial Studies*, ed. Crystal Bartolovich and Neil Lazarus (Cambridge: Cambridge University Press, 2002), 240–256.

52. Nehru, *The Discovery of India*, 59–61.

53. On Pal, see Manu Goswami, "Autonomy and Comparability: Notes on the Anticolonial and Postcolonial," *boundary 2* 32, no. 2 (summer 2005): 201–225. For Chatterjee's discussion of this episode in *The Discovery of India*, see his *Nationalist Thought and the Colonial World*, 147.

54. Jawaharlal Nehru, *An Autobiography* (Delhi: Oxford University Press, 1985), 406.

55. See Chatterjee, *Nationalist Thought and the Colonial World*, vii, 43, 50.

56. See ibid., 155.

57. One important exception, of course, is the work of Gyanendra Pandey. See *Construction of Communalism in Colonial India* (Delhi: Oxford University Press, 1990).

58. See Muzaffar Alam, *The Languages of Political Islam: India, 1200–1800* (Chicago: University of Chicago Press, 2004).

59. See, for instance, Shail Mayaram, *Resisting Regimes: Myth, Memory and the Making of a Muslim Identity* (Delhi: Oxford University Press, 1997); and idem, *Against History, Against State: Counterperspectives from the Margins* (New York: Columbia University Press, 2003).

60. See Nicholas B. Dirks, *Castes of Mind: Colonialism and the Making of Modern India* (Princeton, N.J.: Princeton University Press, 2001). In my view this work develops to the utmost and brings to a conclusion certain lines of investigation begun in the work of the late Bernard Cohn, who was Dirks's mentor at the University of Chicago, by inflecting them through the form of knowledge critique inaugurated in Said's work.

61. For a superb historical critique of the ahistoricism of contemporary debates about the cosmopolitan and the vernacular, see Sheldon Pollock, "Cosmopolitan and Vernacular in History," *Public Culture* 12, no. 3 (2000): 591–625.

62. Fredric Jameson, *Singular Modernity: Essay on the Ontology of the Present* (London: Verso, 2002), 12; Slavoj Žižek, "The Ongoing 'Soft Revolution,'" *Critical Inquiry* 30 (winter 2004): 295–296. Also see Goswami, "Autonomy and Comparability," esp. 203.

63. Dipesh Chakrabarty, *Provincializing Europe: Postcolonial Thought and Historical Difference* (Princeton, N.J.: Princeton University Press, 2000), 17.

64. See Aamir R. Mufti, "Global Comparativism," *Critical Inquiry* 31 (winter 2005): 472–489.

65. See Gayatri Chakravorty Spivak, *The Death of a Discipline* (New York: Columbia University Press, 1993).

Chapter One
Jewishness as Minority

1. Karl Marx, "On the Jewish Question," in *The Marx-Engels Reader*, ed. Robert C. Tucker, 2nd ed. (New York: Norton, 1978), 35–36.

2. On the political and intellectual background of Marx's essay, see Julius Carlebach, *Karl Marx and the Radical Critique of Judaism* (London: Routledge, 1978); Robert Wistrich, *Revolutionary Jews from Marx to Trotsky* (London: Harrap, 1977); Dennis K. Fischman, *Political Discourse in Exile: Karl Marx and the Jewish Question* (Amherst: University of Massachusetts Press, 1991); and Elisabeth de Fontenay, *Les Figures Juives de Marx: Marx dans l'Ideologie Allemande* (Paris: Editions Galilée, 1973).

3. The literature on "the Jews and modernity" has burgeoned in recent years and produced a new interdisciplinary space of critique and theoretical speculation. See, for instance, the following rather diverse set of works: Zygmunt Bauman, *Modernity and Ambivalence* (Ithaca: Cornell University Press, 1991); Gillian Rose, *Judaism and Modernity: Philosophical Essays* (Oxford: Blackwell, 1993); Jean-François Lyotard, *Heidegger and "the Jews"*; Vassilis Lambropoulos, *The Rise of Eurocentrism: Anatomy of Interpretation* (Princeton, N.J.: Princeton University Press, 1993); and Cheyette and Marcus, *Modernity, Culture, and "the Jew."* This renewal of interest takes not only Marx's own essay as precursor, but such mid-twentieth-century works as Sartre, *Anti-Semite and Jew*; Horkheimer and Adorno, "Elements of Anti-Semitism: Limits of Enlightenment," in idem, *Dialectic of Enlightenment*; and Arendt, *The Origins of Totalitarianism*.

4. These terms are Jonathan Boyarin's; see his, *Storm from Paradise*.

5. For a genealogy of the term "Jewish emancipation," see Jacob Katz, "The Term 'Jewish Emancipation': Its Origin and Historical Impact," in *Studies in Nineteenth-Century Jewish Intellectual History*, ed. Alexander Altmann (Hanover, N.H.: University Press of New England, 1981), 1–25.

6. On the (logical) priority of "citizen" over "Man" in the Enlightenment, see Balibar, "Citizen Subject."

7. See, for instance, the now classic work of political sociology by Rogers Brubaker, *Citizenship and Nationhood in France and Germany* (Cambridge, Mass.: Harvard University Press, 1992).

8. See Arendt, *The Origins of Totalitarianism*, 275.

9. Isaiah Berlin, "Kant as an Unfamiliar Source of Nationalism," in *The Sense of Reality: Studies in Ideas and their History*, ed. Henry Hardy (London: Pimlico, 1996), 234.

10. Arendt, *The Origins of Totalitarianism*, 275.

11. See, for instance, Katz, "The Term 'Jewish Emancipation,'" 1–3. For a somewhat different chronology, which would move the beginnings of this era to a century earlier, in seventeenth-century responses to religious strife, see Salo W. Baron, *A Social and Religious History of the Jews*, vol. 2 (New York: Columbia University Press, 1937), 164.

12. For a fascinating interpretation of the significance of these events in eighteenth-century English culture, see James Shapiro, *Shakespeare and the Jews*, chap. 6. Concern that the state demonstrate "consistency" in this regard is, of course, voiced as early as 1689 in Locke's second *Letter of Toleration*, but only towards the end of the eighteenth century did such ideas become dominant.

13. For a detailed and evocative account of this friendship, see Alexander Altmann, *Moses Mendelssohn: A Biographical Study* (Philadelphia: Jewish

Publication Society of America, 1973), on which I rely a great deal in what follows. On friendship and the Enlightenment, see also Klaus L. Berghahn, "Lavater's attempt to compel the conversion of Moses Mendelssohn abuses the friendship cult surrounding Jewish and Christian intellectuals," in *Yale Companion to Jewish Writing and Thought in German Culture, 1096–1996*, ed. Sander L. Gilman and Jack Zipes (New Haven: Yale University Press, 1997), 61–67; Hannah Arendt, "On Humanity in Dark Times: Thoughts about Lessing," in idem, *Men in Dark Times* (New York: Harcourt Brace, 1983), 3–31; and Willi Goetschel, "Lessing, Mendelssohn, Nathan: German-Jewish Myth-Building as an Act of Emancipation," *Lessing Yearbook* 32 (Detroit: Wayne State University Press, 2000), 341–360.

14. Alexander Altmann, "Moses Mendelssohn as the Archetypal German Jew," in *The Jewish Response to German Culture: From the Enlightenment to the Second World War*, ed. Jehuda Reinharz and Walter Schatzberg (Hanover, N.H., and London: University Press of New England, 1985), 21.

15. See George L. Mosse, *German Jews beyond Judaism* (Bloomington: Indiana University Press, 1985), 15–16.

16. See William Baker, *George Eliot and Judaism* (Salzburg: Institut für Englische Sprache und Literatur, Universität Salzburg, 1975), 32–33.

17. See *George Eliot's "Daniel Deronda" Notebooks*, ed. Jane Irwin (Cambridge: Cambridge University Press, 1996), 233, 508.

18. See Altmann, *Moses Mendelssohn*, 569. On the figure of the noble Jew in the literature of the Enlightenment, including Lessing's work, see Charlene A. Lea, "Tolerance Unlimited: 'The Noble Jew' on the German and Austrian Stage (1750–1805)," *German Quarterly* 64, no. 2 (spring 1991): 166–177.

19. Horkheimer and Adorno, *Dialectic of Enlightenment*, 138. For a historical survey of the play's critical reception over the last two centuries, see Jo-Jacqueline Eckardt, *Lessing's Nathan the Wise and the Critics: 1779–1991* (Columbia, S.C.: Camden House, 1993).

20. On the ideal of *Bildung* in the history of Jewish emancipation, see George L. Mosse, "Jewish Emancipation: Between *Bildung* and Respectability," in *Confronting the Nation: Jewish and Western Nationalism* (Hanover, N.H.: University Press of New England, 1993), 131–145; and David Sorkin, *The Transformation of German Jewry, 1780–1840* (New York: Oxford University Press, 1987).

21. On the philo-Semitic strand in nineteenth- and early-twentieth-century English culture, see William D. Rubinstein and Hilary L. Rubinstein, *Philosemitism: Admiration and Support in the English-Speaking World for Jews, 1840–1939* (New York: St. Martin's, 1999).

22. See Aziz Ahmad, "Islam d'Espagne et Inde musulmane moderne," in *Études d'orientalisme dédiées a la mémoire de Lévi-Provençal*, vol. 2 (Paris: G.-P. Maisonneuve et Larosse, 1962), 461–470.

23. See, for instance, Ernst Cassirer, *The Philosophy of the Enlightenment* (Princeton, N.J.: Princeton University Press, 1968), 169, where the "fable of the rings" is read within the context of the discussion of the place of "toleration" in the Enlightenment. In the story, whose source for Lessing is a tale in *Decameron*, the third story of the first day, a man who dwelled in Eastern lands

possesses a magical ring that grants whoever wears it the love of God and men. At different times during his life, he promises it to each of his three sons. As death approaches, unable to choose between his sons, he secretly has two identical copies of the ring made and gives one to each son. After the man dies, each son produces the ring as a sign that he is the legitimate heir. The matter is brought before a judge who provides the moral lesson of the parable:

> Accept the matter wholly as it stands.
> If each one from his father has his ring,
> Then let each one believe his ring to be
> The true one.—Possibly the father wished
> To tolerate no longer in his house
> The tyranny of just one ring!

See Gotthold Ephraim Lessing, *Nathan the Wise: A Dramatic Poem in Five Acts* (New York: Frederick Unger, 1987), 3.7.17, 22, 126–131.

24. "Das leidige, verwünschte Geld!" See Gotthold Ephraim Lessing, *Gesammelte Werke*, vol. 2 (Berlin: Aufbau-Verlag, 1954), 362. The translations are all from the Frederick Unger edition, which I have changed slightly where necessary. This passage is at 2.2.116.

25. See Arthur Hertzberg, *The French Enlightenment and the Jews: The Origins of Modern Anti-Semitism* (New York: Columbia University, 1968), 280–283; and Jacob Katz, *From Prejudice to Destruction: Anti-Semitism, 1700–1933* (Cambridge, Mass.: Harvard University Press, 1980), chaps. 2–3.

26. Michael Ragussis, *The Figures of Conversion: "The Jewish Question" and English National Identity* (Durham, N.C.: Duke University Press, 1995), 39.

27. Gotthold Ephraim Lessing, "On the Origin of Revealed Religion" (1763–64?), in *Lessing's Theological Writings*, ed. Henry Chadwick (Stanford: Stanford University Press, 1956), 105.

28. See Selma Stern, *The Court Jew* (Philadelphia: Jewish Publication Society of America, 1950); and Arendt, *The Origins of Totalitarianism*, 11–28. For Mendelssohn's commercial activities, see Altmann, *Moses Mendelssohn*.

29. Gayatri Chakravorty Spivak, "Speculation on Reading Marx: After Reading Derrida," in *Poststructuralism and the Question of History*, ed. Derek Attridge et al. (Cambridge: Cambridge University Press, 1987), 34; and Karl Marx, *Capital: A Critique of Political Economy*, vol. 1, trans. Ben Fowkes (Harmondsworth: Penguin, 1976), 226.

30. Marx, *Capital*, 1: 226.

31. Ibid., 1: 222.

32. For a very different reading of this metaphor, see Marc Shell, *Money, Language, and Thought: Literary and Philosophical Economies from the Medieval to the Modern Era* (Berkeley: University of California Press, 1982).

33. See Hans Aarsleff, "The Tradition of Condillac: The Problem of the Origin of Language in the Eighteenth Century and the Debate in the Berlin Academy before Herder," in idem, *From Locke to Saussure: Essays on the Study of Language and Intellectual History* (Minneapolis: University of Minnesota Press, 1982). For

this influence on Lessing per se, see Dorothea E. von Mücke, *Virtue and the Veil of Illusion: Generic Innovation and the Pedagogical Project in Eighteenth-Century Literature* (Stanford: Stanford University Press, 1991), chap. 1.

34. On "progressivist semiotics" in Lessing, see David Wellbery, *Lessing's Laocoon: Semiotics and Aesthetics in the Age of Reason* (Cambridge: Cambridge University Press, 1984), 228–231.

35. Suzanne Gearhart, *The Interrupted Dialectic: Philosophy, Psychoanalysis and Their Tragic Other* (Baltimore, Md.: Johns Hopkins University Press, 1992), 189.

36. Denis Diderot, *Oeuvres Esthétiques* (Paris: Garnier, 1988), 312. All subsequent references to this collection are indicated within parentheses in the text.

37. Gearhart, *The Interrupted Dialectic*, 201–202.

38. Karl Marx, *Grundrisse: Foundations of the Critique of Political Economy (Rough Draft)* (New York: Penguin, 1993), 189; emphasis added.

39. Georg Simmel, "The Stranger," *The Sociology of Georg Simmel*, ed. Kurt H. Wolff (New York: Free Press, 1950), 402.

40. Etienne Balibar, "Citizen Subject," 53.

41. Thus much of this critique takes the form of engagement with the welfare statist arguments of the work of T. H. Marshall. See, for instance, several of the contributions to *Citizenship: Critical Concepts*, ed. Bryan S. Turner and Peter Hamilton, vols. 1 and 2 (London: Routledge, 1994), as well as those in *Citizenship and Social Theory*, ed. Bryan S. Turner (London: Sage 1993).

42. Marx, "On the Jewish Question," 35.

43. Immanuel Kant, "An Answer to the Question: 'What Is Enlightenment?'" in *Political Writings*, ed. Constance Garnett, 2nd ed. (Cambridge: Cambridge University Press, 1991), 54. And we must not ignore the meaning of childhood as explained to the Templar by the Patriarch of Jerusalem: "For is / Not all that's done to children done by force?" (4.2.74–75).

44. Jacob Katz, "The Jewish Diaspora: Minority Position and Majority Aspirations," *The Jerusalem Quarterly* 25 (fall 1982): 76.

45. On the motif of incestuous union in the literature of the Enlightenment, see Horst S. Daemmrich, "The Incest Motif in Lessing's *Nathan der Weise* and Schiller's *Braut von Messina*," *Germanic Review* 42 (1967): 184–196.

46. Mosse, *German Jews Beyond Judaism*, 16. See also Eike Geisel, "The Cultural League is formed to concentrate all 'Jewish' cultural life in one central organization under Nazi supervision," in Gilman and Zipes, *Yale Companion to Jewish Writing and Thought in German Culture, 1096–1996*, 508.

47. Arendt, *Men in Dark Times*, 17–18.

48. Hannah Arendt, "The Jew as Pariah: A Hidden Tradition," in idem, *The Jew as Pariah: Jewish Identity and Politics in the Modern Age*, 68.

49. See, for instance, Hannah Arendt, "From the Dreyfus Affair to France Today," *Jewish Social Studies* 4 (July 1942): 195–240.

50. See Bernstein, *Hannah Arendt and the Jewish Question*, 29–30.

51. Arendt, "The Jew as Pariah," 81.

52. Hannah Arendt, "'Eichmann in Jerusalem': An Exchange of Letters between Gershom Scholem and Hannah Arendt," in idem, *The Jew as Pariah*, 246.

53. Arendt, "The Jew as Pariah," 68.

54. Horkheimer and Adorno, *Dialectic of Enlightenment*, 4.

55. For a comparative reading of *The Jews* and *Nathan the Wise*, see Willi Goetschel, "Lessing's 'Jewish' Questions," *Germanic Review* 78 (2003): 62–73.

56. Gotthold Ephraim Lessing, *Nathan the Wise, Minna von Barnhelm, and other Plays and Writings*, ed. Peter Demetz (New York: Continuum, 1991), 168–169.

57. See Berghahn, "Lavater's attempt to compel the conversion of Moses Mendelssohn abuses the friendship cult surrounding Jewish and Christian intellectuals," 61–67; and Altmann, *Moses Mendelssohn*, 194–263.

58. See Edward Breuer, "Politics, Tradition, History: Rabbinic Judaism and the Eighteenth-Century Struggle for Civil Equality," *Harvard Theological Review* 85, no. 3 (1992): 360–361; Altmann, *Moses Mendelssohn*, 502–513; Allan Arkush, *Moses Mendelssohn and the Enlightenment* (Albany: State University of New York Press, 1994), 158–161; and *The Jew in the Modern World: A Documentary History*, ed. Paul R. Mendes-Flohr and Jehuda Reinharz (New York: Oxford University Press, 1980), 81–85.

59. I am not speaking here of the general sociological phenomenon of baptism as the means to social and professional mobility, an important aspect of the process of assimilation in the nineteenth century. Rather, I refer to the more specific *intellectual* concern with the mutual relations of Judaism, Christianity, and enlightened modernity. The latter, of course, also played a certain role in the former.

60. See Mosse, *German Jews Beyond Judaism*, 10. The painting is dated 1856.

61. See Michael Ragussis, *The Figures of Conversion*, 17–56, 174–211.

62. See Altmann, *Moses Mendelssohn*, chap. 6; and Katz, "The Term 'Jewish Emancipation,'" 14.

63. For the details of the debate as a whole, see Breuer, "Politics, Tradition, History," 357–383; Altmann, *Moses Mendelssohn*, chap. 6; and Mendes-Flohr and Reinharz, *The Jew in the Modern World*, 27–43.

64. See Le Comte de Mirabeau, *Sur Moses Mendelssohn, sur la réforme politique des Juifs: et en particulier sur la révolution tentée en leur faveur en 1753 dans la Grande Bretagne* (Paris: Editions d'Histoire Sociale, 1968); Henri Grégoire, *Essai sur la régénération des Juifs* (Paris: Editions d'Histoire Sociale, 1968); and Dominique Bourel, preface to Christian Wilhelm Dohm, *De la réforme politique des Juifs* (Paris: Editions Stock, 1984), 11.

65. See Edward Breuer, *The Limits of Enlightenment: Jews, Germans, and the Eighteenth-Century Study of Scripture* (Cambridge, Mass.: Harvard University Press, 1996), 22–23.

66. See Alexander Altmann, *Essays in Jewish Intellectual History* (Hanover, N.H.: University Press of New England, 1981), 170–189.

67. Altmann, *Essays in Jewish Intellectual History*, 159.

68. Mendes-Flohr and Reinharz, *The Jew in the Modern World*, 103–104. For the full debate, see Achille-Edmond Halphen, *Recueil des lois, décrets, ordonnances, avis du conseil d'état, arrêtés et règlements concernant les israélites depuis la révolution de 1879* (Paris: Bureaux des archives israélites, 1851), 184–191.

69. Mendez-Flohr and Reinharz, *The Jew in the Modern World*, 104.

70. See Condillac, *An Essay on the Origin of Human Understanding* (Gainesville, Fla.: Scholars' Facsimilies and Reprints, 1971), pt. 2, sec. 1, chaps. 1, 9–11, 13–14. See also von Mücke, *Virtue and the Veil of Illusion*, chap. 1; Aarsleff, "The Tradition of Condillac"; and G. A. Wells, "Condillac, Rousseau and Herder on the Origin of Language," *Studies on Voltaire and the Eighteenth Century*, vol. 230 (1985): 233.

71. Mendelssohn does not refer in *Jerusalem* to Condillac's essay nor to the work of William Warburton, *The Divine Legation of Moses* (1738–41), on whose chapter concerning hieroglyphs Condillac had heavily relied. Alexander Altmann cites Warburton as the source of Mendelssohn's ideas on this subject, and, according to Aarsleff, the Condillac framework would have been familiar to Berlin intellectuals from the linguistic debates of the Berlin Academy during the 1750s and 1760s. See Aarsleff, "The Tradition of Condillac."

72. As Amos Funkenstein has noted, Mendelssohn's account of fetishization "is a forerunner to later theories of 'Verdinglichung,' for example, Marx's account of the fetishization of the commodity" and of the money-form. See Amos Funkenstein, *Perceptions of Jewish History* (Berkeley: University of California Press, 1993), 226.

73. For eighteenth-century European theories about the nature of Egyptian hieroglyphs, see Erik Iverson, *The Myth of Egypt and Its Hieroglyphs in European Tradition* (Princeton, N.J.: Princeton University Press, 1993), chap. 4.

74. Lessing, "The Education of the Human Race," in *Lessing's Theological Writings*, 104–105.

75. Hannah Arendt, "We Refugees," in idem, *The Jew as Pariah: Jewish Politics and Identity in the Modern Age*, 66.

76. Bathja Bayer, "Jerusalem," in *Encyclopedia Judaica*, vol. 9 (Jerusalem: Macmillan, 1971), 1559–1560, 1568; and Žižek, "The Ongoing 'Soft Revolution,'" 323.

77. See J. J. Shulim, "Napoleon as the Jewish Messiah: Some Contemporary Conceptions in Vienna," *Jewish Social Studies* 7 (1945): 275–280. On the relationship of the secular to the theological in the history of Zionism, see Jacques Derrida, "The Eyes of Language: The Abyss and the Volcano," in *Acts of Religion*, ed. Gil Anidjar (New York: Routledge, 2002), 191–227. Derrida's main preoccupation here is with the themes of Gershom Scholem's open letter on Hebrew and secularization to Franz Rosenzweig, to which I return in a later chapter.

78. Quoted in Simon Schwarzfuchs, *Napoleon, the Jews and the Sanhedrin* (London: Routledge and Kegan Paul, 1979), 82.

79. See Joseph Lémann, *Napoléon et les Juifs* (Paris: Avalon, 1989), 17–20; Schwarzfuchs, *Napoleon, the Jews and the Sanhedrin*, 24–27; and Franz Kobler, *Napoleon and the Jews* (New York: Schocken Books, 1975). Although the issuing of this proclamation was announced in Paris in May 1791 in the *Moniteur Universel*, there apparently is no text extant and the whole matter may be a hoax. Kobler claims to have discovered a text that purports to be a German translation of the proclamation, a claim that Schwarzfuchs considers doubtful.

80. Edward W. Said, *Orientalism* (New York: Vintage, 1978), 42.

81. Ibid., 121.

82. Karl Marx and Friedrich Engels, *The German Ideology*, ed. C. J. Arthur (New York: International, 1984), 99.

83. See Schwarzfuchs, *Napoleon, the Jews and the Sanhedrin*, 50–52.

84. Ibid., 57.

85. Ibid., 72.

86. Quoted in ibid., 205 n. 56.

87. Ibid., 118.

88. See, for instance, Frederick Beiser, "Early Romanticism and the *Aufklärung*," in *What Is Enlightenment? Eighteenth-Century Answers and Twentieth-Century Questions*, ed. James Schmidt (Berkeley: University of California Press, 1996), 317–329; and Berlin, "Kant as an Unfamiliar Source of Nationalism."

89. See Le Comte Emmanuel Siéyès, *Qu'est-ce que le Tiers Etat?* (Paris: Sociéte de l'Histoire de la Révolution Française, 1888).

90. Quoted in Leah Greenfield, *Nationalism: Five Roads to Modernity* (Cambridge, Mass.: Harvard University Press, 1992), 361.

91. Etienne Balibar, *Masses, Classes, Ideas: Studies on Politics and Philosophy before and after Marx* (New York: Routledge, 1994), 194.

92. Johann Gottlieb Fichte, *Addresses to the German Nation*, ed. George Armstrong Kelly (New York: Harper and Row, 1968), 111. This work will henceforth be cited parenthetically in the text as *AGN*.

93. Foucault, *Language, Counter-Memory, Practice*, 148.

94. Marx and Engels, *The German Ideology*, 100.

95. See David Martyn, "Borrowed Fatherland: Nationalism and Language Purism in Fichte's *Addresses to the German Nation*," *Germanic Review* 72 (fall 1997): 1–13.

96. Deborah Sadie Hertz, *Jewish High Society in Old Regime Berlin* (New Haven: Yale University Press, 1988), 125. Chapters 3 and 5, in particular, list in detail the members of the German intelligentsia who were regular visitors at the Berlin salons.

97. See also Greenfield, *Nationalism*, 384–386.

98. Excerpted in Mendes-Flohr and Reinharz, *The Jew in the Modern World*, 257.

99. Hannah Arendt, *Rahel Varnhagen: The Life of a Jewish Woman*, rev. ed. (New York: Harcourt Brace Jovanovich, 1974), 131.

100. See Jürgen Habermas, "The German Idealism of the Jewish Philosophers," in idem, *Philosophical-Political Profiles* (Cambridge, Mass.: MIT Press, 1990), 21. Habermas proceeds here by outlining what he considers the influence of Jewish mystical thought, especially the Kabbalah, on German idealism.

101. Theodor W. Adorno, "On the Question 'What is German?'" in *Critical Models: Interventions and Catchwords* (New York: Columbia University Press, 1998), 205.

102. See, in particular, ibid., 205–214; "Words from Abroad," in *Notes on Literature*, vol. 1 (New York: Columbia University Press, 1991), 185–199; "On the Use of Foreign Words," in Adorno, *Notes on Literature*, vol. 2 (New York:

Columbia University Press, 1992), 286–91; and "The Meaning of Working through the Past," in Adorno, *Critical Models*, 89–104.

103. Adorno, "On the Question 'What is German?,'" 213, 207.

104. See Edward W. Said, "Reflections on Exile," *Granta* 13 (autumn 1984): 159–172.

105. Adorno, *Minima Moralia: Reflections from Damaged Life*, 110.

106. See Katie Trumpener, *Bardic Nationalism: The Romantic Novel and the British Empire* (Princeton, N.J.: Princeton University Press, 1997), xiii, passim. As a child in Pakistan in the 1970s, I read the novel in at least three forms—abridged, as "illustrated classic," and finally the actual novel.

107. See Christopher Hill, "The Norman Yoke," in idem, *Puritanism and Revolution: Studies in Interpretation of the English Revolution of the 17th Century* (London: Secker and Warburg, 1958); and Asa Briggs, "Saxons, Normans, and Victorians," in idem, *The Collected Essays of Asa Briggs*, vol. 2 (Urbana: University of Illinois Press, 1985).

108. Sir Walter Scott, *Ivanhoe* (Harmondsworth: Penguin Books, 1986), 536. All further references to this edition are cited in parentheses in the text as *I*.

109. See Ragussis, *The Figures of Conversion.*

110. M. Samuel, *Conversion of the Jews: An Address from an Israelite to the Missionary Preachers Assembled at Liverpool to Promote Christianity among the Jews* (Liverpool: W. Wales, n.d.), 15; and H. H. Norris, *The Origin, Progress, and Existing Circumstances of the London Society for Promoting Christianity among the Jews* (London: 1825), 502. Quoted in Ragussis, *The Figures of Conversion*, 18, 20.

111. George Eliot, *Daniel Deronda*, ed. Graham Handley (New York: Oxford University Press, 1990), 640.

112. Georg Lukács, *The Historical Novel* (Lincoln, Neb.: University of Nebraska Press, 1983), 24–25, 257. See James Chandler, *England in 1819: The Politics of Literary Culture and the Case of Romantic Historicism* (Chicago: University of Chicago Press, 1998).

113. Lukács, *The Historical Novel*, 53.

114. See Trumpener, *Bardic Nationalism*, 128–133.

115. On the history of Marxism's theoretical and practical engagement with the Jewish question, see Enzo Traverso, *The Marxists and the Jewish Question: The History of a Debate, 1842–1943*, trans. Bernard Gibbons (Atlantic Highlands, N.J.: Humanities, 1994).

116. See Fredric Jameson's introduction to Lukács, *The Historical Novel*, 21; and *Heinrich Heine: A Biographical Anthology*, ed. Hugo Beiber and Moses Hadas (Philidelphia: Jewish Publication Society of America, 1956), 196.

117. Lukács, *The Historical Novel*, 30.

118. See, for instance, Gershom Scholem, *Walter Benjamin: The Story of a Friendship* (London: Faber and Faber, 1982), 159–60.

119. Homi K. Bhabha, "Introduction: Narrating the Nation," in *Nation and Narration*, ed. Homi K. Bhabha (London: Routledge, 1990), 2–3.

120. On the life of the young Heine, see parts 1 and 2 of Jeffrey L. Sammons, *Heinrich Heine: A Modern Biography* (Princeton, N.J.: Princeton University Press, 1979).

121. Heinrich Heine, *Jewish Stories and Hebrew Melodies* (New York: Markus Wiener, 1987), 23. All further references are to this edition and are cited parenthetically in the text of the chapter as *JS*.

122. Hannah Arendt uses "Princess Sabbath" in this way in "The Jew as Pariah," 69–75.

123. See Heinrich Heine, "Concerning the History of Religion and Philosophy in Germany," trans. Helen Mustard, in idem, *The Romantic School and Other Essays* (New York: Continuum, 1985), 128–244.

124. See Gershom Scholem, "The Science of Judaism—Then and Now," in idem, *The Messianic Idea in Judaism and Other Essays on Jewish Spirituality* (New York: Schocken, 1971), 304–313.

125. Jeffrey L. Sammons, "Heine's *Rabbi von Bacherach*: The Unresolved Tensions," *German Quarterly*, 32, no. 1 (January 1964): 37.

126. Theodor W. Adorno, "Heine the Wound," in *Notes on Literature*, ed. Rolf Tiedemann, trans. Shierry Weber Nicholsen, 2 vols. (New York: Columbia University Press, 1991–92), 1: 85.

Chapter Two
Inscriptions of Minority in British Late Imperial Culture

1. George Eliot, *Daniel Deronda*, ed. Graham Handley (New York: Oxford University, 1990), 327. This edition is henceforth cited in the text as *DD*.

2. See Israel Zangwill, *Dreamers of the Ghetto* (London: William Heinemann, 1898), 261–299. Incidentally Zangwill refers to Mendelssohn throughout this text exclusively as "Nathan the Wise."

3. Amy Levy, *The Complete Novels and Selected Writings of Amy Levy, 1861–1889*, ed. Melvyn New (Gainesville: University of Florida Press, 1993), 238.

4. See David Feldman, *Englishmen and Jews: Social Relations and Political Culture, 1840–1914* (New Haven: Yale University Press, 1994), 46.

5. The work of the critics, including such scholars as Edward Said, Catherine Hall, Mike Davis, Gauri Viswanathan, and Simon Gikandi, among numerous others, is now too voluminous and well known to require or bear citation here. For notable instances of the recent neo-imperial turn, see Niall Ferguson, *Empire: How Britain Made the Modern World* (London: Allen Lane, 2003); and David Cannadine, *Ornamentalism: How the British Saw Their Empire* (Oxford: Oxford University Press, 2001).

6. Virginia Woolf, *Mrs. Dolloway* (New York: Harcourt Brace Jovanovich, 1953), 26, 274.

7. See Edward W. Said, "Zionism from the Standpoint of Its Victims," *Social Text* 1 (1979): 5–78; and idem, *The Question of Palestine* (New York: Times Books, 1979), 56–114. A shorter version, abridged by me, has appeared in *Dangerous Liaisons: Gender, Nation, and Post-Colonial Perspectives*, ed. Anne

McClintock, Aamir Mufti, and Ella Shohat (Minneapolis: University of Minnesota Press, 1997), 15–38.

8. Said, *Orientalism*, 49–73.

9. Amanda Anderson, "George Eliot and the Jewish Question," *Yale Journal of Criticism*, 10.1 (1997): 56–57. See Boyarin and Boyarin, "Diaspora: Generation and the Ground of Jewish Identity."

10. Already discussed at some length in the previous chapter is the appeal of this idea in England earlier in the century.

11. Levy, *The Complete Novels*, 238.

12. Susan Meyer, " 'Safely to Their Own Borders': Proto-Zionism, Feminism, and Nationalism in *Daniel Deronda*," *ELH* 60 (1993): 745, 748. This essay has since appeared as the final chapter in Susan Meyer, *Imperialism at Home* (Ithaca: Cornell University Press, 1996), 157–201.

13. The classic study of this dimension in Eliot's work is still Suzanne Graver, *George Eliot and Community: A Study in Social Theory and Fictional Form* (Berkeley: University of California Press, 1984).

14. Barbara Hardy, "The Moment of Disenchantment," in *George Eliot*, ed. Harold Bloom (New York: Chelsea House, 1986), 52; and Said, *The Question of Palestine*, 61.

15. *George Eliot: The Critical Heritage*, ed. David Carroll (London: Routledge and Kegan Paul, 1971), 32.

16. George Eliot, *Middlemarch*, ed. David Carroll (New York: Oxford University Press, 1991), 3.

17. Said, *The Question of Palestine*, 62.

18. See Tony E. Jackson, "George Eliot's 'New Evangel': *Daniel Deronda* and the Ends of Realism," *Genre* (summer/fall 1992): 234–35.

19. Marx, "On the Jewish Question," 49.

20. See Anthony McCobb, *George Eliot's Knowledge of German Life and Letters* (Salzburg: Institut für Anglistik und Amerikanistik, Universität Salzburg, 1982); and William Baker, *George Eliot and Judaism*.

21. See Baker, *George Eliot and Judaism*, chap. 7.

22. See ibid., 9; and Gordon S. Haight, *George Eliot: A Biography* (Harmondsworth: Penguin Books, 1985), 145–48.

23. *The George Eliot Letters*, ed. Gordon S. Haight, vol. 1 (New Haven: Yale University Press, 1954), 185 (November 12, 1854).

24. See Baker, *George Eliot and Judaism*, 37.

25. "Heine's Poems," *Leader*, vi (September 1, 1855): 843–44; "German Wit: Heinrich Heine," *Westminster Review*, lxv (January 1856): 1–33; "Heine's Book of Songs," *Saturday Review*, i (April 26, 1856): 523–24; and "Recollections of Heine," *Leader* 7 (August 23, 1856): 811–12.

26. See McCobb, *George Eliot's Knowledge of German Life and Letters*, 72–77.

27. Haight, *The George Eliot Letters*, 247 (February 11, 1848).

28. See Barbara Spackman, *Decadent Genealogies: The Rhetoric of Sickness from Baudelaire to D'Annunzio* (Ithaca: Cornell University Press, 1989); Gilman, *The Jew's Body*; and Mosse, *Confronting the Nation: Jewish and Western Nationalism*.

29. V. N. Vološinov, *Marxism and the Philosophy of Language*, trans. Ladislav Matejka and I. R. Titunik (Cambridge, Mass.: Harvard University Press, 1973), 123.

30. See Tucker, *A Probable State: the Novel, the Contract, and the Jews*, 105.

31. See Haight, *George Eliot: A Biography*, 7, 15, 21, 39, passim.

32. George Eliot, *Essays of George Eliot*, ed. Thomas Pinney (London: Routledge and Kegan Paul, 1963), 326. See Ragussis, *Figures of Conversion*, 266.

33. Eliot, *Middlemarch*, 217: "Your pier-glass or extensive surface of polished steel made to be rubbed by a housemaid, will be minutely and multitudinously scratched in all directions; but place now against it a lighted candle as a center of illumination, and lo! the scratches will seem to arrange themselves in a fine series of concentric circles round that little sun. It is demonstrable that the scratches are going everywhere impartially, and it is only your candle which produces the flattering illusion of a concentric arrangement, its light falling with an exclusive optical selection. These things are a parable. The scratches are events, and the candle is the egoism of any person now absent."

34. A. W. Ward and A. R. Waller, *The Cambridge History of English Literature,* vol. 13: *The Nineteenth Century, Part Two* (Cambridge: Cambridge University Press, 1933), 443.

35. See F. R. Leavis, *The Great Tradition: George Eliot, Henry James, Joseph Conrad* (New York: New York University Press, 1964). I have never seen the same said of *Middlemarch*, also a novel with a "double plot."

36. George Eliot, *The Complete Works of George Eliot: Impressions of Theophrastus Such and Miscellaneous Essays* (New York: Harper and Brothers, n.d.), 213, 203, 211.

37. Ibid., 203.

38. Ibid., 203.

39. Hannah Arendt, "Zionism Reconsidered," in idem, *The Jew as Pariah: Jewish Identity and Politics in the Modern Era*, 136.

40. P. Hardy, *The Muslims of British India* (Karachi: Cambridge University Press, 1972), 60, 62, 61.

41. W. W. Hunter, *The Indian Musalmans, Are They Bound in Conscience to Rebel against the Queen?* (Lahore: Premier Book House, 1974), 209. David Lelyveld, *Aligarh's First Generation: Muslim Solidarity in British India* (Princeton, N. J.: Princeton University Press, 1978) is a superbly nuanced and still the classic study of the emergence of the Aligarh movement.

42. Mohammad Mujeeb, "The Partition of India in Retrospect," in *India's Partition: Process, Strategy and Mobilization*, ed. Mushirul Hasan (Delhi: Oxford University Press, 1993), 396–407.

43. See Vasudha Dalmia, *The Nationalization of Hindu Traditions: Bhār atendu Hariśchandra* and *Nineteenth-Century Banaras* (Delhi: Oxford University Press, 1999).

44. Rudyard Kipling, "On the City Wall," in idem, *The Man Who would Be King and Other Stories* (Oxford: Oxford University Press, 1987), 221–243. This source is henceforth referred to as CW.

45. See, for instance, Louis L. Cornell, introduction to CW, xxxii.

46. Benita Parry, *Delusions and Discoveries: India in the British Imagination, 1880–1930* (London: Verso, 1998), 212.

47. See Sara Suleri, *The Rhetoric of English India* (Chicago: University of Chicago Press, 1993), 104–110; and Lelyveld, *Aligarh's First Generation*, 4–6.

48. Edward W. Said, *Culture and Imperialism* (New York: Knopf, 1993), 134.

49. Thomas R. Metcalfe, *Ideologies of the Raj* (New York: Cambridge University Press, 1995), x.

50. Uday Singh Mehta, *Liberalism and Empire: A Study in Nineteenth-Century British Liberal Thought* (Chicago: University of Chicago Press, 1999), 121.

51. Rudyard Kipling, *Barrack-Room Ballads and Departmental Ditties and Other Verses* (New York: Grosset and Dunlap, n.d.), 20.

52. The now classic conceptual analysis of the dynamics of this anxiety is to be found, of course, in Homi K. Bhabha, *The Location of Culture* (New York: Routledge, 1994); but see also Ashis Nandy, *The Intimate Enemy*. For a fuller intellectual history of ideologies of British rule in the nineteenth century, see Metcalfe, *Ideologies of the Raj*.

53. Charles Carrington, *Rudyard Kipling: His Life and Work* (Harmondsworth: Penguin, 1986), 137.

54. See Mehta, *Liberalism and Empire*, chap. 4.

55. Said, *Culture and Imperialism*, 74.

56. Typical, perhaps exemplary, in this regard is the attitude of Henry James, who wrote a glowing preface for the American publication of *Mine Own People* but spoke with concern in private of the author's "brutality." Oscar Wilde dismissed Kipling as "our best authority on the second-rate." See Carrington, *Rudyard Kipling*, 400–402.

57. Said, "Representing the Colonized: Anthropology's Interlocutors," *Critical Inquiry* 15, no. 2 (1989): 223.

58. Asha Varadharajan, *Exotic Parodies: Subjectivity in Adorno, Said and Spivak* (Minneapolis: University of Minnesota Press, 1995), xxv.

59. E. M. Forster, *A Passage to India* (New York: Harcourt Brace Jovanovich, 1984), 102–103. This edition is referred to henceforth as *PI*.

60. See *PI*, 358.

61. Parry, *Delusions and Discoveries*, 233.

62. Joseph Conrad, *Heart of Darkness*, ed. Robert Kimbrough, 3rd ed. (New York: Norton, 1988), 10, 38.

63. E. M. Forster, "What I Believe," *A Bloomsbury Group Reader*, ed. S. P. Rosenbaum (Oxford: Blackwell, 1993), 165–172.

64. Ibid., 165, 167, 169. The reference is, of course, to Shakespeare's sixty-fifth sonnet.

65. In the 1953 preface to *The Hill of Devi* (New York: Harcourt Brace Jovanovich, 1984), 9, Forster writes: "And throughout I use 'India' in the old, and as it seems to me the true, sense of the word to designate the whole subcontinent. Much as I sympathize with the present government at New Delhi, I wish it had not chosen "India" to describe its territory. Politicians are too prone to plunder the past."

66. Sara Suleri, *The Rhetoric of English India*, 133–134.
67. See, for instance, E. M. Forster, *The Hill of Devi*, 127, 323.
68. Forster, "What I Believe," 169.
69. Suleri, *The Rhetoric of English India*, 133.

Chapter Three
Jawaharlal Nehru and Abul Kalam Azad

1. See Maulana Abul Kalam Azad, *Ġhubār-e ḳhāṯir* (New Delhi: Sāhitya Academy, 1991), 29. This edition hereafter is referred to as *G*.
2. On the history of the movement launched by the passage of the resolution, see Arun Chandra Bhuyan, *The Quit India Movement: The Second World War and Indian Nationalism* (Delhi: Manas, 1975).
3. Sarvepalli Gopal, *Jawaharlal Nehru: A Biography*, vol. 1 (London: Jonathan Cape, 1975), 298, 299.
4. See D. D. Kosambi, "The Indian Bourgeoisie Comes of Age," *Social Scientist* 10.4 (1946): 392–398. I am grateful to Janaki Bakhle for making me aware of this review.
5. Chatterjee, *Nationalist Thought and the Colonial World*, 51.
6. Stanley Corngold and Michael Jennings, "Walter Benjamin/Gershom Scholem," *Interpretation: A Journal of Political Philosophy* 12.2, 12.3 (May, September 1984): 357–366.
7. According to Azad's most distinguished editor, Malik Ram, Cheetah Khan is identified in medieval histories as a "eunuch" ("ḳhvāja sarā") (*G*, 310–311 n. 7).
8. Nehru, *An Autobiography*, 466, 448.
9. See, for instance, Nehru on the Khilafat movement, the Indian Muslim agitation on behalf of the Ottoman Caliphate after its defeat in the First World War (*DI*, 350); Nirad Chaudhuri, *Autobiography of an Unknown Indian* (London: Macmillan, 1951); and Suniti Kumar Chatterji, *Indo-Aryan and Hindi*, 2nd ed. (Calcutta: Firma K. L. Mukhopadhyay, 1960), 220.
10. Beni Prasad, *India's Hindu-Muslim Questions* (London: Allen and Unwin, 1946), 68.
11. Arendt, *The Origins of Totalitarianism*, 289. For the drafting of the Minorities Treaties and the League's exercise of its protective authority in the following decade, the authoritative study, by an official of the League of Nations Union, is C. A. Macartney, *National States and National Minorities* (London: Oxford University Press, 1934). The history of the treaties with respect to Jewish populations in particular is described in great detail by Oscar I. Janowsky, *The Jews and Minority Rights (1898–1919)* (New York: Columbia University Press, 1933). Janowsky provides an accessible summary of the League's labyrinthine procedures regarding treaty enforcement in *Nationalities and National Minorities (with Special Reference to East-Central Europe)* (New York: MacMillan, 1945), 110–134.
12. Macartney, *National States and National Minorities*, 507.

13. See, for instance, Syed Ahmed Khan's classic biography by his follower and publicist, Altaf Husain Hali, *Ḥayāt-e jāvēd* (New Delhi: Taraqqī-e Urdū Bureau, 1990). Hali is perhaps the original author of this interpretive convention.

14. See Chatterjee, *Nationalist Thought and the Colonial World*, 143.

15. The historical literature and relevant debates are voluminous. For the more important highlights, see Paul Brass, *Language, Religion and Politics in North India* (New York: Cambridge University Press, 1974), part 3; Amrit Rai, *A House Divided: The Origin and Development of Hindi/Hindavi* (Delhi: Oxford University Press, 1984); Christopher King, *One Language, Two Scripts: The Hindi Movement in Nineteenth-Century North India* (Bombay: Oxford University Press, 1994); Vasudha Dalmia, *The Nationalization of Hindu Traditions*, esp. chaps. 2 and 4; Francesca Orsini, *The Hindi Public Sphere, 1920–1940: Language and Literature in the Age of Nationalism* (Delhi: Oxford University Press, 2002); and two important recent works, one by Alok Rai, *Hindi Nationalism* (Delhi: Orient Longman, 2000), and the other by Shamsur Rahman Faruqi, *Early Urdu Literary Culture and History* (Delhi: Oxford University Press, 2001). A shorter version of this latter book has appeared as one of the four chapters devoted to Urdu and Hindi in *Literary Cultures in History: Reconstructions from South Asia*, ed. Sheldon Pollock (Delhi: Oxford University Press, 2001). These two short, polemical works, almost companion volumes, have given a new direction to the ongoing discussion on the history of the Hindu-Urdu conflict.

16. See Hali, *Ḥayāt-e jāvēd*, 139–144; Lelyveld, *Aligarh's First Generation*, 97–101; Francis Robinson, *Separatism among Indian Muslims: The Politics of the United Provinces' Muslims, 1860–1923* (Delhi: Oxford University Press, 1994), 96–98; and Rai, *Hindi Nationalism*.

17. For a general history of the college, see Sisir Kumar Das, *Sahibs and Munshis: The College of Fort William* (New Delhi: Orion, 1978); on Hindi and Urdu, see Sadiq-ur-Rahman Kidwai, *Gilchrist and the "Language of Hindoostan"* (New Delhi: Rachna Prakashan, 1972).

18. On vernacularization and the nation-state, the classic theoretical study is Benedict Anderson, *Imagined Communities: Reflections on the Origins and Spread of Nationalism* (London: Verso, 1983). Beyond the emergence of the modern European vernaculars, I have in mind such language "revolutions" as "May 4" in China, *genbun itchi* in Japan, the Bengal Renaissance, and the *nahḍa* in the Arab world, especially in Egypt and the Levant.

19. On Punjab, see Ayesha Jalal, *Self and Sovereignty: Individual and Community in South Asian Islam since 1850* (New York: Routledge, 2002), chap. 3; and on late-nineteenth-century Bengal, see Rafiuddin Ahmed, *The Bengal Muslims, 1871–1906: A Quest for Identity*, 2nd ed. (Delhi: Oxford University Press, 1996), 106–132.

20. Tej Bahadur Sapru, foreword to Ram Babu Saksena, *A History of Urdu Literature* (Lahore: Sang-e Meel, 1996), iii.

21. See Faruqi, *Early Urdu Literary Culture and History*, 13–62.

22. See ibid., 23–29.

23. See ibid., 23 n. 4.

24. See John Gilchrist, *The British Indian Monitor* (Edinburgh: n.p., 1806).

25. See Das, *Sahibs and Munshis*, 123.

26. Ram Babu Saksena, for instance, speaks of Gilchrist as "the father of Urdu prose." See Saksena, *A History of Urdu Literature*, 267.

27. Kidwai, *Gilchrist and the "Language of Hindoostan,"* 31–32. Quoted in Faruqi, *Early Urdu Literary Culture and History*, 37 n. 36.

28. This nineteenth-century involvement of Urdu with the *kachahrī* or lower courts is still visible to us in the seemingly trivial fact that, in the musicals of "Hindi" cinema today, one of the common moments of the surfacing of an unmistakably "Urdu" register is the courtroom scene, in which speech forms distinctly marked as "Urdu" suddenly predominate in a seemingly unself-conscious manner. The other such "scene" of Urdu speech and culture in "Hindi" cinema is the *kōṭhā* or courtesan's salon, a question of some interest to which I return in the next chapter.

29. See Robinson, *Separatism among Indian Muslims*, 98; and Hali, *Ḥayāt-e jāvēd*, 140.

30. Anonymous [Madan Mohan Malaviya], *Court Character and Primary Education in the N.-W. Provinces & Oudh* (Allahabad: Indian Press, 1897), 24, 25. For a detailed discussion of Malaviya's text and its moment, see Rai, *Hindi Nationalism*, 17–49.

31. Anonymous, *A Defence of the Urdu Language and Character (Being a reply to the pamphlet called "Court Character and Primary Education in N.-W. P. and Oudh")* (Allahabad: Liddell's N.-W. P. Printing Press, 1900), 2, 5, 7, 10.

32. See, for instance, Robert Alter, *The Invention of Hebrew Prose: Modern Fiction and the Language of Realism* (Seattle: University of Washington Press, 1988); and Naomi Seidman, "Lawless Attachments, One-Night Stands: The Sexual Politics of the Hebrew-Yiddish Language War," in Boyarin and Boyarin, *Jews and Other Differences*, 279–305.

33. See Anderson, *Imagined Communities*, 77. Here Anderson relies upon, and quotes from, Tom Nairn, *The Break-Up of Britain* (London: New Left Books, 1977).

34. On the sense in Urdu circles that modern Hindi was vulgar or rustic speech, see T. Graham Bailey, "Does Khari Boli Mean Nothing More Than Rustic Speech," *Bulletin of the School of Oriental and African Studies, University of London* 8, no. 2/3 (1936): 363–371. See Rai, *Hindi Nationalism*.

35. Among the more interesting accounts of this episode in the history of the Hindi-Urdu conflict, from opposing perspectives, are R. B. Saksena, *Gandhiji's Solution of the Language Problem of India* (Bombay: Hindustani Prachar Sabha, 1972), 9–11; and Dr. Akhtar Husain Raipuri, *Gard-e rāh* (Karachi: Maktaba-e Afkār, 1984), 102–107. For a selection of Gandhi's interventions in the language debates during this period, see *Our Language Problem*, ed. Anand T. Hingorani (Karachi: Anand T. Hingorani, 1942).

36. Gandhi, *Our Language Problem*, 2, 4.

37. Ibid., 27–28; emphases added.

38. Ibid., 2.

39. For one such journal, launched for this purpose from the mofussil (*mufaṣṣil*) town of Moradabad, see Rashid Kamali, "ʿArẓ-e niāz," *Hindustānī* 1, no. 1 (August 1937): 2–5. The journal editor was this author's father, writing under his pen-name.

40. See Orsini, *The Hindi Public Sphere*, 357–379.

41. See Maulvi Abdul Haq, *Ḵhuṭbāt-e ʿAbd al-Ḥaq*, ed. Ibadat Barelvi (Karachi: Anjuman-e Taraqqī-e Urdū, 1952), 154; Raipuri, *Gard-e rāh*, 104; and Saksena, *Gandhiji's Solution*, 11. For a small sampling of Abdul Haq's numerous accounts of his dealings with Gandhi and his followers in 1936, see *Ḵhuṭbāt-e ʿAbd al-Ḥaq*, 150–151, 504–505. On Jinnah, see Stanley Wolpert, *Jinnah of Pakistan* (Delhi: Oxford University Press, 1988), 100–102.

42. See his letters of 1947–48 to Gandhi, Azad (then the education minister in independent India), and Tej Bahadur Sapru (nominally the president of the Anjuman) in Maulvi Abdul Haq, *Makātīb-e ʿAbd al-Ḥaq* (Karachi: Urdū Academy Sindh, 1963), 409–424, 428–431, 432–438.

43. Jawaharlal Nehru, *The Question of Language*, with a foreword by Mahatma Gandhi (Allahabad: K. M. Ashraf on behalf of the Political and Economic Information Department of the All-India Congress Committee, 1937), 16–22. On the evolution of Nehru's views and policies regarding the politics of language after partition, see Robert D. King, *Nehru and the Language Politics of India* (Delhi: Oxford University Press, 1997).

44. Something like a mirror reflection of this process can also be seen, of course, in the development of Hindi as a distinct version of the vernacular. See Dalmia, *The Nationalization of Hindu Traditions*.

45. Syed Sulaiman Nadvi, *Nuqūsh-e Sulaimānī* (Karachi: Urdū Academy Sindh, 1967), *jīm*.

46. See Gershom Scholem, "Confession on the Subject of Our Language," in Jacques Derrida, *Acts of Religion*, trans. Gil Anidjar (New York: Routledge, 2002), 227, 226, 227, 226.

47. See Stéphane Mosès, "Langage et secularization chez Gershom Scholem," in *Archives de Sciences Sociales des Religions* 60, no. 1 (July–September 1985): 85–96; and Jacques Derrida, "The Eyes of Language: The Abyss and the Volcano," in idem, *Acts of Religion*, 191–226.

48. On the instrumental, but also uncontrollable, use of Islam by the central government in the early years of Pakistan, see Ayesha Jalal's superb historical narrative in *The State of Martial Rule: The Origins of Pakistan's Political Economy of Defence* (Karachi: Verso, 1991), 277–294.

49. The word is of Persian etymology, but I am referring here to the complex of ritual practices and concepts of purity that it signifies in *sharīf* (that is, upper-*caste*) Muslim culture in North India.

50. See, for instance, Aijaz Ahmad, "Azad's Careers: Roads Taken and Not Taken," in *Islam and Indian Nationalism: Reflections on Abul Kalam Azad*, ed. Mushirul Hasan (Delhi: Manohar, 1992), 139–150, and passim; and Rajat Ray, "Revolutionaries, Pan-Islamists and Bolsheviks: Maulana Abul Kalam Azad and the Political Underworld in Calcutta, 1905–1925," in *Communal and Pan-Islamic Trends in Colonial India*, ed. Mushirul Hasan (Delhi: Manohar,

1985), 101–124. Nothing reveals more clearly the pervasiveness of these rumors and uncertainties than that Nehru felt it necessary to lay to rest one of them—Azad's purported education at al-Azhar—in the brief speech he made in Parliament on the latter's death in 1958. See Jawaharlal Nehru, "The Passing of a Great Man," in *Maulana Azad: A Memorial Volume*, ed. Humayun Kabir (London: Asian Publishing House, 1959), 1–4. In *The Discovery of India*, Nehru had stated baldly that Azad "had received his early education in Al Azhar Universty of Cairo" (*DI*, 347).

51. See Gail Minault, *The Khilafat Movement: Religious Symbolism and Political Mobilization in India* (New York: Columbia University Press, 1982); Francis Robinson, *The ʿUlama of Farangi Mahall and Islamic Culture in South Asia* (London: C. Hurst, 2001); and Ian Henderson Douglas, *Abul Kalam Azad: An Intellectual and Religious Biography*, ed. Gail Minault and Christian W. Troll (Delhi: Oxford University Press, 1989), 170–188. This is the most comprehensive biography of Azad in English to date and was written as a Ph.D. dissertation at Oxford in the 1960s under the supervision of Albert Hourani. The Ali brothers were formal disciples of Abdul Bari, having taken *baiʿat* with him during the political mobilization.

52. On the emergence of "English" education, the classic study is Gauri Viswanathan, *Masks of Conquest: Literary Study and British Rule in India* (New York: Columbia University Press, 1989); see also Kumkum Sangari, "Relating Histories: Definitions of Literacy, Literature, Gender in Nineteenth-Century Calcutta and England," in *Rethinking English: Essays in Literature, Language, History*, ed. Svati Joshi (New Delhi: Trianka, 1991), 32–123.

53. See Viswanathan, *Masks of Conquest*, 36, and passim.

54. See Louis Massignon, "My Meetings with Maulana Azad," in Kabir, *Maulana Azad*, 27–29. On Azad's essay, see Christian W. Troll, "Abul Kalam Azad and Sarmad, the Martyr," in Hasan, *Islam and Indian Nationalism*, 28–42. For a critical but sympathetic assessment of Massignon's place in the history of Orientalism, see Said, *Orientalism*, 264–275.

55. This enormous work, which has been published in four large volumes by the Sahitya Academy in India, deserves a sustained engagement that is beyond the scope of the present work and must be left for another occasion. The more than four-hundred-page first volume is an explication—historical, philological, theological, philosophical—of the opening chapter of the Qur'an, "al-Fātiḥa," which is a mere four to five lines long.

56. See Nikki R. Keddie, *An Islamic Response to Imperialism: Political and Religious Writings of Sayyid Jamal ad-Din "al-Afghani"* (Berkeley: University of California Press, 1983), 3–97.

57. See, for instance, David Berman, *A History of Atheism in Britain: From Hobbes to Russell* (London: Routledge, 1988), 206–221. In a long footnote—one of a handful in the entire book—Azad explains to his readers the basic principles of the Higher Criticism by using as example the question of the multiple authorship of the Book of Isaiah (*G*, 121).

58. See Saiyid Athar Abbas Rizvi, *A History of Sufism in India*, vol. 1 (Delhi: Munshiram Manoharlal, 1983), 41–42.

59. See Annemarie Schimmel, *Mystical Dimensions of Islam* (Chapel Hill: University of North Carolina Press, 1975), 267.

60. See Alam, *The Languages of Political Islam*, 91–98.

61. See Mushirul Hasan, *Nationalism and Communal Politics in India* (Delhi: Manohar, 1994), 207–210, 214–215; and Robinson, *Separatism among Indian Muslims*, 338–339.

62. See Jalal, *Self and Sovereignty*, 177–178; and Aijaz Ahmad, *Lineages of the Present: Ideology and Politics in South Asia* (New York: Verso, 2000), 12–13.

63. Abul Kalam Azad, *Ḳhuṭbāt-e Āzād*, ed. Malik Ram (New Delhi: Sāhitya Academy, 1990), 297; henceforth, *K*.

64. Nadvi, *Nuqūsh-e Sulaimānī*, 155–156.

65. Schimmel, *Mystical Dimensions of Islam*, 79.

66. I owe my understanding of the fascinating Turkish-Greek context in part to conversations with Asli Igsiz, for which I extend my thanks.

67. See Hardy, *The Muslims of British India*, 50–51. For a somewhat spotty but nevertheless useful survey of *hijrah* in Islamic thought and in political practice across the Muslim world, see Zafarul-Islam Khan, *Hijrah in Islam* (New Delhi: Pharos Media and Publishing, for the Muslim Institute, London, 1997).

68. Muhammad Khalid Masud, "The Obligation to Migrate: The Doctrine of *hijra* in Islamic Law," in *Muslim Travellers: Pilgrimage, Migration, and the Religious Imagination*, ed. Dale F. Eickelman and James Piscatori (Berkeley: University of California Press, 1990), 29.

69. See Masud, "The Obligation to Migrate," 31.

70. See Minault, *The Khilafat Movement*, 106–107; and M. Naeem Qureshi, "The 'Ulama of British India and the Hijrat of 1920," *Modern Asian Studies* 13, no. 1 (1979): 43.

71. See Qureshi, "The 'Ulama of British India and the Hijrat of 1920," 50, 45. For a firsthand account of the emigration to Afghanistan and a voluminous documentary history of the *hijrat* movement, see Syed Rais Ahmed Jaafri, *Aurāq-e gum gashta* (Lahore: Muḥammad ʿAlī Academy, 1968).

72. The title of Attar's work, *Manṭiq al-ṭā'ir*, is often translated as "Conference of the Birds," although perhaps *manṭiq* is slightly better rendered as "discourse," "disputation," or "conversation."

Chapter Four
Saadat Hasan Manto

1. Mahnaz Ispahani, "Saadat Hasan Manto," *Grand Street* 7, no. 4 (summer 1988): 193. For the reported Urdu original, see Sahba Lakhnavi, *Manṭō: ēk kitāb* (Lahore: Maktaba-e Afkār, 1994), 66.

2. Manto's own remarks on this stormy relationship are to be found in "Jaib-e kafan," in *Manṭōnāma* (Lahore: Sang-e Mīl, 1990), 221–229. All references to this volume are identified henceforth as *MN*. Also see Leslie Fleming, *Another Lonely Voice: The Life and Works of Saadat Hassan Manto* (Lahore: Vanguard, 1985), 27–30. This edition is henceforth identified as *AV*.

3. Georg Lukács, *The Theory of the Novel: A Historico-Philosophical Essay on the Forms of Great Epic Literature*, trans. Anna Bostock (Cambridge, Mass.: MIT, 1989), 88, 92–93.

4. Sandhya Shetty, "(Dis)figuring the Nation: Mother, Metaphor, Metonymy," *differences: A Journal of Feminist Cultural Criticism*, 7, no. 3 (1995): 50.

5. Salman Rushdie, *The Moor's Last Sigh* (New York: Vintage, 1995), 137.

6. Studies of North Indian literatures that include analyses of this trope include Sudhir Chandra, *The Oppressive Present: Literature and Social Consciousnes in Colonial India* (Delhi: Oxford University Press, 1992), 27–30; and Sudipta Kaviraj, *The Unhappy Consciousness: Bankimchandra Chattopadhyay and the Formation of Nationalist Discourse in India* (Delhi: Oxford University Press, 1995), 137ff. The history of the figure in modern painting is briefly touched upon in Partha Mitter, *Art and Nationalism in Colonial India, 1850–1922: Occidental Orientations* (Cambridge: University of Cambridge Press, 1994), part 3.

7. See Fareed Kazmi, "Muslim Socials and the Female Protagonist: Seeing a Dominant Discourse at Work," in *Forging Identities: Gender, Communities and the State*, ed. Zoya Hasan (New Delhi: Kali for Women, 1994), 226–243; and Mukul Kesevan, "Urdu, Awadh and the Tawaif: The Islamicate Roots of Hindi Cinema," in Hasan, *Forging Identities*, 244–257.

8. The more important of these include Partha Chatterjee, "The Nationalist Resolution of the Women's Question," *Recasting Women: Essays in Colonial History*, ed. Kumkum Sangari and Sudesh Vaid (New Brunswick, N.J.: Rutgers University Press, 1990), 233–253; Gayatri Chakravorty Spivak, "A Literary Representation of the Subaltern," *In Other Worlds: Essays in Cultural Politics* (New York: Routledge, 1988), 241–268; and idem, "Woman in Difference: Mahasweta Devi's 'Douloti the Bountiful,'" *Nationalisms and Sexualities*, ed. Andrew Parker et al. (New York: Routledge, 1992), 96–117; and Sandhya Shetty, "(Dis)figuring the Nation."

9. See Carlo Coppola, "The All-India Progressive Writers' Association: The European Phase," in *Marxist Influences and South Asian Literature*, vol. 1, Occasional Papers no. 23, South Asia series, ed. Carlo Coppola (Lansing: Michigan State University, 1974), 1–34. For a documentary history of the AIPWA, see *Marxist Cultural Movement in India, Chronicles and Documents*, vol. 1, ed. Sudhi Pradhan (Calcutta: Pustak Bipani, 1985). For a collection of documents as well as interpretive and historical essays pertaining to the influence of the AIPWA in Urdu literature per se, see *Taraqqī pasand adab: pachās sāla safar*, ed. Qamar Raees and Syed Ashore Kazmi (Delhi: Educational Publishing House, 1987). For Urdu, the standard historical study is still Khalilur Rahman Azmi, *Urdū mēñ taraqqī pasand adabī taḥrīk* (Aligarh: Anjuman-e Taraqqī-e Urdū, 1972). Zaheer's own authoritative insider's account is to be found in *Raushnā'ī* (Karachi: Dānyāl, 1986).

10. Askari and Raipuri each wrote only a small but influential body of short fiction. The former, as already discussed, went on to become a leading literary critic in Pakistan after Partition and a major antagonist of Progressivist aesthetics, and the latter largely withdrew from literary life for the next several decades.

11. The critique of classical Urdu poetry (of the period from the late seventeenth to the mid-nineteenth century) associated with the Aligarh movement "reformers" like Altaf Husain Hali and Muhammad Husain Azad is discussed at length in Frances W. Pritchett, *Nets of Awareness: Urdu Poetry and Its Critics* (Berkeley: University of California Press, 1994), and I return to it in the next chapter. For the (Indian) nationalist view of the Urdu poetic tradition, a reliable source, as we have seen in the previous chapter, is Suniti Kumar Chatterji, author of *Indo-Aryan and Hindi* [1942]: "A language and literature which came to base itself upon an ideology which denied on the soil of India the very existence of India and Indian Culture [*sic*], could not but be met with a challenge from the sons of India, adherents of their natural culture; and that challenge was in the form of highly Sanskritized Hindi." Quoted in Aziz Ahmad, *Studies in Islamic Culture in the Indian Environment* (Oxford: Clarendon, 1969), 255. It is significant that Ahmad, whose position throughout this book may be described as Pakistani nationalist, is in perfect agreement with Chatterji and cites the latter only as a cap to his own argument about the inwardness and autonomy of the "Muslim psyche" in India as revealed in classical Urdu poetry.

12. See Asif Farrukhi, *Ḥarf-e man o tū* (Karachi: Nafīs Academy, 1989), 73.

13. On the novel and the nation, the classic study is, of course, Benedict Anderson's *Imagined Communities*.

14. The standard histories in English include Shaista Akhtar Banu Suhrawardy, *A Critical Survey of the Development of the Urdu Novel and Short Story* (London: Longmans Green, 1945); and Ram Babu Saksena, *A History of Urdu Literature*, chaps. 15–17; Also see the following somewhat impressionistic works by Ralph Russell: "The Development of the Modern Novel in Urdu," in *The Novel in India: Its Birth and Development*, ed. T. W. Clark (Berkeley: University of California Press, 1970); and *The Pursuit of Urdu Literature: A Select History* (Delhi: Oxford University Press, 1992).

15. On the contours of this process in another colonial setting, namely, Ireland, see David Lloyd, "Violence and the Constitution of the Novel," in idem, *Anomalous States*, 88–124.

16. See Michael Scriven and Dennis Tare, eds. *European Socialist Realism* (Oxford: Berg, 1988).

17. See Pradhan, *Marxist Cultural Movement*, 22–23.

18. Lukács, *The Theory of the Novel*, 50–51.

19. Saadat Hasan Manto, "Hatak," in *Manṭōrāmā* (Lahore: Sang-e Mīl, 1990), 904. This volume is henceforth identified as *MR*. The corresponding passage in the Tahira Naqvi translation can be found in *AV*, 248.

20. "Bābū Gōpīnāth," in *MN*, 276–291. A translation can be found in Saadat Hasan Manto, *Kingdom's End and Other Stories*, trans. Khalid Hasan (New Delhi: Penguin Books, 1987), 133–148. This latter volume is henceforth referred to as *KE*.

21. See, for instance, Dr. Wazir Agha, "Manṭō kē afsānōñ mēñ ʿaurat," *Timṡāl* 1.1 (1992): 35–50. Bhisham Sahni, writing from a Progressive position far removed from the deconstructionism of Agha's argument, has also argued that

Manto's women seem ultimately incapable of rebellion against their state. See "Saadat Hasan Manto: A Note," *Life and Works of Saadat Hasan Manto*, ed. Alok Bhalla (Shimla: Indian Institute for Advanced Study, 1997), 172–174. I am grateful to Zoya Khan for bringing this latter reference to my attention.

22. Sahni, "Saadat Hasan Manto," 172.

23. See Adorno, *Notes on Literature*, 1: 190.

24. Manto, "Lazzat-e sañg," in *MN*, 619–620.

25. Michel Foucault, "The Subject and Power," *Critical Inquiry* 8 (summer 1992): 790. For two studies of the governmentalization of power in South Asian colonial society, see David Scott, "Colonial Governmentality," *Social Text* 43 (fall 1995): 191–220; and Milind Wakankar, "Body, Crowd, Identity: Genealogy of a Hindu Nationalist Ascetics," *Social Text* 45 (winter 1995): 45–73.

26. The historical reference here is, of course, to the Government of India Act of 1935, which promised limited self-government to Indians at the local and provincial levels.

27. If at first it appears faintly ridiculous to speak of nationalist hopes for the flush toilet, we need think only of the conclusion to Anand's *Untouchable*, where it is suggested that the practice of untouchability, socially tied to the demeaning labor of removing human filth, will disappear upon introduction of that modern technology.

28. Saadat Hasan Manto, "Safēd jhūṭ," in *MN*, 674–683.

29. See, for instance, Veena Talwar Oldenburg, "Lifestyle as Resistance: The Case of the Courtesans of Lucknow, India," *Feminist Studies* 16, no. 2 (summer 1990): 259–287.

30. See Shetty, "(Dis)figuring the Nation," 55–56; and Kaviraj, *The Unhappy Consciousness*, 139.

31. On the conception of India at the turn of the century as "a collection of communities," see the seminal work by Gyanendra Pandey, *The Construction of Communalism in Colonial North India*, 210. As for the stylization of the courtesan figure in its post-Partition articulations, in the cinematic "Muslim social" genre, for instance, the courtesan encodes (the marked) "Muslim" selfhood as merely style, that is, as an excess beyond the (unmarked) self that is representative of the nation. In other words, it encodes "the Muslim" as minority.

32. Susan Buck-Morss, "The Flâneur, the Sandwichman, and the Whore: The Politics of Loitering," *New German Critique* 39 (1986): 99–140.

33. See Charles Bernheimer, *Figures of Ill Repute: Representing Prostitution in Nineteenth-Century France* (Durham, N.C.: Duke University Press, 1997).

34. Claire Wills, "Joyce, Prostitution, and the Colonial City," *South Atlantic Quarterly* 95, no. 1 (winter 1996): 79–95.

35. While I admire and applaud the wide-ranging contemporary critical efforts—in the work, among others, of Edward Said, David Lloyd, Seamus Deane, Luke Gibbons, Joe Cleary, and Wills herself—to rethink Irish cultural experience in modernity as that of a colonial and postcolonial society, I do think that this move requires extra caution that we not simply conflate an experience such as Ireland's with that of Third World societies like India or Egypt.

36. See Rai, *Hindi Nationalism*, 94.

37. See, for instance, Imtiaz Ahmad, "Secularism and Communalism," *Economic and Political Weekly* (July 1969): 1137–1158.

38. Saadat Hasan Manto, "Gunāh kī bēṭīyañ, gunāh kē bāp," in *MR*, 332.

39. See Buck-Morss, "The Flâneur, the Sandwichman, and the Whore," 119–120.

40. Wills, "Joyce, Prostitution, and the Colonial City," 93. Wills is referring here to the function of the prostitute in Joyce's fictions as an unmasking of the claims of Irish nationalism.

41. The string "āf dī" could be read as a Punjabi pronunciation of the English "of the." The second word is clearly written in the original in the same way as the Punjabi feminine possessive "dī." On constative versus performative statements in speech act theory, see James Lyons, *Semantics*, vol. 2 (Cambridge: Cambridge University Press, 1977), 726–727.

42. Saadat Hasan Manto, "Zaḥmat-e mahr-e darakḥshāñ," in *MN*, 352.

43. See Saadat Hasan Manto, *Manṭōnumā* (Lahore: Sang-e Mīl, 1991), 455–458.

44. See ibid., 389–512. Many of these pieces are included in translation in Saadat Hasan Manto, *Mottled Dawn: Fifty Sketches of Partition*, trans. Khalid Hasan (New Delhi: Penguin, 1997).

45. Saadat Hasan Manto, *Manṭō kahānīyāñ* (Lahore: Sang-e Mīl, 1995), 11. Henceforth cited as *MK*. A translation inexplicably titled "The Return" can be found in Manto, *Mottled Dawn*, 11–14. Henceforth cited as *MD*.

46. Manto, "Zaḥmat-e mahr-e darakḥshān," 354.

47. See, for instance, Urvashi Butalia, *The Other Side of Silence: Voices from the Partition of India* (Karachi: Oxford University Press, 1998); Ritu Menon and Kamla Bhasin, *Borders and Boundaries: Women in India's Partition* (Delhi: Kali for Women, 1998); and Veena Das, *Critical Events: An Anthropological Perspective on Contemporary India* (Delhi: Oxford University Press, 1995), 55–83.

48. See Urvashi Butalia, "Community, State and Gender: On Women's Agency during Partition," *Economic and Political Weekly* 28, no. 17 (24 April 1993), esp. WS-18.

49. See Manto, *Manṭōnumā*, 135; and Saadat Hasan Manto, *Stars from Another Sky: The Bombay Film World of the 1940s*, trans. Khalid Hasan (Delhi: Oxford University Press, 1998), 73.

50. Askari, *Majmūʿa*, 140.

51. Ibid., 142–143.

52. See Azmi, *Urdū mēñ taraqqī pasand adabī taḥrīk*, 93. It is remarkable that in *Raushnāʾī*, his memoir of the AIPWA, Zaheer makes not a single reference to this entire episode.

53. Quoted in Fleming, *Another Lonely Voice*, 28–29.

54. Lukács, *The Theory of the Novel*, 50.

Chapter Five
Faiz Ahmed Faiz

1. The standard work in English on these debates in the late nineteenth century is Pritchett, *Nets of Awareness*.

2. See Agha Shahid Ali, "Introduction: Translating Faiz Ahmed Faiz," in Faiz Ahmed Faiz, *The Rebel's Silhouette: Selected Poems*, rev. ed., trans. Agha Shahid Ali (Amherst: University of Massachusetts Press, 1995), xiv; and V. G. Kiernan, introduction to *Poems by Faiz* by Faiz Ahmed Faiz, trans. V. G. Kiernan (Lahore: Vanguard Books, 1971), 40. This work will be cited as *PF*.

3. Adorno, "On Lyric Poetry and Society," in idem, *Notes to Literature*, 1: 42, 38.

4. See, for instance, Syed Sibte Hassan, "Faiẓ kā ādarsh," in *Faiẓ Aḥmad Faiẓ: tanqīdī jā'iza*, ed. Khaleeq Anjum (New Delhi: Anjuman-e Taraqqī-e Urdū, 1985), 119, 121.

5. In matters of citing translations, I have set the following principles for myself: wherever possible, I work with Kiernan's translation, the "literal" one if I am engaging in a line-by-line analysis, as this is closest to the original in terms of line content, and the "non-literal" where the object is to convey a sense of the whole, in either case altering the translations as necessary. Where a poem or fragment is not available in a Kiernan translation, I either provide my own "literal" translation or turn to the more freely translated versions of Agha Shahid Ali (see note 2) or Naomi Lazard—see *The True Subject: Selected Poems of Faiz Ahmed Faiz*, trans. Naomi Lazard (Princeton, N.J.: Princeton University Press, 1988)—depending, again, on the specific purpose at hand.

6. See Kiernan, introduction to *PF*, 38. On Gandhi and Urdu, see chap. 3, above.

7. Kiernan, introduction to *PF*, 38.

8. See "Faiẓ—az Faiẓ," in Faiz Ahmed Faiz, *Nuskhahā'-e vafā* (Lahore: Maktaba-e Kārvāñ, 1986), 308–311. This work will be cited as *NV*.

9. See *PF*, 90–95; and *NV*, 89–91.

10. See *NV*, 308–311.

11. This biographical summary is based on the following sources: Kiernan, introduction to *PF*; Khaleeq Anjum, "Faiẓ bītī," in Khaleeq Anjum, *Faiẓ Aḥmad Faiẓ: tanqīdī jā'iza*, 14–37; Faiz, "Faiẓ—az Faiẓ," in *NV*, 307–314; Faiz, "Ahd-e ṯiflī sē 'unfuvān-e shabāb tak," in *NV*, 489–497; "Bachpan kī qir'at sē Jōsh kī buzurgī tak," in Faiz Ahmed Faiz, *Matā'-e lauḥ o qalam* (Karachi: Dānyāl, 1985), 112–121; and Faiz Ahmed Faiz, *Māh o sāl-e āshnā'ī: yādoñ kā majmū'a* (Karachi: Dānyāl, 1983), 5–20.

12. See Carlo Coppola, "The Angare Group: The Enfants Terribles of Urdu Literature," *Annual of Urdu Studies*, no. 1 (1981): 57–69.

13. *Naqsh-e faryādī* (Remonstrance) was published in 1941, to be followed, during his lifetime, by *Dast-e ṣabā* (Fingers of the wind, 1952), *Zindāñ-nāma* (Prison thoughts, 1956), *Dast-e tah-e sañg* (Duress, 1965), *Sar-e vādī-e Sīna* [Mount Sinai, 1971], *Shām-e shahr-e yārāñ* [Twilight over the city of friends, 1978], and *Mirē dil mirē musāfir* (My heart, my fellow traveler, 1981). His late and previously uncollected poems have been collected as *Ġhubār-e ayyām* (Dust of days). The first four translations here are Kiernan's, the rest mine.

14. Quoted in Azmi, *Urdū mēñ taraqqī pasañd adabī taḥrīk*, 109.

15. See Hasan Zaheer, *The Times and Trial of the Rawalpindi Conspiracy 1951: The First Coup Attempt in Pakistan* (Karachi: Oxford University Press, 1998).

16. Said, "Reflections on Exile," 160. Faiz appears briefly in Mahmoud Darwish's memoir of the Israeli siege. See Mahmoud Darwish, *Memory for Forgetfulness*, trans. and with an introduction by Ibrahim Muhawi (Berkeley: University of California Press, 1995), 65.

17. On the early years of the Aligarh movement, see Lelyveld, *Aligarh's First Generation*; on a particular strain of religious neo-orthodoxy, see Barbara Daly Metcalf, *Islamic Revival in British India: Deoband, 1860–1900* (Princeton, N.J.: Princeton University Press, 1982); and an intriguing study of culture and space by Faisal Fatehali Devji, "Gender and the Politics of Space: The Movement for Women's Reform, 1857–1900," in Hasan, *Forging Identities*, 22–37.

18. See Altaf Husain Hali, *Muqaddama-e shiʿr o shāʿirī*, ed. Dr. Waheed Qureishi (Aligarh: Educational Publishing House, 1993), 116–117, 153–154, 158, 178–185. On the popularity of the *ġhazal*, and hence the greater importance of its "reform" (*iṣlāḥ*) than all other genres of poetry, see 179.

19. For a full-length account of these debates, see Pritchett, *Nets of Awareness*.

20. See Gopi Chand Narang, *Sāḳhtīyāt, pas-sāḳhtīyāt, aur mashriqī shiʿrīyāt* (Delhi: Educational Publishing House, 1994), 9.

21. Regrettably Kiernan did not include this very beautiful poem among his excellent translations. Agha Shahid Ali has a lovely interpretation, although not in his Faiz volume. This translation is my own. I have tried to keep it as literal as possible—with almost no attention to meter or rhyme scheme—and to remain true to the content of the lines, even at the cost of syntactical awkwardness, as in lines 9 and 10. The punctuation and capitalization in the original are, of course added. (Urdu lacks the latter and makes sparing use of the former.) My analysis stays close to the original, with the translation meant merely as a rough guide for readers unfamiliar with the Urdu.

22. Theodor W. Adorno, "Subject and Object," in *The Essential Frankfurt School Reader*, ed. Andrew Arato and Eike Gebhardt (New York: Continuum, 1988), 500.

23. Faiz, *NV*, 438. Again the translation is mine, the literal meaning my immediate goal with some attention to the rhyme scheme.

24. For the classical *ġhazal* and its symbolic and thematic universe, see Russell, *The Pursuit of Urdu Literature*, chap. 2; and Annemarie Schimmel, *A Two-Colored Brocade: The Imagery of Persian Poetry* (Chapel Hill: University of North Carolina Press, 1992), pt. 2; on the erotics of *ġhazal* imagery, see Schimmel, "Eros—Heavenly and Not So Heavenly—in Sufi Literature and Life," *Society and the Sexes in Medieval Islam*, ed. Afaf Lutfi al-Sayyid-Marsot (Malibu: Undena, 1979), 119–141.

25. See *PF*, 276–277, for Kiernan's rendition, which I have altered slightly; and *NV*, 429.

26. See Schimmel, "Eros—Heavenly and Not So Heavenly—in Sufi Literature and Life," 134–135.

27. This evocative, but largely free, translation is Agha Shahid Ali's. See Faiz, *The Rebel's Silhouette*, 85; and *NV*, 524–525.

28. Adorno, "Lyric Poetry and Society," 46.

29. See Gérard Genette, *Paratexts: Thresholds of Interpretation*, trans. Jane E. Lewin (Cambridge: Cambridge University Press, 1997); and Georg Stanizek, "Texts and Paratexts in Media," *Critical Inquiry* 32 (autumn 2005): 27–42.

30. See C. M. Naim, "The Consequences of Indo-Pakistani War for Urdu Language and Literature," *Journal of Asian Studies* 38, no. 2 (February 1969): 269–283. Also see Aijaz Ahmad, "Some Reflections on Urdu," *Seminar* 359 (July 1989): 29.

31. This is a slight modification of Kiernan's translation. See *PF*, 268–271. Also, in *NV*, the lineation is slightly different, and Kiernan's line 12 is broken into two after "siyāhmast" and line 16 after "hō kē"; see 409–410.

32. Ahmad Faraz, "Main kyūñ udās nahīñ," in *Nāyaft* (Lahore: Māvrā, 1989), 29–30. The title itself is ambiguous and could be translated as either "Why do I not grieve?" or "Why I do not grieve." I am not concerned here with the explicitly jingoistic verse that was produced in response to the war. For a discussion of some of this work and its context, see Naim, "The Consequences of Indo-Pakistani War for Urdu Language and Literature."

33. Kiernan translates the title "Mauẓūʿ-e sukhan" as "Poetry's Theme." This leaves out the grammatical and philosophical senses that "mauẓūʿ" shares with "subject."

34. For a rather different reading of "Mujh sē pahlī sī maḥabbat . . ." by an Orientalist "lover" of the classical *ġhazal* tradition, see Russell, *The Pursuit of Urdu Literature*, 230–231, 243–244. In line with his literal readings of Urdu poetry in general, Russell notes sarcastically that he is not impressed with the discovery "that there are other things in life besides love of women" (243). His entire chapter on Faiz would be laughable—he considers Faiz a second-rate poet—if it did not border on the scurrilous, accusing Faiz of self-promotion and political insincerity and cowardice.

35. See Faruqi, *Early Urdu Literary Culture and History*, chap. 1.

36. Some of these matters are discussed in chapter 3 above.

37. This summary of Faiz's views on the problem of "Pakistani culture" is based on the following essays, lectures, and interviews: "Pākistānī tahzīb kā mas'ala" and "Jahān-e nau hō rahā hai paidā," in Faiz Ahmed Faiz, *Mīzān* (Karachi: Urdū Academy Sindh, 1987), 87–96, 97–101; "Ġhālib," in Faiz, *Matāʿ-e lauḥ o qalam*, 134–139; and the four lectures and one interview collected in Faiz Ahmed Faiz, *Hamārī qaumī śaqāfat*, ed. Mirza Zafarul Hasan (Karachi: Idāra-e Yādgār-e Ġhālib, 1976).

38. Faiz, "Pākistānī tahzīb kā mas'ala," 94.

39. Ibid., 94–95.

40. Etienne Balibar, "The Nation Form: History and Ideology," in Etienne Balibar and Immanuel Wallerstein, *Race, Nation, Class: Ambiguous Identities* (New York: Verso, 1991), 86–87.

41. For an example of the form such contortions take today, see Aitzaz Ahsan, *The Indus Saga and the Making of Pakistan*. (Karachi: Oxford University Press, 1996).

42. Hali, *Muqaddama-e shiʿr o shāʿirī*, 158.

43. Faiz himself argues that much of what Hali is credited with having originated in poetry—the turn to "nature," the rejection of "artificial" affect, the rejection of abstraction and esotericism—can, in fact, be traced to Nazir Akbarabadi, who wrote almost a century earlier. Hali's uniqueness lies in the "national" (*qaumī*) nature of his poetry and poetics. See his important essay, "Naẕīr aur Ḥālī," in Faiz, *Mīzān*, 169–170, 179–183.

44. The English here is a modification of Agha Shahid Ali's very free but lovely translation. See Faiz, *The Rebel's Silhouette*, 30.

45. Theodor W. Adorno, "The Fetish Character in Music and the Regression of Listening," trans. Arato and Gebhardt, *The Frankfurt School Reader* (New York: Continuum, 1982), 275.

46. Theodor W. Adorno, *Negative Dialectics*, trans. E. B. Ashton (New York: Seabury, 1973), 3. On Adorno and lateness, see Fredric Jameson, *Late Marxism: Adorno, or the Persistence of the Dialectic* (London: Verso, 1990); and Edward W. Said, "Adorno as Lateness Itself," *Apocalypse Theory and the Ends of the World*, ed. Malcolm Bull (Oxford: Blackwell, 1995), 264–281.

47. See Fanon, *The Wretched of the Earth*, 40.

48. I am grateful to Stathis Gourgouris and Eduardo Cadava for elucidating the need for this clarification.

49. Adorno, "On Lyric Poetry and Society," 40.

50. See Kiernan's notes to selections 10, 32, 47, 48, 49, and 54, in *PF*.

51. See Muhammad Abd-Al-Rahman Barker and Shah Abdus Salam, *Classical Urdu Poetry*, vol. 1 (Ithaca, N.Y.: Spoken Languages Services, 1977), xliv.

52. Hali speaks of the "unbearable confinements" ("na qābil-e bardāsht qaidēñ") of rhyme scheme in the *ġhazal*. See Hali, *Muqaddama*, 178–179.

53. *Radīf* (refrain) "hōtā." See Mirza Asadullah Khan Ghalib, *Dīvān-eĠhālib* (Aligarh: Educational House, 1991), 63.

54. I am grateful to Tahsin Siddiqi of the University of Michigan, Ann Arbor, for his help in identifying this couplet from Mushafi.

55. See Carla Petievich, *Assembly of Rivals: Delhi, Lucknow and the Urdu Ghazal* (Delhi: Manohar, 1992), x, xvi n. 14; and Annemarie Schimmel, *Classical Urdu Literature from the Beginnings to Iqbal* (Wiesbaden: Otto Harrossovitz, 1975), 191, 198.

56. See Amrit Rai, *A House Divided*, 32–33.

Epilogue

1. See Bishnupriya Ghosh, *When Borne Across: Literary Cosmopolitics in the Contemporary Indian Novel* (New Brunswick, N.J.: Rutgers University Press, 2004). This use of the term derives from *Cosmopolitics: Thinking and Feeling beyond the Nation*, ed. Pheng Cheah and Bruce Robbins (Minneapolis: University of Minnesota Press, 1998).

2. Meenakshi Mukherjee, *Twice Born Fiction: Themes and Techniques of the Indian Novel in English* (New Delhi: Heinemann, 1971), i.

3. Rushdie, *The Moor's Last Sigh*, 87; henceforth cited in the text as *MLS*.

4. Amitav Ghosh, *In an Antique Land* (Delhi: Ravi Dayal, 1992), 236, 237.

5. See ibid., 338–342.

6. Anita Desai, *Baumgartner's Bombay* (New York: Penguin Books, 1989), 92; henceforth cited in the text as *BB*.

7. Arendt, *The Origins of Totalitarianism*, xv.

8. On the "voluntary" phase of the Aryanization of Jewish businesses, see Raul Hilberg, *The Destruction of the European Jews*, rev. ed., vol. 1 (New York: Holmes and Meier, 1985), 94–102.

9. Said, *Orientalism*, 332.

10. See Joachim Oesterheld, "British Policy towards German-speaking Emigrants in India, 1939–1945," in *Jewish Exile in India, 1933–1945*, ed. Anil Bhatti and Johannes H. Voigt, 25–44 (Delhi: Manohar, 2005).

11. Adorno, *Minima Moralia: Reflections from Damaged Life*, 193.

12. Sartre, *Anti-Semite and Jew*, 57.

13. Arendt, *The Origins of Totalitarianism*, 284.

14. If we assume that Desai is not taking license with historical chronology here, this is a representation not of *Kristallnacht* but of the pogroms of early 1933.

15. Aijaz Ahmad, *In Theory: Classes, Nations, Literatures* (New York: Verso, 1992), 13.

16. For a recent rehashing of these themes, see, for instance, Arif Dirlik, "The End of Colonialism? The Colonial Modern in the Making of Global Modernity," *boundary 2* 32, no. 1 (2005): 1–31.

17. Aijaz Ahmad, "A Response," *Public Culture* 6, no. 1 (fall 1993): 163.

18. Adorno, *Negative Dialectics*, 203.

19. Ibid., xx–xxi.

20. Ibid., 18.

21. Ibid., 17–18.

Works Cited

Aarsleff, Hans. "The Tradition of Condillac: The Problem of the Origin of Language in the Eighteenth Century and the Debate in the Berlin Academy before Herder." In idem, *From Locke to Saussure: Essays on the Study of Language and Intellectual History*. Minneapolis: University of Minnesota, 1982.

Abdul Haq, Maulvi. *Ḵhuṭbāt-e ʿAbd al-Ḥaq*. Edited by Ibadat Barelvi. Karachi: Anjuman-e Taraqqī-e Urdū, 1952.

———. *Makātīb-e ʿAbd al-Ḥaq*. Karachi: Urdū Academy Sindh, 1963.

Adorno, Theodor W. "The Fetish Character in Music and the Regression of Listening." In Arato and Gebhardt, *The Essential Frankfurt School Reader*, 119–132.

Adorno, Theodor W. "Heine the Wound." In *Notes to Literature*, 1: 80–85.

———. *Minima Moralia: Reflections from Damaged Life*. London: Verso, 1989.

———. *Minima Moralia: Reflexionen aus dem beschädigten Leben*. Berlin: Suhrkampf Verlag, 1951.

———. *Negative Dialectics*. Translated by E. B. Ashton. New York: Continuum, 1973.

———. *Notes on Literature*. Edited by Rolf Tiedemann. Translated by Shierry Weber Nicholsen. 2 vols. New York: Columbia University Press, 1991–92.

———. "On Lyric Poetry and Society." In idem, *Notes on Literature*, 1: 37–54.

———. "On the Question 'What Is German?'" In idem, *Critical Models: Interventions and Catchwords*, 205–214. New York: Columbia University Press, 1998.

———. "On the Use of Foreign Words." In idem, *Notes on Literature*, 2: 286–291.

———. "Perennial Fashion—Jazz." In idem, *Prisms*, 119–132. Cambridge, Mass.: MIT Press, 1988

———. "Subject and Object." In Arato and Gebhardt, *The Essential Frankfurt School Reader*, 497–511.

———. "Words from Abroad." In idem, *Notes on Literature*, 1: 185–199.

Agha, Wazir. "Manṭō kē afsanōn̄ mēn̄ 'aurat.'" *Timṡāl* 1, no. 1 (1992): 35–50.

Ahmad, Aijaz. "Azad's Careers: Roads Taken and Not Taken." In M. Hasan, *Islam and Indian Nationalism*, 122–175.

———. *In Theory: Classes, Nations, Literatures*. London: Verso, 1992.

———. *Lineages of the Present: Ideology and Politics in South Asia*. New York: Verso, 2000.

———. "Some Reflections on Urdu." *Seminar* 359 (July 1989): 23–29.

———. "A Response." *Public Culture* 6, no. 1 (1993): 143–191.

Ahmad, Aziz. "Islam d'Espagne et Inde musulmane moderne." In *Études d'orientalisme dédiées a la mémoire de Lévi-Provençal*, vol. 2. Paris: G.-P. Maisonneuve et Larosse, 1962, 461–470.

———. *Studies in Islamic Culture in the Indian Environment*. Oxford: Clarendon, 1969.

Ahmad, Imtiaz. "Secularism and Communalism." *Economic and Political Weekly* (July 1969): 1137–1158.

Ahmed, Rafiuddin. *The Bengal Muslims, 1871–1906: A Quest for Identity*. 2nd ed. Delhi: Oxford University Press, 1996.

Ahsan, Aitzaz. *The Indus Saga and the Making of Pakistan*. Karachi: Oxford University Press, 1996.

Alam, Muzaffar. *The Languages of Political Islam: India, 1200–1800*. Chicago: University of Chicago Press, 2004.

Ali, Agha Shahid. "Introduction: Translating Faiz Ahmed Faiz." In Faiz Ahmed Faiz, *The Rebel's Silhouette: Selected Poems*, rev. ed., translated by Agha Shahid Ali. Amherst: University of Massachusetts Press, 1995.

Alter, Robert. *The Invention of Hebrew Prose: Modern Fiction and the Language of Realism*. Seattle: University of Washington Press, 1988.

Altmann, Alexander. *Essays in Jewish Intellectual History*. Hanover, N.H.: University Press of New England, 1981.

———. *Moses Mendelssohn: A Biographical Study*. Philadelphia: Jewish Publication Society of America, 1973.

———. "Moses Mendelssohn as the Archetypal German Jew." In *The Jewish Response to German Culture: From the Enlightenment to the Second World War*, edited by Jehuda Reinharz and Walter Schatzberg, 17–31. Hanover, N.H.: University Press of New England, 1985.

Anderson, Amanda. "George Eliot and the Jewish Question." *Yale Journal of Criticism* 10, no. 1 (1997): 39–61.

Anderson, Benedict. *Imagined Communities: Reflections on the Origin and Spread of Nationalism*. London: Verso, 1983.

Anjum, Khaleeq. "Faiẓ bītī." In *Faiẓ Aḥmad Faiẓ: tanqīdī jā'iza*, edited by Khaleeq Anjum. New Delhi: 14–37. Anjuman-e Taraqqī-e Urdū, 1985.

Anonymous. *A Defence of the Urdu Language and Character (Being a reply to the pamphlet called "Court Character and Primary Education in N.-W. P. and Oudh."* Allahabad: Liddell's N.-W. P. Printing Press, 1900.

Appadurai, Arjun. *Modernity at Large*. Minneapolis: University of Minnesota Press, 1998.

Arendt, Hannah. "From the Dreyfus Affair to France Today." *Jewish Social Studies* 4 (July 1942): 195–240.

———. *The Jew as Pariah: Jewish Politics and Identity in the Modern Age*. Edited by Ron H. Feldman. New York: Grove, 1978.

———. "The Jew as Pariah: A Hidden Tradition." In idem, *The Jew as Pariah*, 67–90.

———. "On Humanity in Dark Times: Thoughts about Lessing." In idem, *Men in Dark Times*, 3–31. New York: Harcourt Brace, 1983.

———. *The Origins of Totalitarianism*. New ed. New York: Harcourt Brace, 1979.

———. *Rahel Varnhagen: The Life of a Jewish Woman*. Rev. ed. New York: Harcourt Brace Jovanovich, 1974.

———. "We Refugees." In idem, *The Jew as Pariah*, 55–66.

———. "Zionism Reconsidered." In idem, *The Jew as Pariah*, 131–163.

Arkush, Allan. *Moses Mendelssohn and the Enlightenment.* Albany: State University of New York Press, 1994.

Askari, Muhammad Hasan. *Majmūʿa.* Lahore: Sang-e Mīl, 1994.

Azad, Maulana Abul Kalam. *Khuṭbāt-e Āzād.* Edited by Malik Ram. New Delhi: Sāhitya Academy, 1990.

———. *Ġhubār-e khāṭir.* New Delhi: Sāhitya Academy, 1991.

Azmi, Khalilur Rahman. *Urdū mēñ taraqqī pasand adabī taḥrīk.* Aligarh: Anjuman-e Taraqqī-e Urdū, 1972.

Bailey, T. Graham. "Does Kari Boli Mean Nothing More than Rustic Speech?" *Bulletin of the School of African and Oriental Studies, University of London* 8, no. 2/3 (1936): 363–371.

Baker, William. *George Eliot and Judaism.* Salzburg: Institut für Englische Sprache und Literatur, Universität Salzburg, 1975.

Balibar, Etienne. *Masses, Classes, Ideas: Studies on Politics and Philosophy before and after Marx* (New York: Routledge, 1994).

———. " 'Rights of Man' and 'Rights of the Citizen': The Modern Dialectic of Equality and Freedom." In idem, *Masses, Classes, Ideas*, 39–59.

———. "The Nation Form: History and Ideology." In Etienne Balibar and Emmanuel Wallerstein, *Race, Nation, Class: Ambiguous Identities*, 86–106. New York: Verso, 1992.

———. "What Is a Politics of the Rights of Man?" In idem, *Masses, Classes, Ideas*, 205–225.

———. "Citizen Subject." In *Who Comes after the Subject?* edited by Eduardo Cadava, Peter Connor, and Jean-Luc Nancy, 33–57. New York: Routledge, 1991.

Barker, Muhammad Abd-Al-Rahman and Shah Abdus Salam. *Classical Urdu Poetry*, vol. 1. Ithaca, N.Y.: Spoken Languages Services, 1977.

Baron, Salo W. *A Social and Religious History of the Jews.* vol. 2. New York: Columbia University Press, 1937.

Basu, Tapan, Pradip Datta, and Sumit Sarkar, et al. *Khaki Shorts and Saffron Flags.* New Delhi: Orient Longman, 1993.

Bauman, Zygmunt. *Modernity and Ambivalence.* Ithaca, N.Y.: Cornell University Press, 1991.

———. *Modernity and the Holocaust.* Ithaca, N.Y.: Cornell University Press, 1989.

Bayer, Bathja. "Jerusalem." In *Encyclopedia Judaica*, vol. 9. Jerusalem: MacMillan, 1971.

Beiber, Hugo, and Moses Hadas, eds. *Heinrich Heine: A Biographical Anthology.* Philadelphia: Jewish Publication Society of America, 1956.

Beiser, Frederick. "Early Romanticism and the *Aufklärung.*" In *What Is Enlightenment? Eighteenth-Century Answers and Twentieth-Century Questions*, edited by James Schmidt, 317–329. Berkeley: University of California Press, 1996.

Berghahn, Klaus L. "Lavater's attempt to compel the conversion of Moses Mendelssohn abuses the friendship cult surrounding Jewish and Christian intellectuals." In Gilman and Zipes, *Yale Companion to Jewish Writing*, 61–67.

Berlin, Isaiah. *The Sense of Reality: Studies in Ideas and Their History.* Edited by Henry Hardy. London: Pimlico, 1996.

Berman, David. *A History of Atheism in Britain: From Hobbes to Russell.* London: Routledge, 1988.

Bernheimer, Charles. *Figures of Ill Repute: Representing Prostitution in Nineteenth-Century France.* Durham: Duke University Press, 1997.

Bernstein, Richard J. *Hannah Arendt and the Jewish Question.* Cambridge, Mass.: MIT Press, 1996.

Bhabha, Homi K. "Editor's Introduction: Minority Maneuvers and Unsettled Negotiations." *Critical Inquiry* 23 (spring 1997): 431–459.

———. *The Location of Culture.* New York: Routledge, 1994.

———, ed. *Nation and Narration.* London: Routledge, 1990.

———. "Anxious Nations, Nervous States." In *Supposing the Subject*, edited by Joan Copjec, 201–217. London: Verso, 1994.

Bhuyan, Arun Chandra. *The Quit India Movement: The Second World War and Indian Nationalism.* Delhi: Manas, 1975.

Bohnert, Christiane. "Enlightenment and Despotism: Two Worlds in Lessing's *Nathan the Wise*." In Wilson and Holub, *Impure Reason*, 344–363.

Bourel, Dominique. Preface to *De la réforme politique des Juifs* by Christian Wilhelm Dohm. Paris: Éditions Stock, 1984.

Boyarin, Daniel, and Jonathan Boyarin. "Diaspora: Generation and the Ground of Jewish Identity." *Critical Inquiry* 19, no. 4 (summer 1993): 693–725.

———, eds. *Jews and Other Differences: The New Cultural Studies.* Minnesota: University of Minnesota Press, 1997.

Boyarin, Jonathan. *Storm from Paradise: The Politics of Jewish Memory.* Minneapolis: University of Minnesota Press, 1992.

———. *Palestine and Jewish History: Criticism at the Borders of Ethnography.* Minneapolis: University of Minnesota Press, 1996.

Brass, Paul. *Language, Religion and Politics in North India.* Cambridge: Cambridge University Press, 1974.

———. *The Production of Hindu-Muslim Violence in Contemporary India.* Delhi: Oxford University Press, 2003.

Briggs, Asa. "Saxons, Normans, and Victorians." In idem, *The Collected Essays of Asa Briggs*, vol. 2. Urbana: University of Illinois Press, 1985, 215–235.

Brubaker, Rogers. *Citizenship and Nationhood in France and Germany.* New York: Columbia University Press, 1992.

Breuer, Edward. *The Limits of Enlightenment: Jews, Germans, and the Eighteenth-Century Study of Scripture.* Cambridge, Mass.: Harvard University Press, 1996.

———. "Politics, Tradition, History: Rabbinic Judaism and the Eighteenth-Century Struggle for Civil Equality." *Harvard Theological Review* 85, no. 3 (1992): 357–383.

Buck-Morss, Susan. "The Flâneur, the Sandwichman, and the Whore: The Politics of Loitering." *New German Critique* 39 (1986): 99–140.

Butalia, Urvashi. "Community, State and Gender: On Women's Agency during Partiton." *Economic and Political Weekly* 28, no. 17 (April 24, 1993): WS12–WS24.

———. *The Other Side of Silence: Voices from the Partition of India.* Karachi: Oxford University Press, 1998.

Cabral, Amilcar. *Return to the Source: Selected Speeches*. New York: Monthly Review Press, 1974.

Cannadine, David. *Ornamentalism: How the British Saw Their Empire*. Oxford: Oxford University Press, 2001.

Carlebach, Julius. *Karl Marx and the Radical Critique of Judaism*. London: Routledge, 1978.

Carrington, Charles. *Rudyard Kipling: His Life and Work*. Harmondsworth: Penguin, 1986.

Carroll, David, ed. *George Eliot: The Critical Heritage*. London: Routledge and Kegan Paul, 1971.

Cassirer, Ernst. *The Philosophy of the Enlightenment*. Princeton, N.J.: Princeton University Press, 1968.

Césaire, Aimé. *Discourse on Colonialism*. New York: Monthly Review Press, 1972.

Chadwick, Henry, ed. *Lessing's Theological Writings*. Stanford: Stanford University Press, 1956.

Chakrabarty, Dipesh. "Radical Histories and Question of Enlightenment Rationalism: Some Recent Critiques of Subaltern Studies." *Economic and Political Weekly* (April 8, 1995): 751–759.

———. *Provincializing Europe: Postcolonial Thought and Historical Difference*. Princeton, N.J.: Princeton University Press, 2000.

Chandler, James. *England in 1819: The Politics of Literary Culture and the Case of Romantic Historicism* (Chicago: Chicago University Press, 1998).

Chandra, Sudhir. *The Oppressive Present: Literature and Social Consciousnes in Colonial India*. Delhi: Oxford University Press, 1992.

Chatterjee, Partha. *Nationalist Thought and the Colonial World: A Derivative Discourse*. Minneapolis: University of Minnesota Press, 1993.

———. "The Nationalist Resolution of the Women's Question." In *Recasting Women: Essays in Colonial History*, edited by Kumkum Sangari and Sudesh Vaid. New Brunswick, N.J.: Rutgers University Press, 1990, 233–253.

Chatterji, Suniti Kumar. *Indo-Aryan and Hindi*. 2nd ed. Calcutta: Firma K. L. Mukhopadhyay, 1960.

Chaudhuri, Nirad. *Autobiography of an Unknown Indian*. London: Macmillan, 1951.

Cheah, Pheng, and Bruce Robbins, eds. *Cosmopolitics: Thinking and Feeling beyond the Nation*. Minneapolis: University of Minnesota Press, 1998.

Cheyette, Bryan. *Constructions of "the Jew" in English Literature and Society: Racial Representations, 1875–1945*. Cambridge: Cambridge University Press, 1993.

Cheyette, Bryan, and Laura Marcus, eds. *Modernity, Culture, and "the Jew"*. Cambridge: Polity, 1998.

Condillac, Abbé de. *An Essay on the Origin of Human Understanding*. Gainesville, Fla.: Scholars' Facsimilies and Reprints, 1971.

Conrad, Joseph. *Heart of Darkness*. 3rd ed. Edited by Robert Kimbrough. New York: Norton, 1988.

Coppola, Carlo. "The All-India Progressive Writers' Association: The European Phase." In *Marxist Influences and South Asian Literature*, edited by

Carlo Coppola, vol. 1, Occasional Papers no. 23, South Asia series. East Lansing: Michigan State University Press, 1974.

———. "The Angare Group: The Enfants Terribles of Urdu Literature." *Annual of Urdu Studies* 1 (1981): 57–69.

Cornell, Louis L. Introduction to *The Man Who Would Be King, and Other Stories* by Rudyard Kipling. Edited by Louis L. Cornell. New York: Oxford University Press, 1987.

Corngold, Stanley, and Michael Jennings. "Walter Benjamin/Gershom Scholem." *Interpretation: A Journal of Political Philosophy* 12, nos. 2–3 (May/September, 1984): 357–366.

Daemmrich, Horst S. "The Incest Motif in Lessing's *Nathan der Weise* and Schiller's *Braut von Messina*." *Germanic Review* 42 (1967): 184–196.

Dalmia, Vasudha. *The Nationalization of Hindu Traditions: Bhāratendu Hariśchandra and Nineteenth Century Banaras*. Delhi: Oxford University Press, 1997.

Darwish, Mahmoud. *Memory for Forgetfulness*. Translated and with an introduction by Ibrahim Muhawi. Berkeley: University of California Press, 1995.

Das, Sisir Kumar. *Sahibs and Munshis: The College of Fort William*. New Delhi: Orion, 1978.

Das, Veena. *Critical Events: An Anthropological Perspective on Contemporary India*. Delhi: Oxford University Press, 1995.

Deleuze, Gilles, and Félix Guattari. *Kafka: Toward a Minor Literature*. Translated by Dana Polan. Minneapolis: University of Minnesota Press, 1986.

Derrida, Jacques. *Acts of Religion*. Translated by Gil Anidjar. New York: Routledge, 2002.

Desai, Anita. *Baumgartner's Bombay*. New York: Penguin Books, 1989.

Devji, Faisal Fatehali "Gender and the Politics of Space: The Movement for Women's Reform, 1857–1900." In Z. Hasan, *Forging Identities*, 22–37.

Devy, G. N. *After Amnesia: Tradition and Change in Indian Literary Criticism*. Hyderabad: Orient Longman, 1995.

Didérot, Denis. *Oeuvres Esthètiques*. Paris: Garnier, 1988.

Dirks, Nicholas B. *Castes of Mind: Colonialism and the Making of Modern India*. Princeton, N.J.: Princeton University Press, 2001.

Dirlik, Arif. "The End of Colonialism? The Colonial Modern in the Making of Global Modernity." *boundary 2* 32, no. 1 (2005): 1–31.

Douglas, Ian Henderson. *Abul Kalam Azad: An Intellectual and Religious Biography*. Edited by Gail Minault and Christian W. Troll. Delhi: Oxford University Press, 1989.

Eckardt, Jo-Jacqueline. *Lessing's Nathan the Wise and the Critics, 1779–1991*. Columbia, S.C.: Camden House, 1993.

Eliot, George. *The Complete Works of George Eliot: Impressions of Theophrastus Such and Miscellaneous Essays*. New York: Harper and Brothers, n.d.

———. *Daniel Deronda*. Edited by Graham Handley. New York: Oxford University Press, 1990.

———. *Essays of George Eliot*. Edited by Thomas Pinney. London: Routledge and Kegan Paul, 1963.

———. "German Wit: Heinrich Heine." *Westminster Review* 65 (January 1856): 1–33.
———. "Heine's Book of Songs." *Saturday Review* 1 (April 26, 1856): 523–524.
———. "Heine's Poems." *Leader* 6 (September 1, 1855): 843–844.
———. *Middlemarch*. Edited by David Carroll. New York: Oxford University Press, 1991.
———. "Recollections of Heine." *Leader* 7 (August 23, 1856): 811–812.
Faiz, Faiz Ahmed. *Poems by Faiz*. Translated by V. G. Kiernan. Lahore: Vanguard Books, 1971.
———. *Hamārī qaumī s̀aqāfat*. Edited by Mirza Zafarul Hasan. Karachi: Idāra-e Yādgār-e Ġhālib, 1976.
———. *Nusḳhahā-e vafā*. Lahore: Maktaba-e Kārvāñ, 1986.
———. *Mīzān*. Karachi: Urdū Academy Sindh, 1987.
———. *Māh o sāl-e āshnā'ī: yādōñ kā majmū'a*. Karachi: Dānyāl, 1983.
———. *Matā'-e lauḥ o qalam*. Karachi: Dānyāl, 1985.
———. *The Rebel's Silhouette: Selected Poems*. Rev. ed. Translated by Agha Shahid Ali. Amherst: University of Massachusetts Press, 1995.
———. *The True Subject: Selected Poems of Faiz Ahmed Faiz*. Translated by Naomi Lazard. Princeton, N.J.: Princeton University Press, 1988.
Fanon, Frantz. *Black Skins, White Masks*. New York: Grove, 1967.
———. *The Wretched of the Earth*. Translated by Constance Farrington. New York: Grove, 1979.
Faraz, Ahmad. "Main kyūñ udās nahīñ." In idem, *Nāyāft*, 29–30. Lahore: Māvarā, 1989.
Farrukhi, Asif. *Ḥarf-e man o tū*. Karachi: Nafīs Academy, 1989.
Faruqi, Shamsur Rahman. *Early Urdu Literary Culture and History*. Delhi: Oxford University Press, 2001.
Feldman, David. *Englishmen and Jews: Social Relations and Political Culture, 1840–1914*. New Haven: Yale University Press, 1994.
Ferguson, Niall. *Empire: How Britain Made the Modern World*. London: Allen Lane, 2003.
Fichte, Johann Gottlieb. *Addresses to the German Nation*. Edited and with an introduction by George Armstrong Kelly. New York: Harper and Row, 1968.
Fischman, Dennis K. *Political Discourse in Exile: Karl Marx and the Jewish Question*. Amherst: University of Massachusetts Press, 1991.
Fleming, Leslie. *Another Lonely Voice: The Life and Works of Saadat Hassan Manto*. Lahore: Vanguard, 1985.
Fontenay, Elisabeth de. *Les Figures Juives de Marx: Marx dans l'Idéologie Allemande*. Paris: Éditions Galilée, 1973.
Forster, E. M. *A Passage to India*. New York: Harcourt Brace Jovanovich, 1984.
———. *The Hill of Devi*. New York: Harcourt Brace Jovanovich, 1984.
———. "What I Believe." In *A Bloomsbury Group Reader*. Edited by S. P. Rosenbaum. Oxford: Blackwell, 1993: 165–172.
Foucault, Michel. "The Subject and Power." *Critical Inquiry* 8 (summer 1982): 777–795.

———. "Nietzsche, Genealogy, History." In *Language, Counter-Memory, Practice: Selected Essays and Interviews*. Edited by Donald F. Bouchard, 139–64. Ithaca, N.Y.: Cornell University Press, 1977.

Freedman, Jonathan. *The Temple of Culture: Assimilation and Anti-Semitism in Literary Ango-America*. New York: Oxford University Press, 2000.

Funkenstein, Amos. *Perceptions of Jewish History*. Berkeley: University of California Press, 1993.

Gandhi, Mohandas Karamchand. *Our Language Problem*. Edited by Anand T. Hingorani. Karachi: Anand T. Hingorani, 1942.

Ganguly, Keya. "Adorno, Authenticity, Critique." In *Marxism, Modernity, and Postcolonial Studies*. Edited by Crystal Bartolovich and Neil Lazarus. Cambridge: Cambridge University Press, 2002, 240–256.

Gearhart, Suzanne. *The Interrupted Dialectic: Philosophy, Psychoanalysis and Their Tragic Other*. Baltimore, Md.: Johns Hopkins University Press, 1992.

Geisel, Eike. "The Cultural League is formed to concentrate all 'Jewish' cultural life in one central organization under Nazi supervision." In Gilman and Zipes, *Yale Companion to Jewish Writing and Thought*, 506–511.

Genette, Gérard. *Paratexts: Thresholds of Interpretation*. Translated by Jane E. Lewin. Cambridge: Cambridge University Press, 1997.

Ghalib, Mirza Asadullah Khan. *Dīvān-e Ġhālib*. Aligarh: Educational Publishing House, 1991.

Ghosh, Amitav. *In an Antique Land*. Delhi: Ravi Dayal, 1992.

Ghosh, Bishnupriya. *When Borne Across: Literary Cosmopolitics in the Contemporary Indian Novel*. New Brunswick, N.J.: Rutgers University Press, 2004.

Gilchrist, John Bothwick. *The British Indian Monitor* (Edinburgh: n.p., 1806).

Gilman, Sander L. *The Jew's Body*. New York: Routledge, 1991.

Gilman, Sander L., and Jack Zipes, eds. *Yale Companion to Jewish Writing and Thought in German Culture, 1096–1996*. New Haven: Yale University Press, 1997.

Godzich, Wlad. *The Culture of Literacy*. Cambridge, Mass.: Harvard University Press, 1994.

Goetschel, Willi. "Lessing, Mendelssohn, Nathan: German-Jewish Myth-Building as an Act of Emancipation." In *Lessing Yearbook*, vol. 32. Detroit: Wayne State University Press, 2000, 341–360.

———. "Lessing's 'Jewish' Questions." *Germanic Review* 78 (2003): 62–73.

Gopal, Sarvepalli. *Jawaharlal Nehru: A Biography*. Vol. 1. London: Jonathan Cape, 1975.

Goswami, Manu. "Autonomy and Comparability: Notes on the Anticolonial and Postcolonial." *boundary 2* 32, no. 2 (summer 2005): 201–225.

Graver, Suzanne. *George Eliot and Community: A Study in Social Theory and Fictional Form*. Berkeley: University of California Press, 1984.

Greenfield, Liah. *Nationalism: Five Roads to Modernity*. Cambridge, Mass.: Harvard University Press, 1992.

Grégoire, Henri. *Essai sur la régénération des Juifs*. Paris: Éditions d'Histoire Sociale, 1968.

Guha, Ranajit. "A Conquest Foretold." *Social Text* 54 (spring 1998): 85–99.

———. *Dominance without Hegemony*. Cambridge, Mass.: Harvard University Press, 1997.

———. *Elementary Aspects of Peasant Insurgency in Colonial India*. Delhi: Oxford University Press, 1986.

———. "On Some Aspects of the Historiography of Colonial India." In Guha and Chakravorty, *Selected Subaltern Studies*, 37–44.

———. "The Prose of Counter-Insurgency." In Guha and Chakravorty, *Selected Subaltern Studies*, 44–88.

Guha, Ranajit, and Gayatri Chakravorty Spivak, eds. *Selected Subaltern Studies*. New York: Oxford University Press, 1988.

Habermas, Jürgen. *Philosophical-Political Profiles*. Cambridge, Mass.: MIT Press, 1990.

Haight, Gordon S. *George Eliot: A Biography*. Harmondsworth: Penguin Books, 1985.

———, ed. *The George Eliot Letters*. Vol. 1. New Haven: Yale University Press, 1954.

Hali, Altaf Hussain. *Ḥayāt-e jāvēd*. New Delhi: Taraqqī-e Urdū Bureau, 1990.

———. *Muqaddama-e shiʿr o shāʿirī*. Edited by Dr. Waheed Qureishi. Aligarh: Educational Publishing House, 1993.

Halphen, Achille-Edmond. *Recueil des lois, décrets, ordonnances, avis du conseil d'état, arrêtés et règlements concernant les israélites depuis la révolution de 1789*. Paris: Bureaux des archives israélites, 1851.

Hardy, Barbara. "The Moment of Disenchantment." In *George Eliot*, edited by Harold Bloom. New York: Chelsea House, 1986.

Hardy, P. *The Muslims of British India*. Karachi: Cambridge University Press, 1972.

Hasan, Mushirul, ed. *Islam and Indian Nationalism: Reflections on Abul Kalam Azad*. Delhi: Manohar, 1992.

———. *Legacy of a Divided Nation: India's Muslims since Independence*. Delhi: Oxford University Press, 1997.

———, ed. *Nationalism and Communal Politics in India*. Delhi: Manohar, 1994.

Hasan, Syed Sibte. "Faiẓ kā ādarsh." In *Faiẓ Aḥmad Faiẓ: tanqīdī jā'iza*, edited by Khaleeq Anjum, 112–125. New Delhi: Anjuman-e Taraqqī-e Urdū, 1985.

Hasan, Zoya, ed. *Forging Identities: Gender, Communities, and the State*. New Delhi: Kali for Women, 1994.

Heine, Heinrich. "Concerning the History of Religion and Philosophy in Germany." In idem, *The Romantic School and Other Essays*, translated by Helen Mustard. New York: Continuum, 1985, 1–127.

———. *Jewish Stories and Hebrew Melodies*. New introduction by Elizabeth Petuchowski. New York: Markus Weiner, 1987.

Hertz, Deborah Sadie. *Jewish High Society in Old Regime Berlin*. New Haven: Yale University Press, 1988.

Hertzberg, Arthur. *The French Enlightenment and the Jews: The Origins of Modern Anti-Semitism*. New York: Columbia University Press, 1968.

Hilberg, Raul. *The Destruction of the European Jews*. Vol. 1. Rev. ed. New York: Holmes and Meier, 1985.

Hill, Christopher. "The Norman Yoke." In idem, *Puritanism and Revolution: Studies in Interpretation of the English Revolution of the 17th Century*. London: Secker and Warburg, 1958.

Horkheimer, Max, and Theodor W Adorno. *Dialectic of Enlightenment: Philosophical Fragments*. Edited by Gunzelin Schmid Noerr. Translated by Edmund Jephcott (Stanford: Stanford University Press, 2002).

Hunter, W. W. *The Indian Musalmans: Are They Bound in Conscience to Rebel against the Queen?* Lahore: Premier, 1974.

Irwin, Jane, ed. *George Eliot's "Daniel Deronda" Notebooks*. Cambridge: Cambridge University Press, 1996.

Ispahani, Mahnaz. "Saadat Hasan Manto." *Grand Street* 7, no. 4 (summer 1988): 183–193.

Iverson, Erik. *The Myth of Egypt and Its Hieroglyphs in European Tradition*. Princeton, N.J.: Princeton University Press, 1993.

Jaafry, Syed Rais Ahmed. *Aurāq-e gum gashta*. Lahore: Muhammad Ali Academy, 1968).

Jackson, Tony E. "George Eliot's 'New Evangel': *Daniel Deronda* and the Ends of Realism." *Genre* (summer/fall 1992): 229–248.

Jalal, Ayesha. *Sole Spokesman: Jinnah, the Muslim League, and the Demand for Pakistan*. Cambridge: Cambridge University Press, 1985.

———. *The State of Martial Rule: The Origins of Pakistan's Political Economy of Defence* (Karachi: Verso, 1991.

———. *Self and Sovereignty: Individual and Community in South Asian Islam since 1850*. New York: Routledge, 2002.

Jameson, Fredric. *Late Marxism: Adorno, or the Persistence of Dialectic*. London: Verso, 1990.

———. *Singular Modernity: Essay on the Ontology of the Present*. London: Verso, 2002.

Janowsky, Oscar I. *The Jews and Minority Rights (1898–1919)*. New York: Columbia University Press, 1933.

———. *Nationalities and National Minorities (with Special Reference to East-Central Europe)*. New York: MacMillan, 1945.

Kabir, Humayan, ed. *Maulana Azad: A Memorial Volume*. London: Asian Publishing House, 1959.

Kamali, Rashid. "ʿArẓ-e niāz." *Hindustānī* 1, no. 1 (August 1937): 2–5.

Kant, Immanuel. "An Answer to the Question: 'What Is Enlightenment?'" In *Political Writings*, 2nd ed., edited by Constance Garnett, Cambridge: Cambridge University Press, 1991 58–64.

Katz, Jacob. *From Prejudice to Destruction: Anti-Semitism, 1700–1933*. Cambridge, Mass.: Harvard University Press, 1980.

———. "The Jewish Diaspora: Minority Position and Majority Aspirations." *Jerusalem Quarterly* 25 (fall 1982): 68–78.

———. "The Term 'Jewish Emancipation': Its Origin and Historical Impact." In *Studies in Nineteenth-Century Jewish Intellectual History*, edited by Alexander Altmann, 1–25. Hanover, N.H.: University Press of New England, 1981.

Kaviraj, Sudipta. *The Unhappy Consciousness: Bankimchandra Chattopadhyay and the Formation of Nationalist Discourse in India*. Delhi: Oxford University Press, 1995.

Kazmi, Fareed. "Muslim Socials and the Female Protagonist: Seeing a Dominant Discourse at Work." In Z. Hasan, *Forging Identities*, 226–243.

Keddie, Nikki R. *An Islamic Response to Imperialism: Political and Religious Writings of Sayyid Jamal ad-Din "al-Afghani."* Berkeley: University of California Press, 1983.

Kesevan, Mukul. "Urdu, Awadh and the Tawaif: The Islamicate Roots of Hindi Cinema." In Z. Hasan, *Forging Identities*, 244–257.

Khan, Zafarul-Islam. *Hijrah in Islam*. New Delhi: Pharos Media and Publishing, for the Muslim Institute, London, 1997.

Kidwai, Sadiq-ur-Rahman. *Gilchrist and the "Language of Hindoostan."* New Delhi: Rachna Prakashan, 1972.

Kiernan, V. G. Introduction to *Poems by Faiz* by Faiz Ahmed Faiz. Translated by V. G. Kiernan. Lahore: Vanguard Books, 1971.

King, Christopher. *One Language, Two Scripts: The Hindi Movement in Nineteenth Century North India*. Bombay: Oxford University Press, 1994.

King, Robert D. *Nehru and the Language Politics of India*. Delhi: Oxford University Press, 1997.

Kipling, Rudyard. *Barrack-Room Ballads and Departmental Ditties and Other Verses*. New York: Grosset and Dunlap, n.d.

———. "On the City Wall." In idem, *The Man Who Would Be King and Other Stories*, 221–243. Oxford: Oxford University Press, 1987.

Kobler, Franz. *Napoleon and the Jews*. New York: Schocken Books, 1975.

Kosambi, D. D. "The Indian Bourgeoisie Comes of Age." *Social Scientist* 10, no. 4 (1946): 392–398.

Lakhnavi, Sahba. *Manṭō: ēk kitāb*. Lahore: Maktaba-e Afkār, 1994.

Lambropoulos, Vassilis. *The Rise of Eurocentrism: Anatomy of Interpretation*. Princeton, N.J.: Princeton University Press, 1993.

Laroui, Abdallah. *L'idéologie arabe contemporaine: essai critique*. Preface by Maxime Rodinson. Paris: François Maspero, 1967.

Lea, Charlene A. "Tolerance Unlimited: 'The Noble Jew' on the German and Austrian Stage (1750–1805)." *German Quarterly* 64, no. 2 (spring 1991): 166–177.

Leavis, F. R. *The Great Tradition: George Eliot, Henry James, Joseph Conrad*. New York: New York University Press, 1964.

Lelyveld, David. *Aligarh's First Generation: Muslim Solidarity in British India*. Princeton, N.J.: Princeton University Press, 1978.

Lémann, Joseph. *Napoléon et les juifs*. Paris: Avalon, 1989.

Lessing, Gotthold Ephraim. *Gesammelte Werke*. Vol. 2. Berlin: Aufbau-Verlag, 1954.

———. *Nathan the Wise: A Dramatic Poem in Five Acts*. New York: Frederick Unger, 1987.

———. *Nathan the Wise, Minna Von Barnhelm, and Other Plays and Writings*. Edited by Peter Demetz. New York: Continuum, 1991.

———. "On the Origin of Revealed Religion." In Chadwick, *Lessing's Theological Writings*, 104–105.

———. "On the Proof of the Spirit and the Power." In Chadwick, *Lessing's Theological Writings*.

———. "The Education of the Human Race." In Chadwick, *Lessing's Theological Writings*.

Lévi-Strauss, Claude. *Structural Anthropology*. Vol. 2. Translated by Monique Layton. Harmondsworth: Penguin Books, 1978.

Levy, Amy. *The Complete Novels and Selected Writings of Amy Levy, 1861–1889*. Edited by Melvyn New. Gainesville: University of Florida Press, 1994.

Lloyd, David. "Violence and the Constitution of the Novel." In idem, *Anomalous States: Irish Writing and the Post-Colonial Moment*, 125–162. Durham: Duke University Press, 1993.

Lloyd, David, with Paul Thomas. *Culture and the State*. New York: Routledge, 1998.

———. *Nationalism and Minor Literature: James Clarence Mangan and the Emergence of Irish Cultural Nationalism*. Berkeley: University of California Press, 1987.

———. "Genet's Genealogy: European Minorities and the Ends of the Canon." *Cultural Critique* 6 (spring 1987): 161–185.

Ludden, David, ed. *Making India Hindu: Religion, Community, and the Politics of Democracy in India*. 2nd ed. Delhi: Oxford University Press, 2005.

Lukács, Georg. *The Theory of the Novel: A Historico-Philosophical Essay on the Forms of Great Epic Literature*. Translated by Anna Bostock. Cambridge, Mass.: MIT Press, 1989.

———. *The Historical Novel*. Lincoln: University of Nebraska Press, 1983.

Lyons, James. *Semantics*. Vol. 2. Cambridge: Cambridge University Press, 1977.

Lyotard, Jean François. *Heidegger and "the jews."* Translated by Andreas Michel and Mark Roberts. Minneapolis: University of Minnesota Press, 1990.

Macartney, C. A. *National States and National Minorities*. London: Oxford University Press, 1934.

[Malaviya, Madan Mohan]. *Court Character and Primary Education in the N.-W. Provinces & Oudh*. Allahabad: Indian Press, 1897.

Manto, Saadat Hasan. *Kingdom's End and Other Stories*. Translated by Khalid Hasan. New Delhi: Penguin Books, 1987.

———. *Manṭōnāma*. Lahore: Sang-e Mīl, 1990.

———. *Manṭōnumā*. Lahore: Sang-e Mīl, 1991.

———. *Manṭōrāmā*. Lahore: Sang-e Mīl, 1990.

———. *Manṭō kahānīyāñ*. Lahore: Sang-e Mīl, 1995.

———. *Mottled Dawn: Fifty Stories and Sketches of Partition*. Translated by Khalid Hasan. Delhi: Penguin India, 1997.

———. *Stars from Another Sky: The Bombay Film World of the 1940s*. Translated by Khalid Hasan. Delhi: Oxford University Press, 1998.

Martyn, David. "Borrowed Fatherland: Nationalism and Language Purism in Fichte's *Addresses to the German Nation*." *Germanic Review* 72 (fall 1997): 1–13.

Marx, Karl. "On the Jewish Question." In *The Marx-Engels Reader*, edited by Robert C. Tucker, 2nd ed., 26–52. New York: Norton, 1978.

Marx, Karl, and Friedrich Engels. *The German Ideology*. Edited by C. J. Arthur. New York: International, 1984.

———. *Grundrisse: Foundations of the Critique of Political Economy (Rough Draft)*. New York: Penguin, 1993.

———. *Capital: A Critique of Political Economy*. Vol. 1. Translated by Ben Fowkes. Harmondsworth: Penguin, 1976.

Massignon, Louis. "My Meetings with Maulana Azad." In *Maulana Azad: A Memorial Volume*, edited by Humayan Kabir, 27–29. London: Asian Publishing House, 1959.

Masud, Muhammad Khalid. "The Obligation to Migrate: The Doctrine of *hijra* in Islamic Law." In *Muslim Travellers: Pilgrimage, Migration, and the Religious Imagination*, edited by Dale F. Eickelman and James Piscatori, 29–49. Berkeley: University of California Press, 1990.

Mayaram, Shail. *Resisting Regimes: Myth, Memory, and the Making of a Muslim Identity* (Delhi: Oxford University Press, 1997).

———. *Against History, Against State: Counterperspectives from the Margins*. New York: Columbia University Press, 2003.

McClintock, Anne, Aamir Mufti, and Ella Shohat, eds. *Dangerous Liaisons: Gender, Nation, and Post-Colonial Perspectives*. Minneapolis: University of Minnesota Press, 1997.

McCobb, Anthony. *George Eliot's Knowledge of German Life and Letters*. Salzburg: Institut für Anglistik und Amerikanistik, Universität Salzburg, 1982.

Mehta, Uday Singh. *Liberalism and Empire: A Study in Nineteenth-Century British Liberal Thought*. Chicago: University of Chicago Press, 1999.

Mendelssohn, Moses. *Jerusalem; or, On Religious Power and Judaism*. Translated by Allan Arkush. Hanover, N.H.: University Press of New England, 1986.

Mendes-Flohr, Paul R., and Jehuda Reinharz, eds. *The Jew in the Modern World: A Documentary History*. New York: Oxford University Press, 1980.

Menon, Ritu, and Kamla Bhasin. *Borders and Boundaries: Women in India's Partition* New Delhi: Kali for Women, 1998.

Metcalf, Barbara Daly. *Islamic Revival in British India: Deoband, 1860–1900*. Princeton, N.J.: Princeton University Press, 1982.

Metcalfe, Thomas R. *Ideologies of the Raj*. New York: Cambridge University Press, 1995.

Meyer, Michael A. *The Making of the Modern Jew*. Detroit: Wayne State University Press, 1967.

Meyer, Susan. *Imperialism at Home*. Ithaca, N.Y.: Cornell University Press, 1996.

———. "'Safely to Their Own Borders': Proto-Zionism, Feminism, and Nationalism in *Daniel Deronda*." *ELH* 60 (1993): 733–758.

Minault, Gail. *The Khilafat Movement: Religious Symbolism and Political Mobilization in India*. New York: Columbia University Press, 1982.

Mirabeau, Le Comte de. *Sur Moses Mendelssohn, sur la réforme politique des juifs: et en particulier sur la revolution tentée en leur faveur en 1753 dans la Grande Bretagne*. Paris: Éditions d'Histoire Sociale, 1968.

Mitter, Partha. *Art and Nationalism in Colonial India, 1850–1922: Occidental Orientations.* Cambridge: Cambridge University Press, 1994.

Mosès, Stéphane. "Langage et secularization chez Gershom Scholem." *Archives de Science Sociales de Religions* 60, no. 1 (July–September 1985): 85–96.

Mosse, George L. *Confronting the Nation: Jewish and Western Nationalism.* Hanover, N.H.: University Press of New England, 1993.

———. *German Jews beyond Judaism.* Bloomington: Indiana University Press, 1985.

Mufti, Aamir R. "Auerbach in Istanbul: Edward Said, Secular Criticism, and the Question of Minority Culture." *Critical Inquiry* 25, no. 1 (autumn 1998): 95–124.

———. "Critical Secularism: A Reintroduction for Perilous Times." *boundary 2* 31, no. 2 (summer 2004): 1–11.

———. "Global Comparativism." *Critical Inquiry* 31 (winter 2005): 472–489.

———. "Reading the Rushdie Affair: 'Islam,' Cultural Politics, Form." In *The Administration of Aesthetics: Censorship, Political Criticism, and the Public Sphere*, edited by Richard Burt, 307–339. Minneapolis: University of Minnesota Press, 1994.

Mujeeb, Mohammad. "The Partition of India in Retrospect." In *India's Partition: Process, Strategy and Mobilization*, edited by Mushirul Hasan. Delhi: Oxford University Press, 1993, 396–407.

Mukherjee, Meenakshi. *Twice Born Fiction: Themes and Techniques of the Indian Novel in English.* New Delhi: Heinemann, 1971.

Nadel, Ira B. *James Joyce and the Jews: Culture and Texts.* (Houndmills, Basingstoke, Hampshire: Macmillan, 1989.

Nadvi, Sulaiman. *Nuqūsh-e Sulaimānī.* Karachi: Urdū Academy Sindh, 1967.

Naim, C. M. "The Consequences of Indo-Pakistani War for Urdu Language and Literature." *Journal of Asian Studies* 38, no. 2 (February 1969): 269–283.

Nairn, Tom. *The Break-Up of Britain.* London: New Left Books, 1977.

Nandy, Ashis. *The Intimate Enemy: Loss and Recovery of Self under Colonialism.* Delhi: Oxford University Press, 1991.

———. "The Politics of Secularism and the Recovery of Religious Tolerance." In *Mirrors of Violence: Communities, Riots and Survivors in South Asia*, edited by Veena Das. Delhi: Oxford University Press, 1992, 69–93.

Narang, Gopi Chand. *Sākhtīyāt, pas-sākhtīyāt, aur mashriqī shiʿrīyāt.* Delhi: Educational Publishing House, 1994.

Nehru, Jawaharlal. *An Autobiography.* Delhi: Oxford University Press, 1985.

———. *The Discovery of India.* Delhi: Oxford University Press, 1989.

———. "The Passing of a Great Man." In *Maulana Azad: A Memorial Volume*, edited by Humayun Kabir. London: Asian Publishing House, 1959, 1–4.

———. *The Question of Language.* Foreword by Mahatma Gandhi. Allahabad: K. M. Ashraf on behalf of the Political and Economic Information Department of the All-India Congress Committee, 1937.

Nora, Pierre, ed. *Les Lieux de Mémoire.* 7 vols. Paris: Editions Gallimard, 1984–92.

———. *Realms of Memory: The Construction of the French Past.* 3 vols. New York: Columbia University Press, 1996–98.

Norris, H. H. *The Origin, Progress, and Existing Circumstances of the London Society for Promoting Christianity among the Jews*. London, 1825.
Oesterheld, Joachim. "British Policy towards German-speaking Emigrants in India, 1939–1945." In *Jewish Exile in India, 1933–1945*, ed. Anil Bhatti and Johannes H. Voigt, 25–44. Delhi: Manohar, 2005.
Oldenburg, Veena Talwar. "Lifestyle as Resistance: The Case of the Courtesans of Lucknow, India." *Feminist Studies* 16, no. 2 (summer 1990): 259–287.
Orsini, Francesca. *The Hindi Public Sphere, 1920–1940: Language and Literature in the Age of Nationalism*. Delhi: Oxford University Press, 2002.
Pandey, Gyanendra. *The Construction of Communalism in Colonial North India*. Delhi: Oxford University Press, 1990.
———, ed. *Hindus and Others: The Question of Identity in India Today*. Delhi: Oxford University Press, 1993.
Parry, Benita. *Delusions and Discoveries: India in the British Imagination, 1880–1930*. London: Verso, 1998.
Petievich, Carla. *Assembly of Rivals: Delhi, Lucknow and the Urdu Ghazal*. Delhi: Manohar, 1992.
Pollock, Sheldon. "Cosmopolitan and Vernacular in History." *Public Culture* 12, no. 3 (2000): 591–625.
———, ed. *Literary Cultures in History: Reconstructions from South Asia*. Delhi: Oxford University Press, 2001.
Pradhan, Sudhi. *Marxist Cultural Movement in India, Chronicles and Documents*. Vol. 1. Calcutta: Pustak Bipani, 1985.
Prakash, Gyan. "Introduction: After Colonialism." In *After Colonialism: Imperial Histories and Postcolonial Displacements*, edited by Gyan Prakash, 3–17. Princeton, N.J.: Princeton University Press, 1995.
Prasad, Beni. *India's Hindu-Muslim Questions*. London: George Allen and Unwin, 1946.
Pritchett, Frances W. *Nets of Awareness: Urdu Poetry and Its Critics*. Berkeley: University of California Press, 1994.
Qureshi, M. Naeem. "The 'Ulama' of British India and the Hijrat of 1920." *Modern Asian Studies* 13, no. 1 (1979): 41–59.
Raees, Qamar, and Syed Ashore Kazmi, eds. *Taraqqī pasand adab: pachās sāla safar*. Delhi: Educational Publishing House, 1987.
Ragussis, Michael. *The Figures of Conversion: "The Jewish Question" and English National Identity*. Durham: Duke University Press, 1995.
Rai, Amrit. *A House Divided: The Origin and Development of Hindi/Hindavi*. Delhi: Oxford University Press, 1984.
Rai, Alok. *Hindi Nationalism*. Delhi: Orient Longman, 2000.
Raipuri, Akhtar Husain. *Gard-e rāh*. Karachi: Maktabā-e Afkār, 1984.
Ray, Rajat. "Revolutionaries, Pan-Islamists and Bolsheviks: Maulana Abul Kalam Azad and the Political Underworld in Calcutta, 1905–1925." In *Communal and Pan-Islamic Trends in Colonial India*, edited by Mushirul Hasan. Delhi: Manohar, 1985, 102–104.
Rizvi, Saiyid Athar Abbas. *A History of Sufism in India*. Vol. 1. Delhi: Munshiram Manoharlal, 1983.

Robinson, Francis. *Separatism among Indian Muslims: The Politics of the United Provinces' Muslims, 1860–1923*. Delhi: Oxford University Press, 1994.

———. *The 'Ulama of Farangi Mahall and Islamic Culture in South Asia*. London: C. Hurst, 2001.

Rose, Gillian. *Judaism and Modernity: Philosophical Essays*. Oxford: Blackwell, 1993.

Rubenstein, William D., and Hilary L. Rubenstein. *Philosemitism: Admiration and Support in the English-Speaking World of Jews, 1840–1939*. New York: St. Martin's, 1999.

Rushdie, Salman. *The Moor's Last Sigh*. New York: Vintage, 1995.

Russell, Ralph. "The Development of the Modern Novel in Urdu." In *The Novel in India: Its Birth and Development*, edited by T. W. Clark. Berkeley: University of California Press, 1970, 102–141.

———. *The Pursuit of Urdu Literature: A Select History*. Delhi: Oxford University Press, 1992.

Sahni, Bhisham. "Saadat Hasan Manto: A Note." In *Life and Works of Saadat Hasan Manto*, edited by Alok Bhalla. Shimla: Indian Institute for Advanced Study, 1997.

Said, Edward W. "Adorno as Lateness Itself." In *Apocalypse Theory and the Ends of the World*, edited by Malcolm Bull. Oxford: Blackwell, 1995.

———. *Beginnings: Intention and Method*. New York: Columbia University Press, 1975.

———. *Culture and Imperialism*. New York: Knopf, 1993.

———. *Orientalism*. New York: Vintage, 1978.

———. *Power, Politics, and Culture: Interviews with Edward W. Said*. Edited by Gauri Viswanathan. New York: Pantheon, 2001.

———. *The Question of Palestine*. New York: Times Books, 1979.

———. "Reflections on Exile." *Granta* 13 (autumn 1984): 159–172.

———. "Representing the Colonized: Anthropology's Interlocutors." *Critical Inquiry* 15, no. 2 (1989): 205–225.

———. *The World, the Text, and the Critic*. London: Faber and Faber, 1983.

———. "Zionism from the Standpoint of Its Victims." *Social Text* 1 (1979): 5–78.

Saksena, R. B. *Gandhiji's Solution of the Language Problem of India*. Bombay: Hindustani Prachar Sabha, 1972.

Saksena, Ram Babu. *A History of Urdu Literature*. Lahore: Sang-e-Mīl, 1996.

Sammons, Jeffrey L. "Heine's *Rabbi von Bacherach*: The Unresolved Tensions." *German Quarterly* 32, no. 1 (January 1964): 26–38.

———. *Heinrich Heine: A Modern Biography*. Princeton, N.J.: Princeton University Press, 1979.

Samuel, M. *Conversion of the Jews: An Address from an Israelite to the Missionary Preachers Assembled at Liverpool to Promote Christianity among the Jews*. Liverpool: W. Wales, n.d.

Sangari, Kumkum. "Relating Histories: Definitions of Literacy, Literature, Gender in Nineteenth Century Calcutta and England." In *Rethinking English: Essays in Literature, Language, History*, edited by Svati Joshi, 32–123. New Delhi: Trianka, 1991.

Sapru, Tej Bahadur. Foreword to *A History of Urdu Literature* by Ram Babu Saksena. Lahore: Sang-e Mīl, 1996.

Sartre, Jean-Paul. *Anti-Semite and Jew*. New York: Schocken Books, 1976.

———. Preface to *The Wretched of the Earth* by Frantz Fanon. Translated by Constance Farrington. New York: Grove, 1979.

Schimmel, Annemarie. *A Two-Colored Brocade: The Imagery of Persian Poetry*. Chapel Hill: University of North Carolina Press, 1992.

———. "Eros—Heavenly and Not So Heavenly—in Sufi Literature and Life." In *Society and the Sexes in Medieval Islam*, edited by Afaf Lutfi al-Sayyid-Marsot. Malibu: Undena, 1979.

———. *Classical Urdu Literature from the Beginnings to Iqbal*. Wiesbaden: Otto Harrossovitz, 1975.

———. *Mystical Dimensions of Islam*. Chapel Hill: University of North Carolina Press, 1975.

Scholem, Gershom. "Confessions on the Subject of Our Language." In Derrida, *Acts of Religion*, 226–227.

———. "The Science of Judaism—Then and Now." In idem, *The Messianic Idea in Judaism and Other Essays on Jewish Spirituality*, 304–313. New York: Schocken, 1971.

———. *Walter Benjamin: The Story of a Friendship*. London: Faber and Faber, 1982.

Schwarzfuchs, Simon. *Napoleon, the Jews and the Sanhedrin*. London: Routledge and Kegan Paul, 1979.

Scott, David. "Colonial Governmentality." *Social Text* 43 (fall 1995): 191–220.

Scott, H. M. "Introduction: The Problem of Enlightened Absolutism." In *Enlightened Despotism: Reform and Reformers in Later Eighteenth-Century Europe*, edited by H. M. Scott. Ann Arbor: University of Michigan Press, 1990.

Scott, Walter, Sir. *Ivanhoe*. Harmondsworth: Penguin Books, 1986.

Scriven, Michael, and Dennis Tate, eds. *European Socialist Realism*. Oxford: Berg, 1988.

Seidman, Naomi. "Lawless Attachments, One-Night Stands: The Sexual Politics of the Hebrew-Yiddish Language War." In Boyarin and Boyarin, *Jews and Other Differences*, 279–305.

Shapiro, James. *Shakespeare and the Jews*. New York: Columbia University Press, 1996.

Shell, Marc. *Money, Language, and Thought: Literary and Philosophical Economies from the Medieval to the Modern Era*. Berkeley: University of California Press, 1982.

Shetty, Sandhya. "(Dis)figuring the Nation: Mother, Metaphor, Metonymy." *differences: A Journal of Feminist Cultural Criticism* 7, no. 3 (1995): 50–79.

Shulim, J. J. "Napoleon as the Jewish Messiah: Some Contemporary Conceptions in Vienna." *Jewish Social Studies* 7 (1945): 275–80.

Siéyès, Le Comte Emmanuel. *Qu'est-ce que le Tiers État?*. Paris: Société de l'Histoire de la Révolution Française, 1888.

Simmel, Georg. "The Stranger." In *The Sociology of Georg Simmel*, edited by Kurt H. Wolff, 402–408. New York: Free Press, 1950.

Sorkin, David. *The Transformation of German Jewry, 1780–1840*. New York: Oxford University Press, 1987.

Spackman, Barbara. *Decadent Genealogies: The Rhetoric of Sickness from Baudelaire to D'Annunzio*. Ithaca, N.Y.: Cornell University Press, 1989.

Spivak, Gayatri Chakravorty. *The Death of a Discipline*. New York: Columbia University Press, 1993.

———. "A Literary Representation of the Subaltern." In idem, *In Other Worlds: Essays in Cultural Politics*. New York: Routledge, 1988.

———. "Speculation on Reading Marx: After Reading Derrida." In *Post-structuralism and the Question of History*, edited by Derek Attridge, Geoff Bennington, and Robert Young, 30–62. Cambridge: Cambridge University Press, 1987.

———. *Outside in the Teaching Machine*. New York: Routledge, 1993.

———. "Woman in Difference: Mahasweta Devi's 'Douloti the Bountiful.' " In *Nationalisms and Sexualities*, edited by Andrew Parker, Mary Russo, et al., 96–117. New York: Routledge, 1992.

Stanizek, Georg. "Texts and Paratexts in Media." *Critical Inquiry* 32 (autumn 2005): 27–42.

Stern, Selma. *The Court Jew*. Philadelphia: Jewish Publication Society of American, 1950.

Stern-Taeubler, Selma. "The Jews in the Economic Policy of Frederick the Great." *Jewish Social Studies* 11 (April 1949): 129–152.

Suhrawardy, Shaista Akhtar Banu. *A Critical Survey of the Development of the Urdu Novel and Short Story*. London: Longmans Green, 1945.

Suleri, Sara. *The Rhetoric of English India*. Chicago: University of Chicago Press, 1993.

Traverso, Enzo. *The Marxists and the Jewish Question: The History of a Debate, 1842–1943*. Translated by Bernard Gibbons. Atlantic Highlands, N.J.: Humanities Press, 1994.

Trumpener, Katie. *Bardic Nationalism: The Romantic Novel and the British Empire*. Princeton, N.J.: Princeton University Press, 1997.

Troll, Christian W. "Abul Kalam Azad and Sarmad, the Martyr." In M. Hasan, *Islam and Indian Nationalism*, 28–42.

Tucker, Irene. *A Probable State: The Novel, the Contract, and the Jews*. Chicago: University of Chicago Press, 2002.

Turner, Bryan S., and Peter Hamilton, eds. *Citizenship: Critical Concepts*. 2 vols. London: Routledge, 1994.

Turner, Bryan S., ed. *Citizenship and Social Theory*. London: Sage, 1993.

Van der Veer, Peter. "Syncretism, Multiculturalism, and the Discovery of Tolerance." In *Syncretism/Anti-Syncretism: The Politics of Religious Synthesis*, edited by Charles Stewart and Rosalind Shaw. London: Routledge, 1994.

Varadharajan, Asha. *Exotic Parodies: Subjectivity in Adorno, Said and Spivak*. Minneapolis: University of Minnesota Press, 1995.

Viswanathan, Gauri. "Beyond Orientalism: Syncretism and the Politics of Knowledge." *Stanford Humanities Review* 5, no. 1 (1996): 18–32.

———. *Masks of Conquest: Literary Study and British Rule in India*. New York: Columbia University Press, 1989.

Vološinov, V. N. *Marxism and the Philosophy of Language*. Translated by Ladislav Matejka and I. R. Titunik. Cambridge, Mass.: Harvard University Press, 1973.

Von Mücke, Dorothea E. *Virtue and the Veil of Illusion: Generic Innovation and the Pedagogical Project in Eighteenth-Century Literature*. Stanford: Stanford University Press, 1991.

Wakankar, Milind. "Body, Crowd, Identity: Genealogy of a Hindu Nationalist Ascetics." *Social Text* 45 (winter 1995): 45–73.

Ward, A. W., and A. R. Waller. *The Cambridge History of English Literature*. Vol. 13, *The Nineteenth Century*. Part 2. Cambridge: Cambridge University Press, 1933.

Weber, Max. *Ancient Judaism*. Glencoe, Ill.: Free Press, 1952.

Wellbery, David. *Lessing's Laocoon: Semiotics and Aesthetics in the Age of Reason*. Cambridge: Cambridge University Press, 1984.

Wells, G. A. "Condillac, Rousseau and Herder on the Origin of Language." In *Studies on Voltaire and the Eighteenth Century*. Vol. 230. (1985): 233–246.

Wicke, Jennifer, and Michael Sprinker. "Interview with Edward Said." In *Edward Said: A Critical Reader*, edited by Michael Sprinker. Oxford: Blackwell, 1992, 221–264.

Wistrich, Robert. *Revolutionary Jews from Marx to Trotsky*. London: Harrap, 1977.

Wills, Claire. "Joyce, Prostitution, and the Colonial City." *South Atlantic Quarterly* 95, no.1 (winter 1996): 79–95.

Wilson, W. Daniel. "Enlightenment's Alliance with Power: The Dialectic of Collusion and Opposition in the Literary Elite." In Wilson and Holub, *Impure Reason*, 364–384.

Wilson, W. Daniel, and Robert C. Holub, eds. *Impure Reason: Dialectic of Enlightenment in Germany*. Detroit: Wayne State University, 1993.

Wolpert, Stanley. *Jinnah of Pakistan*. Delhi: Oxford University Press, 1988.

Woolf, Virginia. *Mrs. Dalloway*. New York: Harcourt, Brace Jovanovich, 1953

Zaheer, Hasan. *The Times and Trial of the Rawalpindi Conspiracy Case 1951: The First Coup Attempt in Pakistan*. Karachi: Oxford University Press, 1988.

Zaheer, Sajjad. *Raushnā'ī*. Karachi: Dānyāl, 1986.

Zangwill, Israel. *Dreamers of the Ghetto*. London: Heinemann, 1898.

Žižek, Slavoj. "The Ongoing 'Soft Revolution.'" *Critical Inquiry* 30 (winter 2004): 292–323.

Index

GPSR Authorized Representative: Easy Access System Europe - Mustamäe tee 50, 10621 Tallinn, Estonia, gpsr.requests@easproject.com

www.ingramcontent.com/pod-product-compliance
Ingram Content Group UK Ltd.
Pitfield, Milton Keynes, MK11 3LW, UK
UKHW010611030426
469651UK00002B/79

9780691057323